Lesbian and Gav Studies

Lesbian and Gay Studies

An Introductory, Interdisciplinary Approach

Edited by
Theo Sandfort, Judith Schuyf,
Jan Willem Duyvendak and Jeffrey Weeks

SAGE Publications
London • Thousand Oaks • New Delhi

Foreword © Mary McIntosh 2000
Editorial arrangement © Theo Sandfort, Judith Schuyf, Jan
Willem Duyvendak and Jeffrey Weeks 2000
Chapter 1 © Jeffrey Weeks 2000
Chapter 2 © Theo Sandfort 2000
Chapter 3 © Ken Plummer 2000
Chapter 4 © Judith Schuyf 2000
Chapter 5 © Gert Hekma 2000
Chapter 6 © Leslie J. Moran 2000
Chapter 7 © André Krouwel and Jan Willem Duyvendak 2000
Chapter 8 © Jon Binnie and Gill Valentine 2000
Chapter 9 © Marco Pustianaz 2000
Chapter 10 © Liana Borghi 2000
Chapter 11 © reneé c. hoogland 2000
Chapter 12 © Theo Sandfort and Hansje Galesloot 2000
Chapter 13 © Rommel Mendès-Leite and Onno de Zwart 2000
Chapter 14 © Judith Schuyf and Theo Sandfort 2000

First published 2000

SAGE Publications Ltd
6 Bonhill Street
London EC2A 4PU

SAGE Publications Inc
2455 Teller Road
Thousand Oaks, California 91320

SAGE Publications India Pvt Ltd
32, M-Block Market
Greater Kailash – I
New Delhi 110 048

British Library Cataloguing in Publication data
A catalogue record for this book is
available from the British Library

ISBN 0 7619 5417 1
ISBN 0 7619 5418 X (pbk)

Library of Congress catalog card number 00 131533

Typeset by Keystroke, Jacaranda Lodge, Wolverhampton
Printed in Great Britain by Athenaeum Press, Gateshead

Contents

List of contributors

Jon Binnie is a Lecturer in the Department of Geography and Earth Sciences at Brunel University, UK. He has written on sexual citizenship, urban sexual cultures and international migration. He is the co-author of *The Sexual Citizen: Queer Politics and Beyond* (Polity Press, 2000), *Contested Bodies* (Routledge, forthcoming) and *Pleasure Zones* (Syracuse University Press, in press). He is currently completing a book on globalization and sexuality for SAGE Publications.

Liana Borghi teaches Anglo-American literature at the University of Firenze. She co-founded in 1985 the women's publishing house Estro, in 1994 the Lesbian division of WISE (Women's International Studies Europe), and in 1996 the Società Italiana delle Letterate (Italian Society of Women in Literature). She has written on Mary Wollstonecraft, nineteenth-century ethics and literature, women travellers and women's fiction. Her interest in contemporary women's writing ranges from poetry to lesbian fiction, science fiction and Jewish-American women's literature. She is editor of two volumes of essays on women's comparative literature.

Jan Willem Duyvendak is Professor in Community Organization at Erasmus University, Rotterdam, and Director of the Research Institute 'Verwey-Jonker'. He has been Research Fellow at the Amsterdam School for Social Science Research (University of Amsterdam) and Assistant Professor at the Roman Catholic University of Nijmegen. He is (co-)editor of *New Social Movements in Western Europe. A Comparative Analysis* (UCL Press, 1995), *The Power of Politics. France: New Social Movements in an Old Polity* (Westview Press, 1995), and *The Global Emergence of Gay and Lesbian Politics. National Imprints of a Worldwide Movement* (Temple University Press, 1999).

Hansje Galesloot is a historian and journalist. She is the (co-)author of several books and articles on the social participation of homeless people, local politics, the communist resistance during the Second World War, and the climate of moral repression in postwar society. Her most recent publication is on the history of buddy care for people with HIV and AIDS in the Netherlands (1999).

Gert Hekma is Lecturer in gay and lesbian studies at the University of Amsterdam and chairs the stream of courses on sexuality, gender and culture. He has published widely on the history, sociology and anthropology of sexual diversity and recently coedited the two volumes of *Sexual Cultures in Europe* (Manchester University Press, 1999).

renée hoogland teaches lesbian cultural studies at the University of Nijmegen, the Netherlands. She is the author of *Elizabeth Bown: A Reputation in Writing* (New York University Press, 1994) and *Lesbian Configurations* (Polity Press/Columbia University Press, 1997). Her current research focuses on the function of fantasy in processes of embodiment in the age of posthumanism.

André Krouwel is Assistant Professor of Comparative Politics at the Vrije Universiteit of Amsterdam. He wrote his PhD on the transformation of political parties in Western Europe. He has also published articles and books on political parties, democratization in Eastern Europe, Dutch local politics and the gay and lesbian movement. Recently he co-edited *The Global Emergence of Gay and Lesbian Politics. National Imprints of a Worldwide Movement* (Temple University Press, 1999).

Mary McIntosh taught sociology at the University of Essex for many years. She has written on a variety of topics: 'The Homosexual Role', *The Organisation of Crime*, 'The State and the Oppression of Women', *The Anti-social Family* (with Michèle Barrett), and *Sex Exposed: Sexuality and the Pornography Debate* (edited with Lynne Segal). She was active in the Gay Liberation Front and the Women's Liberation Movement and was a founding editor of *Feminist Review*.

Rommel Mendès-Leite is a sociologist and social anthropologist affiliated with the 'sexuality' team of the Laboratoire d'Anthropologie Sociale (Collège de France, Paris). He is also an associate researcher at the Centre d'Etudes Africaines (Centre National de la Recherche Scientifique, Paris). His primary interests are the discrepancies between the sexual practices of men who have sex with men and their sexual identities and behaviours, the construction of gay male rationales and HIV prevention. His recent books include: *Penser les (homo)sexualités* (Paris, 2000), *Trois essais sur les (homo)sexualités* (with B. Proth and P.-O. de Busscher, Paris, 2000) and *Gay Studies from the French Cultures* (with P.-O. de Busscher, Harrington Press, 1993).

Leslie Moran is Reader in the School of Law at Birkbeck College, University of London. His work on law is interdisciplinary, drawing heavily on social theory, and with particular emphasis on gender and sexuality scholarship. He has written extensively on matters relating to gay issues in the law. His monograph, *The Homosexual(ity) of Law* was published by Routledge in 1996. He edited a special edition of *Social and Legal Studies* entitled *Legal Perversions* in 1997 and co edited *Legal Queeries* (Cassells) with colleagues in 1998. His current work is on homophobic violence and safety. This work is part of the largest study of lesbians, gay men, violence and safety undertaken in the UK. It is funded by the Economic and Social Research Council as part of a 20-project initiative on violence research.

Ken Plummer is Professor of Sociology at the University of Essex. He is the author of *Sexual Stigma* (1975), *Documents of Life* (1983), *Telling Sexual Stories* (1995) and (with John Macionis) *Sociology: A Global Introduction* (1998), as well as being the author of many articles. He has edited *The Making of the Modern Homosexual* (1981), *Symbolic Interactionism* (1991), *Modern Homosexualities*

(1992), and *Chicago Sociology* (1997); and is the founding editor of the journal *Sexualities*.

Marco Pustianaz teaches English Literature at the University of Eastern Piedmont in Italy. He has written on English Renaissance culture, queer and gender studies. He is currently involved in a research project on the discourse of fashion in Renaissance England.

Theo Sandfort is senior researcher at the Department of Clinical Psychology, Utrecht University, and directs research at the Netherlands Institute of Social Sexological Research (NISSO, Utrecht). His research focuses on sexual health issues in the general population as well as in gay men and lesbians. His most recent publications as a (co-)editor are *The Dutch Response to HIV: Pragmatism and Consensus* (UCL Press, 1998), *Sexual Behaviour and HIV/AIDS in Europe: Comparisons of National Surveys* (UCL Press, 1998), *AIDS in Europe: New Challenges for Social Sciences* (Routledge, 2000) and *Child Sexuality: International Perspectives* (Haworth, 2000).

Judith Schuyf is one of the founder-members of the Lesbian and Gay Studies Department at Utrecht University. Her research interests include lesbian and gay history, politics, media and senior lesbians and gays. She has written various books on these subjects. She chairs the Dutch National Platform for Lesbian and Gay Seniors. At present she works as Director of Research of the Dutch National Institute for Victims of War (ICODO) and is engaged in writing a biography of a Dutch homosexual war victim.

Gill Valentine is Professor of Geography at Sheffield University. Her research interests include geographies of technology, food, childhood, sexuality and the fear of crime. She is the co-editor of *Mapping Desire: Geographies of Sexualities* (Routledge, 1995), co-author of *Consuming Geographies: Where We Are What We Eat* (Routledge, 1997) and *Cool Places: Geographies of Youth Culture* (Routledge, 1998).

Jeffrey Weeks is currently Professor of Sociology and Dean of Humanities and Social Science at South Bank University London. He is the author of numerous articles and various books on the history and social organization of sexuality. Among his publications are *Coming Out: Homosexual Politics in Britain from the Nineteenth Century to the Present* (Quartet, 1977/1990), *Sexuality and its Discontents* (Routledge, 1985), *Invented Moralities* (Polity Press, 1995), *Making Sexual History* (Polity Press, 2000) and *Families of Choice and Other Life Experiments* (with Brian Heaphy and Catherine Donovan, forthcoming).

Onno de Zwart is employed by the Municipal Health Service – Rotterdam Area. Initially, he served there as HIV/AIDS Policy Co-ordinator, and at present he is the acting head of the Department of Infectious Diseases. He was previously a researcher at the Lesbian and Gay Studies Department at Utrecht University, where he focused on HIV prevention policy directed at gay men and the meaning of anal sex for gay men.

Foreword

Mary Mcintosh

I wonder now what I would have thought thirty years ago if I had been told that there would be a whole book, of fourteen chapters no less, on lesbian and gay studies. I would certainly not have believed that we could reach such a degree of acceptance, to be represented in almost every discipline and in the most respected institutions – at least in northern Europe and the English-speaking world, to be published by reputable academic publishers and in international refereed journals. Perhaps I would not have wanted to see this, either. At that time, we wanted above all to challenge heterosexual assumptions, rather than to set up our own stall alongside theirs. We could not imagine having enough strength to sustain that subversive project within the very bastions of respectability. Nor did we think that academia, respectable as it might be, was a seat of power. It was an ivory tower, set beside the main stream, with a good view, perhaps, but little influence. The serious battles lay elsewhere, in the 'real' world. In our most optimistic moments, we would have thought that these battles would have been won and there would be no more distinction between gay and straight and no need for lesbian and gay studies to exist.

As it turns out, the gay/straight divide has become even clearer as each has become naturalized as a way of life rather than a state of moral being and more lesbians and gays have become visible to the straight world. There is much more to study, and more of us to study it. In this, academia is not divided off from the world outside, but is deeply influential and even playing a leading role. Already there can be few professional people, journalists or media workers under 50 who have not been to a university with a student gay society. In the future, all of these people will have glimpsed some form of lesbian or gay studies, at least at the periphery of their vision, and many will have had a closer encounter. In the short term academia may be isolated, but in the longer term and as higher education expands it plays a significant part in shaping social consciousness. At the very least, the media will purvey an understanding that gays and lesbians exist and that they have their own pride, their own perspectives and concerns.

Yet it is often said that we in lesbian and gay studies are remote from the ordinary gay world and from the gay movement because we are aware of the lesbian and gay identities as the product of a particular period or culture, whereas the average lesbian or gay has a folk-essentialist view and, indeed, likes to think that 'we' have always been there, throughout historical and cultural oppression.

Similarly, it is sometimes said that queer theory is threatening and destabilizing to the movement because it challenges identity. I think, on the contrary, that queer theory may be debilitating because it is obscure, elitist and merely fashionable. In fact folk-essentialism and the naturalizing tendency are part of lesbian and gay studies. Whatever theories to the contrary are promulgated within them, the very fact that lesbian and gay studies have taken on an institutional form tends to confirm a naturalized perception of sexualities as ways of life, suggesting a pluralist multicultural mutual tolerance rather than a fundamental challenge to heterosexual hegemony. Just as in day-to-day life outside the academy, the naturalized perception is the one we have to live by and we have built networks, organizations and media and colonized social spaces on that basis.

The opposition between transgression and liberal collusion that has so plagued the gay movement has an obvious relation to contrasting theories within lesbian and gay studies, or better, contrasting moments within lesbian and gay studies. At moments we explore differences between categories that we accept as given, or power relations between groups that we treat as pre-defined. At others, we deconstruct the whole idea of gay and straight, feminine and masculine, and even woman and man. The shift towards culture and away from structure in lesbian and gay studies, as in intellectual life in general, emphasizes the deconstructive moment so that the naturalizing one is seen as old-fashioned, unsophisticated or outdated. But in practice, the two are not mutually exclusive and neither needs to displace the other. The movement, which gains its momentum from identity politics, despite recurrent 'queer' manifestations, needs research that is apparently humanistic to support its equal rights campaigning; as well as research that challenges the whole heterosexual order in which we are identified, showing the straight world how bizarre it seems from a lesbian or gay perspective. And as well as research that explores and problematizes questions of lesbian and/or gay identity, we need research that supports campaigning by presenting positive images and by increasing our understanding of the forces arrayed against us, and we also need research on issues of concern to us as people living lesbian or gay lives in present-day society. In addition, since the seed bed of movement activity is a rich and flourishing gay culture and an imaginable community, lesbian and gay studies needs to support that culture by participating in it and giving it wider currency.

We should be wary of presuming to play a leading role in the long run. An unfortunate imperative of the academic milieu is that we each make our name by saying something new and that we know we have moved forward only when we have discredited something old. We are prey to fashion, in a way that mirrors the succession of styles in dress and music which serve to distinguish generations and set them against each other, rather than representing real progression. Nevertheless, we have much that is important to offer and a considerable responsibility, especially as a growing proportion of the population pass through our classrooms. What, I wonder now, lies in store in the next thirty years?

1 The Challenge of Lesbian and Gay Studies

Jeffrey Weeks

Bringing scholars together to discuss lesbian and gay studies, whether in a book or in a conference, invites a series of stark questions: as a start, at the very least 'What?' 'Why?' 'How?' 'Where?' In this book we show the range of challenging studies that is now encompassed by the broad title, while in this introduction I will attempt to answer some at least of the questions.

The 'where?' question is the easiest to address, although the answers reveal the ambiguous status of lesbian and gay studies. Since the 1970s a vast amount of work has been produced that can broadly fall under the label. Originally much of this emerging work came from outside the universities, as a grassroots response to the emergence of the lesbian and gay movements after 1970, but increasingly it became part of the university curriculum in universities across Europe, North America and Australasia. Serious study of homosocial and homosexual life is now undertaken in all Western, and many non-Western countries, though often it lacks academic respectability. There are major intellectual achievements. But there is still a sense of vulnerability about the area of work. Lesbian and gay studies still hover on the borders of full respectability.

Yet it is conducted on a wide scale, and seems to have a life of its own, despite vicissitudes in certain countries and institutions: at various times over the past generation particular countries and universities appear to have taken the lead, then faded. Other foci have then emerged. In recent years the American influence has been most obvious, but as this book demonstrates there has been a major and continuing European input, with distinctive intellectual and political implications. Recent collections of work on lesbian and gay studies underline the importance of the two-way flow across cultures and academic traditions, and the major formative influence of European work is obvious (see, for example, Abelove et al., 1993; Medhurst and Munt, 1997; Nardi and Schneider, 1998). If, as we argue, lesbian and gay studies is best seen as a dialogue across disciplines, experiences and differences, then an account of developments in one part of the world is a vital part of understanding the rich tapestry that this field of work has become. Hence the concentration in this book on the specifically European contributions to the development of lesbian and gay studies. The conversation that is lesbian and gay studies requires that all voices are heard fully.

This nevertheless pinpoints a paradox at the heart of lesbian and gay studies. Many participants spend a great deal of time on deconstruction, showing differences, divisions, tensions. But the proliferation of monographs, readers, articles, colloquia and conferences suggest that we need to find a space where certain common themes are discussed. And that same paradox informs what we want to say in this introduction. Because a simultaneous recognition of difference, by gender, nationality, discipline, career, position or whatever, and a search for common ground, may actually constitute what lesbian and gay studies is and can be (Adam et al., 1998). In other words, at the heart of the enterprise is the attempt to find a common language in which we can speak, in different accents.

The diversity of lesbian and gay studies

Lesbian and gay studies means many things to people, at different times, in different countries. In fact, it often seems easier to define what it is not rather than what it is. There is a general agreement that it is not a single discipline with a single object of study. Obviously, there are common themes and there is a lot of coming together at various times. The object of study has to a large extent often been the lives of lesbian and gay people themselves: identities, experience of oppression, struggles for recognition, through history and in literature and so on. But we are also concerned with other things outside that, from legal codes to cultural representation, defining parts of lived life, certainly, but developing modes of interpretation and audiences that are often distinctive, and throw stark light on heterosexuality as much as homosexuality. So it is very difficult to see this area as a single discipline that will lie alongside other disciplines, although sometimes we may want to argue for that. There is something that inherently holds those involved together, but it is not a common disciplinary focus.

Similarly, it is difficult to detect a single theoretical position that unifies lesbian and gay studies. The history of work in lesbian and gay studies over the last twenty-five years has seen a number of major theoretical differences. During the 1980s, most of the debates at conferences and in journals were on the wearisome theme of essentialism versus constructionism, that is the degree to which homosexuality can be seen as the focus of an essential core identity and minority experience consistent across time and place, or as an historically variable and culturally specific phenomenon, a 'historical invention' (Altman et al., 1989; Foucault, 1979; Stein, 1990). More recently, many have been, to a large extent, concerned with the impact of 'queer studies' and what its relationship is to other studies and to politics (for example, Jagose, 1996; Seidman, 1996; Warner, 1993). Queer studies has questioned the fixity of sexual and gender boundaries, and offered a picture of sexual categories as fluid and changeable, in a way that builds on, and consciously radicalizes, constructionist insights. It claims a personal and critical stance which is deliberately subversive and transgressive of taken-for-granted categories of thought and experience. Throughout, feminist controversies have interwoven with lesbian and gay debates, and produced different inflections, for example concerning the complex relationship of male and female homosexuality, and the significance of male power. But though influential, such intellectual and political interventions have never managed to obliterate alternative voices. Different theoretical positions have been put forward and argued for, have informed debates, and raised the temperature. But it is difficult to find a theoretical position which has become hegemonic, despite the sometimes fevered accusations of polemicists.

That intellectual diversity has been a strength. It is important here to bear in mind that even the arguments that some of us, at least, find profoundly wrong – like the biological arguments announcing the gay gene or the gay brain – are a necessary part of the debate in lesbian and gay studies and cannot be excluded from it, because they have social consequences; they matter to the constituency of lesbian and gay studies and they have to be answered even if many of us disagree fundamentally with them. And there is another key point to make here: it is clearly wrong to read on from any theoretical position, whether it is self-styled as essentialist or constructionist, any single political implication. There is no necessary political belonging to any theoretical position. There are obvious examples of this: the biological essentialist arguments of the first generation of writers on homosexuality were used both to argue for rights for lesbian and gay people, and by the Nazis in the 1930s to argue for the suppression and even extermination of homosexuals (Weeks, 1986). Similarly today, although the lesbian and gay movement (in the United States particularly) has taken up and used the argument for a gay gene or a gay brain – often very enthusiastically – to back the claim for full civil rights, the very same arguments have been used by moral Conservatives to campaign for exactly the opposite. For example, in Britain, the former Chief Rabbi argued that the theory of a gay gene was an important breakthrough because it meant that we could then learn how to eliminate the gene. So a theory which is taken up in one position to argue for a particular case, can be used in exactly the opposite way. It is dangerous to get too trapped on specific theoretical battlefields. The greater priority is to find and articulate the values we can share than the issues that divide.

Just as there is no common theoretical core, lesbian and gay studies does not have a single methodology. Although some people have argued for a stronger methodological purity, it should surely be axiomatic that various approaches, whether quantitative or qualitative methodologies, can be used. Large- or small-scale quantifiable and comparative surveys have their uses, just as personal narratives have theirs (Plummer, 1995). They can complement each other, and which one we use has to be a pragmatic decision and not one made a priori. But that does not mean that the thinking about methodologies is irrelevant. For example, within lesbian and gay studies, borrowing to a large extent from the debates of feminists, the emphasis on the reflexive approach, which involves listening to, engaging with, and responding to the people we are researching, has been crucial because it relates us as actors to the participants in our research. At the same time, the development of 'objective knowledge', based on the models of traditional social scientific empirical research, can often prove an effective weapon in engaging with public authorities, as studies relating to AIDS have demonstrated (for example, Hubert et al., 1998).

If there is diversity in theoretical and methodological approaches, lesbian and gay studies is not, either, unified by a common politics in the sense that participants can possibly agree on everything, or sometimes, anything. Lesbian and gay politics is always to a certain extent inflected by the wider politics that individuals feel they belong to, whether it is left or right, radical, liberal or conservative. Lesbians and gays are divided by arguments, and experiences, around gender, around class, around race and ethnicity, around nationality. And of course there is significant differentiation by age and generation. Queer studies and queer activism, more transparently, have spent an enormous amount of energy rejecting the pioneers of the 1970s as if they had achieved little: what Gayle Rubin describes as a theoretical 'erasure' (Rubin and Butler, 1994: 82), whereas in fact there are strong continuities in themes, tone and content: you do not build a house without a strong base.

But there is a common political root to lesbian and gay studies. Its origins lie in the new lesbian and gay movements as they emerged in the early 1970s. All those involved would claim some affinity in a commitment to sexual justice, greater legal and social equality for non-heterosexual people, and in a willingness to be identified as lesbian and gay in the academy. Without that, lesbian and gay studies would lack defining characteristics. But this raises questions about the validity of the work conducted under that description. Just as women's studies has often been criticized for speaking from one standpoint, and therefore opening itself to the charge of 'bias' or 'subjectivity', so lesbian and gay studies is open to the same charge. Both are involved in what Epstein (1996) calls 'credibility struggles', in which the nature of knowledge is contested, and where the boundaries are being redrawn on who is allowed to speak with authority and credibility on a particular subject. One of the issues this raises is to what extent lesbian and gay studies can be 'scientific' in its approach. There is a problem of language here. In Britain, when using the word 'science', people tend to think of the natural sciences or a particular form of social sciences. On the continent of Europe it is used much more in relation to higher levels of scholarship. Whatever the value of the term 'scientific', there can be little disagreement that if it is to be credible, lesbian and gay studies should certainly be scholarly – which does not mean that it has to be abstract, or esoteric. Again, there is a problem in the different ways disciplines are expressed, but we should not abandon the protocols of the discipline that we work within, unless we can criticize them appropriately. And the work we do must be good work, not shoddy. However, lurking in lesbian and gay studies is the question of whom its practitioners are speaking for. Awareness of audience requires that 'science' or 'scholarship' is balanced by accessibility, precisely because of the underlying broad political stance which can alone give lesbian and gay studies meaning.

What lesbian and gay studies is – or could be

So what is lesbian and gay studies? We can offer broad descriptions. It is clearly pluralist; it is disputatious; it is often full of tensions and divisions. Yet, it follows from the existence of books like this that there are enough shared values and perspectives to keep us plugging on together and that is very important. So what do we have in common?

First of all, lesbian and gay studies must be about the recognition of the need to learn to live with differences and to find ways of resolving differences in dialogue with one another in an open and democratic fashion. Easier said than done, but that is surely a prerequisite of living in a pluralist society, and coming to terms with sexual diversity. It is the fundamental challenge in the wider political world too. It is not easy, as we know, to find what we have in common as well as recognizing what differentiates us. Nevertheless, that seems to be the supreme challenge in the postmodern world.

Secondly, although there cannot be a single political position, lesbian and gay studies is rooted in a specific if broad political and cultural stance, one claiming sexual justice. The changing social contexts and influences have shaped what can be said at particular times, and it is essential to remember here how some of the key and most influential works in lesbian and gay studies emerged in the context of specific political debates.

Let us choose a few at random. Mary McIntosh's article on the homosexual role (McIntosh, 1981; see also Weeks, 1998a), a key document in the new historical approach to homosexuality, and in providing insights into the significance of changing identities, was written before gay liberation in a specific political context in Britain: the campaign to change the law. It has been enormously influential because it both reflected the debates of the late 1960s and offered an alternative way of analysing lesbian and gay history and the nature of homosexuality. It challenged the idea of homosexuality as a specific 'condition', and instead suggested it was a complex social creation. It opened up crucial new avenues for exploration and debate. But as McIntosh makes clear (1981) the history of its publication was tempered by political caution – a reluctance on her part to undermine the arguments of law reformers, in a difficult climate, that homosexuality was an unfortunate condition for which individuals should not be punished – just as its subsequent impact was shaped by the emergence of gay liberation.

Another quite different but extremely influential body of work is that of the American historian, John Boswell (1980, 1994). One of the interesting features of Boswell's work is that it again, covertly at least, is engaged in a political struggle in a particular political context, this time on the role of the Christian Church in shaping homophobia. He not only offers major new insights into lesbian and gay history, but also fundamentally challenges the protocols of the faith that he belonged to (the Roman Catholic Church). His work is emotionally geared, it appears, to the argument that the Roman Catholic Church has abandoned its tolerant origins and early history, and that it has gone wrong on sexual and moral issues. And from his book on homosexuality and Christian toleration in ancient and early medieval times to his last book on same sex partnerships and 'marriage', you can see this dialogue going on all the time with the traditions of Roman Catholicism.

A further example is provided by the French gay theorist, Guy Hocquenghem. His early work on 'homosexual desire' (published in France in 1972, English edition 1978) represented a juncture of certain French theoretical debates, strongly influenced by the delirium of 1968, and gay liberation. The flavour of that book cannot be divorced from the political and cultural conjuncture in which he wrote. His subsequent writings, not least on paedophilia, remained on the controversial cutting edge of sexual debate, and embroiled him in ongoing scandal. But what survives is the sense of the moral case for homosexual emancipation battling against an intractable social categorization and normalization, which necessarily shapes the terms of the intervention (see Marshall, 1996).

So politics in a broad sense is inescapably part of lesbian and gay studies, but impacts in different ways at different times. In this lesbian and gay studies is in principle the same as other specialized fields (and perhaps the same as knowledge in general). But lesbian and gay studies has had to engage with societal assumptions about the nature of sexuality, which has given research on the erotic a tinge of 'danger'.

Thirdly, this very sense of danger has provided a more specific unifying standpoint: at the core of all the best work that has been undertaken is a questioning of the sexual orthodoxy, and a fundamental critique of the heterosexual norm. The claim to lesbian and gay rights, for equality and justice, demands a basic challenge to the historical privileging of heterosexuality. So lesbian and gay studies cannot simply be about what lesbians and gays do. It must also be about the way societies have structured sexuality throughout time and the impact of that structuring on the very existence of non-heterosexual ways of life.

It follows that lesbian and gay studies is rooted in a distinctive form of politics that has developed around this understanding – identity politics – which simultaneously affirms the validity of homosexual life choices and confronts the various forms of power which deny lesbian and gay life chances. It could hardly be anything else. At the core is a sense of rooted belonging that comes from identity and forms of community (although these vary greatly, and are often problematic). We cannot escape the way identity is constructed as a means of political mobilization and political legitimization in the contemporary world. Whether that form of identity is around nationalism, or around race, or even just around the construction of a Conservative or Social Democratic political position, what politics is about is the construction of an identity. Lesbian and gay identity formation, identity politics, therefore offers a particular stance on the nature of modern society, about the possibilities of a pluralistic and democratic society. Even that position which has challenged the traditions of lesbian and gay politics over the last few years – the queer insurgency – is simultaneously about identity and the construction of identity (Weeks, 1995). It is in part about the rejection of the way lesbian and gay politics has gone, but nevertheless it is also about forming an identity – not so much around sexual orientation, but about style, about stance, about choice. It appears that however much we might reject the notion of a fixed identity, we cannot easily escape the fact that lesbian and gay studies is rooted in identity politics.

Within that identity politics there is an interesting tension, between what has been described as a moment of transgression and the moment of citizenship (Weeks, 1995). There have been periods in the history of all the new social movements since the 1960s when there has been an emphasis on confronting the status quo through subversion and transgression (by defiantly flaunting sexual difference; the way we dress; the way we want to live together, the way we want to challenge the dominant codes). But at times there has also been a strong stress on claiming full equality, the moment of citizenship, where we campaign for rights; where we fight for changes in the law on sex; when we claim partnership recognition, as many in Europe have done. The interesting point about these two moments is that it is not a matter of 'either/or'. These two moments are necessary to each other. But there's also something significant in that distinction between transgression and citizenship, because, not only are they necessary politically to each other, they are also quite important to each other in the way we define citizenship. What the campaigns for rights have done is to redefine the notions of citizenship, and to put on to the agenda of citizenship what Ken Plummer, in *Telling Sexual Stories* (1995), talks about as intimate citizenship: a notion of citizenship which goes beyond the traditional preoccupation with political, social and economic rights to the role of the intimate, and the need to protect and enhance the spaces for private life (see also Weeks, 1998b). And that is something that lesbian and gay studies is addressing in a variety of ways and should go on addressing.

Fourthly, lesbian and gay politics is about contesting existing knowledge, at first from the outside, by redefining who has the expertise to speak about homosexuality. What lesbian and gay researchers have tried to do in various ways over the past thirty years, whether it is in history or sociology or anthropology, or in other subjects, is to transform the way we see the world. Some of our earliest intellectual efforts were concerned to challenge the claims of dominant forms of knowledge that distorted or excluded the realities of lesbian and gay lives. So, for example, psychiatry and psychiatric institutions and the dominance of psychological and sexological models of homosexuality were critiqued. The exclusion of homosexuality from history was sharply questioned. The ignorance of sociology about the sexual was highlighted, and addressed. In doing all that, we began to create for ourselves knowledge that was from us; for us. We began to reverse the terms of the debate. And in all sorts of ways you can see the intellectual effort that has gone on in lesbian and gay studies as precisely the evolution of an alternative expertise, a 'grassroots' and situated knowledge, based on the insurgency of subjugated knowledges and the creation of new knowledge. This was especially important in shaping the response to the HIV/AIDS crisis. As Epstein has very clearly shown in *Impure Science* (1996), lesbians and gay men were able to engage in the 'credibility struggles' with 'experts' both over the definition of AIDS and HIV, and in the treatment and care agenda, because of the expertise built up in the lesbian and gay communities over the previous decade. And many, if not all, of those involved were inspired to ask the questions they did, to do the work that has been so influential, by a sense of political alignment and moral commitment. Many of the earliest proponents of lesbian and gay studies and AIDS activists (and sometimes they were the same people) have been, in Gramscian terms, 'organic intellectuals' – that is they were linked to social movements, in the same way as feminist theorists, historians, literary critics and the like were directly linked to the women's movement. Inevitably, perhaps, a split has developed between those who are now in leading academic positions and have become well-known writers or researchers (who get grants), and who travel around the world from conference to conference, and those they claim to be speaking for and to, which is why we always need a reality check. We need to check what we say and do in accordance with the experience of those we claim to speak for and come from. There is always a danger of becoming ivory tower academics, and many appear to believe that much of the work around queer studies has indeed become extremely ivory tower. It is not the only work that has; you can see it in all sorts of disciplines. It is about speaking to a small group of people (our peers in our disciplines, probably) rather than informing the movement or community. Perhaps that says something about the way academic life is structured, but in terms of lesbian and gay studies there is obviously a danger: a danger of the separation of intellectuals from their constituencies. With that in mind, we must continue to validate the non-academic work and interests that go on in the lesbian and gay communities and recognize that much of our work started in the same way.

When we think of the development of lesbian and gay studies in the United States, for instance, we can see the way in which the slide shows and other forms of independent scholarship about lesbian and gay history began to inform wider academic debate. One thinks of Alan Berube's work on the military, begun as a slide show in San Francisco (Berube, 1990); or Jonathan Katz's work as an independent researcher on gay history (1976, 1983); both were enormously influential, and Katz's work in particular significantly contributed to the debate around constructionism and essentialism which became so vital. It is necessary to recognize the diverse roots of lesbian and gay studies, and the ways that they have grown because of these beginnings. And it is perhaps because of that sense that lesbian and gay studies, in the end, is not simply an academic discipline, but speaks to a wider cultural constituency, that many reputable publishers in the past decade have wanted to jump on the bandwagon. Of course they have their own agendas; of course they want to make money out of it; of course they are doing it because it increases markets. And yes, of course there is a danger of consumerism, of marketization, and of commodification, as many nostalgic for an earlier simpler world complain. Nevertheless, we must take advantage of the opportunities for publishing that certainly did not exist twenty years ago – it is a major gain for everyone.

There is, however, a paradox in this discursive explosion: in Great Britain and the United States it seems to be undeniably true, if painful, that the biggest expansion of the lesbian and gay community occurred under governments hostile to those communities. Under Reagan in the USA and Thatcher in Britain there was a huge expansion of the lesbian and gay constituency during the 1980s despite, or perhaps because of, the impact of HIV and AIDS. It may have been because of the opposition; it may have been because of the expansion of the economy and the integration of gay culture into the mainstream of the market; it may have been because of the growing maturation of the community; it may have been because of the epidemic, and the sense of embattlement that resulted – whatever the reasons, there has been this expansion, as the increase in the number of publishers, authors and publications illustrates. And that says something we ought to bear in mind about the relationship between the particular politics of lesbian and gay people, and the wider politics of Western countries. They are inextricably linked, but not necessarily in obvious ways. Things can change for the better, even in the most hostile circumstances – sometimes because of the hostile circumstances – and we should never forget the unanticipated consequences of events.

This raises again the question of who we are doing this work for. There must be an assumption that it should be of some use for the constituencies we wish to speak for and from; if not directly, then by opening avenues that others can explore. That in turn, however, reveals a tension that exists between validity and use in lesbian and gay studies. We can all think of examples of the way in which the results of specific studies can be seen to go against the necessities of our political commitments. Two things can be said on this. First, and most obviously, it is important to tell the truth as we see it. There is no point in doing poor work simply because it serves a political purpose. We have to tell our truth, on the basis of our research, while recognizing that there are many potential truths. But it is always possible to use the truth pragmatically, and this is the second point. Is it always appropriate to say something if, in the short term, it may have adverse effects? The genesis of Mary McIntosh's article on the homosexual role illustrates the dilemma. In her 1981 postscript to her essay, McIntosh describes the circumstances which shaped its political tact:

> I remember writing a letter to the Homosexual Law Reform Society at one stage, supporting the cause in general, but saying that I had lots of reservations about the nature of the arguments they were putting forward because I could not really accept the view that homosexuality was a sickness. And they wrote back and said that they had a lot of sympathy with my position but at that time they had to use the arguments that were suited to the moment. I quite understood that. . . . (McIntosh, 1981: 44–5)

This is the pragmatic sanction which often shapes not only what, but how, a piece of work is disseminated and used.

At its most basic, lesbian and gay studies is a standpoint perspective. It is a perspective developed from a particular position, a particular history of a different culture, which is committed to the understanding of societal hostility towards homosexuality. It is concerned with the power of heterosexual privilege; it is concerned with understanding the ways in which a hierarchy of sexual values and sexual power is constructed. It is concerned with the categorizations of sexuality as they have emerged and changed over time and it is concerned with the ways in which the development of these hegemonic forms have subordinated various categories of people, whether lesbian or gay, or other 'minority' groupings. Is it, then, necessarily partisan, which is how conservative critics have often caricatured it? Is there a 'lavender establishment', a 'homintern' elite pumping out propaganda for its own deviant concerns?

Lesbian and gay studies is committed certainly, but not to any orthodoxy. The ferocity of some of the internal controversies should undermine any such assumption. It is aligned, yes, but not to any broader political movement, or to a single truth. At its best, lesbian and gay studies stand for a questioning of accepted truths, a problematization of the taken for granted, a proliferation of truths. The standpoint is one of seeking justice, a level playing field, and a claim to equality. If that is bias or partisanship, so be it.

For in the end lesbian and gay studies constitutes a sort of intellectual and political diaspora. It is not fixed in a single place, or confined to a single disciplinary approach; yet there is a common sense of belonging that transcends differences of country and nation, of gender and of culture. There is a sense of common concerns within dispersal, a network rather than a fixed positionality, confirmed by informal as much as formal ties, by common reading rather than geographical propinquity, just as likely today to be part of a dialogue on the Internet as of formal conferencing (though that grows exponentially too). There is something there which is amorphous if we try to define it too closely, but is nevertheless significant. It constitutes, we could argue, in the terms of information science, an 'invisible college', that is to say, it is defined by links that go beyond the formal institutional parameters that constitute most disciplines, yet has a sense of identity which has been shaped by common preoccupations. A number of issues have made the solidification of the college essential. AIDS is an example of the way in which pre-existing ties were both necessary and then strengthened by the urgency of the crisis (see Mendès-Leite and de Zwart, Chapter 13 in this volume). Gay studies, especially concerning identity and sexual behaviour, has been an indispensable basis for intellectual work around AIDS, and for understanding the social aspects of the epidemic. At the same time, the impact of AIDS has shifted much of the work in lesbian and gay studies, redirecting it in large part towards enquiries which could illuminate the epidemiology, representations and social, political, cultural and personal consequences of the syndrome. In many ways lesbian and gay studies came of age in its work around the epidemic.

Finally, lesbian and gay studies is about the creation of space. It is about the creation of a space for debate; for analysis; for negotiation; for rows occasionally, and for finding a common cause. Now, space, as we know, can be filled. It can be fought over. It cannot obliterate differences, in fact it may be the arena where differences have to be worked out, or worked through sometimes in quite difficult struggles. But if we can construct the space in which we can work together, then we can try, sometimes fail, sometimes succeed, to build little houses; little buildings – arenas for debate.

The current situation

If lesbian and gay studies is by its nature a broad church, what state of repair is it now in? Perhaps its current state could be best described, to use an old Marxist phrase, as a mixture of combined and uneven development. It is a combined development in the sense that everyone involved is familiar with at least the parameters of the debates in Western countries. Whatever our different cultural backgrounds and interests, we are all likely today to be familiar with the impact of the queer studies debate, and the need to address it. That indicates that within obvious limits (we cannot possibly keep up with everything in all disciplines) we share certain common themes, which vary from time to time. It is uneven in the sense that different disciplines, countries and cultures may be in different phases of development.

There are, first of all, different phases in the impact of different disciplines. We need to be aware of the way in which anthropology set the terms of a debate on homosexuality from the late nineteenth century, by putting on the agenda the whole question of cultural relativism (see Hekma, Chapter 5 in this volume). By the 1980s, however, its overall impact had weakened, though it continues to provide a vital strand. In the 1970s a new lesbian and gay history set the terms of the debate, especially by reshaping the way we thought about the whole idea of identity (Schuyf, Chapter 4 in this volume). This was complemented by new tendencies within sociology in documenting difference and theorizing social construction and so on (Plummer, Chapter 3 in this volume). But while anthropology, history and sociology, we could argue, dominated the first phase – whether directly or indirectly – the current phase is dominated more by geography and the spatial dimensions of difference and the queering of literature (see the chapters by Binnie and Valentine, Borghi, hoogland, and Pustianaz in this volume). And in many ways the would-be hegemonic form today is not social science but literary studies, though guided by a cultural theory that would have been unrecognizable to earlier practitioners of the genre.

Those differences, over time, have been shaped by influences from other developments: most obviously the development of feminist theory over the last thirty years (see Sandfort and Galesloot, Chapter 12 in this volume), but also Marxism in the 1970s/early 1980s, the return of psychoanalysis, largely under the impact of feminism, and latterly the radical impact of post-structuralism, and the advent of postmodernism, all of which have informed queer studies.

Lesbian and gay studies is structured by national rhythms. It would be difficult, for example, to divorce the institutionalization of lesbian and gay studies in the Netherlands in the 1980s from the broader political and cultural framework which emphasized a pluralism rooted in confessional difference. In France, the peculiarities of a tolerated but privatized homosexuality, combined with the existence of intellectual superstars like Foucault, who were notably but not publicly gay, posed challenges for the development of a distinctive theoretical tradition around lesbian and gay studies. In Britain there was another peculiarity: it is a very centralized country which is historically weak on the notion of individual rights. But at the same time there is a history of pragmatic adaptation to social change, and a history of institutionalizing major social movements like the Labour movement, which paradoxically created space for the development of a certain form of lesbian and gay studies. So each culture shapes the fashion in which lesbian and gay studies has developed.

There are obviously variations across disciplines, with different paces in different countries at different times. Some disciplines, such as sociology, have been more receptive than others, such as psychiatry and psychology, to lesbian and gay studies (Sandfort, Chapter 2 in this volume). Law has been too locked into the traditions of individual jurisdictions for the development of a much broader sense of European law (but see Waaldijk and Clapham, 1993). The developing discourse of human rights has been very important in changing the situation (Moran, Chapter 6 in this volume). In politics, political science, the analysis of social movements and the impact of political theory have been extremely important – beginning to reshape and putting on the agenda new thinking about what is political (Krouwel and Duyvendak, Chapter 7 in this volume).

There is another thing that has come up throughout the debate – the dialogue of different subjects. A brief examination of references in books or papers will quickly reveal the cross-disciplinary influences, which says something significant.

You cannot ultimately do any of the things that lesbian and gay scholars want to do by simply sticking in one disciplinary framework. And it may be that that is why subjects like sociology or cultural studies are much more amenable to lesbian and gay studies, because they are traditionally less driven to orthodoxy – they are more open, more pluralist in the nature of their approach – than some older disciplines.

Finally, we must recognize a problem of 'translation'. We speak different languages in Europe, but lesbian and gay scholars, in order to be heard in English-speaking countries, where the largest markets are, have to write and publish in English. So there is a literal problem of translation, which is fundamental. But there is also a problem in the translation of feelings, which makes some of our debates difficult. We do not necessarily have the same understanding of concepts and traditions. But there are other problems we are more familiar with – the different languages of men and women; lesbians and gay men; different ethnicities – white and black and people of colour; and of different generations. But the fact that we are continuing the dialogue, however heatedly at times, suggests that despite all these differences, a lesbian and gay Esperanto is developing – some sort of common language (a mixture of languages) which allows us to communicate with each other freely and openly, in a common cause. That is advertisement enough for the existence of something called lesbian and gay studies.

References

Abelove, H., Barale, M. and Halperin, D. (eds) (1993) *Lesbian and Gay Studies Reader.* New York and London: Routledge.

Adam, B., Duyvendak, J.-W. and Krouwel, A. (eds) (1999) *The Global Emergence of Gay and Lesbian Politics. National Imprints of a Worldwide Movement.* Philadelphia: Temple University Press.

Altman, D., Vance, C., Vicinus, M., Weeks, J. and others (1989) *Homosexuality, Which Homosexuality?* London: GMP Publishers.

Berube, A. (1990) *Coming Out Under Fire.* New York: The Free Press.

Boswell, J. (1980) *Christianity, Social Tolerance, and Homosexuality. Gay People in Western Europe from the Beginning of the Christian Era to the Fourteenth Century.* Chicago and London: University of Chicago Press.

Boswell. J. (1994) *Same-Sex Unions in Premodern Europe.* New York: Villard Books.

Epstein, S. (1996) *Impure Science. AIDS, Activism and the Politics of Knowledge.* Berkeley: University of California Press.

Foucault, M. (1979) *The History of Sexuality, Volume 1: An Introduction.* London: Allen Lane.

Hocquenghem, G. (1978) *Homosexual Desire.* London: Allison & Busby.

Hubert, M., Bajos, N. and Sandfort, T. (eds) (1998) *Sexual Behaviour and HIV/AIDS in Europe.* London: UCL Press.

Jagose, A. (1996) *Queer Theory.* Melbourne: Melbourne University Press.

Katz, J. N. (1976) *Gay American History: Lesbians and Gay Men in the USA.* New York: Thomas Y. Crowell.

Katz, J. N. (1983) *Gay/Lesbian Almanac: A New Documentary.* New York: Harper & Row.

Marshall, B . (1996) *Guy Hocquenghem. Theorising the Gay Nation.* London: Pluto Press.

McIntosh, M. (1981) 'The homosexual role' and 'Postscript', in Plummer (1981), pp. 30–49.

Medhurst, A. and Munt, S. M. (eds) (1997) *Lesbian and Gay Studies: A Critical Introduction.* London and Washington: Cassell.

Nardi, P.M. and Schneider, B. E. (eds) (1998) *Social Perspectives in Lesbian and Gay Studies. A Reader.* London and New York: Routledge.

Plummer, K. (ed.) (1981) *The Making of the Modern Homosexual.* London: Hutchinson.

Plummer, K. (1995) *Telling Sexual Stories: Power, Change and Social Worlds.* London: Routledge.

Rubin, G., with Butler, J. (1994) 'Sexual traffic', *Differences. A Journal of Feminist Cultural Studies*, 6 (2 and 3): 62–99.

Seidman, S. (ed.) (1996) *Queer Theory/Sociology.* Oxford: Blackwell.

Stein, E. (ed.) (1990) *Forms of Desire: Sexual Orientation and the Social Constructionist Controversy.* New York and London: Garland Publishing.

Waaldijk, K. and Clapham, A. (eds) (1993) *Homosexuality. A European Community Issue. Essays in Lesbian and Gay Rights in European Law and Policy.* Dordrecht, Boston and London: Martinus Nijhoff.

Warner, M. (ed.) (1993) *Fear of a Queer Planet: Queer Politics and Social Theory.* Minneapolis and London: University of Minnesota Press.

Weeks, J. (1986) *Sexuality.* Chichester, London and New York: Ellis Horwood/ Tavistock.

Weeks, J. (1995) *Invented Moralities. Sexual Values in an Age of Uncertainty.* Cambridge: Polity Press; New York: Columbia University Press.

Weeks, J. (1998a) 'The "homosexual role" after 30 years: an appreciation of the work of Mary McIntosh', *Sexualities*, 1 (2): 131–52.

Weeks, J. (1998b) 'The sexual citizen', *Theory, Culture and Society*, 15 (3–4): 35–52.

2 Homosexuality, Psychology, and Gay and Lesbian Studies

Theo Sandfort

Psychology was one of the first scientific disciplines to become involved in the study of homosexuality. Since its early involvement, both the perspective of and the attention to homosexuality have developed within psychology in several respects. In the beginning, a pathological approach was dominant. Subsequently, extensive research has been carried out to prove the normality of homosexuality and to criticize heterosexual assumptions within psychology. At a later stage, gay affirmative psychology was developed, predominantly by researchers who were gay or lesbian, as an alternative to the traditional psychological approach. A diversity of aspects of gay and lesbian lives became the focus of this new approach. These researchers were, however, hardly affected by the simultaneous development of gay and lesbian studies and the later queer studies. Its relative independence is illustrated by the fact that gay and lesbian psychology is the only scientific discipline addressing homosexuality to have 'gay and lesbian' as part of its name. This gay affirmative psychology applied various traditional psychological theories. The outcomes of its research affected mainstream psychology to some extent. In the 1980s and 1990s, AIDS attracted a great deal of attention and energy from gay psychologists. As will be shown, the current state of affairs within the psychological approach in gay and lesbian studies can be criticized for several reasons. This chapter, however, will also demonstrate that homosexuality has been a rich topic for psychological research and theorizing, and can continue to be such.

Psychology and its relevance to the study of homosexuality

Showing the relevance of psychology as a perspective in the study of homosexuality first requires a definition of psychology. It is not easy to describe exactly what psychology actually is. Since its inception, various definitions have been presented and definitions continue to change. The unity that the term suggests is contradicted by divergence in the practice of psychological research and theorizing. Psychology encompasses a rich variety of theoretical perspectives, paradigms and related methodologies and subdisciplines, as well as relatively diverse fields of application. The unifying element in this diversity is psychology's subject of study: human behaviour in the broadest sense of the word, ranging from perceptual processes to relations between groups of people.[1] The general aim of psychology is to describe, categorize, understand, explain and, ultimately, predict this behaviour, although the latter aim is rarely achieved. Obviously, psychology encompasses more than the usually limited lay understanding of it as only dealing with people's mental health problems.

Human behaviour is the subject of other scientific disciplines as well. Characteristic of the psychological perspective is that behaviour is studied with the objective of identifying psychic processes, and factors within individuals, affecting or determining their behaviour in specific situations.[2] In this respect, psychology can be distinguished from sociology, which primarily aims to identify the ways in which societal structures and institutions affect people's behaviour. Social psychology can be considered an intermediate subdiscipline between psychology and sociology.[3]

With human behaviour as the central element, it is easy to illustrate why psychology is at least an interesting perspective for the study of homosexuality. Here are some examples of questions, which, although not exclusively, are relevant from a psychological perspective. Which factors determine that people have homosexual desires? What are the causes of discriminatory behaviour regarding gays and lesbians and how can this be influenced? Does being gay or lesbian affect one's health status, psychological functioning or general well-being? What determines successful adaptation to a rejecting social climate in gays and lesbians? Why do some gays and lesbians experience homosexuality as central to their identity, while others experience it as peripheral? Why do some gay men develop more effeminate behaviour than others? How do children of lesbian and gay parents develop? What determines the attitude of gays and lesbians towards other (sexual) minorities? As will be shown, most of these questions have received some attention in psychological research, although some questions clearly more than others.

The questions that are actually addressed, and the kind of answers looked for, depend on such related things as the tradition in which a researcher is working, historical circumstances, the available intellectual and practical resources, but also the objectives of the researchers. It will be obvious that from the perspective of gay and lesbian lives, not all of the questions mentioned are equally relevant; research is particularly relevant if it is helpful in:

- supporting people in their expression of homosexual desires and in building gay and lesbian identities and lifestyles;
- counteracting homophobic tendencies and actions;
- promoting the emancipation of homosexuality.

Psychological research that meets these criteria can be defined as gay and lesbian. Although this perspective seems self-evident, it can be operationalized in various ways. What is relevant depends on the actual situation of gays and lesbians in a specific society, as well as on the ideology and strategy of the gay and lesbian movement.[4] However, some questions, such as how gays and lesbians can successfully be converted into heterosexuals, have little or no relevance from this perspective. Consequently, not all psychological research into homosexuality necessarily qualifies as gay and lesbian psychology. This implies that the label 'gay and lesbian psychology' refers to a loosely demarcated field of research.

An exponential growth in diversity and number of empirical studies

Since the publication of what is considered one of the first empirical psychological works about homosexuality – Evelyn Hooker's (1957) study of the psychological functioning of gay men – the growth in number and diversity of studies has been exponential. In 1977 Morin presented one of the first overviews of studies which were published in the preceding eight years. By looking under homosexuality and lesbianism in the register of *Psychological Abstracts*, he identified 139 empirical studies and developed a taxonomy to classify the research questions explored. His overview shows that in those days, the question most frequently studied was the cause of male and female homosexuality. More than one-third of the studies he collected addressed this issue. Twenty-seven of the 139 studies dealt with assessment or diagnosis. Another substantial part, 33 per cent, dealt with 'adjustment' or, more simply put, with the question of whether homosexuals are mentally ill. A small number of studies addressed attitudes towards homosexuality.[5] Overall, Morin observed an intensification of the interest in the struggle to free homosexuality of stigma.

This latter characterization does not apply to the over 2,000 references in the bibliography compiled by Anderson and Adley (1997), of publications abstracted in the *Psychological Abstracts* between 1985 and 1996.[6] This overview shows that the psychological interest in homosexuality has evolved further. There is still an interest in gay and lesbian health issues, but seldom from a psychopathological perspective. The interest in attitudes towards homosexuality has intensified. Most striking, however, is the enormous attention to a wide range of aspects of gay and lesbian lives. This change in perspective is probably best explained by the fact that research is no longer predominantly carried out by heterosexual researchers and that gay and lesbian researchers themselves have started to define the issues to be studied. The result of this increase in studies is also reflected in Cabaj and Stein's (1996) *Textbook of Homosexuality and Mental Health*, in anthologies such as those edited by Dynes and Donaldson (1992a, 1992b) and Garnets and Kimmel (1993), in bibliographies (cf. Maggiore, 1992), in the series on psychological perspectives on lesbian and gay issues edited by Greene and Herek (1994; Herek and Greene, 1995; Green, 1997; Herek, 1998), and in books such as those edited by D'Augelli and Patterson (1995; Patterson and D'Augelli, 1998). One qualification to this ostensible abundance is that most of these empirical studies have been carried out in the United States.

In the next part of this section an overview will be presented of the kinds of studies that have been carried out, the topics addressed, and some of the outcomes. Given the huge number of studies, this overview cannot be exhaustive. Priority has been given to review studies and studies by scholars who should be considered as having contributed extensively to gay and lesbian psychology. To counterbalance the predominance of American studies, extra effort has been made to include non-US studies.

Psychological research into homosexuality can be divided into the following five categories: the origins of homosexuality; anti-homosexual attitudes and behaviours; psychological functioning; becoming and being gay and lesbian; and sexuality, intimate relationships and parenting. Within these categories, studies have applied a variety of research designs. While studies into anti-homosexual attitudes predominantly focus on non-gays and non-lesbians, several apply a design in which homosexual and heterosexual samples are compared.[7] In other studies, focusing on issues specific to gays or lesbians, data are collected from predominantly self-identified homosexual persons only.

Theorizing the existence and origin of homosexuality

The first psychological theories about homosexuality dealt with its origin and were developed from the middle of the nineteenth century and in the early twentieth century by writers such as Ulrichs and Hirschfeld (Hekma, 1994). From our current perspective, these theories appear somewhat simplistic, romanticized, and rather ideologically inspired. The latter also applies to the more sophisticated theory developed by Freud, the founder of psychoanalysis. Although he had a relatively accepting attitude, Freud considered homosexuality the outcome of a disturbed psychosexual development in which the child's relationships with his or her parents were the sole determining factor in homosexual orientation (Drescher, 1996).

Empirical studies into the psychological origins of homosexuality were carried out in the 1960s and 1970s in particular. Psychologists, independently or in collaboration with professionals from other disciplines such as endocrinology and genetics, looked for a variety of causes. These studies applied either a psychoanalytic or social learning perspective and studied factors such as parental background and parenting styles, family constellations, birth order, sibling sex ratios, parental age, sex-role enforcement, gender non-conforming behaviour and sexual abuse experiences in childhood. Several researchers compared lesbian and heterosexual women to see whether negative childhood and adolescent sexual experiences with men were predictors of a homosexual orientation. Some did not find any support for this hypothesis (Brannock and Chapman, 1990; Peters and Cantrell, 1991). Beitchman et al. (1992), however, concluded in their review paper that adult women with child sexual abuse experiences had more homosexual experiences in adolescence and adulthood. Dancey (1990) also compared lesbian and heterosexual women and could not find any effect of various personality factors, either in combination with or independent from family attitudes and behaviours, such as sex-role enforcement, educational styles, parental protectiveness and maternal supportiveness.

Probably because of the lack of convincing results, psychological research into the origins of homosexuality is becoming rare. This could also be because the biological approach, offering some support for both genetic and prenatal hormonal explanations, seems more encouraging. These explanations are supported by findings from studies of twins. Whitman et al. (1993) showed that homosexuality was more often present in both persons if the twins are monozygotic instead of bizygotic. Other researchers looked at the composition of families and found that, compared to heterosexual women, homosexual women had a significantly higher proportion of homosexual sisters (Bailey and Benishay, 1993; see also Blanchard, 1997).

Researchers looking for the origins of homosexuality seldom state the aims of their studies, more or less assuming that their relevance is self-evident. Studies into origins are heavily disputed, biological studies in particular (see for instance De Cecco and Parker, 1995). When advocates and opponents of the biological approach enter into discussion, they seem to speak different languages. This is illustrated in Bailey et al. (1998), where the biological position is defended by some while others reject it as essentialist and claim that women's sexuality is fluid and dynamic rather than static and fixed. It seems that neither side is willing to see that each perspective may contribute to the understanding of how (homo)sexual behaviour develops and is expressed.

Anti-homosexual attitudes and attempts to change them

One of the major topics in psychological research is people's attitudes towards homosexuality; various labels, such as homophobia, anti-homosexual sentiments, anti-gay prejudice, and homonegativity are applied. Within this category, a variety of issues have been studied, looking at various populations and applying divergent approaches. Studies have most often focused on attitudes towards gay men; studies that specifically focus on attitudes toward lesbians are relatively rare (Kite and Whitley, 1998).

In the classical approach, studies tried to identify demographic, social and psychological correlates of anti-homosexual attitudes. Less favourable attitudes are more or less systematically found to be more prevalent among men than women, older people than young people, among less educated and religious people, and people who live in rural rather than urban areas (Herek, 1991; Kite, 1994).

More sophisticated studies look at different dimensions and the underlying structure of anti-gay attitudes, including the functions these attitudes have for the persons involved. In trying to assess whether anti-homosexual sentiments are a result of sexual conservatism or social prejudice, as measured by racist and sexist beliefs, Ficarrotto (1990) found that both independently predicted anti-homosexual attitudes. Bhughra (1987) presents an overview of research into homophobia as an irrational fear or intolerance of homosexuality and the various underlying reasons for this. Haddock and Zanna (1998) showed that anti-gay attitudes are not directly related to stereotypic ideas about homosexual men, but only if these ideas imply a violation of important values held by a person.

Attitudes have been studied in a variety of populations. However, as in psychological research in general, students are most frequently studied since they are easily accessible for most researchers. Other populations frequently studied are specific professional groups. One of the most important among them is counsellors and therapists. Rudolph (1988) reviewed various studies of this population and concluded that these attitudes are reflections of people's beliefs in both the potential health and the pathology of homosexuality. Stevens (1993) in her review of lesbian healthcare research, concluded that healthcare providers quite often hold prejudiced views and that these findings are mirrored by studies in which lesbians report the negative experiences they have had with healthcare providers.

Studying attitudes towards homosexuality lends itself to different approaches to data collection from the traditional written questionnaires. Tsang (1994) studied the responses of male and female shoppers who were approached by an Asian or white female experimenter either wearing a shirt identifying her as a lesbian or not and asking for change. Neither the race of the experimenter nor the sex of the shopper made a difference; what really seemed to matter was the shirt. The shoppers were less likely to give change to women identified as lesbian. A similar technique is to drop postcards with a neutral, or a gay and lesbian, message at a phone booth and checking whether there is a difference in return rate (Levinson et al., 1993).

The consequences of homophobic attitudes for heterosexual people themselves have also been studied, especially in men. Homophobia in men seems to be inversely related to their level of social intimacy (Monroe, et al., 1997). Roese et al. (1992) found support for the idea that homophobic attitudes result in less touching in casual contacts with people of the same sex (see also Stark, 1991).[8]

Given the detrimental effects of homophobia, both on homosexual as well as heterosexual people, one would expect that many studies would have been carried out evaluating attempts to change these attitudes. This does not however appear to be the case. As Stevenson (1988) shows in his overview, most of these studies are performed among students; although positive changes of participating in specific courses are reported, the extent and duration of these changes are not clear. It is also not clear what causes the established changes and whether the findings apply to groups of people other than students.

Findings from Herek and Glunt (1993) strongly support the idea that physical proximity to a homosexual individual plays a major role in attitude change. They demonstrated that, while controlling for a variety of demographic and social psychological variables, prior exposure to homosexual men had a positive effect on heterosexuals' attitudes towards gay men. Having been in contact with homosexuals also seems to be related to theories lay people have about homosexuality.[9]

A final development consists of the studies that look at reciprocal perceptions of homosexual and heterosexual men, or at the images lesbians have of bisexual women. Although the notion of the gay and lesbian movement assumes harmony between gay men and lesbians, they do not constitute one group and do not necessarily hold positive attitudes towards each other. The collaboration that does occur between them predominantly results from strategic considerations. Kristiansen (1990) for instance studied feminist lesbians, gay movement lesbians and gay males. While feminist lesbians seemed to share an intergroup relationship with gay men, the gay movement lesbians and the gay men shared an intragroup relationship. As with heterosexual people, the factor affecting feminist lesbians' attitudes is the perception that gay men placed less importance on values they themselves regarded as important. Rust (1992) studied the tension between lesbian- and bisexual-identified women and concluded that this tension was the result of the threat that bisexuality poses to lesbians, personally and politically.

Psychological functioning

The first studies assessing the psychological functioning of gay and lesbian people primarily focused on the mental health status not so much of the people studied, but of homosexuality *per se*. In comparing homosexual and heterosexual people, the aim was to challenge the generally accepted idea that homosexuality is a mental disease. The classical example in this approach is Evelyn Hooker's study (1957), in which she let professionals blindly judge the responses of homosexual men and heterosexual men to various projective tests. She found that these professionals were unable to distinguish between the two groups and concluded that the groups of men did not differ in their level of psychological adjustment. In 1991 Gonsiorek reviewed the studies that applied this approach and concluded that 'the issue of whether homosexuality per se is a sign of psychopathology, psychological maladjustment, or disturbance has been answered, and the answer is not' (1991: 135). This does not imply that this kind of defensive research was no longer being carried out. Depending on the social circumstances, these studies may still even have some practical relevance. However, current studies examining psychological health in gays and lesbians, more often start from the perspective that health has been impaired by societal oppression or that stress has been increased as a result of homophobia.

Acknowledging the socially oppressive climate, 'self-esteem' has been a central concept in research among gays and lesbians since the early 1970s. Hammersmith and Weinberg (1973) who introduced this line of research showed that psychological adjustment, including positive self-esteem, was a consequence of what they then called 'commitment to a deviant identity'. In line with these findings, Frable et al. (1997) showed that the more stigma gays and lesbians thought to be related to homosexuality, the more negatively they perceived themselves.

Self-esteem has a central place in the psychological study of gays and lesbians, and continues to be studied both as a determinant and as an outcome of various issues, such as coming out to parents, general disclosure, intimacy, problem-solving in relationships, and relationship satisfaction. Walters and Simoni (1993) showed that higher self-esteem resulted from having a positive attitude to the group identity, which means identifying with the social category of gays or lesbians.[10]

Internalized homophobia, which has been studied frequently as well, is in some way the homosexual opposite of self-esteem. This individual characteristic is assumed to result from internalizing the anti-homosexual attitudes encountered as part of a traditional, heterosexist socialization. In a study among gay men, Ross and Rosser (1996) identified four independent dimensions of internalized homophobia: (1) concern about being publicly identified as being gay, (2) concern about the stigma associated with being gay outside the gay world, (3) feelings of comfort with other gay men, and (4) the moral and religious acceptability of being gay. As is the case with self-esteem, internalized homophobia is also studied in relation to a variety of aspects of gay and lesbian lives and seems, amongst others, to predict mental health problems, problems with intimacy in relationships, and AIDS-related risk-taking behaviour (Meyer and Dean, 1998).

Given the issues gay and lesbian people have to deal with when they come out and develop a homosexual lifestyle, it has been assumed that they have more problems with alcohol and drugs, and also think of suicide and actually attempt it more often. To test this, several studies have made comparisons between heterosexual and homosexual people. Bux (1996) discusses various theories as to the aetiology of drinking problems in homosexual populations and reviews research on the prevalence of problem drinking in gay men and lesbians. He concludes that gay men are not at a higher risk than heterosexual men are, but that lesbian woman are as compared to heterosexual women.[11] He also concluded that theories about heavy and problematic drinking in gay men and lesbians have minimal empirical support. Regardless of the prevalence, there are gays and lesbians who do have alcohol-related problems, which to some extent will result from the stress they experience from having a stigmatized lifestyle. Various clinical reports have been written about the treatment of gay and lesbian alcoholics illustrating aspects of the treatment that are specific to homosexual people, such as fostering greater acceptance of one's homosexual orientation (see for instance Hall, 1994 and Israelstam, 1986).

Several studies looked at intended and attempted suicide in gays and lesbians, particularly in relation to the coming-out process (Remafedi, 1994). Rotheram-Borus et al. (1994) showed that gay adolescents who attempted suicide reported more gay-related stressors than those who did not. Another study showed that gay and lesbian adolescents who did attempt or consider suicide had less skills and resources to cope with discrimination, loneliness and isolation (Proctor and Groze, 1994). Hershberger et al. (1997) found within a group of gays and lesbians that those who attempted suicide had disclosed more completely their sexual orientation to others, had lost more friends because of their disclosure, and had experienced more victimization due to their orientation

Whether suicide is more prevalent among gays and lesbians is studied by Remafedi et al. (1998) in a population-based study of adolescents. They found that for males, but not for females, homosexuality was indeed related to suicidal intent and actual attempts. Bagley and Tremblay (1997) found in a random sample of males that homosexual and bisexual males are over 13 times more at risk of a serious suicide attempt than their heterosexual counterparts.[12] Since suicide rates differ widely between countries, these figures naturally cannot be generalized.

In a Dutch study, the prevalence of psychiatric disorders was assessed in a national probability sample (Sandfort et al., 1999). The study showed that lifetime and 12-month prevalence of various disorders – especially mood and anxiety disorders – were significantly higher for homosexual than heterosexual men. Regardless of sexual orientation, women in this study reported more mood and anxiety disorders than men. Comparing heterosexual and homosexual women, there was a significantly higher lifetime prevalence of major depression in homosexual women. There were no differences in the prevalence of other mood disorders and anxiety disorders. Homosexual women also reported more alcohol and drug dependency (lifetime and 12-months) than heterosexual women. Although the study does not allow for any causal interpretations of the findings, it is likely that the differences partly result from the stresses gay men and lesbians have to cope with in a society that does not accept homosexuality.

A topic which has more recently received attention from researchers is that of physical appearance and eating disorders. Like heterosexual women, gay men seem to have lower ideal weights and tend to be more preoccupied with their weight than are heterosexual men (Brand et al. 1992); this is suggested to be a consequence of their shared desire to attract and please men. Lesbians and heterosexual men are supposed to be less concerned with their physical attractiveness and, consequently, are less dissatisfied with their bodies and less vulnerable to eating disorders (Siever, 1994).

Psychological dimensions on which gays and lesbians are frequently compared with heterosexual persons are masculinity and femininity. Homosexual men appear to be systematically more gender atypical than heterosexual males (Hiatt and Hargrave, 1994). For lesbians, the results of these studies are less systematic. Finlay and Scheltema (1991) showed that higher masculinity scores in lesbians resulted from higher self-ratings of independence compared to heterosexual women; higher masculinity scores for heterosexual men were the result of higher self-ratings as competitive, compared to homosexual men. Peters and Cantrell (1993) looked at gender roles and social roles such as a worker, daughter and intimate partner, and the potential conflicts between these roles in lesbian and heterosexual feminist women. They found that lesbians and heterosexual women did not differ in gender role orientation. However, heterosexual women reported more conflict between their roles as daughter and worker. The lesbians reported more conflict between their roles as daughter and intimate partner, primarily resulting from their perceived disapproval of their intimate relationships.

Becoming and being gay and lesbian

One of the major challenges in the lives of people with homosexual desires is to integrate these desires in the sexual and social understanding of oneself and to cope with the stigma attached to these desires. Many studies have tried to explore the processes involved or have focused specifically on the situation of young gays and lesbians.

Most studies into the process of coming out are based on retrospective accounts of people who self-identify as gay or lesbian.[13] Based on this research various models have been developed describing the stages people subsequently go through (Cass, 1996; Troiden, 1989). Usually, these models include stages in which there is an awareness of being different from peers ('sensitization'), and in which people start to question their sexual identity ('identity confusion'). Subsequently, they start to explore practically the option of being gay or lesbian and learn to deal with the stigma ('identity assumption'). In the final stage, they integrate their sexual desires into a positive understanding of self ('commitment').[14]

Although the stage models are very helpful in understanding the ways in which people deal with the various issues they are confronted with, they have also been criticized. One of the criticisms is that the transition from one stage to the next is not self-evident. The model has also been criticized as ahistorical. Based on a study of coming-out processes in lesbian- and bisexual-identified women, Rust (1993) concluded that coming out is not a linear, goal-oriented, developmental process, but continues during maturity and takes place in a changing social context. The processes of coming out are also not completely identical for lesbians and gay men (De Monteflores and Schultz, 1978).

Many studies have explored the specific situation of lesbian and gay youth. D'Augelli and Hershberger (1993) for instance looked at the personal challenges youth face due to their sexual orientation and the way they respond to these.[15] As mentioned previously, alcohol and drug abuse, and suicidality have been studied frequently in gay and lesbian youth. Other studies focused on social background and on parents' role. Newman and Muzzonigro (1993) assessed the effects of traditional family values on the coming-out process of gay male adolescents. They showed that families with a strong emphasis on traditional values – implying the importance of religion, an emphasis on marriage and having children – were less accepting of homosexuality than were low-traditional families. Holtzen and Agresti (1990) studied parental responses to gay and lesbian children and found parents with negative responses to have lower self-esteem and negative attitudes towards women; negative feelings about homosexuality in parents decreased the longer they were aware of their child's homosexuality.[16]

Even when gay and lesbian people acquire a 'committed sexual identity', this does not mean that the issue of whether or not being open about one's orientation is solved once and for all. Several studies looked at whether or not people are open about their orientation and its consequences. There seems to be a hierarchy of persons to whom people are open regarding their homosexuality. Berger (1992) showed that among the gay men he studied, friends and siblings were more likely to be aware of their homosexuality than were co-workers, parents, and more distant relatives.

'Passing' – not being open about one's homosexuality or presenting oneself as heterosexual – used to be understood as an indication of a late stage in the process of coming out, in which one does not yet fully accept one's homosexuality. Harry (1993) showed however that among adult homosexual men being open is determined much more by income, occupation, where one lives, and the nature of one's friends. Likewise, Franke and Leary (1991) showed that among male and female homo- and bisexuals, openness depends much more on concern about the opinions of others and the consequences of disclosing, than on self-acceptance as homosexuals. These studies show that whether people are open should not just be understood from an intrapsychic perspective. The practical circumstances in which people operate vary and may set limits on the opportunities to be open.

Being open about one's homosexual orientation generally seems to promote individual well-being. Jordan and Deluty (1998) showed in a study of a large sample of lesbians, that disclosure of sexual orientation was negatively related to anxiety and positively to self-esteem and levels of social support. Berger (1990a) found that homosexual men and women who were less open were more likely to report less satisfaction with their relationships, although they did not love their partners less. Day and Schoenrade (1997), who studied gays and lesbians in work environments, showed that being closeted was related to a lesser affective commitment to the organization where one worked, to lesser job satisfaction, lesser belief in support from the top management, more role conflict and more conflict between work and home issues.

Cole et al. (1996a, 1996b) showed various detrimental health effects of not being open about one's homosexuality. HIV-negative men who concealed their homosexual identity experienced a significantly higher incidence of cancer and several infectious diseases. In HIV-positive men, the infection appears to progress more rapidly in gay men who conceal their homosexual identity. In both studies, the observed effect could not be attributed to various other factors, such as age, coping style or health behaviours. The effects are interpreted as negative health consequences of psychological inhibition.

The consequences of being homosexual have been studied in relation to various social situations, one of them being work. Sexual orientation first seems to be of influence on career decision-making. Etringer et al. (1990), studying the effect of both orientation and gender, found that gay men had the highest level of uncertainty about making a career choice, while lesbian women had the lowest level. Gay men, together with heterosexual women, also showed more dissatisfaction with their career choice than heterosexual men and lesbians. Sandfort and Bos (1998) showed that being homosexual negatively affected people's level of experienced social support at work and their job satisfaction. Both resulted in a higher level of burnout, and more reported sick leave.[17]

Experiences that several gay men and lesbian women have in common are discrimination and violence. D'Augelli (1992) described undergraduates' experiences of verbal insults and physical violence; few students reported victimization to the authorities; the most frequent victimizers were other students. Herek et al. (1997) showed that what they call 'hate crime victimization' was experienced by almost half of their sample and had almost exclusively been perpetrated by men. Having had these experiences was related to higher levels of depression, anxiety, anger and symptoms of post-traumatic stress.[18]

Gay men and lesbians' experiences of medical and mental health care have frequently been studied. The specific issues they have to cope with, such as coming out, dealing with a stigmatized identity, discrimination and violence, might negatively affect their health status.[19] Dunkle (1994) presents an overview of studies assessing the outcomes of psychotherapy with male homosexual clients, carried out since 1975. He identified four main goals of therapy: (1) facilitating gay male identity, (2) developing strategies for coping with AIDS, (3) increasing relationship satisfaction, and (4) helping a partner or a couple overcome sexual dysfunction. Dunkle criticizes the research in this field for its limited methodological quality. MacDonald (1998) discusses issues in therapy with gay and lesbian couples. Stevens (1993) shows in an overview of various studies that the experiences of mistreatment, hostility and rejection, which lesbian women had with healthcare providers, had a negative impact in delaying the seeking of healthcare.[20]

Psychological and social adjustment in ageing homosexual men and women has been addressed in several studies.[21] Whether the process of ageing is different for homosexual and heterosexual people is not clear. Lee (1987) suggests that older homosexual and heterosexual men are more similar than different, and that a generational class conflict is the major problem facing all aged. In his own study, Lee (1989) documented how liberated homosexual communities do not seem to be willing to make room for the elderly, which he sees as a consequence of the cultural differences between young and old members of gay communities, particularly where privacy and intimacy are concerned.

Schuyf (1996) assessed gay men's and lesbians' opportunities for successful ageing. She observed major differences between elderly lesbians and gay men, gay men usually being better off in both material and psychic respects. The social networks of the men were more varied than those of the lesbians. General differences in socialization between men and women, resulting in different attitudes toward sexuality and intimacy, make it easier for gay men to build and maintain their network of friends. For women, preferring to experience sex and intimacy with one partner, there is a higher risk of becoming isolated, since it becomes harder to find new partners as one becomes older.[22]

Adelman (1990) found the quality of the adjustment to ageing among elderly gays and lesbians to be related to the coming-out process. High life satisfaction, low self-criticism, and few psychosomatic problems were related to high satisfaction with being gay and to gay experimenting before defining oneself as gay or lesbian. Pope and Schulz (1990) focused on the sexual aspect of ageing in gay men and found that most of the men they studied continued to be sexually active. While some reported a decrease in the enjoyment of sexuality, almost the same proportion of men showed an increase.

Sexuality, intimate relationships and parenthood

Although sexuality is at the basis of homosexual identities, surprisingly little research used to be carried out into the sexual behaviour of gay men and lesbians. Only after the onset of the AIDS epidemic did the sexual behaviour of gay men, or more generally sexuality between men, become an issue of serious attention, predominantly from the perspective of health promotion.[23] Given the strong impact of sex role socialization on sexuality, it is generally assumed that sexuality is affected more by gender than by sexual orientation. The fact that the sexual relationships of gay men are more often 'open' than heterosexual relationships is often understood from this perspective.[24] In an overview of studies on lesbian sexuality, Schreurs (1993) also showed that lesbian couples have more in common with heterosexual women than with gay men. Compared to other couples, lesbians have sex less frequently, although they seem to be more satisfied with their sex lives.

A few studies compared the sexual functioning of homosexual and heterosexual people. Crowden and Koch (1995) showed that sexual orientation had a greater effect on sexual attitudes than gender. Compared to heterosexual people, homosexual people for instance had a better sexual self-understanding, and showed less guilt regarding masturbation and sexuality in general. Hurlbert and Apt (1993), who only studied women, showed several differences based on sexual orientation. In lesbian women they observed greater interpersonal dependency, compatibility and intimacy; the heterosexual women, however, evidenced more positive dispositions toward sexual fantasies, greater sexual assertiveness, stronger sexual desire, and higher frequencies of sexual activity. The two groups did not differ in sexual satisfaction.

Wells (1990), studying the sexual vocabulary people use for communicating erotically with sexual partners, found differences related to gender and orientation. Lesbians and gay males seemed to use erotic or arousing vocabulary with a spouse or lover more often than heterosexual females and males did. Gay males also more often used slang with a spouse or lover than did heterosexual males and females. Keating and Over (1990) studied sexual fantasies of heterosexual and homosexual men. They found that in each group, sensual and genital fantasies, corresponding to one's orientation, were more arousing than either public-sex or dominance-submissive fantasies. The latter were in turn more arousing than aggressive-sex fantasies. The more experience one had of a specific sexual activity, the more arousing the fantasy about that activity. Hawkins (1990) compared how men in heterosexual and homosexual relationships dealt with sexual jealousy. He found that men in heterosexual couples have higher levels of sexual jealousy than men in homosexual couples, and that sexual jealousy is less strong in men who focus on personal growth and fully employ their personal potentials.

Still very little is known of the prevalence of sexual problems in lesbians and gay men.[25] In one study, Shires and Miller (1998) compared gay and heterosexual men with erectile dysfunctions and found that for heterosexual men performance anxiety was a dominant factor, while gay men were more strongly affected by anxiety about HIV, internalized homophobia and intimacy issues.

Klinkenberg and Rose (1994) explored dating scripts used by gay men and lesbians. Gay men's scripts seemed to be more sexually oriented and less emotionally and intimacy focused than lesbians' scripts. Some aspects of traditional heterosexual, gender-typed roles were lacking. Girls for example were less likely to inform their parents about dates. Some actions were unique to this gay and lesbian population, in particular addressing the issue of safe sex. On a more abstract level, Bailey et al. (1997) studied the preference among gays and lesbians for either masculine or feminine partners. They found that gays and lesbians both preferred partners who have the gender traits that belong to their biological sex.

Several studies have looked at gay and lesbian intimate relationships. Some offer descriptions of these relationships (Berger, 1990b; Akkermann et al., 1990a 1990b), focusing on issues such as where partners had met – for men this is most frequently the gay bar – and what most conflicts are about – finances and relations with family members, it is suggested. Other studies looked at processes within gay and lesbian relationships in greater depth. If a rationale is offered for studying gay and lesbian intimate relationships, it usually relates to the specific challenges gays and lesbians must cope with. Among these challenges are the limited oppor-tunities for finding partners, the lack of social and institutional support, and the stigma that homosexual relationships have to cope with. Specific characteristics, such as the fact that both partners have had the same sex-role socialization, are also offered as a rationale for studying these relationships. Meyer (1989) is one of the few researchers who actually assessed the issue of the support heterosexual and homosexual couples receive from their social network and found that homosexual couples indeed experienced less support. Meyer suggests that this leads to less stability, shorter duration and less monogamy in gay relationships.

Based on extensive interviews with male couples, McWhirter and Mattison (1984) developed a model of relationship development in gay men. According to their theory, there are six stages in the development of relationships, each with its own characteristics, challenges and problems, respectively labelled blending, nesting, maintaining, building, releasing and renewing.

Steinman (1990), applying the social exchange theory in gay couples in which there was a big age difference between partners, studied how intrinsic and extrinsic resources were exchanged. He observed that in most couples the younger partner was much more likely than the older one to grant or refuse sexual gratification as a means of securing or maintaining equity in the social exchange. The sexual resources, however, were not necessarily exchanged for non-sexual, extrinsic resources such as financial compensation. The intrinsic resources, which the older partner had to offer, such as intelligence and social accomplishments, were often as strongly attractive to younger partners as material possessions.

Rosenbluth and Steil (1995) have addressed the issue of power, comparing women in lesbian and heterosexual relationships. They found, among other differences, that the uses of direct, bilateral influence strategies, which were more frequently observed in lesbian relationships, predicted the level of intimacy in the relationship. The use of indirect strategies to influence the partner, more common if one is in a position of relatively less power, was related to lower levels of intimacy, especially for women in heterosexual relationships. Based on their findings, the researchers suggest that power inequality, which generally characterizes heterosexual couples, impedes intimacy.

An exceptional study focused specifically on the allocation of household labour among gay, lesbian and heterosexual couples (Kurdek, 1993). Lesbian couples tended to share tasks more often than both married and gay couples. Compared with lesbian couples, gay couples and married couples were likely to have one or the other partner perform the tasks; and in heterosexual married couples, this was likely to be the wife. Finally, in contrast with married couples, gay couples and lesbian couples were likely to split tasks in such a way that each partner performed an equal number of different tasks.

Domestic violence is a relatively often researched issue, mainly in lesbian relationships. In one of these studies it was shown that slightly more than half of the 1,099 lesbians surveyed reported that they had been abused by a female lover (Lie and Gentlewarrier, 1991). Reviews of studies indicate that the reported rates of intimate abuse vary, depending on the types of question actually posed to respondents. It is also not clear whether it happens more often in gay or lesbian couples compared to heterosexual couples (Renzetti, 1998; West, 1998). It is quite likely, though, that the underlying dynamics in homosexual couples differ from those in heterosexual couples, since there is either no male person who abuses (in lesbian couples) or there are two men who, based on their socialization as men, are equally likely to be the abuser. Mutual battering would also be more likely in male homosexual relationships than in heterosexual relationships. Furthermore, homosexual couples can use different 'weapons', such as threatening to tell other people that the victim is homosexual or telling the victim that this is what she deserves for being a lesbian. With respect to the potential origins of gay and lesbian intimate abuse, it is likely that the same determinants, such as violence in the family of origin, substance abuse and power imbalances, play a role, as in heterosexual relationships, although internalized homophobia could promote abuse as well.

Schilit, Lie and Montagne (1990) showed that alcohol or drugs were systematically involved before or during incidents of battering. The more often one drank, the more often one committed abusive acts as well as being the victim of abusive acts. Reported aggression with a previous male partner is more often described by lesbians as an act of self-defence, while aggression in relationships involving a female partner was most frequently described as mutual (Lie et al., 1991). In gay men, intimate abuse was more frequently observed in relationships in which partners shared decision-making authority in such a way that each partner makes decisions in different domains.

Hickson et al. (1994) studied the prevalence of non-consensual sex among 930 homosexually active men and found that over 27 per cent of them had had such an experience at least once in their life; in one-third of the cases they were having consensual sex with the same men as well. Waldner-Haugrund and Gratch (1997) found that sexual coercion was not more frequent in lesbian than in gay relationships; they did not find any differences regarding the type of coercion and the severity of the outcomes of sexual coercion.

Kurdek (1991a), and Eldridge and Gilbert (1990) have studied relationship satisfaction in gay and lesbian couples. The latter, studying lesbian couples, found that dyadic attachment, intimacy, self-esteem, life satisfaction, etc. all correlated positively with relationship satisfaction. Role conflict and personal autonomy were found to correlate negatively with relationship satisfaction, as did differences between the partners' levels of career commitment. As was found earlier in heterosexual relations (Doi and Thelen, 1993), relationship satisfaction is higher in gay and lesbian couples when there is less fear of intimacy; fear of intimacy was more frequently observed when there was little self-disclosure and when partners felt less comfortable with emotional closeness in the relationship (Greenfield and Thelen, 1997). Deenen et al. (1994) also showed that emotional intimacy was the best predictor of relationship satisfaction in gay men, although the factors that predicted relationship and sexual satisfaction differed according to relationship duration and age of the partner. Caron and Ulin (1997) found that the quality of lesbian relationships is better when a couple is able to be open about their relationship towards family and friends.

Using a longitudinal design, Kurdek (1992) also studied which gay and lesbian relationships lasted and which ones ended. In another study, he examined reactions to breaking up in both partners of gay and lesbian couples. He found that persons adjusting better had completed more years of education, had known his or her partner for fewer months, had lived with that partner for fewer months, had not pooled finances with the partner, reported little love for the partner, and placed a low value on attachment to the partner (Kurdek, 1991b). In a later study, he showed that levels of distress resulting from breaking up did not differ between gay, lesbian and heterosexual people. If lack of relational cohesion was the cause of breaking up, individuals expressed less distress as a result of the separation compared to individuals who said that communication problems were the cause of the separation (Kurdek, 1997).

A final area of research deals with homosexual parenting. Most of these studies are quite recent and focus on lesbians and their children. Most research in this field addresses what is probably central to (heterosexual) objections to lesbian and gay parenthood: the potential negative consequences for the children involved.[26] Studies have, however, shown that regardless of the various challenges lesbian families are confronted with, they are able to create nurturing, egalitarian families in which they are bearing and raising well-functioning, well-adjusted and socially tolerant children (Parks, 1998; Patterson, 1997). Tasker and Golombok (1997) present data from a longitudinal study of 25 children raised in lesbian mother families and a comparison group raised by single heterosexual mothers.

A few studies have started to assess the interactions of parents and children within lesbian and gay families. Mitchell (1998) explored the way in which lesbian mothers deal with the issues of sexuality and reproduction in relation to their children. Patterson et al. (1998) looked at children's relationships with adults outside the immediate family and found that children were more likely to be in contact with relatives of the biological mother than with those of the non-biological mother. Bigner and Jacobsen (1992) showed that gay and non-gay fathers had comparable parenting styles and attitudes toward fathering.[27]

Challenges for gay and lesbian psychology

Taken as a whole, the studies offer valuable and, in a few cases, somewhat trivial insights. Some of these studies are theory driven, but they are relatively few. A more critical point is that in most of these studies gay and lesbian persons appear as if they are interchangeable representatives of a clearly distinguishable static human species, sharing a common psychology or personality type. In some studies being gay or lesbian *as such* is even implied to be the explanation for differences found from heterosexual groups. This basic assumption can be criticized at a practical as well as a conceptual level. Scrutinizing this assumption will help to determine the direction in which gay and lesbian psychology should develop further.

Another way to phrase the issue at stake is: who are these gays and lesbians being studied? Which people are these studies about? Whose homosexuality are we dealing with when we talk about gays and lesbians? At a practical level these questions can be answered in terms of how representative the groups are that are being studied.[28] Researchers are usually aware of this issue. The statement that samples of gay and lesbian people studied are selective has almost become a platitude. In the case of homosexual men, the sample quite often consists of white, well-educated, upper-middle-class men.[29] The fact that most samples of gay men and lesbians are selective is usually a consequence of the way they are composed. Since there is no inventory of all gays and lesbians from which random samples can be drawn, researchers are usually dependent on convenience samples. Respondents are recruited via magazines, groups, organizations, meeting places, and snowball sampling.

The fact that selective samples are used affects the meaning of the findings. In studies with descriptive aims, it becomes unclear to what extent percentages and proportions are accurate reflections of larger groups of gays and lesbians. Studies might give both deflated as well as inflated images of reality. From a strategic perspective, it might be helpful to have inflated figures when problems are to be exposed. The pictures that emerge from these studies may however also support existing stereotypes of gays and lesbians.[30] It is quite likely that the same qualification applies to studies that aim at exploring relationships between variables or testing hypotheses.

A practical solution to solve the issue of representativeness is to apply large, general sample frames, and to screen for individuals with homosexual behaviour, interests or self-identification. In practice, however, these procedures are rather costly. A way to circumvent this problem is to include some identifying questions in general population surveys set up by other researchers to study phenomena such as mental health or work experiences, which are also relevant from a gay and lesbian perspective.

At a conceptual level, the issue of representativeness is more complicated. The mere fact that most studies of gays and lesbians are overpopulated with self-identified, white, well-educated, upper-middle-class people is not just a consequence of sampling.[31] It is also a reflection of the way homosexuality is organized and expressed. Gay and lesbian identities do not only encompass a variety of homosexual expressions and experiences; homosexuality is also expressed beyond the context of these identities. Research in the field of AIDS has made clear that labelling oneself as gay is, although not exclusively, a rather 'white' phenomenon. As a consequence, the term 'men who have sex with men' is used in AIDS research next to 'gay men', acknowledging the fact that same gender sexuality can be experienced and expressed not only in the context of a gay identity but in a variety of other ways as well. Gay and lesbian psychology should find ways to acknowledge this variety.

Even when studies focus on gay and lesbian people, it is important not to isolate their experiences from the social context in which these come about. One might seriously pose the question as to whether for instance gay men in the Netherlands have more in common with gay men in the US than with heterosexual men in the Netherlands. Experiences also vary from a historical perspective. In view of the fact that the way in which homosexuality is expressed depends so much on cultural and historical factors, it makes no sense to talk of gays and lesbians in unqualified terms. The diversity of experiences assembled under the label gay and lesbian should be acknowledged and even become a focus of study. Furthermore, the cultural contexts of experiences have to be taken into account and should be addressed. This implies that historical and cross-cultural comparisons and the development of theories that transcend these specific contexts are fruitful.

Except for cross-cultural comparisons, it is difficult for empirical research to include social context in the study, since one has to specify the unit of analysis, be it individuals or relationships. Consequently, people usually appear in empirical studies as isolated entities. Social context can only appear when the outcomes are interpreted. To make gay and lesbian sense of research findings, a well-developed cultural and historical framework is a prerequisite. This implies that gay and lesbian psychology can only be practised in conjunction with other disciplines, in particular sociology and history. A major challenge for gay and lesbian psychology is to contextualize empirical studies and to incorporate the diversity of homosexual expression.

Although social and cultural contexts should be integrated in psychological studies about homosexuality, it does not mean that there is no communality across the various cultures. Wherever one goes, homosexuality, because of its relatively infrequent occurrence, is attributed specific symbolic value, which affects the ways it is expressed and experienced. In Western societies homosexuality is, in varying degrees, not a legitimate form of sexual expression and is not equally valued with heterosexuality. This affects the lives of people who engage in homosexual practices and who develop gay and lesbian identities, as well as their psychological make-up. A task people involved in homosexual behaviour have in common is to process and overcome societies' negative evaluations. Lacking clear-cut models, gays and lesbians have more leeway for experimentation with identities and within intimate relationships. Less social and legal support for relationships, however, makes it harder to develop and maintain relationships. This shared aspect of being a member of a differently valued minority group – which membership, unlike ethnicity and religion, only becomes clear at a later stage in life and always in an environment without like-minded people – is the most convincing argument for the existence of gay and lesbian psychology.

Gay and lesbian studies and mainstream psychology

In the 1960s and 1970s, psychology played a major role in the study of gay and lesbian issues, especially with respect to taking homosexuality out of the realm of psychopathology and replacing bias by facts. Nowadays, gay and lesbian studies is dominated by other disciplines such as history, cultural studies and literary studies. This becomes apparent when one examines recent compilations of gay and lesbian texts, such as *The Lesbian and Gay Studies Reader* (Abelove et al., 1993) and *Queer Studies: A Lesbian, Gay, Bisexual, and Transgender Anthology* (Beemyn and Eliason, 1996), which contain no contributions from the field of psychology. It seems that after psychology had served its function in depathologizing homosexuality, psychological questions about gays and lesbians themselves lost their interest and are no longer valid. As a response to the pathologizing approach dominant in early psychology, this is understandable. It is, however, interesting to see that although these new perspectives have a different object of study, they include various psychological statements. The need to empirically verify these statements seems to be less pressing. The lack of connection between gay and lesbian psychology and gay and lesbian studies or queer studies is certainly a consequence of differences in the respective paradigms.

Research methods that are predominantly used within psychology are not considered valid ways of acquiring knowledge within the perspectives that are now dominant in the study of gay and lesbian issues.[32]

Gay and lesbian psychology seems to be better connected to mainstream psychology than to gay and lesbian studies or queer studies. It is quite likely that consequently the way homosexuality is dealt with within psychology in general has changed substantially in recent decades. A closer look at what is published in scientific journals and in introductory psychology textbooks suggests, however, that the impact of gay and lesbian psychology is still limited – it goes without saying that homosexuality is still addressed in these textbooks as if all the readers are heterosexual. There are, however, several other signs indicating more serious attention for homosexuality within mainstream psychology.

Various authors have reviewed psychology's attention to homosexuality. Rivers (1997) concluded in his overview that the last twenty years have seen a marked increase in the number of journal articles and books in the field of lesbian and gay psychology and psychotherapy. Clark and Serovich (1997), however, who surveyed 13,217 articles published in 17 different marriage and family therapy journals, reached a less optimistic conclusion: only 0.006 per cent of these articles focused on gay, lesbian and/or bisexual issues, or used sexual orientation as a variable. Weitz and Bryant (1997) observed a change in models of homosexuality in their overview of American textbooks published between 1980 and 1995. In recent textbooks, homosexuality is no longer described as an illness while in 1980 30 per cent of the books still used this description. The perspective of homosexuals as a minority group is gaining strength, although these authors also observe that the concept of homosexuality as a sin has gained new life with the emergence of the AIDS epidemic.

Although general psychology's attention to homosexuality has increased and has become more neutral, several introductory psychology textbooks still do not address homosexuality at all. At the same time, homosexuality remains a compulsory topic for textbooks on abnormal psychology. If homosexuality is addressed in textbooks, almost all attention is invariably given to its potential biological and psychological causes. Homosexuality also quite often figures in the discussions of the role of hormones in determining human behaviour. The treatment of this issue is usually somewhat critical. Most authors strongly stress that research is still inconclusive and that the 'causes' of homosexuality are unknown, 'as they are for heterosexuality', as is sometimes added. Huffman et al. (1997) cautiously suggest that it might even be that looking at the causes of homosexuality, and not heterosexuality, is a form of covert prejudice.[33] Most authors of these textbooks conclude that causes are quite likely to be 'multifaceted' and include both biological and psychological factors. That homosexuality itself is a multi-faceted phenomenon is, however, not acknowledged in the discussion of causes. There is also no acknowledgement of sociohistorical factors. In addition, homosexual behaviour is usually implicitly equated with being homosexual. While several authors in general textbooks try to dispel myths, others myths are, maybe inadvertently, reinforced.[34]

Given the original perspective of homosexuality as an illness, it is understandable that most textbooks discuss therapeutic treatment. Arguments are presented pro and con treatment, usually with the additional statement that homosexuality is a rather stable disposition. Homosexuality recurrently figures as an example of how changing societal norms affect thinking about mental disorders.

More extensive discussions are usually to be found in introductory textbooks in social psychology, although not all address homosexuality, not even in the obvious section on societal attitudes towards minority groups. A common issue in these textbooks is intimate relationships. Some authors stress the similarities between heterosexual and homosexual people. Some go to great lengths to stress the normality of homosexuality. Comer (1995) for instance asserts: 'It is impossible to identify a characteristic that consistently separates them [homosexuals] from the rest of the population other than their sexual preference' (1995: 515). Other authors also pay attention to differences between heterosexual and homosexual people. Franzoi (1996) refers to research showing that same gender friendships among gay men quite often result from sexual interaction, while in heterosexual men friendships with the opposite gender sometimes result in sex, which usually means the end of the relationship. Costin and Draguns (1989) explain that cross-dressing in gay men differs from transvestism in heterosexual men since the latter usually lacks sexual motivation. These social psychology textbooks also pay attention to stereotypes about homosexuality and its consequences, homophobia or heterosexism, discrimination, and the gay and lesbian movement and its accomplishments.

Although inspection of psychology textbooks suggests that the impact of gay and lesbian psychology on mainstream psychology is limited, other signs produce a more optimistic picture. Where relevant, various psychological contributions to journals and books include a homosexual perspective.[35] Furthermore, papers dealing with gay and lesbian issues are not only published in specialized journals such as the *Journal of Homosexuality*, *Journal of Sex Research*, *Journal of Sex and Marital Therapy* and *Archives of Sexual Behavior*, but also in major psychological journals such as *Developmental Psychology*, *Journal of Personality and Social Psychology*, and the interdisciplinary journal *Sex Roles*. It must be added, though, that from a lesbian and gay perspective, the relevance of the papers published in these latter journals is less evident than of those in the more specialized gay and lesbian sources. Finally, the gay and lesbian perspective is also represented in various psychological handbooks.[36]

Compared to other disciplines involved in the study of gay and lesbian issues, gay and lesbian psychology is clearly present in the mainstream discipline. There are various related reasons why this is the case. The first has to do with the fact that homosexuality was studied within psychology before a clear gay and lesbian perspective was developed, and the development of that perspective took place in dialogue with traditional psychology. Another reason is that in studying gay and lesbian issues use was made of existing psychological theories, dealing for instance with self-esteem, attitudes, and intimate relationships. Sometimes the same issues which were studied in a heterosexual population were studied in a gay and lesbian population as well. A third reason is that, as Kitzinger (1997) has pointed out, gay and lesbian psychology mainly applied research methods that were dominant in mainstream psychological research. More qualitatively oriented approaches, such as those used within critical psychology, have rarely been applied. Kitzinger's (1987) own work is an outstanding exception in this respect. Adopting mainstream methods made it possible to continue to participate in mainstream psychological discourse, while focusing on what, from the dominant perspective, is a marginal and not a reputable topic. In line with the former reasons, gay and lesbian psychology, in its empirical approach, is less affected by the postmodern epistemologies which contribute to the alienation between other gay and lesbian perspectives and their basic discipline.

A critical note is in order. Although the situation appears favourable, it should be realized that the most relevant contributions to gay and lesbian psychology still come from gay and lesbian researchers themselves. It is quite likely that if they stopped researching these issues, attention to these topics would disappear and homophobia would more strongly inform the questions that researchers explore. Gay and lesbian psychologists have to continue to fulfil their critical function within psychological academia. This implies that without giving up one's gay and lesbian psychological network, integration into academic networks continues to be important.

Conclusion

Homosexuality has been and for various reasons will continue to be a fruitful subject for psychological research. There continues to be a practical need for this research. For instance, in order to effectively counteract homonegativity it is of crucial importance to understand its underlying dynamics as well as the reasons for success or failure in attempts to influence it. Understanding gay and lesbian relationships is also relevant to relationships in general, since same sex relationships provide an opportunity to examine relationship dynamics in the absence of differing sex role socialization. Homosexuality is also an interesting test case for psychological theories based on heterosexuals, to see whether their applicability is inclusive or needs adjustment in order to account for experiences of homosexual people. Such research could also identify what is specific to homosexual lives and relationships. Future research could focus on, or at least acknowledge, the diversity of gay and lesbian people.

The changing social climate as well as the fact that new generations of gay and lesbian people step forward will also present new issues for study. Examples of these are the consequences of the legal recognition of gay and lesbian relationships on the way people build and experience these relationships. The fact that gay and lesbian people less self-evidently abandon the wish to become parents will also change the formation and maintenance of their relationships. People who came out after Stonewall, having seen a larger range of options for themselves, will age differently than former generations did. A final example is the consequence on the coming-out process of the Internet's role in facilitating contact with others and the opportunity it provides to explore and experiment with (sexual) identities.

Particularly in the case of homosexuality, the social and historical context is pertinent to its psychological understanding. By focusing only on individuals, psychology runs the risk of losing sight of this. Relevant elements of this context are the omnipresent assumption of heterosexuality, the lower status of homosexuality, the unequal valuation of feminine and masculine behaviours, and the inability to accommodate sexual diversity. For its further development, gay and lesbian psychology would profit from the development of an articulated programme, integrating input from other disciplinary approaches to homosexuality and general psychological theories, as well as an analysis and valuation of the needs of gay and lesbian people and their respective social contexts. Such a programme would give coherence to individual studies and a direction for further research endeavours.

Notes

I would like to thank Gregory Herek, Jeffrey Weiss and the editors of this book for their valuable comments on earlier drafts of this chapter.

1. Within psychology, there is also a subdiscipline dealing with animal behaviour.

2. Psychology not only refers to theory and research, it is also applied in practice by professionals such as counsellors and psychotherapists, vocational advisers, organizational consultants, health educators and medical psychologists. People who practise psychology also sometimes publish their work, either in books or in scientific journals. This seems to be particularly true in the case of homosexuality. In doing so, these practitioners contribute fruitfully to the theorizing about various aspects of homosexuality. These works should be distinguished from studies based on systematic and objective observation, which are characteristic of empirical psychology. Depending on one's scientific paradigm, no sharp dividing lines can be drawn between these two approaches.

3. Especially in the study of a multifaceted phenomenon such as homosexuality, exact demarcations between disciplines are hard to draw, though. Consequently, this overview will also include a few references to sociological studies.

4. Illustrative in this respect is the difference in appreciation of biological research into the origins of homosexuality. In the US, gays and lesbians generally value these kinds of studies, mainly because it is expected that proof of a biological basis for homosexuality will promote acceptance. Regardless of whether this is true or not, biological studies are looked upon less positively by, for example, Dutch gays and lesbians, partly because this approach is seen as too deterministic a view of homosexuality and does not acknowledge the wide variety of homosexual expression.

5. The remaining studies were categorized as dealing with special topics, including coming out, relationships, paedophilia, married homosexuals, and homosexuality in prisons.

6. These references not only include empirical studies but clinical descriptions and theoretical reflections.

7. In some of these studies, both a between-subgroup as well as a within-group analysis is carried through. This can contribute substantially to the understanding of the role homosexually related variables play. Frable et al. (1997) for instance found that the predominantly white, young, educated and middle-class cohort of gays they studied did not differ as a group from non-stigmatized (meaning non-gay) samples in self-esteem and psychological distress. Within the gay group itself, however, they were able to show a clear relation between the cultural stigma experienced by the men and their psychological well-being.

8. See Kimmel (1997) for an in-depth theoretical discussion of the relation between homophobia and masculinity.

9. For a more general review of the literature on teaching on homosexuality, see Watter (1987), and Sears and Williams (1997).

10. That the situation is not simple is shown by Vincke and Bolton (1994) who found higher levels of self-acceptance among gay men who attached importance to being gay and who identified with the gay group; these men had, however, also more depressive symptoms than others. Gay men with more intensive group identification socialized less exclusively with fellow gay men and perceived themselves to be more respected.

11. These findings are confirmed by a study in a probability sample of the Dutch population (Sandfort et al., 1999).

12. See McBee and Rogers (1997) for an overview of research into suicidal behaviour among gays and lesbians, and Muehrer (1995) for a critical assessment of methodological limitations of most of these studies.

13. Although Boxer and Cohler (1989) recommended long ago that longitudinal, prospective research should be applied to the study of homosexual development, no such projects have been undertaken as yet.

14. See Brady and Busse (1994) for the development of a measure of homosexual identity formation, the Gay Identity Questionnaire.

15. See Radkowsky and Siegel (1997) for an extensive overview of the available research on gay and lesbian youth.

16. Strommen (1989) and Savin-Williams (1998) present overviews of the empirical research that addresses coming out to family members.

17. See also Croteau (1996) for a review of related studies and Diamant (1993) for a collection of papers on various homosexual issues in the workplace.

18. See Comstock (1991) and Herek and Berrill (1992) for extensive overviews of research into discrimination and violence against homosexual people.

19. Apart from alcohol use, health issues themselves seem to be predominantly studied among lesbians (see for instance Bradford et al., 1994).

20. See also Platzer (1998) for an overview of studies of lesbians' reasons for and experiences of seeking counselling.

21. An extensive qualitative and quantitative study of ageing in gay men has been carried out by Berger (1996).

22. See also Kehoe (1988), who in her study of elderly lesbians comes to similar conclusions.

23. See however Zwart, van Kerkhof and Sandfort (1998) who studied the meaning of anal sex and the way it is scripted in sexual interactions between men.

24. What has been labelled 'promiscuity' among gay men has also been understood as resulting from an unsuccessful coming-out process, in which a person has been unable to integrate sexuality and intimacy. Another explanation of the fact that male homosexual relationships are more open is offered by evolutionary psychology. Given the fact that the actual difference in the proportion of open sexual relationships among homosexual and heterosexual men is not extremely big (Sandfort, 1997), it is quite likely that the image of promiscuity among homosexual men is also a result of the greater visibility of open sexual lifestyles as well as of male heterosexual projection.

25. See however Bhugra and Wright (1995), who present an overview of the literature on the diagnosis and management of sexual dysfunction in gay men.

26. For a discussion on gay and lesbian parenting from a perspective of parenting as a socially constructed phenomenon, see Allen (1997).

27. Bozett (1989) and Patterson and Chan (1996) present an overview of research on gay fathers.

28. To prevent any misunderstandings: representativeness is not always a prerequisite in psychological research. A study does not have to be representative if one wants to demonstrate that a phenomenon occurs or that a specific phenomenon is not universal. Furthermore, if one wants to test hypotheses derived from a theory, selective samples are not necessarily an impediment. For the further development of these theories it is however necessary to replicate such studies, to see in which situations these findings hold and for

which circumstances they have to be refined or rejected. If one wants to generalize findings to a specific population, for instance all gay and lesbian people, one does, however, need a representative sample (assuming that that is practically possible). Regarding the latter, it should be realized that we are not dealing with a dichotomy. Depending upon the way probability samples are composed, the amount of error due to sampling will differ.

29. It is quite likely that in studies which assess attitudes toward homosexual people, respondents answer questions with these white, well-educated, upper-middle-class men in mind, regardless of the respondents' own ethnic or cultural background, and omitting lesbians.

30. This is for instance the case with respect to the frequency of extra-relational sex in gay men. In a recent study, the proportion of Dutch gay men in open relationships in various convenience samples were compared with findings from a substantial, probability sample of homosexual men (Sandfort, 1997). The percentages of men in open relationships found in the various convenience samples which ranged from 65 per cent to 50 per cent, differed significantly from the percentage (24 per cent) found in the random sample. Findings such as these should make us reticent about drawing general conclusions based on findings from selective samples.

31. Although more psychological attention has been paid recently to minority groups within the gay and lesbian population (see for instance Greene, 1997), these studies usually do not solve the problem. The gay men or lesbians studied cannot be considered representative of that specific minority.

32. The reverse is true as well: research methods generally used in literature studies and in the humanities are usually not seen as legitimate means of data collection by psychologists. There are some psychological studies on homosexuality, mainly applying to qualitative research methods, which are more connected to the new paradigms in gay and lesbian studies. An example of this is Kitzinger's study (1987) on the social construction of lesbianism.

33. Some authors seem somewhat more 'knowledgeable' in discussing potential causes. Witterman and Cohen (1990) for instance conclude, 'homosexuality has considerable etiological similarity with transsexuality' (p. 541), which they identify as extreme cross-gender behaviour in early childhood.

34. This is illustrated by the subsequent, arbitrary examples. In discussing eye contact, Zanden (1987), for instance, states: 'Homosexuals often identify one another by means of extended eye contact, followed by a backward glance after a few paces. If the other reciprocates with a backward glance, a pickup is in the offing' (1987: 86). This author also discusses homosexuality in the context of transvestism and transsexuality. He stresses the distinctions between these phenomena, but also states: 'these categories, however, are not necessarily exclusive. Overlap may occur, as in the case of transvestite homosexuals' (1987: 508). The author could have avoided his heterocentrism by saying that transvestites and transsexuals can have either a homosexual or a heterosexual preference. Costin and Draguns (1989) discuss homosexuality at length in a chapter called 'Unconventional sexual preference and sexual dysfunctions', reinforcing its dysfunctional outlook. In discussing the various potential causes of homosexuality they state 'it may well be that *accidents of life* contribute more toward the development of homosexuality than systematic research is able to reveal' (1989: 247; emphasis added). Witterman and Cohen, in discussing cross-gender behaviour as a precursor of homosexuality write: 'adult male homosexuals often report fantasies about being and dressing as females' (1990: 547). I would like to stress that these examples are given here without the intention to specifically discredit the respective authors. It would have been easy to give numerous other examples.

35. This is for instance the case in Bolton and MacEachron's (1988) literature review on adolescent male sexuality, and in various studies of relationships such as Rusbult, Morrow and Johnson's (1987) study of the role of self-esteem in problem-solving behaviour in close relationships.

36. Examples are Julien, Arellano and Turgeon's (1997) overview of gender issues in heterosexual, gay and lesbian couples in the *Clinical Handbook of Marriage and Couples*

Interventions; West's (1998) literature review of partner violence in same sex couples in *Partner Violence: A Comprehensive Review of 20 Years of Research* and Nardi and Bolton's (1991) discussion of gay-bashing in the 76th volume of *Advances in Psychology*. The carry-over from gay and lesbian psychology to mainstream psychology is also illustrated by books such as *Preventing Heterosexism and Homophobia* (Rothblum and Bond, 1996) published as the 17th volume in the series *Primary Prevention of Psychology*.

References

Abelove, H., Barale, M.A. and Halperin, D.M. (eds) (1993) *The Lesbian and Gay Studies Reader*. New York: Routledge.

Adelman, M. (1990) 'Stigma, gay lifestyles, and adjustment to aging: a study of later-life gay men and lesbians', *Journal of Homosexuality*, 20 (3–4): 7–32.

Akkermann, A., Betzelt, S. and Daniel, G. (1990a) 'Nackte Tatsachen: Ergebnisse eines lesbischen Forschungsprojekts I', *Zeitschrift für Sexualforschung*, 3 (1): 1–24.

Akkermann, A., Betzelt, S. and Daniel, G. (1990b) 'Nackte Tatsachen: Ergebnisse eines lesbischen Forschungsprojekts II', *Zeitschrift für Sexualforschung*, 3 (2): 140–65.

Allen, K.R. (1997) 'Lesbian and gay families', in T. Arendell (ed.), *Contemporary Parenting: Challenges and Issues*. Thousand Oaks, CA: Sage. pp. 96–218.

Anderson, C.W. and Adley, A.R. (eds) (1997) *Gay & Lesbian Issues. Abstracts of the Psychological and Behavioral Literature, 1985–1996*, Vol. 17, *Bibliographies in Psychology*. Washington: American Psychological Association.

Bagley, C. and Tremblay, P. (1997) 'Suicidal behaviors in homosexual and bisexual males', *Crises*, 18 (1): 24–34.

Bailey, J.M. and Benishay, D.S. (1993) 'Familial aggregation of female sexual orientation', *American Journal of Psychiatry*, 150 (2): 272–7.

Bailey, J.M., Kim, P.Y., Hills, A. and Linsenmeier, J.A.W. (1997) 'Butch, femme, or straight acting? Partner preferences of gay men and lesbians', *Journal of Personality & Social Psychology*, 73 (5): 960–73.

Bailey, J.M., Pillard, R.C., Kitzinger, C. and Wilkinson, S. (1998) 'Sexual orientation: is it determined by biology?', in M.R. Walsh (ed.), *Women, Men, & Gender: Ongoing Debates*. New Haven: Yale University Press. pp. 181–203.

Beemyn, B. and Eliason, M. (1996) *Queer Studies: A Lesbian, Gay, Bisexual and Transgender Anthology*. New York: New York University Press.

Beitchman, J.H., Zucker, K.J., Hood, J.E., DaCosta, G.A. et al. (1992) 'A review of the long-term effects of child sexual abuse', *Child Abuse & Neglect*, 16 (1): 101–18.

Berger, R.M. (1990a) 'Passing: impact of the quality of same sex couple relationships', *Social Work*, 35 (4): 328–32.

Berger, R.M. (1990b) 'Men together: understanding the gay couple', *Journal of Homosexuality*, 19 (3): 31–49.

Berger, R.M. (1992) 'Passing and social support among gay men', *Journal of Homosexuality*, 23 (3): 85–97.

Berger, R.M. (1996) *Gay and Gray: The Older Homosexual Man*, 2nd edn. New York: Harrington Park Press.

Bhughra, D. (1987) 'Homophobia: a review of the literature', *Sexual & Marital Therapy*, 2 (2): 169–77.

Bhugra, D. and Wright, B. (1995) 'Sexual dysfunction in gay men: diagnosis and management', *International Review of Psychiatry*, 7 (2): 247–52.

Bigner, J.J. and Jacobsen, R.B. (1992) 'Adult responses to child behavior and attitudes toward fathering: gay and nongay fathers', *Journal of Homosexuality*, 23 (3): 99–112.

Blanchard, R. (1997) 'Birth order and sibling sex ratio in homosexual versus heterosexual males and females', *Annual Review of Sex Research*, 8, 27–67.

Bolton, F.G. and MacEachron, A.E. (1988) 'Adolescent male sexuality: a developmental perspective', *Journal of Adolescent Research*, 3 (3–4): 259–73.

Boxer, A.M. and Cohler, B.J. (1989) 'The life course of gay and lesbian youth: an immodest proposal for the study of lives', *Journal of Homosexuality*, 17 (3–4): 315–55.

Bozett, F.W. (1989) 'Gay fathers: a review of the literature', *Journal of Homosexuality*, 18 (1–2): 137–62.

Bradford, J., Ryan, C. and Rothblum, E.D. (1994) 'National Lesbian Health Care Survey: implications for mental health care. Special section: mental health of lesbians and gay men', *Journal of Consulting and Clinical Psychology*, 62 (2): 228–42.

Brady, S. and Busse, W.J. (1994) 'The Gay Identity Questionnaire: a brief measure of homosexual identity formation', *Journal of Homosexuality*, 26 (4): 1–22.

Brand, P.A., Rothblum, E.D. and Solomon, L.J. (1992) 'A comparison of lesbians, gay men, and heterosexuals on weight and restrained eating', *International Journal of Eating Disorder*, 11 (3): 253–9.

Brannock, J.C. and Chapman, B.E. (1990) 'Negative sexual experiences with men among heterosexual women and lesbians', *Journal of Homosexuality*, 19 (1): 105–10.

Bux, D.A. Jr. (1996) 'The epidemiology of problem drinking in gay men and lesbians: a critical review', *Clinical Psychology Review*, 16 (4): 277–98.

Cabaj, R.P. and Stein, T.S. (eds) (1996) *Textbook of Homosexuality and Mental Health*. Washington, DC: American Psychiatric Press.

Caron, S.L. and Ulin, M. (1997) 'Closeting and the quality of lesbian relationships', *Families and Society*, 78 (4): 413–19.

Cass, V. (1996) 'Sexual orientation identity formation: a Western phenomenon', in R.P. Cabaj and T.S. Stein (eds) (1996) *Textbook of Homosexuality and Mental Health*. Washington, DC: American Psychiatric Press. pp. 227–51.

Clark, W.M. and Serovich, J.M. (1997) 'Twenty years and still in the dark? Content analysis of articles pertaining to gay, lesbian, and bisexual issues in marriage and family therapy journals', *Journal of Marital & Family Therapy*, 23 (3): 239–53.

Cole, S.W., Kemeny, M.E., Taylor, S.E. and Visscher, B.R., (1996a) 'Elevated physical health risk among gay men who conceal their homosexual identity', *Health Psychology*, 15 (4): 243–51.

Cole, S.W., Kemeny, M.E., Taylor, S.E., Visscher, B.R. and Fahey, J.L. (1996b) 'Accelerated course of Human Immunodeficiency Virus infection in gay men who conceal their homosexuality', *Psychosomatic Medicine*, 58: 219–31.

Comer, R.J. (1995) *Abnormal Psychology*, 2nd edn. New York: W.H. Freeman (1st edn 1992).

Comstock, G.D. (1991) *Violence against Lesbians and Gay Men. Between Men – between Women: Lesbian and Gay Studies*. New York: Columbia University Press.

Costin, F. and Draguns, J.G. (1989) *Abnormal Psychology. Patterns, Issues, Interventions*. New York: John Wiley & Sons.

Croteau, J.M. (1996) 'Research on the work experiences of lesbian, gay and bisexual people: an integrative review of methodology and findings', *Journal of Vocational Behavior*, 48 (2): 195–209.

Crowden, C.R. and Koch, P.B. (1995) 'Attitudes related to sexual concerns: gender and orientation comparisons', *Journal of Sex Education & Therapy*, 21 (2): 78–87.

Dancey, C.P. (1990) 'The influence of familial and personality variables on sexual orientation in women', *Psychological Record*, 40 (3): 437–49.

D'Augelli, A.R. (1992) 'Lesbian and gay male undergraduates' experiences of harassment and fear on campus', *Journal of Interpersonal Violence*, 7 (3): 383–95.

D'Augelli, A.R. and Hershberger, S.L. (1993) 'Lesbian, gay and bisexual youth in community settings: personal challenges and mental health problems', *American Journal of Community Psychology*, 21 (4): 421–48.

D'Augelli, A.R. and Patterson, C.J. (eds) (1995) *Lesbian, Gay, and Bisexual Identities over the Lifespan: Psychological Perspectives*. New York: Oxford University Press.

Day, N.E. and Schoenrade, P. (1997) 'Staying in the closet versus coming out: relationships between communication about sexual orientation and work attitudes', *Personnel Psychology*, 50 (1): 147–63.

De Cecco, J.P. and Parker, D.A. (eds) (1995) *Sex, Cells, and Same-Sex Desire: The Biology of Sexual Preference*. Binghamton, NY: Haworth Press.

Deenen, A.A., Gijs, L. and Naerssen, A.X. van (1994) 'Intimacy and sexuality in gay male couples', *Archives of Sexual Behavior*, 23 (4): 421–31.

De Monteflores, C. and Schultz, S.J. (1978) 'Coming out: similarities and differences for lesbians and gay men', *Journal of Social Issues*, 34 (3): 59–72.

Diamant, L. (ed.) (1993) *Homosexual Issues in the Workplace. Series in Clinical and Community Psychology*. Washington, DC: Taylor & Francis.

Doi, S.C. and Thelen, M.H. (1993) 'The Fear-of-Intimacy scale: replication and extension', *Psychological Assessment: A Journal of Consulting and Clinical Psychology*, 5: 373–83.

Drescher, J. (1996) 'Psychoanalytic subjectivity and male homosexuality', in R.P. Cabaj and T.S. Stein (eds) (1996) *Textbook of Homosexuality and Mental Health*. Washington, DC: American Psychiatric Press. pp. 173–89.

Dunkle, John H. (1994) 'Counseling gay male clients: A review of treatment efficacy research: 1975 – present', *Journal of Gay and Lesbian Psychotherapy*, 2 (2): 1–19.

Dynes, W.R. and Donaldson, S. (eds) (1992a) *Homosexuality and Psychology, Psychiatry, and Counseling*, Vol. 11, *Studies in Homosexuality*. New York: Garland.

Dynes, W.R. and Donaldson, S. (eds) (1992b) *Homosexuality: Discrimination, Criminology, and the Law*, Vol. 6, *Studies in Homosexuality*. New York: Garland.

Eldridge, N.S. and Gilbert, L.A. (1990) 'Correlates of relationship satisfaction in lesbian couples', *Psychology of Women Quarterly*, 14 (1): 43–62.

Etringer, B.D., Hillerbrand, E. and Hetherington, C. (1990) 'The influence of sexual orientation on career decision-making: a research note', *Journal of Homosexuality*, 19 (4): 103–11.

Ficarrotto, T.J. (1990) 'Racism, sexism, and erotophobia: attitudes of heterosexuals toward homosexuals', *Journal of Homosexuality*, 19 (1): 111–16.

Finlay, B. and Scheltema, K.E. (1991) 'The relation of gender and sexual orientation to measures of masculinity, femininity, and androgony: a further analysis', *Journal of Homosexuality*, 21 (3): 71–85.

Frable, D.E.S., Wortman, C. and Joseph, J. (1997) 'Predicting self-esteem, well-being, and distress in a cohort of gay men: the importance of cultural stigma, personal visibility, community networks, and positive identity', *Journal of Personality*, 65 (3): 599–624.

Franke, R. and Leary, M.R. (1991) 'Disclosure of sexual orientation by lesbians and gay men: a comparison of private and public processes', *Journal of Social and Clinical Psychology*, 10 (3): 262–9.

Franzoi, S. (1996) *Social Psychology*. Madison, WI: Brown & Benchmark.

Garnets, L.D. and Kimmel, D.C. (eds) (1993) *Psychological Perspectives on Lesbian and Gay Male Experiences*. New York: Columbia University Press.

Gonsiorek, J.C. (1991) 'The empirical bases for the demise of the illness model of homosexuality', in J.C. Gonsiorek and J.D. Weinrich (eds), *Homosexuality: Research Implications for Public Policy*. Newbury Park, CA: Sage. pp.115–36.

Greene, B. (ed.) (1997) *Ethnic and Cultural Diversity among Lesbians and Gay Men*, Vol. 3, *Psychological Perspectives on Lesbian and Gay Issues*. Thousand Oaks, CA: Sage.

Greene, B. and Herek, G.M. (eds) (1994) *Lesbian and Gay Psychology. Theory, Research, and Clinical Applications*, Vol. 1, *Psychological Perspectives on Lesbian and Gay Issues*. Thousand Oaks, CA: Sage.

Greenfield, S. and Thelen, M. (1997) 'Validation of the fear of intimacy scale with a lesbian and gay male population', *Journal of Social & Personal Relationships*, 14 (5): 707–16.

Haddock, G. and Zanna, M.P. (1998) 'Authoritarianism, values, and the favorability and structure of antigay attitudes', in G.M. Herek (ed.), *Stigma and Sexual Orientation. Understanding Prejudice against Lesbians, Gay Men, and Bisexuals*, Vol. 4, *Psychological Perspectives on Lesbian and Gay Issues*. Thousand Oaks, CA: Sage. pp. 82–107.

Hall, J.M. (1994) 'Lesbians recovering from alcohol problems: an ethnographic study of health care experiences', *Nursing Research*, 43 (4): 238–44.

Hammersmith, S.K. and Weinberg, M.S. (1973) 'Homosexual identity: commitment, adjustments, and significant others', *Sociometry*, 36 (1): 56–78.

Harry, J. (1993) 'Being out: a general model', *Journal of Homosexuality*, 26 (1): 25–39.

Hawkins, R.O. (1990) 'The relationship between culture, personality, and sexual jealousy in men in heterosexual and homosexual relationships', *Journal of Homosexuality*, 19 (3): 67–84.

Hekma, G. (1994) '"A female soul in a male body": sexual inversion as gender inversion in nineteenth-century sexology', in G. Herdt (ed.), *Third Sex, Third Gender. Beyond Sexual Dimorphism in Culture and History*. New York: Zone Books. pp. 213–39.

Herek, G.M. (1991) 'Stigma, prejudice, and violence against lesbians and gay men', in J.C. Gonsiorek and J.D. Weinrich (eds), *Homosexuality: Research Implications for Public Policy*. Newbury Park, CA: Sage. pp. 60–80.

Herek, G.M. (ed.) (1998) *Stigma and Sexual Orientation. Understanding Prejudice against Lesbians, Gay Men, and Bisexuals*, Vol. 4, *Psychological Perspectives on Lesbian and Gay Issues*. Thousand Oaks, CA: Sage.

Herek, G.M. and Berrill, K.T. (eds) (1992) *Hate Crimes: Confronting Violence against Lesbians and Gay Men*. Newbury Park, CA: Sage.

Herek, G.M. and Glunt, E.K. (1993) 'Interpersonal contact and heterosexuals' attitudes toward gay men: results from a national survey', *Journal of Sex Research*, 30 (3): 239–44.

Herek, G.M. and Greene, B. (eds) (1995) *AIDS, Identity, and Community. The HIV Epidemic and Lesbians and Gay Men*, Vol. 2, *Psychological Perspectives on Lesbian and Gay Issues*. Thousand Oaks, CA: Sage.

Herek, G.M., Gillis, J.R., Cogan, J.C. and Glunt, E.K. (1997) 'Hate crime victimization among lesbian, gay, and bisexual adults', *Journal of Interpersonal Violence*, 12 (2): 195–215.

Hershberger, S.L., Pilkington, N.W. and D'Augelli, A.R. (1997) 'Predictors of suicide attempts among gay, lesbian, and bisexual youth', *Journal of Adolescent Research*, 12 (4): 477–97.

Hiatt, D. and Hargrave, G.E. (1994) 'Psychological assessment of gay and lesbian law enforcement applicants', *Journal of Personality Assessment*, 63 (1): 80–8.

Hickson, F.C.I., Davies, P.M., Hunt, A.J., Weatherburn, P., McManus, T.J. and Coxon, A.P.M. (1994) 'Gay men as victims of nonconsensual sex', *Archives of Sexual Behavior*, 23 (3): 281–94.

Holtzen, D.W. and Agresti, A.A. (1990) 'Parental responses to gay and lesbian children: differences in homophobia, self-esteem, and sex-role stereotyping', *Journal of Social & Clinical Psychology*, 9 (3): 390–9.

Hooker, E. (1957) 'The adjustment of the male overt homosexual', *Journal of Projective Techniques*, 21: 18–31.

Huffman, K., Vernoy, M. and Vernoy, J. (1997) *Psychology in Action*. New York: Wiley.

Hurlbert, D.F. and Apt, C. (1993) 'Female sexuality: a comparative study between women in homosexual and heterosexual relationships', *Journal of Sex and Marital Therapy*, 19 (4): 315–27.

Israelstam, S. (1986) 'Alcohol and drug problems of gay males and lesbians: therapy, counselling and prevention issues', *Journal of Drug Issues*, 16 (3): 443–61.

Jordan, K.M. and Deluty R.H. (1998) 'Coming out for lesbian women: its relation to anxiety, positive affectivity, self esteem and social support', *Journal of Homosexuality*, 35 (2): 41–63.

Julien, D., Arellano, C. and Turgeon, L. (1997) 'Gender issues in heterosexual, gay and lesbian couples', in W.K. Halford and H.J. Markman (eds), *Clinical Handbook of Marriage and Couples Interventions*. Chichester: John Wiley & Sons. pp. 107–27.

Keating, J. and Over, R. (1990) 'Sexual fantasies of heterosexual and homosexual men', *Archives of Sexual Behavior*, 19 (5): 461–75.

Kehoe, M. (1988) 'Lesbians over 60 speak for themselves', *Journal of Homosexuality*, 16 (3–4): 1–111.

Kimmel, M.S. (1997) 'Masculinity as homophobia: fear, shame and silence in the construction of gender identity', in M.M. Gergen and S.N. Davis (eds), *Toward a New Psychology of Gender*. New York: Routledge. pp. 223–42.

Kite, M.E. (1994) 'When perceptions meet reality: individual differences in reactions to lesbians and gay men', in B. Greene and G.M. Herek (eds), *Lesbian and Gay Psychology. Theory, Research, and Clinical Applications*, Vol. 1, *Psychological Perspectives on Lesbian and Gay Issues*. Thousand Oaks, CA: Sage. pp. 25–53.

Kite, M.E. and B.E. Whitley (1998) 'Do heterosexual women and men differ in their attitudes toward homosexuality?' in G.M. Herek (ed.), *Stigma and Sexual Orientation. Understanding Prejudice against Lesbians, Gay Men, and Bisexuals*, Vol. 4, *Psychological Perspectives on Lesbian and Gay Issues*. Thousand Oaks, CA: Sage. pp. 39–61.

Kitzinger, C. (1987) *The Social Construction of Lesbianism*. London: Sage.

Kitzinger, C. (1997) 'Lesbian and gay psychology: a critical analysis', in D. Fox and I. Prilleltensky (eds), *Critical Psychology: An Introduction*. London: Sage. pp. 202–16.

Klinkenberg, D. and Rose, S. (1994) 'Dating scripts of gay men and lesbians', *Journal of Homosexuality*, 26 (4): 23–35.

Kristiansen, C.M. (1990) 'The symbolic/value-expressive function of outgroup attitudes among homosexuals', *Journal of Social Psychology*, 130 (1): 61–9.

Kurdek, L.A. (1991a) 'Correlates of relationship satisfaction in cohabiting gay and lesbian couples: integration of contextual, investment, and problem-solving models', *Journal of Personality and Social Psychology*, 61 (6): 910–22.

Kurdek, L.A. (1991b) 'The dissolution of gay and lesbian couples', *Journal of Social and Personal Relationships*, 8 (2): 265–78.

Kurdek, L.A. (1992) 'Relationship stability and relationship satisfaction in cohabiting gay and lesbian couples: a prospective longitudinal test of the contextual and interdependence models', *Journal of Social and Personal Relationships*, 9 (1): 125–42.

Kurdek, L.A. (1993) 'The allocation of household labor in gay, lesbian, and heterosexual married couples', *Journal of Social Issues*, 49 (3): 127–39.

Kurdek, L.A. (1997) 'Adjustment to relationship dissolution in gay, lesbian, and heterosexual partners', *Personal Relationships*, 4 (2): 145–61.

Lee, J.A. (1987) 'What can homosexual aging studies contribute to theories of aging?' *Journal of Homosexuality*, 13 (4): 43–71.

Lee, J.A. (1989) 'Invisible men: Canada's aging homosexuals: can they be assimilated into Canada's "liberated" gay communities?', *Canadian Journal on Aging*, 8 (1): 79–97.

Levinson, K.S., Pesina, M.D. and Rienzi, B.M. (1993) 'Lost-letter technique: attitude toward gay men and lesbians', *Psychological Reports*, 72 (1): 93–4.

Lie, G. and Gentlewarrier, S. (1991) 'Intimate violence in lesbian relationships: discussion of survey findings and practice implications', *Journal of Social Service Research*, 15 (1–2): 41–59.

Lie, G., Schilit, R., Bush, J., Montagne, M. and Reyes, L. (1991) 'Lesbians in currently aggressive relationships: how frequently do they report aggressive past relationships?' *Violence and Victims*, 6 (2): 121–35.

MacDonald, B.J. (1998) 'Issues in therapy with gay and lesbian couples', *Journal of Sex and Marital Therapy*, 24 (3): 165–90.

Maggiore, D.J. (1992) *Lesbianism: An Annotated Bibliography and Guide to the Literature*. Metuchen, NJ: Scarecrow Press.

McBee, S.M. and Rogers, J.R. (1997) 'Identifying risk factors for gay and lesbian suicidal behavior: implications for mental health counselors', *Journal of Mental Health Counseling*, 19 (2): 143–55.

McWhirter, D.P. and Mattison, A.M. (1984) *The Male Couple. How Relationships Develop*. Englewood Cliffs, NJ: Prentice-Hall.

Meyer, I.H. and Dean, L. (1998) 'Internalized homophobia, intimacy, and sexual behavior among gay and bisexual men', in G.M. Herek (ed.), *Stigma and Sexual Orientation. Understanding Prejudice against Lesbians, Gay Men, and Bisexuals*, Vol. 4,

Psychological Perspectives on Lesbian and Gay Issues. Thousand Oaks, CA: Sage. pp. 160–86.

Meyer, J. (1989) 'Guess who's coming to dinner this time? A study of gay intimate relationships and the support for those relationships', *Marriage & Family Review*, 14 (3–4): 59–82.

Mitchell, V. (1998) 'The birds, the bees . . . and the sperm banks: how lesbian mothers talk with their children about sex and reproduction', *American Journal of Orthopsychiatry*, 68 (3): 400–9.

Monroe, M., Baker, R.C. and Roll, S. (1997) 'The relationship of homophobia to intimacy in heterosexual men', *Journal of Homosexuality*, 33 (2): 23–37.

Morin, S. (1977) 'Heterosexual bias in psychological research on lesbianism and male homosexuality', *American Psychologist*, 32: 629–37.

Muehrer, P. (1995) 'Suicide and sexual orientation: a critical summary of recent research and directions for future research', *Suicide & Life-Threatening Behavior*, 25 (Supplement): 72–81.

Nardi, P.M. and Bolton, R. (1991) 'Gay-bashing: violence and aggression against gay men and lesbians', in R. Baenninger (ed.), *Targets of Violence and Aggression*, Vol. 76, *Advances in Psychology*. Amsterdam: North-Holland. pp. 349–400.

Newman, B.S. and Muzzonigro, P.G. (1993) 'The effects of traditional family values on the coming out process of gay male adolescents', *Adolescence*, 28 (109): 213–26.

Parks, C.A. (1998) 'Lesbian parenthood: a review of the literature', *American Journal of Orthopsychiatry*, 68 (3): 376–89.

Patterson, C.J. (1997) 'Children of lesbian and gay parents', *Advances in Clinical Child Psychology*, 19: 235–82.

Patterson, C.J. and Chan, R.W. (1996) 'Gay fathers', in M.E. Lamb (ed.), *The Role of the Father in Child Development* (3rd edn). New York: John Wiley & Sons. pp. 245–60.

Patterson, C.J. and D'Augelli, A.R. (eds) (1998) *Lesbian, Gay, and Bisexual Identities in Families. Psychological Perspectives*. New York: Oxford University Press.

Patterson, C.J., Hurt, S. and Mason, C.D. (1998) 'Families of the lesbian baby boom: children's contact with grandparents and other adults', *American Journal of Orthopsychiatry*, 68 (3): 390–9.

Peters, D.K. and Cantrell, P.J. (1991) 'Factors distinguishing samples of lesbians and heterosexual women', *Journal of Homosexuality*, 21 (4): 1–15.

Peters, D.K. and Cantrell, P.J. (1993) 'Gender roles and role conflict in feminist lesbian and heterosexual women', *Sex Roles*, 28 (7–8): 379–92.

Platzer, H. (1998) 'The concerns of lesbians seeking counseling: a review of the literature', *Patient Education and Counseling*, 33 (3): 225–32.

Pope, M. and Schulz, R. (1990) 'Sexual attitudes and behavior in midlife and aging homosexual males', *Journal of Homosexuality*, 20 (3–4): 169–77.

Proctor, C.D. and Groze, V.K. (1994) 'Risk factors for suicide among gay, lesbian, and bisexual youths', *Social Work*, 39 (5): 504–13.

Radkowsky, M. and Siegel, L.J. (1997) 'Stressors, adaptations, and psychosocial interventions', *Clinical Psychology Review*, 17 (2): 191–216.

Remafedi, G. (ed.) (1994) *Death by Denial. Studies of Suicide in Gay and Lesbian Teenagers*. Boston, MA: Alyson Publications.

Remafedi, G., French, S., Story, M., Resnick, M.D. and Blum, R. (1998) 'The relationship between suicide risk and sexual orientation: results of a population-based study', *American Journal of Public Health*, 88 (1): 57–60.

Renzetti, C.M. (1998) 'Violence and abuse in lesbian relationships: theoretical and empirical issues', in R.K. Bergen (ed.), *Issues in Intimate Violence*. Thousand Oaks, CA: Sage. pp. 117–27.

Rivers, I. (1997) 'Lesbian, gay and bisexual development: theory, research and social issues', *Journal of Community & Applied Social Psychology*, 7 (5): 329–43.

Roese, N.J., Olson, J.M., Borenstein, M.N., Martin, A. and Shores, A.L. (1992) 'Same-sex touching behavior: the moderating role of homophobic attitudes', *Journal of Nonverbal Behavior*, 16 (4): 249–59.

Rosenbluth, S.C. and Steil, J.M. (1995) ' Predictors of intimacy for women in heterosexual and homosexual couples', *Journal of Social and Personal Relationships*, 12 (2): 163–75.

Ross, M.W. and Rosser, B.R.S. (1996) 'Measurement and correlates of internalized homophobia: a factor analytic study', *Journal of Clinical Psychology*, 52 (1): 15–21.

Rothblum, E.D. and Bond, L.A. (eds) (1996) *Preventing Heterosexism and Homophobia*, Vol. 17, *Primary Prevention of Psychopathology*. Thousand Oaks, CA: Sage.

Rotheram-Borus, M.J., Hunter, J. and Rosario, M. (1994) 'Suicidal behavior and gay-related stress among gay and bisexual male adolescents', *Journal of Adolescent Research*, 9 (4): 498–508.

Rudolph, J. (1988) 'Counselors' attitudes toward homosexuality: a selective review of the literature', *Journal of Counseling and Development*, 67 (3): 165–8.

Rusbult, C.E., Morrow, G.D. and Johnson, D.J. (1987) 'Self-esteem and problem-solving behaviour in close relationships', *British Journal of Social Psychology*, 26 (4): 293–303.

Rust, P.C. (1992) 'The politics of sexual identity: sexual attraction and behavior among lesbian and bisexual women', *Social Problems*, 39 (4): 336–86.

Rust, P.C. (1993) '"Coming out" in the age of social constructionism: sexual identity formation among lesbian and bisexual women', *Gender and Society*, 7 (1): 50–77.

Sandfort, T.G.M. (1997) 'Sampling male homosexuality', in J. Bancroft (ed.), *Researching Sexual Behavior: Methodological Issues*. Bloomington: Indiana University Press. pp. 261–75.

Sandfort, T. and Bos, H. (1998) *Sexual Preference and Work. This is What Makes the Difference*. Zoetermeer: ABVAKABO FNV.

Sandfort, Th.G.M., Graaf, R. de, Bijl, R.V. and Schnabel, P. (1999) 'Sexual orientation and mental health: data from the Netherlands Mental Health Survey and Incidence Study (NEMESIS)', poster presented at the Twenty-Fifth Annual Meeting of the International Academy of Sex Research, 23–27 June, Stony Brook, New York.

Savin-Williams, R.C. (1998) 'The disclosure to families of same sex attractions by lesbian, gay, and bisexual youths', *Journal of Research on Adolescence*, 8 (1): 49–68.

Schilit, R., Lie, G. and Montagne, M. (1990) 'Substance use as a correlate of violence in intimate lesbian relationships', *Journal of Homosexuality*, 19 (3): 51–65.

Schreurs, K.M.G. (1993) 'Sexuality in lesbian couples: the importance of gender', *Annual Review of Sex Research*, 4: 49–66.

Schuyf, J. (1996) *Oud Roze. De positie van lesbische en homoseksuele ouderen in nederland*. Utrecht: Homostudies.

Sears, J.T. and Williams, W.L. (eds) (1997) *Overcoming Heterosexism and Homophobia. Strategies that Work*. New York: Columbia University Press.

Shires, A. and Miller, D. (1998) 'A preliminary study comparing psychological factors associated with erectile dysfunctions in heterosexual and homosexual men', *Sexual and Marital Therapy*, 13 (1): 37–49.

Siever, M.D. (1994) 'Sexual orientation and gender as factors in socioculturally acquired vulnerability to body dissatisfaction and eating disorders', *Journal of Consulting & Clinical Psychology*, 62 (2): 252–60.

Stark, L.P. (1991) 'Traditional gender role beliefs and individual outcomes: an exploratory analysis', *Sex Roles*, 24 (9–10): 639–50.

Steinman, R. (1990) 'Social exchanges between older and younger gay male partners', *Journal of Homosexuality*, 20 (3–4): 179–206.

Stevens, P.E. (1993) 'Lesbian health care research: a review of the literature from 1970 to 1990', in P.N. Stern (ed.), *Lesbian Health. What Are the Issues?* London: Taylor & Francis. pp. 1–30.

Stevenson, M.R. (1988) 'Promoting tolerance for homosexuality: an evaluation of intervention strategies', *Journal of Sex Research*, 25 (4): 500–11.

Strommen, E.F. (1989) '"You're a what?": family member reactions to the disclosure of homosexuality', *Journal of Homosexuality*, 18 (1–2): 37–58.

Tasker, F.L. and Golombok, S. (1997) *Growing up in a Lesbian Family: Effects on Child Development*. New York: Guilford Press.

Troiden, R.R. (1989) 'The formation of homosexual identities', *Journal of Homosexuality*, 17 (1–2): 43–73.

Tsang, E. (1994) 'Investigating the effect of race and apparent lesbianism upon helping behaviour', *Feminism & Psychology*, 4 (3): 469–71.

Vincke, J. and Bolton, R. (1994) 'Social support, depression, and self-acceptance among gay men', *Human Relations*, 47 (9): 1049–62.

Waldner-Haugrund, L.K. and Gratch, L.V. (1997) 'Sexual coercion in gay/lesbian relationships: descriptives and gender differences', *Violence and Victims*, 12 (1): 87–98.

Walters, K.L. and Simoni, J.M. (1993) 'Lesbian and gay male group identity attitudes and self-esteem: implications for counseling', *Journal of Counseling Psychology*, 40 (1): 94–9.

Watter, D.N. (1987) 'Teaching about homosexuality: a review of the literature', *Journal of Sex Education & Therapy*, 13 (2): 63–6.

Weitz, R. and Bryant, K. (1997) 'The portrayals of homosexuality in abnormal psychology and sociology of deviance textbooks', *Deviant Behavior*, 18 (1): 27–46.

Wells, J.W. (1990) 'The sexual vocabularies of heterosexual and homosexual males and females for communicating erotically with a sexual partner', *Archives of Sexual Behavior*, 19 (2): 139–47.

West, C.M. (1998) 'Leaving a second closet: Outing partner violence in same sex couples', in Jana L. Jasinski and L.M. Williams (eds), *Partner Violence: A Comprehensive Review of 20 Years of Research*. Thousand Oaks, CA: Sage. pp. 163–83.

Whitman, F.L., Diamond, M. and Martin, J. (1993) 'Homosexual orientation in twins: a report on 61 pairs and three triplet sets', *Archives of Sexual Behavior*, 22 (3): 187–206.

Witterman, L. and Cohen, D.B. (1990) *Psychopathology*. New York: McGraw-Hill.

Zanden, J.W. vander (1987) *Social Psychology* (4th edn). New York: Random House (1st edn 1977).

Zwart, O. de, Kerkhof, M. van and Sandfort, T. (1998) 'Anal sex and gay men: the challenge of HIV and beyond', *Journal of Psychology and Human Sexuality*, 10 (3–4): 89–102.

3 Mapping the Sociological Gay: Past, Presents and Futures of a Sociology of Same Sex Relations

Ken Plummer

> *The first rule of sociology is this: things are not what they seem.*
> *Peter Berger* (1963)

Born of industrialization and a concern with how the modern world develops, sociology studies how societies – and their institutions – are historically constructed, socially patterned and turned into personal (or subjective) realities in which human lives are lived. Sociology may be celebratory – looking with awe at the patterning and ordering of societies; or it may be critical – looking at the oppression, marginalization and inequality that pervades societies. At its best, it is both. It looks at how private worries become public troubles; and its mission is to challenge assumptions and everyday thinking, especially those that see the world as 'natural' and 'individualistically' explained. And it does all this through theory, conceptualization and empirical research. From this perspective, 'homosexuality' must be viewed as a social fact. The sociological perspective steers right away from the idea that homosexuals are distinctive sorts of individuals, or from arguments that highlight biology and the 'natural'. It problematizes the very idea of the 'homosexual', seeing same sex experience as being historically organized in different ways. It therefore asks questions about the ways in which same sex experiences get historically produced, socially organized and turned into subjective or personal realities.

Despite its potential, for most of its history, sociology has rarely looked at the personal life and hardly ever looked at matters erotic. It has paid even less attention to same gender relations. Hence the links between sociology and homosexuality may be speedily summarized (see Figure 3.1). There was an almost total neglect until the 1950s. Slowly comes the gradual appearance of studies of 'sociological aspects of homosexuality' through the 1950s and mid-1960s. This is followed during the 1960s and 1970s by studies linked to 'deviance theory' and gender and power issues alongside a more empirical 'sociology of lesbian and gay lives'. Two forces interrupt this in the 1980s: the spectre of HIV/AIDS which generates its own research momentum and leaves room for little else to be considered; and the turn to discourse analysis of real world events – what might be called the Foucauldian deluge, after its key thinker. With the popularization and ascendancy of lesbian and gay studies from the late 1980s onwards (chronicled in Escoffier, 1992 and

Plummer, 1992), new disciplines come to dominate sociology. 'Queer' becomes a key concern, and with that a taste for somewhat 'wilde' textual theorizing (e.g. Doty, 1993). When the benchmark *Lesbian and Gay Studies Reader* (Abelove et al.) is published in 1993, only three of its 42 contributors are sociologists. There seems to have been a spectacular rise and fall of sociological analysis around same gender experience. This short account aims to briefly explain and review these trends, assess the impact of sociology on lesbian and gay studies and turn to some directions for the future.

1 Nineteenth century	Perversion	Denial
2 Mid-twentieth	Homosexuality	Liberal research
3 Mid 1960s – early 1980s	Gay	Rise of labelling theory
1970s–1980s	lesbian and gay Lives	Rise of gender theory
4 1980s	HIV and AIDS and the Foucauldian deluge	Survey research/ cultural studies
		Discourse theory
5 Late 1980s	Queer	Post-structuralism

FIGURE 3.1 *A sketch of the emergence of lesbian and gay studies*

Genealogies of sociology and homosexuality

There can be no straightforward or linear history of the study of homosexuality so in what follows I seriously oversimplify. Five 'moments' might be highlighted, each of which feeds into and works on the others.

The modernist silencing of the 'homosexual' voice: up to the 1950s

Which classical sociological treatise has ever mentioned the love which dare not speak its name? I can find evidence of none. For the first hundred years of sociology, the discipline betrayed its conservative side by showing almost no concern for the subject. It seems to be a history of neglect, erasure, denial and ignorance. It is indeed one future topic for study: to see if any sociological research was done in this early period, work which may have subsequently become hidden from history. Recent historical studies in the USA such as George Chauncey's *Gay New York*, Alan Berube's *Coming Out Under Fire*, and Esther Newton's *Cherry Grove* make it very clear that there were large hidden social worlds of homosexuality throughout this century and it would be surprising if a few sociologists had not investigated them. And yet currently the history of the sociology of homosexuality can be written as if nothing at all happened in the pre-World War II period. Indeed, whilst the public domain was full of discussion of sex, sociologists remained silent on every aspect of it. As Seidman (1996: 2) has tellingly remarked:

> If our view of modernity is derived exclusively from the sociological classics, we would not know that a central part of the great transformations consisted of efforts to organize bodies, pleasures, and desires as they relate to personal and public life, and this entailed constructing sexual (and gender) identities.

Whilst it is true that the earliest self-conscious accounts of modern lesbian and gay experiences start to be written in the late nineteenth century, they seem to have nothing whatsoever to do with sociology, which was evolving at the same time. Which makes it all the odder. At the very moment when the homosexual category was being established alongside the binary split of homosexuality/heterosexuality that has organized much of Western modernity's thinking (Sedgwick, 1991), sociologists generally had other things on their mind. Any notion of these profound gender shifts is missing from the classic writings of the founders – Marx, Durkheim and Weber. Only Simmel takes gender as a partial focus, but even for him same sex relationships are beyond the pale. And yet this was, after all, the very time when the earliest homophile rights movement was creating the first wave of 'gay liberation'. It is true that in Europe a number of 'scientists' and scholars did become engaged in attempts to explain and understand the difference that was eventually called homosexuality. Some of the studies could well be seen as the harbingers of empirical sociology, studying the experiences of self-classified inverts or homosexuals. Magnus Hirschfield, for example, created the Scientific Humanitarian Committee and Institute for Sex Research in Germany to study the lives of thousands of 'homosexuals' (Lauritsen and Thorstad 1974; Weeks, 1990). Yet, despite this, there was not a single sociological analysis in sight for the first 150 years of the discipline! The important challenge of linking 'homosexuality' to modernity had not commenced, and ironically, the main contribution of sociology for the first century of its existence was a systematic neglect, almost certainly structured by a deep (and then unarticulated) heterosexism and homophobia (cf. Adam, 1998). It would seem that sociology – like most of the social sciences – lags behind the world of real events and issues.

Founding 'a sociology of homosexuality': the 1950s

Whilst a few non-sociologists – Hirschfield in Germany, Henry and Kinsey in the USA – carried out important social studies (Ericksen and Steffen, 1999), the formal history of the sociology of homosexuality might be seen to start with two major clandestine, yet 'popular', studies produced in the early 1950s. The first clear Anglo-American sightings are from Donald Webster Cory in the USA and Gordon Westwood in the UK: both produced books in the early 1950s with titles like 'The Homosexual and Society'; both authors' names were pseudonyms for sociologists who went on to make further contributions in their real names (Sagarin, 1975; Schofield, 1965); and both were primarily concerned with a simple documentation of the social lives of homosexuals and with observing the ways in which discrimination/ prejudice and hostility affected these lives – working largely within a framework of 'minority groups and prejudice studies'. Schofield's study was possibly the first to announce the word 'sociology' in its very title: *Sociological Aspects of Homosexuality* (1965). (It was certainly the first sociology book I came across in this field.) These studies came at a time when the emerging homophile world was also developing its own institutes and magazines, like the Institute for Homophile Studies in Los Angeles (Dorr Legg, 1994) and others in the Netherlands (Tielman, 1982).

At this time a scattering of papers appear in Anglo-American sociology: Leznoff and Wesley's 'Homosexual community' is generally seen as the first article – a short empirical study of a small gay community in a small Canadian town. It now has some historical value, and it also draws out a key distinction between the overt and the covert homosexual, signalling the importance of the closet as form of social organization that pervades twentieth-century gay life. A little later, Nancy Achilles wrote about the 'Homosexual (note: not gay) bar as an institution', suggesting the centrality of 'bars' in structuring gay life. These are amongst the earliest field reports – using interviews and observation – of an empirical sociology. They started to take the study of homosexuality away from the more clinical studies prevalent at the time, by interviewing and observing homosexuals who lived in the community.

Enter labelling , 'new deviance' and constructionism: the late 1960s and the 1970s

By the early 1960s, the discipline of sociology was rapidly expanding and its theories and methods were in ferment. One aspect of this was the flurry of interest in so-called 'deviance' and 'labelling theory'. This development marked a turn away from 'deviant' people (like homosexuals) in favour of examining the societal reactions towards attributed deviance. It produced a major relativizing and critical thrust, whilst highlighting how deviance was *socially constructed* and organized (cf. Becker, 1963; Berger and Luckmann, 1966). In the US it was associated with the newly formed Society for the Study of Social Problems; in the UK, it led to the formation of a group of radical young sociologists clustered around an organization known as the (York) National Deviancy Conference. Eventually this led to the European Group for the Study of Deviance and Control (Bianchi et al., 1975). Several papers appeared in North America which applied labelling theory to homosexuality: John Kitsuse's (1962) study of student responses, Edwin Schur's (1965) account of criminalization and its effects, and William Simon and John Gagnon's (1967) formulation of a broader sociological perspective which highlighted both the importance of the metaphor 'scripting' in approaching sexuality in general, and the overlap of gay and straight in particular (see Nardi and Schneider, 1998).

It was, however, the functionalist paper published by the English sociologist Mary McIntosh in 1967 which, some suggest, has become the single most influential paper in sociology. McIntosh argued that homosexuality should not be approached as a medical condition, but as a historically specific social role. She claimed that 'The creation of a specialized, despised and punished role of homosexual keeps the bulk of society pure in rather the same way the similar treatment of some kinds of criminal keeps the rest of society law-abiding' (1981: 32). In noting this, she firmly established what subsequently became known as the constructionist–essentialist debate. For her, homosexuality was clearly not a universal condition but a historically specific, 'socially constructed' role (McIntosh, 1981; Weeks, 1998).

By the early 1970s an exciting moment had been reached. It was the time for sociology. A series of important studies started both to document lesbian and gay lives and to develop theorizations around the very notion of 'the homosexual'. There is no space here to consider the details of all these contrasting theories and methods: in summary, it could be said that sociology – feeding into and from anthropology and history – helped to shape a radical new approach to same gender relations. Broadly, it worked on two levels – theoretical and empirical.

Theoretically, sociology problematized the notion of 'the homosexual', asking questions about the nature, origins, conditions of application, and impact of the category (Plummer, 1981) and setting up what was to become known as the essentialist–constructionist debate (a debate which hence appears in sociology before the popularity of either Foucault or queer theory). It turned attention to the societal reactions towards homosexuality. Never being happy with the simplistic psychological concept of 'homophobia', its historically grounded comparative analysis culminated in David Greenberg's (1988) massive, important and too neglected *Construction of Homosexuality*. This book codified a major series of responses to homosexuality in different cultures including those that were generational based, gender based, class based and equality based. Hence major new social typologies of same sex experience emerged. Sociology questioned the meanings of sexualities – offering new social metaphors like script in preference to biological reductive ones like drive (especially in the vital work of Gagnon and Simon, 1973). It explored the concept of identity long before it had become fashionable, providing valuable accounts of how identities get assembled (in the work of Dank, 1971; Ponse, 1978; Plummer, 1975; Epstein, 1987 and others: see Nardi and Schneider, 1998). It investigated the social organization and meanings of culture and community (both Warren, 1974 and Ponse, 1978 applied the insights of a phenomenological interactionism to highlight the links between community and identity. See also Ferguson, 1991). My own account laid out an interactionist theory of sexual stigma (Plummer, 1975). It challenged the baselines of much research by identifying a 'heterosexual assumption' behind much study (Ponse, 1978) and inserted political analysis into much study of sex, broadening the arena of debate beyond gay politics *per se* (Rubin, 1984; Weeks, 1985). And although versions of symbolic interactionism dominated much of this stage of analysis, there were also attempts to bring in wider, more structural approaches, such as Barry Adam's (1978) study of oppression and Gayle Rubin's (1984) concern with 'sex hierarchy'. Continental Europe produced several influential works of social theory in the writings of Guy Hocquenghem (1978), Mario Mieli (1980), and Martin Dannecker (1981). It showed a plurality of 'homosexualities' (the title of a leading book by Bell, Weinberg and Williams, 1978) whilst demonstrating the 'normalization of homosexuality'. This was quite a lot to achieve in a short space of time.

Empirically, sociology started investigations of the institutions of gay life – especially those connected to sociability (bars, etc.) and sexualities. Laud Humphreys brought an ethnographic turn into sharp focus through his investigation of 'public sex in tea rooms' (1971: this was to become a widely discussed socio-logical classic, largely due to its methodology); and after this there was a proliferation of writing on public sex in this, the pre-AIDS era in the work of Delph, Troiden and others; along with analyses of the whole ecosystem of 'getting sex' (Lee, 1978). This period also saw early explorations of patterns of gay friendships, couples, lifestyles and communities. It examined the the tales of 'coming out' in the voices of lesbian and gays. It perused the links between gay and lesbian lives and problems of gender, and it examined the social reactions to homosexuals both historically and situationally.

Again, and even though I was part of it all, I do think all of this was quite an achievement. During this period, sociology was in a kind of Golden Age generally and it was reflected in all sorts of areas – not least in the creation of gender studies and in the nascent analysis of an emergent lesbian and gay life. But a caution is in order. Although this was (certainly by contrast with any earlier time in its history), an important period of productivity, there was a downside. For these 'discoveries' were the work of very few sociologists and their work was largely marginalized and ignored by the mainstream of sociology. Indeed, for most sociologists, lesbian and gay matters remained of no interest, and could be shunted into a ghetto and ignored. Even while sociology made the contributions listed above, over-whelmingly it brought the now more widely recognized traditional biases of white middle-class men, and these remained the main focus. Curiously, too, lesbianism (as a focus of enquiry) had been ignored in sociology – probably as feminist sociologists focused attention on women, gender issues and lesbianism. Most of the key contributions to lesbian studies came from outside sociology (for example, Faderman, 1981, 1991; Newton, 1972, 1984). Prominent exceptions are Diane Richardson, Barbara Ponse, Beth Schneider, Betsi Ettore, Gayle Rubin and Susan Krieger (see Wilton, 1995). In the UK, as elsewhere, there were several attempts to organize a gay and lesbian sociologists section of the British Sociological Association but they proved to be short-lived. The US was more successful, with a Gay and Lesbian Caucus being initiated in 1974 and continuing to this day.[1] In the Netherlands, there were several emergent centres of lesbian and gay studies, though generally with a limited focus on sociology (Tielman, 1982). In Germany, the work of Rüdiger Lautmann (1993) was prominent, as was the work of Michael Pollak in France (1985).

The arrival of AIDS and the Foucauldian deluge: the 1980s

The heyday of sociological research was probably the late 1970s. Some of this work continues to the present day, but during the early 1980s two events helped shift atention from much of the above. One was AIDS. Not surprisingly, a new set of concerns arose from the urgent need for more research on aspects of the health crisis. AIDS was studied both as disease and as symbol. Studies of changing sexual behaviour were initially to the fore; subsequently, studies of social movement change, responses to and adaptations to AIDS, and media/'discourse' analysis became key areas of investigation for sociologists, borrowing heavily from some areas of sociology like the sociology of medicine, media and stigma. For a while a new generation of scholars actually seemed to desert the earlier styles of gay and lesbian research, with the dire needs of AIDS activist research taking precedence over all other concerns. Much more funding was made available for this kind of work, with its pressing policy concerns. An enormous international culture of AIDS research and writing was generated (Hert and Lindenbaum, 1992; Mendès-Leite and de Busscher, 1993). At the same time, there was the tragic loss of a number of leading gay scholars: the pioneers Philip Blumstein, Marty Levine, Richard Troiden, Michel Foucault and Michael Pollak amongst them.

Whilst AIDS generated specific kinds of research, the arrival of Foucault and his major theoretical challenge to all orthodoxies heralded a distinctive turn towards homosexuality through discourse analysis. Though Foucault was popular amongst some sociologists in England throughout the 1970s, it was the publication in 1978 of the English translation of his book *The History of Sexuality Vol. 1: An Introduction* that pushed him to the fore in the nascent lesbian and gay studies. Here the focus shifts from what might be called 'real world events' to a pre-occupation with the power-language spirals through which social life is constituted. Foucault himself became a major intellectual symbol for gay academics – not just because of his theories, which came to dominate much 'left' discourse in the 1980s and 1990s, but also because his own life history as a sex radical came slowly to the fore after his death. James Miller's hugely polemical *The Passion of Michel Foucault* (1993) and David Halperin's *Saint Foucault* (1995) both highlight how important, yet controversial, his work was. Ultimately much of this 'decon-structivist turn' may be seen to lead to the queer studies, discussed in the next section. Foucault is hard to characterize in terms of a discipline: he was, after all, a 'Professor of the History of Systems of Thought' (Smart, 1985: 13). His impact on certain more theoretical wings of sociology from around the early 1970s in the UK, and a little later in the USA, was profound.

Onwards: the queering of academia

Despite a flourish of analysis and research using sociology in the early days of lesbian and gay studies, its impact weakened during much of the 1980s: almost all significant sociological work turned its attention to AIDS or became enmeshed in making discourse analyses. And once lesbian and gay studies started to establish itself in the late 1980s, the mantle of influence passed from the social science to humanistic/literary scholars who were developing queer theory. These key trends are discussed elsewhere in this book, but three cautions may help here. First, this is overwhelmingly a North American tradition – one which grows out of US literary studies; and whilst prevalent there for much of the 1990s, it remains much weaker in Europe. Secondly, it is a transgressive tradition which brings with it a concern for dismantling any notion of the 'gay' or 'lesbian', and which claims the moral and political high ground for transgressive sexualities and genders – hence bisexualities and transgender politics become much more central in this work than in the earlier lesbian and gay studies. Finally, it is a generational tradition: its followers are part of a new generation of research seeking the new and often the postmodern. Sociology did not easily fit into these new developments and for the most part – and to the detriment of both queer studies and sociology – they ignored each other. I return to this below.

The difficulties of a lesbian and gay sociology

There are a number of reasons why sociology started to play a lesser role in lesbian and gay studies during the 1990s. These centre upon tensions that have emerged from four key sources – a sociological community that marginalizes lesbian and gay concerns (little credit or recognition is gained by such work); a lesbian and gay community that militates against the theoretical constructionism of most sociological analyses ('constructionism' is simply not the way most lesbians and gays think); a generationally based queer studies that favours cultural studies over sociological studies (the earlier work has come to be seen as 'old-fashioned'); and a number of linked social movement schisms that see much of sociology as inevitably skewed to white male biases. Sociological work can be situated at the intersection of these tensions: its future will depend in part upon how it handles them (see Figure 3.2).

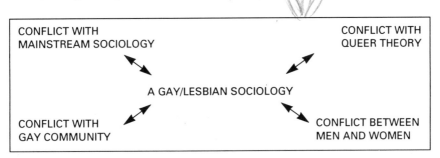

FIGURE 3.2 *Sources of tension and difficulties for a gay/lesbian sociology*

Sociological myopia

Most obviously, it remains the case that the sociological community has little room for lesbian and gay study – indeed, it still marginalizes and minimizes our work. This is not a matter of direct discrimination – few sociologists, hopefully, would wish to be seen as homophobic or discriminatory these days. It is simply that when sociologists in general study the world, they elect to ignore dimensions that are of direct relevance to lesbian and gay lives. The study of social movements and the study of identities are good examples. In both of these research areas, gay and lesbian sociology has contributed much: lesbians and gays have been key protagonists in the emergence of 'identity politics' debates. Thus, there is a significant amount of primary material available about the lesbian and gay movements – its schisms and conflicts, its history and rhetorics, its campaigns and manifestos.

Of all contemporary social movements, it may be that the lesbian and gay movement has proved one of the most successful (along with the women's movement and the green movement). Yet to read mainstream social movement texts would lead one to think it didn't exist – key theorists like Touraine, Snow, Melucci and Oberschall do not even give passing reference to Barry Adam's key book, *The Rise of a Lesbian and Gay Movement* (1995); and a brief review of major journals, yearbooks and textbooks finds almost total neglect. This is also the case with the fully blossoming 'identity studies' (cf. Phelan, 1989). For instance Craig Calhoun's *Social Theory and the Politics of Identity* (1994) is written as if the sociology of lesbian and gay identity added nothing to the debate, whereas it is not only central to it but has been for a very long time (there is a brief mention of the work of Diane Fuss, 1989, who provides one of the key debates on 'essentialized identity'). Sociologists of lesbian and gay lives have been debating the politics of identity for the past twenty years. Is this wilful ignorance among major social theorists, or even latent homophobia? It is certainly very puzzling. A further development within social theory has been the arrival of queer theory. Hardly any sociologists even recognized the existence of queer theory until a 1994 issue of the journal *Sociological Theory* presented a symposium on it (Seidman, 1994, 1996). Yet today, most theory books, readers and texts in sociology still manage to ignore this completely – presumably seeing it as a passing fad or worse? Wherever one looks in sociology, lesbian and gay concerns are shunted to the margins; hence it is not surprising that few sociologists decide to follow these lines of enquiry.

Queering the field

Newer 'postmodern' developments in lesbian and gay studies take routes that do not encourage what is often seen as a more traditional or modernist sociology. The radical deconstruction of much queer theory centres around 'texts', and 'plays' more and more fancifully with a wide array of poems, novels and films. Such interests have tended to push aside the important research which remains to be done in the empirical world. For instance, we now have numerous studies in which the 'queer theorist' re-reads a Hollywood movie or a Victorian novel: but very little indeed which investigates empirically the fragmented natures of aged/classed/racialized audiences of differing sexualities actually making sense of media forms. The queer theorist usually has little time for the seemingly more mundane concerns of sociology, and has claimed dominance over the field – at least in the USA. A major problem emerges here for sociology through what may be termed the 'overtextualization of lesbian and gay experiences'. Queer theory has pushed more traditional sociological concerns to the margins.

Community tensions

There has been a long and uneasy relationship between the sociology of lesbian and gay communities, and the lesbian and gay communities themselves. Some lesbian and gay sociologists are part of this movement but it often leaves them in a curiously contradictory tension – their theories and their politics often seem ill at ease. Community members often believe passionately in a 'folk essentialism' – that 'homosexuals' are born this way – whilst sociologists much more generally take a constructionist line. The popularity of the work of Simon Levay (1993), celebrating our shrinking hypothalamus, meets with disbelief in sociological circles. This tension has long been recognized and is widely discussed, but it cannot be easily resolved. Likewise, movement members may take for granted the power and significance of Stonewall whilst for sociologists Stonewall is a symbol, a sign, best seen as a shared collective memorial useful for rewriting history (Bravmann, 1997). This does not weaken its importance, but it does give rise to a very different perspective. Further it is apparent that movement members have their own schisms and conflicts – from assimilationists to tribalists! – something that sociologists can recognize as driving forces in all social movements. This makes them strangers to some of the movement's activities. At the very least, the sociological imagination has to permit multiple ways of seeing – and recognize that every way of seeing is a way of not seeing. This makes the taking of sides in such schisms much harder. Yet even with an eye for the multiplicity of meanings, sociologists have not been attentive to key differences in identity and community that are shaped by racial, ethnic and national cultures. The articulation of these issues has occurred primarily within the anthologizing efforts of lesbian and gay people of colour, and some authors and poets (e.g. Anzaldua, Lorde, Moraga and Smith: in Nardi and Schneider, 1998: 521–50). Once again, sociologists have not been leading the way!

Men and women

A tension also exists between men and women, which has been present since the very inception of lesbian and gay studies. Although we talk of 'lesbian and gay studies', the idea that these two terms can be happily juxtaposed is a problem. The issues that lesbians and gay men confront in the Western world seem at times to be of such a different order, and indeed seem so deeply antagonistic, that enmity rather than collaboration has been the rule of the day. Some parts of 'modern lesbianisms' have become embedded within the women's movement, feminism and its analysis of male domination and patriarchy since their inception. As Celia Kitzinger has argued: 'Central to radical feminism is the belief that patriarchy (not capitalism or sex roles or socialization or individual sexist men) is the root of all forms of oppression; that all men benefit from and maintain it and are, therefore, our political enemies' (Kitzinger, 1987: 64).

In this quote, does 'All men' include gay men? For the past twenty years, this argument has been repeated on many occasions – from personal rejections of phallocentric gay men (Stanley, 1982) to critiques of the organization of some gay male sexualities into such features as cruising, pornography and sadomasochism (e.g. Jeffreys, 1989); to analyses which suggest that the central organizing force of patriarchy is male sexuality, of which male gay sexuality is a part (MacKinnon, 1987). Such arguments can lead to a lesbian feminist separatism and to a much lesser concern with gay issues within sociology. Often women sociologists have come to identify much more with lesbian-feminist concerns than with sociology.

Future directions for sociology

A dominant trend in recent lesbian and gay studies has been a concern with discourse, text, stories and identities. For instance, in a recent and important collection of readings on sociology and queer theory, an unsuspecting reader might be forgiven for believing that sociology has become the study of identity. Almost every one of the contemporary readings deals with some aspect of identity and identity politics: Asian American identities, black identities, AIDS identities, lesbian identities, queer identities, Dutch gay identities, social movement identities, bisexual identities (Seidman, 1996) . Now whilst I would be the first to agree that the study of identity is important, I cannot believe that it should be the exclusive or paramount concern of a lesbian/gay/queer sociology. Nor can I believe that the other major preoccupation – with texts – should be given such hegemony in the field. For this all too easily cuts us off from the analysis of real world events and turns to a stream of analyses which see only language, rhetoric and discourse.

Yet there are some signs that sociology is starting to push forward again into newer fields. There have been quite a few recent empirical studies: of the Australian dance scene (e.g. Lewis and Ross, 1995) , the 'gay village' in Manchester (Whittle, 1994); two generational cohorts of Californian lesbians (Stein, 1997); gay men's friendships (Nardi, 1999); the relationships between straight men with gay friends (Fee, 1996), and 'white trash gays' talking on tabloid television (Gamson, 1998) amongst them. There have also been interesting syntheses of studies, such as Stephen O. Murray's *American Gay* (1996). Henning Bech, a prominent gay Danish sociologist, has addressed the issue of modernity and homosexuality, arguing that a distinctive form of existence – the *homosexual form of existence* – has appeared in modernity in the conditions of the city. He dissects the features of this modern social type along with the social world he inhabits. It is a world of sex and gazes, of public venues like railway stations and discotheques, as well as an experience of dreams and longings. Take this 'homosexual form' away and society as we know it would not be. As he says:

> The homosexual is an important figure in modern societies. He supplies raw material for science and fund raises for it; he provides a significant contribution to the generation of the psychic self and the sensitive self of modern superficiality, hence also the modern schism between self and surface; he creates art and entertainment, styles and images, enjoyments and sensitivity; he performs vital functions in the modern economy, ensures the circulation of capital and sets capitalists' wives' hair and creates their dresses; he incarnates evil and helps to keep up the gender system and the nuclear family. (Bech 1996: 191)

For Bech, then, society has become so 'homosexualized' that soon men will be with men everywhere; and more, the rigid category of existence of the recent modern past will vanish. This is a challenging sociology at its best: charting new ways of seeing.

At the British Sociological Association's conference on sexualities in 1994 a surprising number of papers had aspects of gayness as a focus (a selection is published in the three volumes edited by Weeks and Holland, 1996) and a new cohort of young sociological gay and lesbian scholars has emerged in the USA – as evidenced by the Gay, Lesbian and Bisexual Sociologists' Caucus. So there are signs of continuing work in sociology. Yet there remains a clear need to bring mainstream sociologists to an awareness of this work, and for them to take lesbian, bisexual, transgendered and queer concerns more seriously and incorporate such understandings in their everyday non-gay research and theory. This would be a major achievement, weakening the ghettoization of lesbian and gay research.

In the end, maybe a much clearer and stronger theoretical and research agenda in gay sociology is required. Indeed, elsewhere I have been busy pointing to a number of potential directions for research. First, in Plummer (1992), I suggested the need for work that would link to *globalization, heterosexism, postmodernism and intimate citizenship*. Secondly, in an essay with Arlene Stein (1994), we suggested three zones for enquiry: *to re-read the classics; to reconsider whole fields of sociology in the light of lesbian/gay/queer studies; and to rethink pedagogy.* Here we urged the placing of homo/hetero/queer debates at the forefront of classic fields of social theory and texts. For instance, what would happen if Durkheim's *Suicide*, or Robert Parks's *The City* were given 'gay' readings? There is no discussion of the links between suicide and sexualities in Durkheim, and Parks's City is a pretty sexless place! Queer sociological re-readings could be very valuable (cf. Bell and Valentine, 1995). In a later book, my prime goal was to suggest a more political concern with the analysis of *social worlds, stories* and their links to what I call *intimate citizenship* (Plummer, 1995). In a more recent earlier version of this essay (Plummer, 1998) I concluded by suggesting a range of substantive areas for research, like *media research, stratification studies* and *heterosexist practices.* Most recently I have urged a renewed interest in more specific studies of the *embodied erotic* (Plummer, forthcoming). I will not detail these concerns here. It seems I have been spending too much time recently producing shopping lists of research projects. But from all this, it does seem very clear that there is still a great deal to be done.

Notes

This chapter is a somewhat revised version of one previously published as 'The past, present and future of the sociology of same sex relations', an afterword to Peter Nardi and Beth Schneider's edited collection, *Social Perspectives in Lesbian and Gay Studies* (1998), pp. 605–14.

1. The British Sociological Association Study Group in the UK held two conferences between 1976 and 1978 and then dissolved! The US group has gone through several name changes, but has remained a flourishing group, meeting annually at the American Sociological Association meetings.

References

Abelove, H., Barale, M.A. and Halperin, D.M. (eds) (1993) *The Lesbian and Gay Studies Reader*. London: Routledge.

Achilles, N. (1967) 'The development of the homosexual bar as an institution', in J. Gagnon and W. Simon (eds) *Sexual Deviance*. New York: Harper and Row. pp. 228–44.

Adam, B. (1978) *The Survival of Domination: Inferiorization and Everyday Life*. New York: Elsevier.

Adam, B. (1995) *The Rise of a Lesbian and Gay Movement* (2nd edn). Boston: Twayne.

Adam, B. (1998) 'Theorizing homophobia', *Sexualities*, 1 (4): 387–404.

Bech, H. (1996) *When Men Meet Men*. Cambridge: Polity.

Becker, H.S. (1963) *Outsiders: Studies in the Sociology of Deviance*. New York: Free Press.

Bell, A., Weinberg, M.S. and Williams, C.J. (1978) *Homosexualities*. London: Mitchell Beazley.

Bell, D. and Valentine, G. (1995) *Mapping Desire*. London: Routledge.

Berger, P. (1963) *Invitation to Sociology*. Harmondsworth: Penguin.

Berger, P. and Luckmann, T.S. (1966) *The Social Construction of Reality*. Harmondsworth: Penguin.

Berube, A. (1991) *Coming Out Under Fire*. New York: Plume.

Bianchi, H., Simondi, M. and Taylor, I. (eds) (1975) *Deviance and Control in Europe*. London: Wiley.

Bravmann, S. (1997) *Queer Fictions of the Past*. Cambridge: Cambridge University Press.

Calhoun, C. (ed.) (1994) *Social Theory and the Politics of Identity*. Oxford: Blackwell.

Chauncey, G. (1994) *Gay New York*. New York: Basic Books.

Connell, R.W. (1992) 'A very straight gay: masculinity, homosexual experience and the dynamics of gender', *American Sociological Review*, 57 (December): 6.

Dank, B. (1971) 'Coming out in the gay world', *Pyschiatry*, 43: 180–97.

Dannecker, M. (1981) *Theories of Homosexuality*. London: Gay Men's Press.

Davis, M. and Kenney, E. (1993) *Boots of Leather, Slippers of Gold: The History of a Lesbian Community*. London: Routledge.

Dorr Legg, W. (1994) *Homophile Studies in Theory and Practice*. San Francisco: ONE Institute, GLB Publishers.

Doty, A. (1993) *Making Things Perfectly Queer*. Minneapolis: University of Minnesota Press.

Epstein, S. (1987) 'Gay politics, ethnic identity: the limits of social contructionism', *Socialist Review*, 17: 9–54.

Ericksen, J. with Steffen, S.A. (1999) *Kiss and Tell*. Cambridge, MA: Harvard University Press.

Escoffier, J. (1992) 'Generations and paradigms: mainstreams in lesbian and gay studies', *Journal of Homosexuality*, 24 (1–2): 7–27.

Faderman, L. (1981) *Surpassing the Love of Men*. London: Junction Books.

Faderman, L. (1991) *Odd Girls and Twilight Lovers*. New York: Columbia University Press.

Fee, D. (1996) 'Coming over: friendship between straight and gay men'. PhD dissertation, University of California at Santa Barbara.

Ferguson, A. (1991) 'Is there a lesbian culture?', in *Sexual Democracy*. Oxford: Westview.

Foucault, M. (1978) *The History of Sexuality: Vol 1*. Harmondsworth: Penguin (1st edn 1976).

Fuss, D. (1989) *Essentially Speaking*. London: Routledge.

Gagnon, J. and Simon, W. (1973) *Sexual Conduct: The Social Sources of Sexual Meaning*. Chicago: Aldine.

Gamson, J. (1998) *Freaks Talk Back*. Chicago: University of Chicago Press.

Greenberg, D. (1988) *The Construction of Homosexuality*. Chicago: University of Chicago Press.

Halperin, D. (1995) *Saint Foucault: Toward a Gay Hagiography*. Oxford: Oxford University Press.

Herdt, G. and Lindenbaum, S. (eds) (1992) *The Time of AIDS*. London: Sage.

Hocquenghem, G. (1978) *Homosexual Desire*. London: Allison & Busby.

Holland, J. and Weeks, J. (eds) (1996) *Sexual Cultures*. London: Macmillan.

Humphreys, L. (1971) *TeaRoom Trade*. London: Duckworth.

Jeffreys, S. (1989) *Anti Climax*. London: Women's Press.

Katz, J. (1995) *The Invention of Heterosexuality*. New York: Dutton.

Kitsuse, J. (1962) 'Societal reaction to deviant behaviour: problems of theory and method', *Social Problems*, 9: 247–56.

Kitzinger, C. (1987) *The Social Construction of Lesbianism*. London: Sage.

Lauritsen, J. and Thorstad, D. (1974) *The Early Homosexual Rights Movement (1864–1935)*. New York: Times Change Press.

Lautmann, R. (ed.) (1993) *Homosexualität. Handbuch der Theories- und Forschungsgeschichte*. Frankfurt: Campus Verlag.

Lee, J.A. (1978) *Getting Sex*: Toronto: General.

Leong, R. (1995) *Asian American Sexualities*. London: Routledge.

Levay, S. (1993) *The Sexual Brain*. Cambridge, MA: MIT Press.

Lewis, L.A. and Ross, M.W. (1995) *A Select Body: The Gay Dance Party Subculture and the HIV/AIDS Pandemic*. London: Cassell.

Leznoff, M. and Wesley, W.A. (1956) 'The homosexual community', *Social Problems*, 3: 257–63.

MacKinnon, C. (1987) *Feminism Unmodified*. Cambridge, MA: Harvard University Press.

McIntosh, M. (1981) 'The homosexual role' and 'Postscript' originally published in *Social Problems* 1967, and reprinted in K. Plummer (ed.) *The Making of the Modern Homosexual*. London: Hutchinson.

Mendès-Leite, R. and de Busscher, P-O. (1993) 'Gay studies from the French cultures', *Journal of Homosexuality*, 25: 1–205.

Mieli, M. (1980) *Homosexuality and Liberation: Elements of a Gay Critique*. London: Gay Men's Press.

Miller, J. (1993) *The Passion of Michel Foucault*. New York: Simon & Schuster.

Murray, S.O. (1984) *Social Theory, Homosexual Realities*. New York: Gai Saber Monographs.

Murray, S.O. (1996) *American Gay*. Chicago: University of Chicago Press.

Nardi, P. (1999) *Gay Male Friendships*. Chicago: University of Chicago Press.

Nardi, P. and Schneider, B. (eds) (1998) *Social Perspectives in Lesbian and Gay Studies*. London: Routledge.

Newton, E. (1972) *Mother Camp*. Englewood Cliffs, NJ: Prentice-Hall.

Newton, E. (1984) 'The mythic mannish lesbian', *Signs*, 9 (4): 557–75.

Newton, E. (1993) *Cherry Grove, Fire Island: Sixty Years in America's First Gay and Lesbian Town*. Boston: Beacon.

Phelan, S. (1989) *Identity Politics: Lesbian Feminism and the Limits of Community*. Philadelphia: Temple University Press.

Plummer, K. (1975) *Sexual Stigma*. London: Routledge.

Plummer, K. (ed.) (1981) *The Making of the Modern Homosexual*. London: Hutchinson.

Plummer, K. (1992) 'Speaking its name: inventing a lesbian and gay studies', in K. Plummer (ed.) *Modern Homosexualities*. London: Routledge.

Plummer, K. (1995) *Telling Sexual Stories*. London: Routledge.

Plummer, K. (1998) 'The past, present and futures of the sociology of same sex relations' (an earlier version of the present chapter), in P. Nardi and B. Schneider (eds), *Social Perspectives in Lesbian and Gay Studies*. London: Routledge. pp. 605–14.

Plummer, K. (forthcoming) 'Power, lust and postmodernism: revisiting symbolic interactionism and sexuality', in J. Irvine (ed.), *Sexuality Revisited*.

Pollak, M. (1985) *Les Homosexuels et le sida. Sociologie d'une épidémie*. Paris: Metailie.

Ponse, B. (1978) *Identities in the Lesbian World*. Westport: Greenwood.

Ringer, R.J. (ed.) (1994) *Queer Words, Queer Images: Communication and the Construction of Homosexuality*. New York: New York University Press.

Rubin, G. (1984) 'Thinking sex', in Carole S. Vance (ed.), *Pleasure and Danger*. London: Routledge.

Sagarin, E. (1975) *Deviants and Deviance: An Introduction to the Study of Devalued People and Behavior*. New York: Praeger.

Schofield, M. (1965) *Sociological Aspects of Homosexuality*. London: Longman.

Schur, E.M. (1965) *Crimes without Victims*. Englewood Cliffs, NJ: Prentice-Hall.

Sedgwick, E.K. (1991) *Epistemology of the Closet*. London: Harvester Wheatsheaf.

Seidman, S. (1990) *Romantic Longings*. London: Routledge.

Seidman, S. (1992) *Embattled Eros*. London: Routledge.

Seidman, S. (ed.) (1994) 'Special issue on queer theory', *Sociological Theory*, 12.

Seidman, S. (ed.) (1996) *Queer Theory/Sociology*. Oxford: Blackwell.

Simon, W. and Gagnon, J. (1967) 'Homosexuality: towards the formulation of a sociological perspective', *Journal of Health and Social Behaviour*, 8: 177–85.

Smart, B. (1985) *Michel Foucault: Key Sociologists*. London: Tavistock.

Stanley, L. (1982) '"Male needs": the problems of working with gay men', in S. Friedman and E. Sarah (eds), *On the Problem of Men*. London: Women's Press. pp. 190–213.

Stein, A. (1997) *Sex and Sensibility: Stories of a Lesbian Generation*. Berkeley: University of California Press.

Stein A. and Plummer, K. (1994) 'I can't even think straight: queer theory and the missing sexual revolution in sociology', *Sociological Theory*, 12 (2 July): 178–87.

Tielman, R. (1982) 'Homosexualty in the Netherlands'. PhD dissertation, University of Utrecht.

Walby, S. (1990) *Theorising Patriarchy*. Cambridge: Polity.

Warren, C. (1974) *Identity and Community in the Gay World*. New York: Wiley.

Weeks, J. (1985) *Sexuality and Its Discontents*. London: Routledge.

Weeks, J. (1990) *Coming Out* (2nd edn). London: Quartet Books.

Weeks, J. (1995) *Invented Moralities*. Cambridge: Polity.

Weeks, J. (1998) 'The "homosexual role" after 30 years: an appreciation of the work of Mary McIntosh', *Sexualities*, 1 (2): 131–52.

Weeks, J. and Holland, J. (eds) (1996) *Sexual Cultures: Communities, Values and Intimacy*. London: Macmillan.

Whittle, S. (ed.) (1994) *The Margins of the City: Gay Men's Urban Lives*. Aldershot: Ashgate.

Wilton, T. (1995) *Lesbian Studies: Setting an Agenda*. London: Routledge.

4 Hidden from History? Homosexuality and the Historical Sciences

Judith Schuyf

Homosexuality and history

The rise of gay and lesbian studies in the early 1980s was preceded and accompanied by a rising interest in what was basically seen as gay and lesbian history, i.e. the way in which people expressed same sex behaviour and feelings in history, in which homosexuality was seen as a history of changing attitudes to an unchanging type of behaviour. Books such as *Homosexuals in History* (Rowse, 1977) and *Homoseksualiteit in middeleeuws West-Europa* (Homosexuality in medieval Western Europe) (Kuster, 1977) bear witness to this attitude. Concurrently the idea was developed that – just as in gay and lesbian studies as a whole – there had been a conspiracy to make gays and lesbians in the past invisible only to wait for the kiss of the gay or lesbian historian to bring them back to life. This was true for the first amateur historians of the reform movements of the 1950s, who wrote short biographies of 'famous homosexuals in history' to legitimize the reform movement, because people such as Plato and Shakespeare could not have been *that* wrong or morally depraved. And it was especially true of early lesbian history, reflecting the long invisibility of lesbians as women and homosexuals (Cook, 1979a). In fact this sense of 'reclaiming' history never went out of fashion, as recent (sub)titles such as 'Reclaiming Lesbians in History' (Lesbian History Group, 1989), 'Reclaiming the Gay and Lesbian Past' show. This last was the subtitle of a compilation of articles on lesbian and gay history called *Hidden from History* (Duberman et al., 1989). However, is homosexuality really hidden from history – or rather hidden *in* history? 'Before it could become classified information, the love that dares not speak its name first of all had to *have* a name' (Smith, 1991: 12–13).

The emphasis on matters of legitimisation is not strange. Ever since E.H. Carr asked the question *What is History?* (Carr, 1961), it has been recognized that history has more to do with our own view of the society in which we live at any particular time than with an exact knowledge of what has happened in the past. Therefore, questions in history are usually questions of legitimization and support, if sometimes hidden under the guise of interest in 'what has happened'.

This idea of contingency, linked to the fact that most historians are averse to 'grand theories', might seem to point in the direction of history as the pre-eminently postmodernist discipline, were it not that at the heart of historical method we find a scientific criticism of the information contained within and around the historical source material (known as 'source criticism'). Therefore at the heart of any historical enquiry there are always specific data about the past which, through the asking of specific questions and careful consideration of sources, become elevated to the special status of 'facts'.

In the case of the history of homosexuality, 1869, the year in which the term 'homosexuality' was used for the first time, has been regarded by many as such a 'fact' (Lautmann, 1993). However, what did this 'fact' mean? Was it an accident of history, did it encode something – more or less exclusive same sex acts – that had been going on for quite a long time (if not, in fact, for ever?) or was this the beginning of a totally new phase in the history of sexuality, when sexual preference started being regarded as an inseparable part of personal identity? Underlying these questions there is the basic philosophical/epistemological problem of the role naming a category plays in the existence of that category.

In this chapter, I shall trace the argument about the importance and meaning of the fact 'homosexuality'. I shall follow two lines of enquiry: the first will deal with the development of discourse about sexuality; and the second will follow recent publications that historicize the body and sexual identity. I shall finish by looking at some recent developments and the relationship (if any) between gay and lesbian and mainstream history. Overall, this chapter will concentrate on the history of European and North American sexuality. This has to do with the fact that fundamentally, the history of homosexuality today is basically the history of Western homosexuality. A comprehensive overview of other sexualities and other cultures remains to be done. I shall start out, however, where lesbian and gay history itself started out, by looking at the role of gay and lesbian icons.

From homosexuals in history to the history of homosexuality

Early gay and lesbian history was built up around the personal and sexual histories of individuals. Although these individuals lived in a past that supposedly had no word for homosexuality, they were deployed as figureheads in the legitimization of present-day homosexuality. Some of these canonical figures were turned into gay and lesbian icons: through their life histories they started living in the text, and by doing so created examples of gay and lesbian lifestyles (Marks, 1979). Sappho is an obvious example, but there are many more: Oscar Wilde, Nathalie Barney, Radclyffe Hall, and others.

In response to these practices, Eve Kosofsky Sedgwick asked in her influential book *Epistemology of the Closet* the question, 'Has there ever been a gay Socrates?' (Sedgwick, 1990: 52). Of course this is meant as a joke; but it is a very apt joke that points a finger at the crucial issue: although it is recognized that the concept of modern homosexuality has eminently been shaped in and through the lives of these icons, asking who was homosexual in a period that had no word for homosexuality is pointless. Much published historical material on homosexuality is of a biographical nature and in many of these biographies it is suggested that, in contrast to earlier studies, the hitherto 'forgotten' homosexual leanings of the protagonist are brought to the fore. This can lead to strange consequences: thus, there is sometimes wild speculation regarding the supposed homosexual identities of people such as Michelangelo, Schubert and Voltaire, to name but three examples. According to the authors of these works (Pomeau, 1986; Royer, 1985; Saslow, 1988; Solomon, 1989), the function of this kind of biography has been to fulfil feelings of personal hero worship (as Terry Castle did in *The Apparitional Lesbian* on Marie Antoinette), or to reclaim personal histories that had been hetero-sexualized, such as Elaine Miller on the relationship between Ellen Nussey and Charlotte Brontë (Lesbian History Group, 1989: 29–55). Here, silence turns into speech, but at the same time, we can ask if this is not all projection.

Precursors of homosexuality?

In the early years of lesbian and gay historical research the question was often debated whether these 'forgotten' same sex relationships should be regarded as precursors of nineteenth-century homosexuality or not. This was even more the case in studies inspired by lesbian-feminist or cultural-feminist paradigms. Within these paradigms, an important role was reserved for (asexual) romantic friendships among women. Such friendships were regarded as the idealistic mode of lesbianism-before-the-fall, in which sisterhood was more important than genital sex, which was at that time viewed as a dirty masculine habit (e.g. Cook, 1979b; Faderman, 1981; Jeffreys, 1989). Some influential early studies were written under this paradigm, such as Caroll Smith-Rosenberg's enquiry into intense forms of friendship among American women in the early nineteenth century (Smith-Rosenberg, 1975), Adrienne Rich's concept of the lesbian continuum (Rich, 1980) and Martha Vicinus's study of boarding-school friendships (Vicinus, 1984). The feminist perspective has continued to inspire some historians (Auchmuty et al., 1992; Bonnet, 1981). It has now, however, become evident that the debate about the precursors is in fact a non-discussion, because this debate disguises the fact that there has been a genuine shift in key concepts concerning the organization of social and sexual life. I shall return to this after considering some epistemological problems.

Epistemological problems

Historians have to face the problem that the subject of homosexuality as regards content and source analysis does not fit in the basically nineteenth-century academization of their discipline. Traditionally the aim of history was to describe 'how things really were'. There was no explicit 'theory of history', but a rather rigid methodology of source criticism that was developed with an epistemology based along more or less positivistic lines. In the early twentieth century, this led to a parcelling of the subject in different spheres of interest, although overall history was viewed predominantly as political history. The French Annales school of (social) historians developed methods of analysing non-traditional subjects (for example, history mentality) by using non-traditional sources, such as economic time series and verbatim records of trials. The Annales concentrated on 'lived experience', the study of daily life. This opened the way to research into various kinds of subject outside the dominant discourse, such as the history of mentalities, family history and sexuality. Traditional source criticism clearly did not suffice to examine mentalities and identities; other sources and methods of analysis were needed as well. These were partly to be found in sociology, although this in itself created another problem, as historians in general are usually not very interested in 'grand theories', which they fear will contaminate the views on their sources. By a curious twist of fortune the rise of social constructivism (not in itself an historical theory), which regarded homosexuality as the result of a social and historical process, not only led to extensive new research from this new angle but also contributed greatly to theory building on the conceptualization of homosexuality and sexuality in general.

Essentialism and social constructionism

Social constructionism in the study of sexuality arose at the end of the 1960s out of two theoretical currents: American symbolic interactionism and French structuralism. Both currents concern themselves with the relation between the individual and society, social forces and 'lived experience'. Within social constructionism two approaches can be distinguished, British constructionism, as embodied by McIntosh (1968), Plummer (1981, 1994) and Weeks (1981a, 1981b), and French constructionism, where in the field of sexuality Foucault is the most important writer. Both focus on the late nineteenth century as the period in which modern homosexuality was first conceptualized. Foucault wrote what he called an 'archaeology of the present'. For Foucault, sexuality is a construct of human imagination, a cultural artefact that changes with time. 'Knowledge' involves talking about sexuality to other people; the subsequent effects of this talking Foucault designated as 'power'. By using the method of deconstructing different discourses about sexuality he hoped to uncover the power structures that had served to regulate human behaviour and led at the end of the nineteenth century to the search for the desire to know the 'truth about sexuality' (*scientia sexualis*). One of the ways individuals could gain this truth was by self-examination of what they saw as their personal identity and subsequent confession (Foucault, 1979, 1986a and 1986b). Weeks uses an historical approach to identity that pays attention to the description of the social conditions under which homosexuality as a category came into existence and the construction of homosexuality as the unification of disparate experiences. Important roads of enquiry are the relation of this categorization to other sociosexual categorizations, and the relationship to certain historical circumstances that have been created by this (Weeks, 1981a: 81). Weeks also sees the late nineteenth century as the formative period of the 'personal identity' conception of homosexuality.

The introduction of social constructionism led to fierce debates between the social constructionists and those who had maintained that there had 'always' been homosexuals in history (such as Bullough, 1979; Dover, 1985). The latter were suddenly labelled 'essentialists', although several writers remarked on the fact that self-confessed essentialists were hard to find. Part of this fierce debate was of a personal nature and reflected old enmities that had little to do with academic debate.

In fact, discussion of the nature of things and categories is a very old philosophical debate (Boswell, 1982–83). Although essentialists were often defamed by constructionists for being uneducated country hicks, within the essentialist grouping there was at least one very respected historian, John Boswell, whose study of sexuality in antiquity led him to believe there was something like a gay consciousness in the Roman period (Boswell, 1980). According to Boswell, constructionists disregard the fact that there are some real problems, summarized in the question of whether society is itself responding to sexual phenomena that are generic to humans or whether these sexual phenomena are created by social structures. He then discusses four areas in which limitations on the validity of constructionism are most apparent. These areas are of four types: philosophical (does an abstract ever relate to reality?); semantic (is it legitimate to ask questions of the past using the categories of the present, regardless of whether they had meaning for the persons being studied, or should the investigator adopt the categories with which denizens of the past would have described their own lives and culture? In other words, does the fact that the Romans had no word for 'religion' mean that they did not have any religion?); political (everybody uses generalizations for political reasons); and empirical (the historical record itself suggests that premodern patterns of sexuality were fundamentally different from modern ones only to a certain extent) (Boswell, 1992).

After well over fifteen years of debate on the essentialist/constructionist divide, we can see that the constructionist paradigm has largely carried the day, at least within intellectual circles. It has not, however, become part of 'popular knowledge', that is, of the people at large, and has been taken up only reluctantly by parts of the political gay movement. For both public and movement, it apparently is safer to stress one's status as an essential group to which members have no choice about belonging. If sexual identity is fixed, it also poses no threat to seduction by older people. Vance (1989: 28) comments on what she calls 'the failure to make a distinction between politically expedient ways of framing an argument and more complex descriptions of social relations.'

The evidence of experience

According to Foucault, every culture has its own distinctive ways of putting sexuality into words – sexuality cannot exist apart from being talked about. The trouble with the gay icons was that they were silent. They could not speak about their experiences because they had no words in which to describe them. Once they started to speak, however, they still had to stay within the discourse that was available to them, thereby also creating methodological problems with those who are speaking. An argument that is often used against constructionism is that when people talk about their (sexual) identities, they often are convinced that they were 'born that way'. Such people refute the idea that there could be such a thing as constructionism. Joan Scott calls this 'the evidence of experience'. She questions this, especially when documenting life-stories of non-dominant groups. The only way to deal with these stories is by comparing them with other narratives. Scott argues against accepting such stories simply at face value: the evidence of experience is not enough. By staying within the epistemological framework of orthodox history, one leaves aside questions about the constructed nature of experience and how subjects are constituted as different in the first place. Whereas individuals have experiences, subjects are constructed by their experiences (Scott, 1991).

The question of knowledge

The discussion about the validity of experience can also be regarded as a discussion about 'knowledge'. Whereas English has only the word 'knowledge', French has two – *connaissance* and *savoir* (Smith, 1991: 13). Whereas *connaissance* refers to knowledge through direct experience, *savoir* – the word used by Foucault – refers to learning beyond direct experience, to erudition and ideas. It is in the latter sense that 'knowledge' plays a role in discussions on the nature of the development of the lesbian sexual role in particular. Exactly because lesbianism (and female sexuality in general) has been so much more invisible than male sexuality, the existence of specific literary sources has been used as evidence that women had 'knowledge' of same sex sexuality. Among these sources we find literature written by men about explicit lesbian activities among distinct groups of women (mostly of a pornographic or adventurous nature, cf. Donoghue, 1993) and coded poems written by women (Van Gemert, 1995). This 'knowledge' has been considered 'transgressive', as it pictured women in an active role in sexual play, and authors such as Donoghue and Van Gemert stressed this transgressiveness as a sure sign of the existence of other sexual heterodoxies such as lesbianism.

It remains to be seen whether this view is correct. It could be the result of a Victorian projection: ever since Victorian times women have been supposed to 'think about England' rather than about sex; therefore, the simple fact that women could acquire some form of knowledge about sexuality was assumed (e.g., by Donoghue, 1993) to be in itself highly transgressive. This is the stance taken by Andreadis (1996). Yet she suggests a connection between the development of sexual knowledge as a printed verbal construct and the increasing availability of vernacular print cultures that in itself was associated with (upper-)class literacy among women.

Class seems to have played an important role in the ideas about sexual practice. Most of the written histories of sex between women are situated within the lower classes. So were (perhaps not incidentally) most of the cases involving females that went to court (Van der Meer, 1984). This has less to do with transgressiveness than with the manner in which the lower classes' sexuality was constructed in the seventeenth and eighteenth centuries. So, Kraakman warns against the tendency to regard eighteenth-century erotic fiction as subversive and transgressive by nature. 'Transgression of political, social and discursive norms can go very well together with the reendorsement of existing sex-roles – how else can we explain the sharp odour of misogyny and sodomophobia that rises from this literature?' At the same time, she recognizes female curiosity in the eighteenth century as the source of sexual curiosity which in itself leads to both learning and knowledge through experience (Kraakman, 1997: 140 ff.). This again takes us to definitions of sexuality that are part of a changing discourse in which elements of class and situations of knowledge play key roles.

The development of sexuality

Homosexuality as we see it today presupposes not only the concept of personal sexual identity but also the notion that this sexual identity has gender as its most important distinguishing feature. The concepts of gender and sexual identities seem to have developed relatively recently. The implicit consequence of this is that we have to investigate sexual object choice in the past and the ways in which this is structured socio-sexually. At which particular point in time was the concept of sexual identity formed and which elements were involved? How was same sex behaviour regarded? Can or should people who engaged in same sex behaviour be seen as precursors of modern homosexuality? When did gender become important and why?

Halperin distinguishes between sex, which is biological, and sexuality, which is cultural. He states, 'Sex has no history. . . . Sex refers to the erogenous capacities and genital functions of the human body. Sex, so defined is a natural fact [. . . and] lies outside history and culture' (Halperin, 1990: intro.). Sexuality, on the contrary, is a cultural product: 'it represents the appropriation of the human body and of its physiological capacities by an ideological discourse'. Padgug in fact implied this in the late 1970s:

> In the pre-bourgeois world sexuality was a group of acts and institutions not necessarily linked to one another. Each group of sexual acts was connected directly or indirectly – that is, formed part of – institutions and thought patterns which we tend to view as political, economic, or social in nature, and the connections cut across our idea of sexuality as a thing, detachable from other things, and as a separate sphere of existence. (Padgug, 1989: 62)

Sexuality does have a history, but, according to Halperin, not a very long one (Halperin, 1989). In classical antiquity there was as yet no sense of either sexuality as an autonomous sphere of existence or the function of sexuality as a principle of individuation in human nature. Foucault had already remarked on the fact that sexuality in antiquity was largely an ethical concern. Recent studies of sexual behaviour in classical antiquity confirm that although there was same sex behaviour, the main distinction was between the sexual behaviour of the free adult male versus that of the rest of the population. Penetration was the main sexual act, but as long as the free male was the perpetrator, the passive partner was not really relevant. The sort of partner he had sex with did not constitute part of his identity, and could equally be a woman, a slave or a young boy (Halperin, 1989; Halperin et al., 1990; Winkler, 1990).

The study of (homo)sexuality in the Middle Ages does not yet incorporate these new perspectives. This is partly because there have been very few recent studies on the subject, but also because the most influential author on the Middle Ages, John Boswell, advocated a more essentialist view of homosexuality, supposing a gay subculture as early as the twelfth century (Boswell, 1980). His study addressed the controversial influence of the Catholic Church on the persecution of gay people. The source material on the medieval period is of a legal nature, focusing on sodomy and other forms of same sex behaviour (Pavan, 1980; Trexler, 1981), and it is probably this kind of material that leads some (such as Goodich, 1979) to the conclusion that effeminacy and the exclusive preference of men for other men that is so prevalent in Italian Renaissance sources were indeed signs of a gay consciousness. On the one hand there is legal prohibition, based on the Church's view of homosexuality as a sin against the world order; yet on the other hand there is an apparently rather profuse 'lived experience' coupled to moral panic over the decadence of the higher classes and fear of extinction (Rousseau and Porter, 1987; Ruggiero, 1985). This fear was the consequence of deep-felt moral precepts embedded in the late medieval and early Renaissance worldviews based on the balance of the God-given universe. Within this moral universe, practising homosexual behaviour became another form of heterodoxy, joining sorcery, religious heresy and treason; a part of the general depravity to which all mankind is subject – dangerous to the continuing existence of the universe and therefore to be condemned, but not a distinct social role as such (Bredbeck, 1991). This ties in with studies that describe the main social division people recognized in sexual behaviour as that between those who were 'honest' (i.e., modest and chaste) and those who were 'dishonest' (lecherous and lustful in all matters of life) (Van der Pol, 1996).

The Renaissance as period of transition

In her groundbreaking article on social constructionism, Mary McIntosh (1968) pointed out that the introduction of what she called the homosexual role had taken place around 1700. As a sociologist, she had no means to prove this at the time, but her conjecture led to a great number of impressive studies focusing on the transitional period of 1600–1700 in England. Discourse on sexuality and same sex relationships at the start of this century turned out to be totally dissimilar to discourse at the end of the century. The first of those studies was by Alan Bray, who considered the development of the homosexual role in the context of this period's great social changes (Bray, 1982). He started by positioning homosexuality in the mental universe and the structure of society, deciding that at the very least homosexuality was the solution to the frustration of sexual needs caused by the universal practice of late marriage. There was a contradiction in the fact that it existed on a large scale despite widespread social condemnation. Bray was unable to explain this contradiction. So were most of his followers, although the Renaissance continued to receive a lot of attention (Coward, 1980; Gerard and Hekma, 1989). Literary historians such as Smith took up the challenge. Following a Foucauldian perspective, Smith set out to investigate not just what was prohibited, but what was actively homo-eroticized – in order to trace *savoir* in the seventeenth century – and found 'a startling ambiguity': a disparity between the extreme punishments prescribed by law and the almost positive valuation of homoerotic desire in the visual arts, literature and political power structure. So, in order to understand Renaissance 'scripts of sexual desire' we must discriminate among various discourses about homosexuality: legal, moral, medical and poetic. Of these the poetic is the most informative, as it tells us about homosexual desire. Smith then describes six (classical) poetic stories (which he calls 'myths') of desire. Each of those represents a different intersection of structures of ideology with power structures, and a different site of sociosexual experience. This ends with an eroticized form of male bonding specific to the culture of early modern England, as demonstrated in Shakespeare's sonnets (Smith, 1991). Little is known about female relationships in this period (Brown, 1986).

The development of gendered sexuality

Smith's study has shown one way in which specific forms of male desire could turn into a specific preference for same sex sexualities rather than just one possible form of behaviour. We still need to analyse the historical process by which this specific preference was taken further in the eighteenth century. This started with an important shift in the organization of sexuality, from hierarchical to gender-based relations.

First, an essential difference between men and women was created that had to become inscribed not only in the body, but also in the soul. The result of this was the recognition that the soul and the emotions were gendered. Men and women were supposed to be and to feel differently. The existing division of humanity into those who were 'honest' and those who were 'dishonest' started to be explained more often in terms of gender than in terms of class. 'Honest' people could control themselves and therefore did not care much about sexuality, whereas 'dishonest' people were perceived to be preoccupied with all sorts of dishonest behaviour, including sexual behaviour. 'Dishonesty' became connected with lasciviousness, which was regarded as a female characteristic. Women were supposed to be unable to control themselves, whereas for men sobriety and moderation were ideal traits. In this way, the gendered soul became embodied in a gendered body. The new male and female identities were realized within different kinds of discourse that were often contradictory. Masculinity was moulded by philosophical and religious discourse about identity in which 'the soul' and 'the self' were described as 'human', that is, 'male'; femininity was described in medical, educational and literary discourse that only served to demonstrate derived identities within the private sphere. Finally, the development of the theory of the self at the end of the eighteenth century liberalized the individuality of emotions. Releasing the reproductive role from the family left room for the introduction of passion and friendship (for a more general background to this see Armstrong, 1987; Nussbaum, 1989).

A prerequisite for perceiving gender differences is to recognize differences between the sexes in general. This remark might seem facetious, but as Thomas Laqueur (1990) has shown, it was only during the eighteenth century that the crucial importance of the physical differences between men and women gained recognition. Before that period the difference between the sexes was seen as one of degree rather than of kind: there was only one sex with two genders, the ideal male and the lesser female. Laqueur describes a radical shift in the eighteenth century from this 'one-sex' system to a 'two-sex' system, in which the anatomical differences between men and women were viewed as significators of important physical and emotional differences as well. Under the 'one-sex' system only one sex and two genders are recognized, whereas under the two-sex system there are two distinct sexes (Trumbach, 1994). In the end, the body itself becomes the bearer of different messages through which the constructed differences between men and women are understood to be the result of natural differences. For women the formation of the two-sex system had the most consequences, as under the 'one-sex system' males formed the universal human standard. Instead of being slightly imperfect versions of universal male perfection, women were suddenly relegated to a distinct category of being with a nature, body and soul that were by definition inferior.

The new ideas about the differences between the sexes led to increasing interest, in both academic discourse and life experience, in the dynamics of sexual relationships between the sexes, to the detriment of the antique systems of attraction through hierarchical differences. This involved a long period of transition that took place throughout the eighteenth century and a large part of the nineteenth. In the sexual vacuum created by this, gay and lesbian identities based on inversion were being formed, although there was probably a time gap of close to a century between the formation of gay and of lesbian identities.

When there was as yet no fixed homosexual role, men who had sex with other men also had sex with women, albeit often with women years older than themselves. For instance, Van der Meer (1995) found, in his Dutch court material of the eighteenth and nineteenth centuries, evidence of the process by which these sexual acts with other males became tied to gendered emotions. According to him, the rise of modernism and especially of the individual at the end of the seventeenth century was the main agent through which desires became gender-related. Within the old hierarchical system, desires were first of all of a purely physical nature. There was room for homosexual behaviour that might not have been exclusive, but was regarded as 'habitual'. As homosexual behaviour was equated with excessive sexuality, these desires were designated as 'female'. Van der Meer sees discourse and life experience (which he calls social reality) drift further apart after the persecution of sodomites in the Dutch republic in the years after 1730. This forced people to face their own feelings and must have played a key part in crystallizing these feelings. Regarding these feelings as 'feminine' became connected to pre-scientific notions of influences on the unborn child that led these sodomites to start seeing their 'female' behaviour as a sign of innateness. According to Van der Meer, these early sodomite subcultures are definite precursors of modern homosexuality. Once these ascribed gender roles became written on the body, the development of male homosexuality became intrinsically linked to unlicensed sexuality and femininity.

The change in thought that led to homosexual men being regarded as 'effeminate' cannot by definition have had the same effect for women. Trumbach (1994) had already surmised that there was a gap of at least seventy-five years between the formation of male and female homosexual identities, although he placed this gap earlier in the eighteenth century, instead of (as now seems more likely) in the late eighteenth century and early nineteenth century. For most of this period, women appear to stay out of the medical and psychiatric discourse about sexual identities that dominated the nineteenth century (Mak, 1997). Class played an important role in the development of ideas about female sexuality. As we have seen, the old ideas about honesty and dishonesty had many undertones of classism and sexism. Women in whom both elements were united – working-class girls and prostitutes in particular – were among the first to be described (by medical doctors commissioned to write reports of social wrongs) as having sexual relations with other women. At the other end of the scale we find the same assumptions about upper-class women, based upon the supposed availability of sexual knowledge as a result of Enlightenment literature and the sort of general 'don't give a damn' attitude that has always been attributed to the nobility (Donoghue, 1993; Kraakman, 1997; Trumbach, 1989). At the same time we witness the rise of the middle-class woman, with her soft female soul and gentle habits, in whom the old notions of honesty developed seamlessly into the bourgeois ideal of sexlessness (with noted unfortunate Victorian consequences). Under the aegis of honest bourgeois enlightenment we can place such former lesbian icons as the Dutch writer-couple Betje Wolff and Aagje Deken, as well as countless other scholarly and literary couples and women who engaged in what later came to be known as 'Boston marriages' (Everard, 1994; Faderman, 1981; Smith-Rosenberg, 1975).

Within bourgeois gentility women who dressed up as men (Dekker and Van der Pol, 1989; Vicinus, 1989) could only create confusion by undermining limits that were becoming ever more fixed. At first they were charged with fraud, not homosexuality (Mak, 1997). Within a one-sex system this is easily explained: sex is not yet an identity, only a status. According to Mak, this status is proclaimed through actions, not yet through words. But this changed during the nineteenth century. As the result of the introduction of the two-sex system, doctors were now increasingly of the opinion that everybody should have 'a true sex'. Gender could be explained in terms of embodied sexed characteristics and thus sexual identity was formed. Because of the intervention of sexologists at the end of the nineteenth century, all women were now supposed to declare their 'true histories' within the narrow definitions of medical discourse. Masculine behaviour was seen as the result of a lack of femininity rather than as a possible mode of behaviour. In this manner inversion – the reversal of the sex role – in women was linked to (homo)sexuality. From this time on a lesbian role, linked to masculinity, existed. The process ended with the internalization by some women of this role, as attested by the publication in 1901 in one of the *Jahrbücher für sexuelle Zwischenstufen* of the autobiography of a lesbian, E. Krause, under the title 'Die Wahrheit über Mich' ('The truth about me'). The homosexual and lesbian role had gained a narrative.

The twentieth century

Consolidation

I have given disproportionate attention to the developments in the seventeenth and eighteenth centuries in relation to the actual number of studies on this subject because it seems to me that this period is on the cutting edge of the development of the study of homosexuality in history. This has not always been the case, however. Some historians still maintain that the late nineteenth century is the period to examine for the conceptualization of homosexuality. These studies emphasize the importance of the sexologists' intervention and the 'medicalization of homosexuality', following Foucault's observation that modern homo- and heterosexual identities were formed only through the development by the medical profession of a *scientia sexualis* in which 'the wish to know' led to confessing the 'truth about one's sexuality' (Foucault, 1979, 1986a and 1986b; Hekma, 1987; Weeks, 1981a). Weeks, who was interested in the intricacies of late Victorian society, also concentrated his argument on the close of the nineteenth century (Weeks, 1977). He regards the years around 1890 as 'the moment of the solidification of that binary opposition between "homosexuality" and "heterosexuality"'. Weeks, working 'on historical questions through the reading of literature, reading literary texts with the grain of contemporary historical knowledge', saw a sense of the historicity and power of our sexual definitions. He found only conflict and disorder, at least suggesting that the process did not run along a clearly defined one-way track. One example to illustrate this is the lawsuit against Oscar Wilde, which probably did more to educate people about the interconnections of dandies, inverts and homosexuals in turn-of-the-century England than the whole abstract discussion on the introduction of the Labouchère Act in 1885, which put male homosexuality back on the statute book (Bristow, 1995). After all, Queensberry accused Wilde of *posing as* a sodomite rather than *being* one!

The process of medicalization has been documented closely (see, among others, Chauncey, 1982–83; Hacker, 1987; Kennedy, 1990; Lautmann, 1993; Steakley, 1975), and the legal punishment and liberation that went hand in hand with this have also been described (e.g., Hütter, 1992; Lauritsen and Thorstad, 1974; Lautmann, 1977). Not yet fully documented are the interrelationships between the development of homosexuality and nationalism, imperialism and concomitant attempts at purity. Nationalistic and imperialistic nations such as Germany and Britain attached great value to maintaining what they defined as 'healthy (hetero)sexuality' as a moral precept that would validate their claim to dominate countries in Africa and Asia. The 'othering' that was the result of this led to the equation of non-white with non-heterosexual and therefore perverse (e.g. Lautmann, 1984; Mosse, 1985; see also Gert Hekma's contribution to this book). Some of this history is rather confusing, as it demonstrates that there were uneasy alliances both between feminism and right-wing anti-sexual movements (using their particular versions of 'femininity' to try to curb a more free expression of sexuality by statutory prohibition) and between early male bonding societies and early Fascism (in celebrating masculine values).

The final phase of conceptualizing the modern homosexual was completed between 1890 and 1914. Foucault pointed to the vicious circle that was the consequence of this conceptualization: as even more people started to recognize themselves as homosexual, more people became aware of the existence of homosexuality. This in itself provoked a repressive reaction from the authorities. The emancipation movement that started up thereafter made homosexuality more visible and public, and attracted more and more support. It is from this point of view of oppression and liberation that the remarkable history of the start of the emancipation movement in the twentieth century has been described.

The company of others like oneself

To the notion that there now was an 'official' homosexual identity, some dissident voices have to be noted. One is that of Lillian Faderman, who claims that the potentially sexual and therefore dangerously transgressive nature of female relationships was recognized only in the wake of what she found to be the stigmatizing writings of sexologists. In the United States, the shift towards a more pathologizing discourse happened only after 1928 (Faderman 1986). Attention has been paid to the conceptualization of other forms of relationship that were not sexual (among women: Rupp, 1989) or not overtly homosexual (among men: Chauncey, 1994). In his study of New York at the beginning of the century, Chauncey found differences between the gay person and his partner based on the perceived female behaviour of the gay person and the masculine image and behaviour of the partner, who did not lose his heterosexual status. According to Chauncey, adaptation was the ability to move between different personas and different lives. It was not so much 'coming out' as such, as coming out *into* the gay world, where men were not divided into 'homosexuals' and 'heterosexuals'. This is a recent distinction that was not made in working-class culture. Men were labelled 'queer' if they took over the gender role of women; the man who responded to this was not considered abnormal so long he adhered to masculine gender conventions. This reminds us of the well-documented behaviour of upper middle-class British writers such as Isherwood, Auden, Forster and Ackerley, who felt sexually attracted only to young working-class boys. Their attraction was based on availability, eroticized class and therefore power. The difference between the 'invert' or core-homosexual and the masculine (rent) boy was maintained by existing social relationships as well as by psychological discourse on inverted behaviour. This changed between the 1930s and the 1950s, marked by class and ethnic differences (Chauncey, 1994), and only fully disappeared under the influence of sexual liberation in the 1960s and 1970s, which led people to regard (sexual) relationships as first of all based on equality.

As many early scholars of lesbian and gay history had backgrounds in the emancipation movement, it comes as no surprise that the history of the movement and of gay and lesbian subcultures itself became a subject for investigation (Altman, 1983; D'Emilio, 1983; Girard, 1981; Tielman, 1982). Most of this research was carried out in the 1980s and can be regarded as quite straightforward attempts at descriptive history, although such studies drew heavily on alternative sources, such as oral history. At the end of the nineteenth century, homosexual men and women developed their own forms of organization. This process was helped along by increasing urbanization in Western Europe and the United States, which created both the space and the people for this. City air again meant freedom. From Berlin in the 1880s to New York, Paris and, to a lesser extent, London, men and women met under various disguises and formed subcultures (e.g. Berlin-Museum, 1984; Chauncey, 1994; Katz, 1983). There have been numerous studies on the development of and habits within subcultures, in particular in relation to the development of subcultural identities. These subcultures are characterized by specific locales, norms and values, and are usually but not always sex-segregated (Benstock, 1987; Casselaer, 1986; Faderman, 1991; Hacker and Vogel, 1984; Hamer, 1996; Kennedy and Davis, 1993; Newton, 1994; and Schuyf, 1994; to name but a few). Local knowledge was needed to be able to make same sexual contacts. This was true in particular in smaller towns in Europe, where we do not find extensive subcultures until the late 1970s. In many towns, the local sexual infrastructure was limited to cruising areas available to men only (see Koenders, 1996, for provincial towns in the Netherlands and Nielssen, 1995, for the town of Göteborg in Sweden).

The history of persecution of homosexuality during World War II can in part be seen as a disruption of the development of lesbian and gay subcultures in the Western world. Part of this history was mapped out through oral history and eyewitness accounts, which were inspired by the total lack of information about the persecution of homosexuality during this period that was maintained by the authorities (Heger, 1972; Plant, 1986). Eventually original source material that had been 'lost' in a number of German archives was located and published (Grau, 1993; Jellonek, 1990). These studies led to the conclusion that it was mainly male homosexuality within the original German Reich that was persecuted, especially in the years between the Nazi take-over and the beginning of the war. According to Nazi ideology, gay men could be re-educated through hard labour, so they were put in labour camps. Although the many thousands that were arrested were not sent to proper extermination camps, a disproportionately large number of them died because they were at the bottom of the camp's pecking order and had no protectors (see Martin Sherman's play *Bent* (1979) for a moving literary representation of this). Schoppmann (1991) wrote about the 'invisible' history of lesbians under Nazism. Lesbians were persecuted as 'asocial' because they did not conform to Nazi population policy and work ethics. Careful consideration of the sources also led Koenders (1996) to the conclusion that there was no extensive persecution of homosexuals outside Germany proper unless German soldiers were actively involved. A number of Dutch homosexuals were active in the Resistance, which may even have formed the kernel of a post-war political movement. Interestingly, in the United States the experiences of many young men and women in sex-segregated army units away from the constricting influences of their small home towns resulted in a heightened gay and lesbian self-consciousness (Berubé, 1990) that, despite a fierce backlash in the 1950s, eventually led to the formation of the modern lesbian and gay movement after the war (Altman, 1983; D'Emilio, 1983).

Countering the taboo: political and emancipation history in the twentieth century

The early emancipation movements made use of a particular kind of legitimising discourse that was based on a mixture of arguments taken from the natural sciences, law and (literary) history. This can be seen almost from the beginning of the movements at the end of the nineteenth century. In reaction to legal pressures on the emerging homosexual identities emancipation movements were founded in Germany as early as 1897 (Wissenschaftlich Humanitäres Komitee in Germany). Its Dutch counterpart, NWHK, was founded in 1911 (Tielman, 1982). There is a remarkable unity in goals and organizational forms among these early movements. Hirschfeld's adagium *per scientia et justitia* seems to have been adopted as their motto: by producing 'scientific evidence' on the nature and manifestations of homosexuality they hoped to change public opinion and contravene the increasingly hostile measures of the authorities. This is also true of the reform movements that were founded after World War II (Adam, 1987; Adam et al., 1999). These movements had to strike a delicate balance between the internal mobilization of the – mainly male – members and keeping up serious appearances externally in order to be accepted by the heterosexual majority. With this, we have strayed into the realm of political history. (For further discussion of this subject see Chapter 7 by Krowel and Duyvendak).

Coda

Undoubtedly the development and ideas of lesbian and gay history have made great contributions to thinking about sexuality in the past as well as in the present (e.g. in gay and lesbian studies). Yet it is striking that it took a long time before the influence of these ideas was felt within mainstream history, let alone by the public. One does not have to look far to find a reason for this, for gay and lesbian studies is methodologically and ideologically suspect in many academic circles (see the introduction to this volume) and the message it carries can be threatening to the male heterosexual world order, which is based on the tenet that heterosexuality is 'natural'. Also, many Foucauldian and postmodern studies are written in the kind of dense argot that those who are not experts in the field find hard to follow. The personal, and especially the sexual, is still not regarded as a subject fit for research; well, perhaps fit for women's history – something that has no status.

But things are slowly changing. Gay and lesbian historians – such as Weeks (1981b) and D'Emilio and Freedman (1988) – have made some efforts to write more general overviews of sexual history. Furthermore, Foucault, well over fifteen years after his death, is finally making some imprint on mainstream history, although this is mostly on studies that deal with the history of culture or literary history. The Dutch cultural historian Frijhoff recently summed up the change in perspective initiated in the study of 'love' (as this was called) as a language of culture and forms rather than something fit for anecdotes. Sex has now become a fully-fledged object of cultural history. The historicization of gender and the body and the introduction to history of concepts such as honour and friendship can be put down to new studies spawned by gay and lesbian studies; unfortunately, this is seldom acknowledged within traditional academic practice (see for instance Frijhoff, 1998). We can add to this new methodological inroads, such as the introduction of the historicization of mentalities – in particular the historicity of the psyche – and the creative use of new types of source in history, such as oral history, which although in itself not a lesbian and gay studies 'invention' has been widely used (Cant and Hemmings, 1988; Kokula, 1986; Marcus, 1995; Newton, 1994; Porter and Weeks, 1991; Vacha, 1985). No longer are these regarded as simple statements of fact, but rather as narratives that can help deconstruct becoming (homo)sexual and other aspects of gay and lesbian lives. 'Telling sexual stories' (Plummer, 1994) is a sign of modernity, of gaining sexual citizenship. New narrative interpretations help to solve the contradictions among theory, discourse and life experience. This shows the space people have created for themselves in countering dominant discourse and helps to break out of the dichotomy between dominance and submission (Marcus, 1995).

So, are there new directions to be found? This outline of the development of the homosexual role has to be fleshed out – in particular for the early nineteenth century and in conjunction with the development of concepts such as 'passion', 'friendship', 'soul' and 'self'. This in itself could lead to new investigations into the Middle Ages. This may appear to take us away from homosexuality *per se*, but will lead us into new and exciting worlds.

Acknowledgements

I wish to thank my co-editors (Jan-Willem Duyvendak, Theo Sandfort and Jeffrey Weeks) and Geertje Mak for their careful comments on this chapter.

References

Adam, B.D. (1987) *The Rise of a Gay and Lesbian Movement*. Boston: Twayne Publishers.

Adam, B.D., Duyvendak, J.W. and Krouwel, A.P.M. (eds) (1999) *The Global Emergence of Gay and Lesbian Politics. National Imprints of a Worldwide Movement*. Philadelphia: Temple University Press.

Altman, D. (1983) *The Homosexualization of America*. Boston: Beacon Press.

Andreadis, H. (1996) 'Tribades, tommies, lollepots and . . . romantic friends? Theorizing early modern lesbianisms', *Thamyris*, 3 (1): 125–37.

Armstrong, N. (1987) *Desire and Domestic Fiction. A Political History of the Novel*. New York and Oxford: Oxford University Press.

Auchmuty, R., Jeffreys, S. and Miller, E. (1992) 'Lesbian history and gay studies: keeping a feminist perspective', *Women's History Review*, 1 (1): 89–108.

Benstock, S. (1987) *Women of the Left Bank. Paris 1900–1940*. London: Virago.

Berlin-Museum (1984) *ELDORADO. Homosexuelle Frauen und Männer in Berlin 1850–1950. Geschichte, Alltag und Kultur*. Berlin: Frölich & Kaufmann.

Bérubé, A. (1990) *Coming out under Fire. The History of Gay Men and Women in World War Two*. New York: Plume Penguin.

Bonnet, M.-J. (1981) *Un Choix sans équivoque: recherches historiques sur les relations amoureuses entre les femmes, XVIIe-XXe Siècle*. Paris: Denoël.

Boswell, J. (1980) *Christianity, Social Tolerance and Homosexuality: Gay People in Western Europe from the Beginning of the Christian Era to the Fourteenth Century*. Chicago: University of Chicago Press.

Boswell, J. (1982–83) 'Revolutions, universals, and sexual categories', *Salmagundi*, 58 (9): 89–113.

Boswell, J. (1992) 'Categories, experience and sexuality', in E. Stein (ed.), *Forms of Desire. Sexual Orientation and the Social Constructionist Controversy*. New York and London: Routledge. pp. 133–73.

Bray, A. (1982) *Homosexuality in Renaissance England*, London: Gay Men's Press.

Bredbeck, G. W. (1991) *Sodomy and Interpretation. Marlowe to Milton*. Ithaca, NY: Cornell University Press.

Bristow, J. (1995) *Effeminate England. Homoerotic Writing after 1885*. Buckingham: Open University Press.

Brown, J. (1986) *Immodest Acts: The Life of a Lesbian Nun in Renaissance Italy*. New York and Oxford: Oxford University Press.

Bullough, V. (1979) *Homosexuality: A History*. New York: New American Library.

Cant, B. and Hemmings, S. (1988) *Radical Records: 30 Years of Lesbian and Gay History*. London: Routledge.

Carr, E.H. (1961) *What Is History?* London: Macmillan.

Casselaer, C. van (1986) *Lot's Wife. Lesbian Paris, 1890–1914*. Liverpool: Janus Press.

Castle, T. (1993) *The Apparitional Lesbian. Female Homosexuality and Modern Culture*. New York: Columbia University Press.

Chauncey, G. (1982–83) 'From sexual inversion to homosexuality: medicine and the changing conceptualization of female deviance', *Salmagundi*, 58 (9): 114–46.

Chauncey, G. (1994) *Gay New York. Gender, Urban Culture, and the Making of the Gay Male World 1890–1940*. New York: Basic Books.

Cook, B.W. (1979a) 'The historical denial of lesbianism', *Radical History Review*, 5 (20): 55–60.

Cook, B.W. (1979b) '"Women alone stir my imagination": lesbianism and the cultural tradition', *Signs*, 4: 719–20.

Coward, D.A. (1980) 'Attitudes to homosexuality in eighteenth century France', *Journal of European Studies*, 10 (4): 231–55.

Dekker, R. and Van der Pol, L. (1989) *The Tradition of Female Transvestism in Early Modern Europe*. London: Macmillan.

D'Emilio, J. (1983) *Sexual Politics, Sexual Communities: The Making of a Homosexual Minority in the United States, 1940–1970*. Chicago: University of Chicago Press.

D'Emilio, J. and Freedman, E.B. (1988) *Intimate Matters. A History of Sexuality in America*. New York: Harper & Row.

Donoghue, E. (1993) *Passions between Women. British Lesbian Culture 1668–1801*. London: Scarlett Press.

Dover, K.J. (1985) *Greek Homosexuality*. New York: Duckworth.

Duberman, M.B., Vicinus, M. and Chauncey Jr, G. (eds) (1989) *Hidden from History: Reclaiming the Gay and Lesbian Past*. New York: New American Library.

Everard, M. (1994) *Ziel en zinnen. Over liefde en lust tussen vrouwen in de tweede helft van de achttiende eeuw*. Groningen: Historische Uitgeverij.

Faderman, L. (1981) *Surpassing the Love of Men. Romantic Friendship & Love between Women from the Renaissance to the Present*. New York: Morrow.

Faderman, L. (1986) 'Love between women in 1928: why progressivism is not always progress', *Journal of Homosexuality*, 12 (1): 23–42.

Faderman, L. (1991) *Odd Girls and Twilight Lovers. A History of Lesbian Life in Twentieth-century America*. New York: Columbia University Press.

Foucault, M. (1979) *The history of sexuality Vol.1: The will to knowledge*. London: Allen Lane.

Foucault, M. (1986a) *The history of sexuality Vol.2: The use of pleasure*. Harmondsworth: Viking.

Foucault, M. (1986b) *The history of sexuality Vol. 3: The care of the self*. London: Allen Lane.

Frijhoff, W. (1998) 'Liefde in Holland: Inleiding', *Historisch Tijdschrift Holland*, 30 (4/5): 191–5.

Gerard, K. and Hekma, G. (eds) (1989) *The Pursuit of Sodomy: Male Homosexuality in Renaissance and Enlightenment Europe*. New York: Harrington Park Press.

Girard, J. (1981) *Le Mouvement homosexuel en France 1945–1980*. Paris: Syros.

Goodich, M. (1979) *The Unmentionable Vice: Homosexuality in the Later Medieval Period.* Santa Barbara, CA: Ross Erikson.

Grau, G. (1993) *Homosexualität in der NS-Zeit. Dokumente einer Diskriminierung und Verfolgung.* Frankfurt am Main: Fischer Verlag.

Hacker, H. (1987) *Frauen und Freundinnen. Studien zur 'Weiblichen Homosexualität' am Beispiel Österreich 1870–1938.* Bernheim and Basel: Beltz.

Hacker, H. and K. Vogel (1984) 'Ist das violette Fieber trivial?', *Unsere kleine Zeitung*, 11: 12–21 and 12: 14–19.

Halperin, D.M. (1989) 'Sex before sexuality: pederasty, politics and power in classical Athens', in M.B. Duberman, M. Vicinus and G. Chauncey (eds), *Hidden from History.* New York: New American Library. pp. 37–53.

Halperin, D.M. (1990) *One Hundred Years of Homosexuality; and Other Essays on Greek Love.* London and New York: Routledge.

Halperin, D.M., Winkler, J.J. and Zeitlin, F.I. (1990) *Before Sexuality: The Construction of Erotic Experience in the Ancient Greek World.* Princeton: Princeton University Press.

Hamer, H. (1996) *Britannia's Glory. A History of 20th-Century Lesbians.* London: Cassells.

Heger, H. (1972) *Die Männer mit dem rosa Winkel.* Hamburg: Merlin.

Hekma, G. (1987) *Homoseksualiteit, een medische reputatie.* Amsterdam: SUA.

Hutter, J. (1992) *Die gesellschaftliche Kontrolle des homosexuellen Begehrens. Medizinische Definitionen und juristische Sanktionen im 19. Jahrhundert.* Frankfurt am Main and New York: Campus Forschung.

Jeffreys, S. (1989) 'Does it matter if they did it?', in Lesbian History Group, *Not a Passing Phase. Reclaiming Lesbians in History 1840–1985.* London: The Women's Press. pp. 19–28.

Jellonek, B. (1990) *Homosexuelle unter dem Hakenkreuz.* Paderborn: Schoeningh.

Katz, J.N. (1983) *Gay/Lesbian Almanac. A New Documentary.* New York: Harper & Row.

Kennedy, E.L. and Davis, M.D. (1993) *Boots of Leather, Slippers of Gold. The History of a Lesbian Community.* New York and London: Routledge.

Kennedy, H. (1990) *Karl Heinrich Ulrichs. Sein Leben und sein Werk.* Stuttgart: Enke.

Koenders, P. (1996) *Tussen christelijk réveil en seksuele revolutie: bestrijding van zedeloosheid in Nederland, met nadruk op de repressie van homoseksualiteit.* Amsterdam: IISG.

Kokula, I. (1986) *Jahre des Glücks, Jahre des Leids. Gespräche mit älteren lesbischen Frauen.* Kiel: Frühlingserwachen.

Kraakman, Th.D. (1997) 'Kermis in de hel. Vrouwen en het pornografisch universum van de "Enfer" 1750–1850'. Dissertation, Amsterdam University.

Kuster, H.J. (1977) *Over homoseksualiteit in middeleeuws West-Europa.* Dissertation, Utrecht University.

Laqueur, T. (1990) *Making Sex.* Berkeley: University of California Press.

Lauritsen, J. and Thorstad, D. (1974) *The Early Homosexual Rights Movement (1864–1935).* New York: Times Change Press.

Lautmann, R. (1977) *Seminar: Gesellschaft und Homosexualität.* Frankfurt am Main: Suhrkamp.

Lautmann, R. (1984) *Der Zwang zur Tugend. Die gesellschaftliche Kontrolle der Sexualitäten.* Frankfurt am Main: Suhrkamp.

Lautmann, R. (ed.) (1993) *Homosexualität. Handbuch der Theorie- und Forschungs-geschichte.* Frankfurt and New York: Campus.

Lesbian History Group (1989) *Not a Passing Phase: Reclaiming Lesbians in History, 1840–1985.* London: The Women's Press.

Mak, G. (1997) *Mannelijke vrouwen. Over de grenzen van sekse in de negentiende eeuw.* Amsterdam and Meppel: Boom.

Marcus, E. (1995) *Making History. The Struggle for Gay and Lesbian Equal Rights 1945–1990. An Oral History.* New York: HarperCollins.

Marks, E. (1979) 'Lesbian intertextuality', in G. Stambolian and E. Marks (eds),

Homosexualities and French Literature: Cultural Contexts/Critical Texts. Ithaca: Cornell University Press. pp. 353–77.

McIntosh, M. (1968) 'The homosexual role', *Social Problems*, 16 (2): 182–92.

Mosse, G.L. (1985) *Nationalism and Sexuality. Respectability and Abnormal Sexuality in Modern Europe.* New York: Howard Fertig.

Newton, E. (1994) *Cherry Grove, Fire Island: Sixty Years in America's First Gay and Lesbian Town.* Boston, MA: Beacon Press.

Nielssen, A. (1995) *Att vara men inte synas. Om mäns homosexuella livsrum i Göteborg decennierna kring andra världskriget.* Göteborg: Sociologiska Institutionen.

Nussbaum, F. (1989) *The Autobiographical Subject. Gender and Ideology in eighteenth Century England.* Baltimore, MD: Johns Hopkins University Press.

Padgug, R. (1989) 'Sexual matters: rethinking sexuality in history', in M.B. Duberman, M. Vinicus and G. Chauncey (eds) *Hidden from History.* New York: New American Library, 54–66.

Pavan, E. (1980) 'Police des moeurs, société et politique à Venise à la fin du moyen âge', *Revue Historique*, 264 (2): 241–88.

Plant, R. (1986) *The Pink Triangle: The Nazi War against Homosexuals.* New York: Henry Holt.

Plummer, K. (ed.) (1981) *The Making of the Modern Homosexual.* London: Hutchinson.

Plummer, K. (1994) *Telling Sexual Stories. Power, Change and Social Worlds.* London: Routledge.

Pomeau, R. (1986) 'Voltaire, du côté de Sodome?', *Revue d'Histoire Littéraire de la France*, 86 (2): 235–47.

Porter, K. and Weeks, J. (eds) (1991) *Between the Acts. Lives of Homosexual Men 1885–1967.* London: Routledge.

Rich, A. (1980) 'Compulsory heterosexuality and lesbian existence', *Signs*, 5: 631–60.

Rousseau, G. and Porter, R. (eds) (1987) *Sexual Underworlds of the Enlightenment.* Manchester: Manchester University Press.

Rowse, A.L. (1977) *Homosexuals in History. A Study of Ambivalence in Society, Literature and the Arts.* London: Weidenfeld & Nicholson.

Royer, J.-M. (1985) 'Voltaire, le gay Candide', *Historama*, 22: 72–8.

Ruggiero, G. (1985) *The Boundaries of Eros: Sex Crime and Sexuality in Renaissance Venice.* New York: Oxford University Press.

Rupp, L. (1989) '"Imagine my surprise": women's relationships in mid-twentieth century America', in M. Duberman et al. (eds), *Hidden from History.* New York: New American Library. pp. 395–410.

Saslow, J.M. (1988) 'A veil of ice between my heart and the fire': Michelangelo's sexual identity and early modern constructs of homosexuality, *Genders*, 2: 77–90.

Schoppmann, C. (1991) *Nationalsozialistische Sexualpolitik und weibliche Homosexualität.* Pfaffenweiler: Centaurus.

Schuyf, J. (1994) *Een stilzwijgende samenzwering. Lesbische vrouwen in Nederland 1920–1970.* Amsterdam: IISG.

Scott, J. (1991) 'The evidence of experience', *Critical Inquiry*, 17: 773–97.

Sedgwick, E.K. (1990) *Epistemology of the Closet.* Berkeley and Los Angeles: University of California Press.

Smith, B.R. (1991) *Homosexual Desire in Shakespeare's England. A Cultural Poetics.* Chicago: University of Chicago Press.

Smith-Rosenberg, C. (1975) 'The female world of love and ritual: relations between women in nineteenth-century America', *Signs*, 1: 1–29.

Solomon, M. (1989) 'Franz Schubert and the peacocks of Benvenuto Cellini', *Nineteenth Century Music*, 12 (3): 193–206.

Steakley, J.D. (1975) *The Homosexual Emancipation Movement in Germany.* New York: Arnold Press.

Tielman, R. (1982) *Homoseksualiteit in Nederland. Studie van een emancipatiebeweging.* Meppel: Boom.

Trexler, R.C. (1981) 'La Prostitution Florentine au XVe siècle: patronages et clientèles', *Annales: Economies, Sociétés, Civilisations*, 36 (6): 983–1015.

Trumbach, R. (1989) 'Gender and the homosexual role in modern Western culture: the eighteenth and nineteenth centuries compared', in D. Altman, C. Vance, M. Vicinus and J. Weeks (eds) *Homosexuality Which Homosexuality?* Amsterdam: Dekker/Schorer; London: GMP Publishers. pp. 149–69.

Trumbach, R. (1994) 'London's Sapphists: from three sexes to four genders in the making of modern culture', in G. Herdt (ed.), *Third Sex, Third Gender. Beyond Sexual Dimorphism in Culture and History*. New York: Zone Books.

Vacha, K. (1985) *Quiet Fire. Memoirs of Older Gay Men*. New York: Grossing Press.

Vance, C.S. (1989) 'Social construction theory: problems in the history of sexuality', in D. Altman, C. Vance, M. Vicinus and J. Weeks (eds), *Homosexuality, Which Homosexuality?* Amsterdam: Dekker/Schorer; London: GMP Publishers. pp. 13–34.

Van der Meer, T. (1984) *De wesentlijke sonde van sodomie en andere vuyligheeden. Sodomieten vervolgingen in Amsterdam 1730–1811*. Amsterdam: Tabula.

Van der Meer, T. (1995) *Sodoms zaad in Nederland. Het ontstaan van homoseksualiteit in de vroegmoderne tijd*. Nijmegen: SUN.

Van der Pol, L. (1996) *Het Amsterdams hoerdom. Prostitutie in de zeventiende en achttiende eeuw*. Amsterdam: Wereldbibliotheek.

Van Gemert, L. (1995) 'Hiding behind words? Lesbianism in seventeenth-century Dutch poetry', *Thamyris*, 2 (1): 11–44.

Vicinus, M. (1984) 'Distance and desire: English boarding school friendships 1870–1920', *Signs*, 9 (4): 600–22.

Vicinus, M. (1989) '"They wonder to which sex I belong": the historical roots of the modern lesbian identity', in D. Altman, C. Vance, M. Vicinus and J. Weeks (eds), *Homosexuality, Which Homosexuality?* Amsterdam: Dekker/Schorer; London: GMP Publishers. pp. 171–98.

Weeks, J. (1977) *Coming Out: Homosexual Politics in Britain from the Nineteenth Century to the Present*. London: Quartet.

Weeks, J. (1981a) 'Discourse, desire and sexual deviance: some problems in the history of homosexuality', in K. Plummer (ed.), *The Making of the Modern Homosexual*. London: Longman. pp. 76–111.

Weeks, J. (1981b) *Sex, Politics and Society. The Regulation of Sexuality since 1800*. London: Longman.

Winkler, J.J. (1990) *The Constraints of Desire: the Anthropology of Sex and Gender in Ancient Greece*. New York: Routledge.

5 Queering Anthropology

Gert Hekma

Anthropology is the social science that used to study non-Western cultures. In the beginning, it mostly surveyed 'primitive tribes' that were largely untouched by colonial cultures. It later went on to explore larger social entities that had been in contact with other cultures for longer periods of time. Its focus was on the social, economic and cultural forms of small groups. Kinship and marriage, with themes such as exchange of women, incest, and the definition of family, formed the basis of analysis. Given anthropology's focus on face-to-face associations, it was no surprise that same sex relations also came to the attention of anthropologists. However, because of its scholarly marginalization in the West, homosexuality never became a central topic of interest.

Over the past few decades, anthropologists have started doing research in Western cultures, and sociologists who traditionally worked exclusively in the Western world have turned to non-Western cultures. This has put an end to the main difference between the disciplines, although some scholars continue to see a distinction because of methodology. In their opinion, anthropology is a kind of micro-sociology that focuses on small groups and intimate relations and has developed its own methods, for example participant observation. As many sociologists have the same focus and use similar methods, I understand the continuing split between anthropology and sociology to be a historical difference that is best explained by the traditional Western/non-Western dichotomy, although the latter has become outdated in an increasingly global world.

The Western/non-Western split was also political and ideological: Western anthropologists researched non-Western cultures while the opposite never happened in the past. The term 'Western' had in those times a series of connotations, such as 'scientific', 'objective' and 'advanced', while 'non-Western' carried the opposite connotations of 'religious' or 'superstitious', 'subjective', 'primitive' and so forth. Non-Western anthropologists have contested this dichotomy while Western anthropologists have become very critical of this heritage.

In this chapter I shall concentrate nonetheless on non-Western forms of male and female homosexuality, as here I discuss the historical development of anthropology and should not overlap with other chapters in the book. Thus, Western forms will be covered marginally. The academic particularity of anthropology can be explained only by its historical development; it has little meaning any more in the contemporary situation where sociology, anthropology, geography and history permanently intertwine and a patchwork of cultural forms has come into existence that can be explained better by other concepts, such as multiculturality or multisexuality, than by the Western/non-Western dichotomy. After a historical introduction, I shall discuss some major topics in contemporary anthropology, then end with perspectives for future research.

Ethnology: the first ruffles

Early work in anthropology was done from the armchair. The first serious anthropologists relied heavily on seamen, missionaries, and traders' reports of 'exotic' cultures. These accounts remained strongly biased by the authors' prejudices, especially when they related to (homo)sexual practices and relations. It is common to find such terms as 'the unmentionable vice', 'the terrible sin of sodomy' or 'the men are addicted to the practice of pederasty'. But based on these narratives, some armchair anthropologists such as Ferdinand Karsch-Haack (1911) and Edward Carpenter (1914) wrote in an apologetic tone about same sex love and practices within the scholarly ideas of their time. They showed that homosexual men in other cultures existed, and, according to their accounts, often were third sexers or sexual intermediaries between male and female, as they were supposed to be in the West. According to these early anthropologists, homosexuality was an innate sexual inclination. Carpenter (1914: 172), for instance, concluded, 'The intermediate types of human being created intermediate spheres of social life and work', interestingly suggesting that social differentiation resulted from sexual differentiation. Sex was rarely given such a central position in the work of other anthropologists.

This early work played an important role in Western homosexual apologies. That other cultures allowed more room for same sex pleasure, sometimes even giving it a central place, countered the homophobic idea that homosexuality did not exist among 'natural peoples' and, where it did, should be understood as a result of decadence and decline. It also fortified the argument that gay men and lesbians should not face discrimination 'at home'.

The focus in these earlier reports was on public manifestations that were assumed to be homosexual, such as cross-dressing, men or women showing tenderness for persons of the same sex, and homosocial institutions with uncertain sexual content, such as women's marriages and male initiation rites. Sexual acts may have been implicated in such observations but were rarely discussed. This situation continues to the present in most research. Anthropologists had and still have great difficulty in going beyond visible traces of same sex desires and exploring the details of same sex practices. They framed public intimacies between same sex partners and cross-dressing as signs of homosexuality, while the absence of such public markers led them to believe there was no homosexuality. This could of course be very erroneous, as transgendered behaviour or public displays of same sex intimacies did not have to result in homosexual practices, which could be common in cultures where such signs were absent. As the private practices and feelings in the explored cultures remained in most cases invisible to the researchers, available data on homosexuality are quite unreliable. In some cases, anthropologists may also have hidden the knowledge that they had because such data were classified as non-objective or obscene or they feared that such information let their subjective feelings shine through. Nevertheless, a very few passionate stories of same sex desires have been handed down by anthropologists (for a sad example about the lonely death of a pederast, see Clastres, 1972: 273–309).

Ethnography: the early fieldwork

In the 1920s, anthropologists such as Bronislaw Malinowski and Margaret Mead left their armchairs and started to spend long periods in the cultures under scrutiny and to investigate for themselves the habits and representations of tribal cultures. These anthropologists discovered many forms of same sex behaviour that could deviate widely from accepted Western ideas and practices. The transgendered behaviour of the Native American *berdache* (third gender) and the promiscuous practices in Melanesian men's houses posed problems of interpretation. Often, the analysis of same sex relations got lost in cultural contexts and explanations. So, Van Baal (1966), who started his research on the Papuan Marind-Anim in the 1930s, submerged orgiastic same sex practices in an extended description of religious cosmogeny. Anthropologists who abhorred the 'filthiness' of extended narratives of same sex affiliations circumvented them by shifting the focus on to something else and hurrying to embrace explanations that were always found outside the sexual system; the explanations were never to be found in same sex systems.

The strange sexual habits of foreign cultures may have been loathed, but some Westerners took a more positive position, understanding such forms to be local manifestations of a universal homosexual desire. According to Devereux (1937), *berdaches* were a distinct way for Native North American cultures to cultivate inborn homosexual instincts. Many other cultures had so-called institutionalized forms of homosexuality or acceptable roles for homosexuals, which were local expressions of a global desire.

As a sequel to Kinsey's survey of white Americans, Ford and Beach (1951) undertook a sex survey of the world's cultures. In the phraseology of the period, they came to the conclusion that studies on homosexual behaviour 'suggest that a biological tendency for inversion of sexual behaviour is inherent in most if not all mammals including the human species' (p. 143). Concerning human homosexuality, they found that the male form was widespread. It was unknown, rare or repressed in only 28 out of the 76 sampled societies, while female homosexuality was known and accepted in 17 of the societies. Finally, homosexuality was more common in adolescence than in adulthood for both sexes. Repression of homosexuality was thus much less general than had been assumed from a Western perspective. Such statistics, based on second-hand reporting, are of course highly questionable both in their essentialism and their suggestion of certainty, given that unreliable data were used. Very disquieting also was the almost total absence of research on female homosexuality.

After Kinsey, and Ford and Beach, the social sciences kept largely silent not only about homosexuality, but even about sexuality. Leading anthropologists did not even include homosexual material they had gathered during their fieldwork in their major monographs, but published it much later, after the 'sexual revolution', in separate publications (Evans-Pritchard, 1970; Van Lier, 1986). Only one article on the anthropology of sexuality can be singled out in the 1950s and 1960s: Mead's (1961) 'Cultural determinants of sexual behavior'.

Gay studies in the house of modern anthropology

When gay and lesbian studies emerged in the 1970s, anthropology, together with political science, was the social science that was least touched by this innovation. Anthropologists such as Newton (1972) who worked on gay and lesbian topics addressed subcultures in the Western world or the *berdache* of the Native North American tribes (Callender and Kochems, 1983; Roscoe, 1991, 1998; Williams, 1986). They applied anthropological methods of participant observation, which was not often used in sociology, to Western cultures. A few sociologists, however, did the same (Delph, 1978; Goode and Troiden, 1974; Humphreys, 1970). Anthropologist Gayle Rubin (1975) made an influential statement about the basic importance of sex and gender to cultural and political analysis while she herself studied the leather scene in San Francisco (Rubin, 1991). The first to explore the non-Western world from the sexual standpoint was Herdt (1981, 1987), who worked on male initiation and 'boy inseminating rituals' in New Guinea. Long a secret topic in Melanesian anthropology (Van Baal, 1966; Williams, 1939; Wirz, 1922), never before had homosexual practices been discussed in such detail. Ethnographic work rapidly became more sophisticated. Whereas Herdt (1984) had discussed the initiation rituals as 'ritualised homosexuality', still suggesting a clear link with Western concepts of same sex desire, the term 'boy inseminating rituals' in his later work (Herdt, 1994a: 30) shatters this link and makes same sex acts and desires culture-bound.

The most important result of recent anthropology has been the confirmation of a wide diversity of same sex pleasures, behaviours and courtship rituals (see however Whitam and Mathy, 1986; and Wieringa, 1989, who see little cultural variety). Notwithstanding their diversity, some major cultural patterns have been recognized. The three most significant are gender- and age-structured forms and egalitarian homosexuality (see Trumbach, 1977; Greenberg, 1988; and Hekma, 1988).

Gender-structured forms

In gender-structured same sex behaviours and pleasures, one of the partners takes the other gender's role (Bleibtreu-Ehrenberg, 1984). These forms disturb the clear male/female dichotomy and add alternative gender positions to both genders. So the *hijra* in India (Nanda, 1990) and *berdache* in North America, who are born with male bodies, take on a female role and may have sexual relations with a man. In some cases, as with the *hijra*, castration can be part of the gender change. Reports of women taking on male roles have been scarcer, but exist both for Native North Americans (see Williams, 1986, who labelled them 'Amazons') and for sub-Saharan cultures, where women's marriages have been quite common (Amadiune, 1987; Tietmeyer, 1985). In these cases it is often unclear to what extent relations are sexual. For the *hijras* the case is quite clear because they prostitute themselves, but for the *berdaches*, Amazons and women's marriages the sexual content of the relations is uncertain because of the lack of reliable research. Of course, sex and gender, like sexuality, are not static categories, and terms such as 'position' and 'performance' underline their variable locations and vocations.

Gender reversals can have different backgrounds and positions. As priests or shamans, third genders carried out religious and medical functions or were particularly skilled in certain crafts. In patrilineal societies women's marriages secured the continuation of families that had no male offspring. The importance of same sex interests in opting for a third-gender role remains unclear. In most cases, however, third genders entertained sexual relations with members of the same sex and the opposite gender, whereas there are no reports they had sex among themselves.

Existing gender dichotomies are broken down by gender blending and bending. Even the gender reversal of post-operative male-to-female transsexuals will always differ from women's position, albeit in different degrees, because such individuals undergo male socialization and notwithstanding all operations none has the reproductive capacities most women have. As female-to-male transsexuals they will occupy a new rather than existing gender position. The same pertains to *hijras*, *berdaches*, eunuchs and all other intermediate genders that have been labelled third sex or third gender. Herdt used this terminology to indicate a wide variety of gender positions and cited Georg Simmel to explain why he used 'third' instead of 'myriad': 'The appearance of the third party indicates transition, conciliation, and abandonment of absolute contrast' (Herdt, 1994b: 19). The difference from earlier uses of this term, for example, by Magnus Hirschfeld (1914), is its cultural or constructionist, rather than biological or essentialist, perspective. Gender is not an innate condition, but a cultural position (see also Sabrina, 1996).

Age-structured forms

Age-structured same sex behaviours and pleasures are relations between persons of the same sex but of different ages. The prime examples are ancient Greek pederasty and the boy-inseminating rituals of the Melanesians. But such relations have also been reported in other parts of the world, e.g., Australia, Indonesia, Japan, Africa, and the Arab world (see Leupp, 1995 for Japan; Evans-Pritchard, 1970, for the Azande in the Sudan; Baldauf, 1988 for Afghanistan; and Rahman, 1989 for Pakistan). For women, reports have again been much scarcer. The most interesting research has been by Gloria Wekker (1994) for Paramaribo, Surinam. She found among lower-class Creole women age-structured *mati* relations of older women – who in most cases had been married and begotten children – with younger women. As in the male cases, these relationships are also a form of sexual and social initiation. The ages of both partners vary widely. In Herdt's (1981, 1987) example of the Sambia, pre-pubescent boys between 6 and 12 years are inseminated by post-pubescent adolescents, while the younger partners in *mati* relations will be between 14 and 30 years of age (compare Bleibtreu-Ehrenberg, 1980). The Sambian boy inseminations were considered to be essential for becoming a man: without sperm donations, boys would not be able to produce sperm themselves. In different Melanesian cultures, other sexual acts were standard: oral and anal penetration as well as the rubbing of sperm on the skin could transmit the masculine essence. For the Greek male elite, intercrural sex was the norm (Dover, 1978: 98).

Egalitarian forms

The most important examples of egalitarian relations without gender or age differences are to be found among contemporary gays and lesbians. They rarely involve large age differences or clear gender divisions, in any case not according to the ideology of gay and lesbian movements. Sexual roles (passive–active, insertive–insertee) are in general interchangeable, as was often not the case with the age- and gender-structured forms. For many gay and lesbian couples, a sharp male/female role dichotomy has little relevance any more either in public or in private, except for reasons of style or play (butch–femme, s/m). Reports of equal same sex relations prior to 1900 are rare, except for homoerotic friendships or romantic loves of which the sexual content has been uncertain in most cases (compare Smith-Rosenberg, 1975). Equality in sexual relations is nowadays considered to be the rule, but it was not in most cultures before 1900 when gender, age, class and ethnicity made a difference and inequalities generated sexual desire. Boswell's (1994) finding of same sex unions between equals in the early Christian Church may have been an exception to this rule, but the phenomenon was probably more marginal than he assumed.

Some considerations

Greenberg (1988) added to these three forms a fourth one that depends on social inequality, namely class-structured same sex relations. This, however, is not a very convincing form as it involves a wide diversity of sometimes quite contradictory subforms. In slave societies it meant that slaves were available for their masters, while in European class societies it most often took the form of well-to-do persons having sex with servants. However, whereas in most slave societies it must have been quite impossible for the male master to reverse roles (to be penetrated), in European class societies such role inversion seems to have been the rule. The first three forms discussed above seem to be by far the most important and coherent, though alongside these forms we should clearly recognize the importance and specifics of sexual relations between persons of different class, religion, ethnicity and so forth.

Identifying such general patterns should not hide the fact that apparently comparable forms may still be very dissimilar. Modern paedophilia is very different in social and psychological status and in ubiquity from Greek pederasty. The meanings that are attributed to it, social contexts and historic backgrounds are in most cases so dissimilar that comparisons have limited value. Moreover, individuals do not always adopt social forms in the same way: there is always some room to develop personal patterns within cultural forms. Anthropology has focused strongly on social forms and seldom on individual expressions of cultural rules. This could be a theme for further work in this field (compare Herdt and Stoller, 1990; Hekma, 1994).

The most surprising result of the division of same sex ambitions into a series of forms is the nearly complete absence of egalitarian same sex relations before the twentieth century. It might be expected that the dominant Western form today should have been observed much more often in other cultures, as humans in general recognize best what they already know. In a similar vein, but with an opposite result, anthropologists seldom found love in our sense in other cultures, because love was not very common in marital relations, which is where anthropologists looked for it, but precisely in other relations between kin, friends, or elsewhere. Their Western perspective made anthropologists look in the wrong direction (Jankowiak, 1994). It seems that egalitarian homosexual relations were largely absent elsewhere and earlier because egalitarian sexual relations were never the norm anywhere. Of course, some people may have formed such bonds beyond the hegemonic models of their culture.

The contemporary situation

Although queer studies in anthropology nowadays lags behind queer studies in other fields, such as history and literature, important work has been done (see Blackwood, 1986b; Caplan, 1987; and Ortner and Whitehead, 1981 for overviews). The results are quite uneven in terms of cultural space and topics. Herdt's (1981, 1984, 1987) work has made the sexual lives of a very small population, the Papua Sambia, well known far beyond anthropology. The work of Williams (1986) and Roscoe (1991, 1998) has contributed clearly to knowledge of the *berdache* in Native North American societies (compare Herdt, 1994b). Thanks to Fry (1986), Trevisan (1986), Parker (1991), Mendès-Leite (1993) and others, Brazil's sexual culture is well researched, while the macho/maricone dichotomy of Spanish-speaking America is being put on the map (Carrier, 1995; Lumsden, 1996; Murray, 1995; Prieur, 1997). But the Islamic world (Bouhdiba, 1975; Murray and Roscoe, 1997; Schmitt and Sofer, 1992), sub-Saharan Africa and major parts of Asia, including China and India, remain largely untrodden fields (see Nanda, 1990 for Indian third genders; Jackson, 1995 for Thailand; for histories of Chinese and Japanese homosexuality, Hinsch, 1990 and Leupp, 1995). Murray (1992) edited a book on *Oceanic Homosexualities* that surveyed the world from Malagasy to Siberia while Manderson and Jolly (1997) covered Southeast Asia and the Pacific. The presence of vast populations of non-Western descent in the West has not stimulated much enquiry into their sexual behaviours and desires. Greenberg (1988) and Blackwood (1986a) have given good summaries of the available research findings on male and female homosexuality, respectively, and Weston (1993) for both. AIDS-related research has yielded more information on same sex behaviours from different parts of the world, but because of cultural, technical and political problems with data-gathering, this information is not always reliable (e.g. Brummelhuis and Herdt, 1995; Herdt, 1997b; Herdt and Lindebaum, 1992; McKenna, 1996; Parker and Gagnon, 1995; Tielman et al., 1991).

Western urban ethnography will be discussed in other chapters in this volume. Examples of this work can be found in Goode and Troiden (1974), Levine (1979) and Herdt (1992). Some anthropologists have taken up research on sexual subcultures such as gay bars (Read, 1980), drag shows (Newton, 1972), the leather world (Rubin, 1991), bathhouses or dark rooms (Bolton et al., 1994; Henriksson, 1995; Mendès-Leite and De Busscher, 1995) as topics of urban ethnography. This research is innovative because it has provided detailed information about cruising and sexual behaviour that was largely missing from the bulk of social science research. Given the growing variety of sexual worlds, this is a very promising direction of research.

Once again, it has to be said that anthropological research on lesbianism remains highly underdeveloped compared with male homosexuality. Blackwood (1986a) has suggested taking a closer look at the places where we might expect to find lesbian loves and desires. We might assume women sequestered inside houses, and especially in polygynous households, to have emotional and erotic relations among themselves. Homosocial situations and spaces, such as girls' initiations, sisterhoods, colleges, dormitories, the world of prostitution or industries dependent on female labour are places to investigate. In the collection that Blackwood (1986b) edited, Sankar discussed a marriage-resisting sisterhood in turn-of-the-century Hong Kong and Gay described 'mummy–baby' relations among adolescent girls in Lesotho. Tietmeyer (1985) and Amadiune (1987) examined women's marriages – the aim of which often was to ensure patrilineal descent in the absence of male offspring but that may have incorporated lesbian loves – that nowadays can be used as models for support of women among women and for lesbianism.

Mati relations among Surinamese women are the best-researched topic of non-Western lesbianism today. Van Lier (1986) described them in detail as they existed in the late 1940s, and explained them as resulting from socio-economic conditions, particularly the absence of males, and from matrifocal families in which unresolved Oedipal conflicts were assumed to promote lesbian desires. Gloria Wekker (1994), in contrast, strongly stressed the importance of lower-class Black African women's cultural heritage. Marie-José Janssens and Wilhelmina van Wetering (1985) have examined the continuation of the Surinamese *mati* tradition in Amsterdam, where many Surinamese settled after the country's independence from the Netherlands, and its difference from modern lesbianism.

There is no longer any need for an anthropology that explains the naturalness and universality of homosexuality. A common thread in discussions within gay and lesbian studies of Western versus non-Western attitudes nowadays is that modern homosexuality is a social construction of recent origin, a product of the Western world, and, according to many people in the non-Western world, an unrequested, unwanted import that is foreign to their own culture. In non-Western countries where sex tourism resulted in the sexual exploitation of boys and young men by Westerners, as it did for girls and women, anti-homosexual and anti-Western sentiments created a strong and poisonous mixture. In those countries, legislation 'to save our children' from sexual abuse (quite a Western argument) is being promoted. Social constructionism, with its position that homosexuality is a recent Western invention, has strengthened the argument that it does not exist outside the Western world, or only in very different forms.

Both positions – the modern one that 'exotic' cultures knew more homosexual freedoms than the Western world and the social constructionist one which holds, with some nuances, that homosexuality is a modern Western invention (Weeks, 1977: 4) – need to be bent. Sexual freedom as an all-encompassing norm will never exist anywhere because sexuality as a social form will always have certain boundaries. Access to sexual possibilities has been socially limited and dependent on gender, age, class or other social denominators in all cultures and periods. Adult men have rarely been allowed the more passive stances in sex and women the more active ones. Even if the possibility existed that such gender-deviant positions could be taken, doing so was rarely well respected. Some contemporary Western cultures may be considered to have reached the pinnacle of adult sexual freedom because of the great variety of sexual possibilities that exist in them today. Age-structured relations, which were widespread in other cultures, are a remarkable exception. On the other hand, and countering more extreme constructionist positions, same sex behaviours and lusts have probably been universal in human cultures. This does not mean that Western concepts of sexual identity, coupling, desire, emancipation and so forth are applicable to those behaviours and pleasures. Nowadays, gay and lesbian identities are coming into existence all over the world. Some may say that this is because of globalization; others will say it reflects deep desires or local developments.

The important contribution that anthropology makes nowadays to research on homosexuality lies in its focus on representations and social contexts. Definitions of same sex interests depend strongly on local knowledge. Similar acts may have different meanings in different contexts. In Western cultures, for example, two men kissing in an urban centre might be gay, but two men hugging and kissing each other on a sports field do so because they scored a goal and the assumption that they might be gay is outrageous to themselves and their public. Interpretation depends on the meanings that are attributed to certain acts, and these meanings vary widely according to performer, place and time within and between cultures. Anthropologists' interpretations are added meanings, not superior or definitive ones, and may be incomprehensible to the people being surveyed. The task of contemporary anthropologists is to transcribe and explain as best as they can the relevant acts, their meanings and their contexts. Definitions of homosexuality will consequently be either situational, dependent on local knowledge, or dependent on the relevant research questions.

Some recent questions from anthropology are of great interest for gay and lesbian studies. Herdt (1994a) has taken up the theme of desire. If we consider homosexuality to be a historical and cultural result, desire should certainly not escape relativistic thinking. Herdt has asked, but not yet clearly answered, the broad question of how to conceive of desire outside the scientific models that reflect Western, but not other, social realities. The question of sexual socialization is also important: how do children learn about and handle sexual habits and meanings in their culture?

Herdt's work has been important for the simple reason that he has used one of the very last opportunities to study a native culture largely untouched by another (major) culture. All cultural forms as they exist at present are a result of mutual influences. Syncretism is the rule of contemporary cultures. Globalization has touched all of them. This is very clear in the case of gay culture, although less so for lesbian culture (see, however, Wieringa, 1989). Gay bar life is becoming quite similar everywhere, as is the gay habitus. A gay man from Asia can easily recognize many signs and habits of gay men in New York, Amsterdam or Mykonos. A global gay culture emanating from the Western world, especially from the United States, has come into existence through networks of gay men, sex tourism, exiles, media representations and so forth. This globalization deeply influences gay experiences everywhere, but the way it is experienced and practised will remain mediated by local and idiosyncratic factors. Local same sex cultures that work on different models of desire, behaviour and courtship continue to exist. However, in many places such worlds have been exterminated, as happened to Melanesian initiations (Herdt, 1997b) or the Uzbek tradition of *bacabozlik* (boygame) under Russian and Soviet rule (Baldauf, 1988). Discussions of global versus local cultures as they have been developing recently are crucial to gay and lesbian studies.

The global gay culture is very much an urban culture. The main difference between small tribes and large cities is social differentiation. The irony of global society is that it replaces a diversity of quite specific sexual forms with a singular form that includes a great variety. Postmodern urban society is once again breaking down the mainstream form of homosexuality into a wide range of separate sexual patterns and producing a wide variety of sexual ambitions for specific acts, fetishes, body parts, skin colours, toys and so forth. The urban world of leisure and pleasure is creating a growing range of desires. The American sex survey concluded that cities produce more men with gay interests (Laumann et al., 1994). It seems likely that postmodern urban centres will create ever more and larger groups with a variety of specific sexual ambitions, which will become a central topic in urban ethnography.

Historical anthropology

Fascinating additions to anthropological research have come from the history of colonialism. Trexler (1995) investigated the harsh persecution of Native American and Spanish sodomites in the early period of the Spanish colonization of Latin America. Stoler (1995) has asked whether the emergence of sexual science, with its production and disciplining of desires and identities, in nineteenth-century European countries was not highly influenced by the countries' status as empires controlling colonies and colonial bodies. The comparisons made in degeneration theory between inferior races and sexual perverts probably resulted from the representation of the exotic other as being sensual and hot. Following this image of nature's primitive children, perverts from the West were seen as regressing to earlier stages of evolution and not being adapted to modern times. A key question persists: why sexology developed most in the least colonial of the European empires, Germany. Stoler's strongest point, however, still holds true: that the division of labour between anthropology and sociology, and between Western and colonial history, is not only outdated, but also responsible for major misunderstandings concerning the interactions of colonial and imperial (sexual) politics.

Bleys (1995; compare Aldrich, 1993) focused specifically on the contribution of travel stories, sailors' diaries and so forth to the unfolding of sexology. His study raises the interesting question of the development of homosexual attribution: at first Westerners perceived the other as perverted and sodomical; nowadays the Western world itself is seen elsewhere as the main den of perversion and homosexuality. Whereas European countries have become more liberal towards homosexuality, many other countries (Cuba, Iran, Afghanistan and Zimbabwe) seem to be going the other way.

Subjectivities and sexual involvements

Recently, a main question in anthropological methodology has been how to handle subjectivity. Most of the data that anthropologists gather are based on intimate relations with some privileged informants. Data on sexuality have often been collected in sexual encounters or love relations. An interesting problem has been posed by these researchers' involvement with their respondents. Because of the ideals of objectivity and privacy, anthropologists with such experiences were reluctant to report on their intimate knowledge. Only recently have scholars started to do so (Kulick and Willson, 1995; Lewin and Leap, 1996) and even stressed the scholarly spin-off that sexual relations might have for research (Bolton, 1995; Newton, 1993). The so-called 'reflexive turn' in anthropology 'makes a problem out of what was once unproblematic: the figure of the fieldworker' (Marylin Strathern quoted in Kulick and Willson, 1995: 2). Nowadays, the opinion is emerging that anthropologists should explain their social and sexual involvements with respondents, reflect on their own position, and learn early on about the erotic intricacies of fieldwork. Situating the anthropologist's subjective position has become an essential part of research methodology. Subjectivity is not opposed to objectivity, or dissolved in intersubjectivity, but has been given an independent place. Participant observation requires that anthropologists state the kinds of participant they have been. With 'experiential' ethnography, Jim Wafer (1996) makes his gay identity an indispensable part of his texts. Anthropologists' relations with and fantasies about their interviewees can shed as much light on their results as do their theoretical perspectives. Some anthropologists might even go so far as to say that all research results in mere personal stories. Criticism has led them to reject all forms of objectivity as if dialogue were impossible.

This 'experiential' trend may seem to be self-indulgent or may well continue a 'tradition of reflecting on others as a means of talking about the self', as Don Kulick summarizes Elspeth Probyn's argument against 'banal egotism'. Kulick cites her alternative that the object of reflection should be a self understood as 'a *combinatoire*, a discursive arrangement that holds together in tension the different lines of race and sexuality that form and re-form our senses of self' (Kulick and Willson, 1995: 13–17). This self is inherently incomplete and partial and problematizes not only itself, but also relations of self and other, of subject and object, of native informant and foreign researcher, of domination and exploitation, of speaking and keeping silent. Such a flexible self produces situated knowledge that might be more interesting and effective than objective knowledge. However, it will remain difficult to find a way through the labyrinth of objectivities and subjectivities.

Gay and lesbian studies in anthropology: the future

The theme of homosexuality has always been present in anthropology, and nowadays perhaps a little more than before, but it is certainly not central to anthropological research and education. Gay and lesbian studies are still marginal in an anthropology that has always focused strongly on kinship but rarely on same sex arrangements. It is not clear why gay and lesbian research got off to a slower start in anthropology than in other disciplines, such as history and sociology. Perhaps history has the advantage that there are many 'amateurs' with an interest in gay and lesbian history, whereas such non-professionals lack the resources to do similar anthropological research. Of course, many governments strongly oppose such studies being carried out in their countries. For several reasons, research on sex in other cultures was hindered by ideologies of privacy and secrecy, by difficulty in getting access to local sexual knowledge, and by the locals' awareness of Western sexophobia, as a result of which local contacts may have resisted divulging their sexual secrets. Gays and lesbians themselves may also have been more attentive to criticisms of anthropology as a neo-colonial enterprise, and therefore more reluctant to 'go native'. They knew from their own experience how distressing straight colonialism of queer cultures and the corresponding research had been and sometimes still are. Because female homosexuality is often more private than its male counterpart, this could explain the even greater lack of research on lesbianism in anthropology. It probably was not because anthropology was a male domain, since many anthropologists were women.

Cultural relativism has been the banner of anthropology for many years, and this relates certainly to sex and gender. As argued before, anthropology defines same sex behaviours and desires as cultural forms that have various social contents, shapes and contexts in different cultures. The meanings and forms of homosexuality have been a central theme of much recent research in anthropology. What has been missing too often – but that is true of most research in gay and lesbian studies – is a focus on the forms and meanings of sexual acts and on individual variability in cultures. We have all too easily forgotten that pleasures take not only distinctive forms in various cultures, but also unique forms in individuals (Herdt and Stoller, 1990). Other important themes for anthropology should be the genders of sexuality; sex and age; combination and separation of love and sex in physical relations; inequality, violence and force in sexual relations; the social structure of sexual relations; geographies of sexuality and what constitute public and private; recreational and cruising cultures; the development of same sex communities; and shifting ideologies of nature and culture with regard to sexual pleasures. The great imbalance in the attention paid to male and female homosexuality, which has not changed much since Ford and Beach did their sexual-culture survey in 1951, should certainly be corrected.

A very promising and under-researched topic remains the connections between global and local gay and lesbian cultures. The internationalization of gay and lesbian culture has affected most countries, while fewer and fewer people with same sex interests will be unaware of Western concepts of homosexuality, although the latter are not uniform. Notwithstanding the trend towards internationalization, local cultures of same sex pleasure still persist and sometimes influence the global culture. The machos and maricones of Latin culture, *hijras* of India and *warias* of Jakarta, and Arab males interested in penetrating other men have not disappeared and have sometimes remained fairly untouched by the global gay culture. Nevertheless, there are also forces of sexual hybridization and replacement of local by global cultures. Both the functioning and the results of these processes are unknown and unclear. The best example of globalization and hybridization might be contemporary Brazil (Parker, 1991). The fact that the main examples of gay and lesbian cultures and politics come from the United States, where the movement operates in a virulently homophobic environment and has been quite unsuccessful in imposing its agenda on general society, is a dangerous development. This privileged example probably points in the wrong direction.

Anthropology has done a poor job in gay and lesbian studies until recently. Too often it has avoided the topic of homosexuality. Many scholars have chosen Western instead of non-Western topics and left the non-Western world to itself. Political correctness has rarely been extended beyond the borders of English-speaking Western cultures and there are few signs that this is changing in the recent boom in anthropological research. However, gay and lesbian studies cannot leave the rest of the world to itself and neglect its struggles for sexual emancipation.

References

Aldrich, R. (1993) *The Seduction of the Mediterranean. Writing, Art and Homosexual Fantasy*. London and New York: Routledge.

Amadiune, I. (1987) 'Male daughters, female husbands', in *Gender and Sex in an African Society*. London: Zed Books.

Baldauf, I. (1988) *Die Knabenliebe in Mittelasien: Bacabozlik* (Ethnizität und Gesellschaft. Occasional Papers 17). Berlin: Verlag Das Arabische Buch.

Balderston, D. and Guy, D.J. (eds) (1997) *Sex and Sexuality in Latin America*. New York: New York University Press.

Blackwood, E. (1986a) 'Breaking the mirror. The construction of lesbianism and the anthropological discourse on homosexuality', in Blackwood (1986b). pp. 1–18.

Blackwood, E. (ed.) (1986b) *The Many Faces of Homosexuality. Anthropological Approaches to Homosexual Behavior*. New York: Harrington Park Press. Also published as *Journal of Homosexuality*, 11 (3/4).

Bleibtreu-Ehrenberg, G. (1980) *Mannbarkeitsriten. Zur institutionellen Päderastie bei Papuas und Melanesiern*. Frankfurt am Main: Ullstein.

Bleibtreu-Ehrenberg, G. (1984) *Der Weibmann. Kultischer Geschlechtswechsel im Schamanismus. Eine Studie zur Travestition und Transsexualität bei Naturvölkern*. Frankfurt am Main: Fischer.

Bleys, Rudi C. (1995) *The Geography of Perversion/Desire: European Etiologies of Male-to-Male Sexualities*. London: Cassell.

Bolton, Ralph (1995) 'Tricks, friends, and lovers: erotic encounters in the field', in Kulick and Willson (1995). pp. 140–67.

Bolton, R., Vincke, J. and Mak, R. (1994) 'Gay baths revisited. An empirical analysis', *GLQ*, 1: 255–74.

Boswell, J. (1994) *Same-Sex Unions in Premodern Europe*. New York: Villard.

Bouhdiba, A. (1975) *La Sexualité en Islam*. Paris: PUF.

Brummelhuis, H. ten and Herdt, G. (eds) (1995) *Culture and Sexual Risk*. New York: Gordon & Breach.

Callender, C. and Kochems, L.M. (1983) 'The North American berdache', *Current Anthropology*, 24: 443–70. Reprinted in Dynes and Donaldson, (1992).

Caplan, P. (ed.) (1987) *The Cultural Construction of Sexuality*. London: Tavistock.

Carpenter, E. (1914) *Intermediate Types among Primitive Folk*. London: Allen & Unwin.

Carrier, J. (1995) *De los otros. Intimacy and Homosexuality among Mexican Men*. New York: Columbia University Press.

Clastres, P. (1972) *Chronique des indiens Guayaki*. Paris: Plon.

Delph, E.W. (1978) *The Silent Community. Public Homosexual Encounters*. Beverly Hills, CA: Sage.

Devereux, G. (1937) 'Institutionalized homosexuality of the Mohave indians', *Human Biology*, 9: 498–527. Reprinted in Dynes and Donaldson (1992).

Dover, K.J. (1978) *Greek Homosexuality*. Cambridge, MA: Harvard University Press.

Dynes, W.R. and Donaldson, S. (eds) (1992) *Ethnographic Studies of Homosexuality*. New York: Garland.

Evans-Pritchard, E.E. (1970) 'Sexual inversion among the Azande', *American Anthropologist*, 72: 1428–34. Reprinted in Dynes and Donaldson (1992).

Ford, C.S. and Beach, F.A. (1951) *Patterns of Sexual Behavior*. New York: Harper.

Fry, P. (1986) 'Male homosexuality and spirit possession in Brazil', in Blackwood (1986b). pp. 137–53.

Gay, J. (1986) '"Mummies and babies" and friends and lovers in Lesotho', in Blackwood (1986b). pp. 55–68.

Goode, E. and Troiden, R. (eds) (1974) *Sexual Deviance & Sexual Deviants*. New York: William Morrow.

Greenberg, D. (1988) *The Construction of Homosexuality*. Chicago: University of Chicago Press.

Hekma, G. (1988) 'Een man of geen man? Een historiografie van mannelijke homoseksualiteit', *Sociologisch Tijdschrift*, 14 (4): 620–44.

Hekma, G. (1994) 'The homosexual, the queen and models of gay history', *Perversions*, 3: 119–38.

Henriksson, B. (1995) *Risk Factor Love. Homosexuality, Sexual Interaction and HIV-Prevention*. Göteborg: Department of Social Work.

Herdt, G. (1981) *Guardians of the Flutes. Idioms of Masculinity. A Study of Ritualized Homosexual Behavior*. New York: McGraw Hill.

Herdt, G. (ed.) (1984) *Ritualized Homosexuality in Melanesia*. Berkeley: University of California Press.

Herdt, G. (1987) *The Sambia. Ritual and Gender in New Guinea*. New York: Holt, Rinehart & Winston.

Herdt, G. (ed.) (1992) *Gay Culture in America. Essays from the Field*. Boston, MA: Beacon Press.

Herdt, G. (1994a) 'Notes and queries on sexual excitement in Sambia culture', *Etnofoor*, 7 (2): 25–41.

Herdt, G. (ed.) (1994b) *Third Sex, Third Gender. Beyond Sexual Dimorphism*. New York: Zone Books.

Herdt, G. (1997a) *Same Sex, Different Cultures. Exploring Gay & Lesbian Lives*. Boulder, CO: Westview Press.

Herdt, G. (ed.) (1997b) *Sexual Cultures and Migration in the Era of AIDS. Anthropological and Demographic Perspectives*. Oxford: Clarendon Press.

Herdt, G. and Lindebaum, S. (eds) (1992) *The Time of Aids*. London: Sage.

Herdt, G. and Stoller, R. (1990) *Intimate Communications. Erotics and the Study of Culture*. New York: Columbia University Press.

Hinsch, B. (1990) *Passions of the Cut Sleeve. The Male Homosexual Tradition in China*. Berkeley: University of California Press.

Hirschfeld, M. (1914) *Die Homosexualität des Mannes und des Weibes*. Berlin: Marcus.

Humphreys, L. (1970) *Tearoom Trade. Impersonal Sex in Public Places*. Chicago: Aldine.

Jackson, P. (1995) *Dear Uncle Go. Male Homosexuality in Thailand*. Bangkok: Bua Luang Books.

Jankowiak, W. (ed.) (1994) *Romantic Passion. A Universal Experience?* New York: Columbia University Press.

Janssens, M.-J. and Wetering, W. van (1985) 'Mati en lesbiennes: homoseksualiteit en etnische identiteit bij Creools-Surinaamse vrouwen in Nederland', *Sociologische Gids*, 32 (5/6): 394–415.

Karsch-Haack, F. (1911) *Das gleichgeschlechtliche Leben der Naturvölker*. Munich: Reinhardt.

Kulick, D. and Willson, M. (eds) (1995) *Taboo. Sex, Identity and Erotic Subjectivity in Anthropological Fieldwork*. London and New York: Routledge.

Laumann, E.O., Gagnon, J.H., Michael, R.T. and Michaels, S. (1994) *The Social Organization of Sexuality. Sexual Practices in the United States*. Chicago: University of Chicago Press.

Leupp, G.P. (1995) *Male Colors. The Construction of Homosexuality in Tokugawa Japan*. Berkeley: University of California Press.

Levine, M.P. (1979) *Gay Men. The Sociology of Male Homosexuality*. New York: Harper & Row.

Lewin, E. and Leap, W.L. (eds) (1996) *Out in the Field. Reflections of Lesbian and Gay Anthropologists*. Urbana and Chicago: University of Illinois Press.

Lumsden, I. (1996) *Machos, Maricones and Gays. Cuba and Homosexuality*. Philadelphia: Temple University Press.

Manderson, L. and Jolly, M. (eds) (1997) *Sites of Desire, Economies of Pleasure. Sexualities in Asia and the Pacific*. Chicago: University of Chicago Press.

McKenna, N. (1996) *On the Margins. Men Who Have Sex with Men and HIV in the Developing World*. London: Panos.

Mead, M. (1961) 'Cultural determinants of sexual behavior', in W.C. Young (ed.), *Sex and Internal Secretions*. Baltimore, MD: Williams & Wilkins. pp. 1433–79.

Mendès-Leite, R. (1993) 'A game of appearances: the "ambigusexuality" in Brazilian culture of sexuality', *Journal of Homosexuality*, 25 (3): 271–82.

Mendès-Leite, R. and De Busscher, P.-O. (1995) *Microgéographie 'sexographique' des back-rooms parisiennes: appropriation de l'espace et gestion de la sexualité face au VIH*. Paris: AFSL (report).

Murray, S.O. (ed.) (1992) *Oceanic Homosexualities*. New York: Garland.

Murray, S.O. (ed.) (1995) *Latin American Male Homosexualities*. Albuquerque: University of New Mexico Press.

Murray, S.O. and Roscoe, W. (eds) (1997) *Islamic Homosexualities. Culture, History, and Literature*. New York and London: New York University Press.

Nanda, S. (1990) *Neither Man nor Woman. The Hijras of India*. Belmont, CA: Wadsworth.

Newton, E. (1972) *Mother Camp. Female Impersonators in America*. Chicago: University of Chicago Press.

Newton, E. (1993) 'My best informant's dress: the erotic equation in fieldwork', *Cultural Anthropology*, 8 (1): 3–23.

Ortner, S. and Whitehead, H. (eds) (1981) *Sexual Meanings: The Cultural Construction of Gender and Sexuality*. Cambridge: Cambridge University Press.

Parker, R.G. (1991) *Bodies, Pleasures and Passions. Sexual Culture in Contemporary Brazil*. Boston, MA: Beacon Press.

Parker, R.G. and Gagnon, J.H. (eds) (1995) *Conceiving Sexuality. Approaches to Sex Research in a Postmodern World*. New York: Routledge.

Prieur, A. (1997) *Mema's House, Mexico City. On Transvestites, Queens, and Machos*. Chicago: University of Chicago Press.

Rahman, G.T. (1989) 'Boy love in the Urdu', *Paidika*, 2 (1): 10–27.

Read, K.E. (1980) *Other Voices. The Style of a Male Homosexual Tavern*. Novato, CA: Chandler & Sharp.

Roscoe, W. (1991) *The Zuni Man-Woman*. Albuquerque: University of New Mexico Press.

Roscoe, W. (1998) *Changing Ones. Third and Fourth Genders in Native North America*. New York: St Martin's Press.

Rubin, G. (1975) 'The traffic in women: notes on the "political economy" of sex', in R.R. Reiter (ed.), *Toward an Anthropology of Women*. New York: Monthly Review Press.

Rubin, Gayle (1991) 'The catacombs: a temple of the butthole', in M. Thompson (ed.), *Leatherfolk. Radical Sex, People, Politics, and Practice*. Boston, MA: Beacon Press. pp. 119–141.

Sabrina, P.R. (ed.) (1996) *Gender Reversals & Gender Cultures. Anthropological and Historical Perspectives*. London and New York: Routledge.

Sankar, A. (1986) 'Sisters and brothers, lovers and enemies: marriage resistance in Southern Kwantung', in Blackwood (1986b). pp. 69–82.

Schmitt, A. and Sofer, J. (eds) (1992) *Sexuality and Eroticism among Males in Moslem Societies*. New York: Harrington Park Press.

Smith-Rosenberg, C. (1975) 'The female world of love and ritual. Relations between women in nineteenth-century America', *Signs*, 1 (1), reprinted in her *Disorderly Conduct. Visions of Gender in Victorian America*. New York: Knopf, 1985.

Stoler, A. (1995) *Race and the Education of Desire. Foucault's History of Sexuality and the Colonial Order of Things*. Durham, NC: Duke University Press.

Tielman, R., Carballo, M. and Hendriks, A.C. (eds) (1991) *Bisexuality & HIV/AIDS. A Global Perspective*. Buffalo: Prometheus Books.

Tietmeyer, E. (1985) *Frauen heiraten Frauen. Studien zur Gynaegamie in Afrika*. Munich: Klaus Renner Verlag.

Trevisan, J.S. (1986) *Perverts in Paradise*. London: GMP.

Trexler, Richard C. (1995) *Sex and Conquest. Gendered Violence, Political Order, and the European Conquest of the Americas*. Ithaca, NY: Cornell University Press.

Trumbach, R. (1977) 'London's sodomites: homosexual behavior and Western culture', *Journal of Social History*, 11 (1): 1–33.

Van Baal, J. (1966) *Dema. Description and Analysis of Marind-Anim Culture (South New Guinea)*. With the collaboration of Father J. Verschueren. The Hague: Martinus Nijhoff.

Van Lier, R. (1986) *Tropische tribaden. Een verhandeling over homoseksualiteit en homoseksuele vrouwen in Suriname*. Dordrecht: Foris.

Wafer, J. (1996) 'Out of the closet and into print: sexual identity in the textual field', in E. Lewin and W.L. Leap (eds) *Out in the Field. Reflections of Lesbian and Gay Anthropologists*. Urbana and Chicago: University of Illinois Press.

Weeks, J. (1977) *Coming Out. Homosexual Politics in Britain, from the Nineteenth Century to the Present*. London: Quartet.

Wekker, G. (1994) *Ik ben een gouden munt, ik ga door vele handen, maar verlies mijn waarde niet. Subjectiviteit en seksualiteit van Surinaamse volksklasse vrouwen in Paramaribo*. Amsterdam: Vita.

Weston, K. (1993) 'Lesbian/gay studies in the house of anthropology', *Annual Review of Anthropology*, 22: 337–67.

Whitam, F.L. and Mathy, R.M. (1986) *Male Homosexuality in Four Societies: Brazil, Guatemala, the Philippines, and the United States*. New York: Praeger.

Wieringa, S. (1989) 'An anthropological critique of constructionism: *berdaches* and butches', in Dennis Altman et al. (eds) *Homosexuality, Which Homosexuality?* London: GMP. pp. 215–38.

Williams, F.E. (1939) *Papuans of the Trans-Fly*. Oxford: Oxford University Press.

Williams, W. (1986) *The Spirit and the Flesh. Sexual Diversity in American Indian Culture*. Boston, MA: Beacon Press.

Wirz, P. (1922 and 1925) *Die Marind-Anim von Holländisch-Süd-Neu-Guinea*. Hamburg: Abhandlungen aus dem Gebiet der Auslandskunde, Vols 10 and 16.

6 Homo Legalis: Lesbian and Gay in Legal Studies

Leslie J. Moran

In the early seventeenth century Sir Edward Coke, a celebrated English judge and legal scholar, completed a four-volume exposition on English law entitled *The Institutes of the Laws of England* (1628). Volume I brings together all the laws relating to land and land tenure. Volume II is a compilation of Acts of Parliament. Volume III collects together all the pleas of the crown; what we would now call serious criminal offences. The fourth volume of the study deals with the procedural rules of the courts. Volume III is of particular interest. In that volume we find a chapter entitled, 'Of Buggery or Sodomy' which is important in various ways. In the four volumes it is the only reference to genital relations between persons of the same sex: it is the first piece of legal scholarship that addresses these relations in English law. Nor is it only of historical significance. It has been repeatedly cited by successive legal scholars writing within the legal tradition founded upon English law, the common law tradition (Moran, 1996: Ch.4). It has become the classic exposition on buggery or sodomy in all jurisdictions influenced by English law.

In the context of my study it has additional significance. It exemplifies a dominant method of scholarship through which same sex relations have become an object of legal scholarship. This method is of fundamental importance as it informs the way we understand the nature of legal studies. In order to consider the significance of lesbian and gay studies for the study of law and the study of law for lesbian and gay studies it will be necessary to examine the nature of the tradition of legal scholarship exemplified in Coke's work. I will explore the way the dominant methodology has influenced the impact of lesbian and gay scholarship and political activism upon legal scholarship. I will then consider the contribution that an informed lesbian and gay legal scholarship might make to legal scholarship and to the wider domain of lesbian and gay studies

The method of legal scholarship

In Coke's exegesis buggery and sodomy are presented as legal terms of art that name genital relations between persons of the same sex in law. Coke documents their use in law and records their most recent deployment in written law: a statute of Queen Elizabeth I. Much of the chapter then takes the form of an exposition on the language of the current statute. Coke summarizes the statutory provision then produces an extended reflection on the meaning of key words and phrases, such as 'buggery' and 'carnal knowledge' in the law. 'Buggery' is a name for acts forbidden by law. 'Buggery', Coke explains, is an act of penetration *per anum* by a man of a man or by a man of a woman. He notes that it is also a term of law that refers to carnal knowledge by mankind with an animal. 'Carnal knowledge' requires penetration. The emission of seed is not required. Coke notes that all human participants are guilty of an offence. He gathers together other references to 'buggery' or 'sodomy' in earlier legal commentaries and in an ancient Parliamentary debate. He documents a formula of words used to describe the offence in the formal charge, records their successful use in a notable case and advises future resort to the same formula. In writing the chapter Coke places these forbidden acts within a hierarchy of other forbidden acts by reference to the seriousness of the wrongful act: 'Of Buggery or Sodomy' is Chapter 10 in a volume of 106 chapters. He also documents the seriousness of the offence by placing 'Of Buggery or Sodomy' close to offences of treason and next to the offence of rape. All are extreme offences for which at that time death was the only punishment. Finally he explains the prohibition by reference to a higher authority, the word of God found in the Bible.

Coke's scholarly method has its roots in the Western legal tradition (Berman, 1983; Goodrich, 1986). The Western legal tradition has two branches: common law associated with English legal systems and civil law with its roots in the legal systems of continental Europe. Legal scholarship in common law and civil law have a common heritage in the method of legal scholarship of medieval continental universities. The first object of study in medieval times was not the contemporary law of the town, city, region or state but the study of the law of an empire that had collapsed, the Roman Empire.[1] As such, legal scholarship began as the study of an already largely dead law: the recently rediscovered texts of Roman law, its written law and ancient commentaries. The study of these ancient texts drew extensively upon another well-established scholarly practice: the monastic practices of reading and commenting upon religious texts. The study of law also developed as a search for the truth (of law) within the text (of law). As a practice of textual analysis the relationship between the legal scholar and the text is very specific. Legal scholars are servants of the law. Scholarship is understood as a passive practice of revelation rather than creation. Legal scholarship has developed as a set of practices dedicated to the language of law: of reading the written law and revealing its meaning; of making commentaries in the margins of the text of law; forging links between the many rules in the text to create a unity out of diversity; of explaining distinctions between various rules; outlining the meaning of concepts in the rules; expounding principles not apparent on the surface of the text but supposedly located below, behind or above the text and always already present in it. The objective of this scholarship was to celebrate law's internal perfection and autonomy. This tradition celebrates and preserves law as an archaic and esoteric language, invests it with special significance and polices its meanings. Through these specific practices of interpretation the lawyer and the legal scholar deploy a particular method of truth to produce the truth of law. That truth is remote from the social origins or significance of law, its political authority or impact, its morality or its relationship to the wider economic or cultural context.

Coke's exposition 'Of Buggery or Sodomy' provides a good example of this method of legal scholarship. Same sex genital relations come into being by way of a text, in this instance the written law found in a statute of Elizabeth I.[2] The written rules are made by those with due authority to make such rules and the ultimate power to enforce them. Where the law is written law judicial decisions are understood merely as a commentary on those rules. Nor are the decisions of others who resort to law, such as state officials, businessmen or lay persons, objects of study. Genital relations are explained by reference to the specific language of the written law. They are given form and meaning by the citation of earlier examples of the use of key terms of art. Thereby these genital relations come into being for legal scholars by way of a methodology that is concerned with the repetition and preservation of archaic terms, recording the sources of authority that name these actions and plotting their durability. They are given meaning by way of practices that seek to limit meaning and to promote consistency of meaning over time and place. An important characteristic of Coke's method is the deployment of the dominant method of legal scholarship not in the context of the law of an empire long since destroyed, but in the context of contemporary domestic English law. This draws attention to the fact that when legal scholarship began to turn towards the contemporary, while the type of law studied may have changed, the method of study remained the same.[3]

Coke's writing on buggery draws attention to the fact that for much of the history of Western legal systems genital relations between persons of the same sex are acts rarely referred to in law. Even where direct reference has appeared, in many jurisdictions they refer only to men. Secondly, genital relations between persons of the same sex have been largely confined to a particular domain of law: the criminal law. References to same sex relations in the wider body of law are limited, as same sex sexuality has for a long time been thought of only in terms of unlawful behaviour. References to 'homosexual' or 'homosexuality', 'gay men' and 'lesbian' have been absent, because they were terms yet to be invented. More importantly they are absent from more contemporary legal scholarship within this tradition as they are not legal terms of art and therefore are beyond the parameters of legal scholarship. They could only have legal significance, and thereby come within the boundary of legal scholarship, by being formally introduced by law-making bodies into the vocabulary of law (Moran, 1996). To criticize criminalization or to try to introduce same sex sexuality in terms other than the archaic legal language of wrongdoing (buggery or sodomy) or in contexts where it did not appear on the surface of the text of law would be, at best, to challenge conventions of legal scholarship or at worst to step beyond the boundaries of legal scholarship and legal studies.

While my example has been drawn from the common law world it would be wrong to conclude that either the form or the stability of legal scholarship is peculiar to legal studies within common law. A similar story could have been told of scholarship within the civil legal tradition. Much of current civil and common law legal scholarship continues to be informed by the long-standing methodological characteristics outlined above. In contemporary legal scholarship this approach is known as positivist legal studies or 'black letter law'. 'Black letter law' continues to take the text of the written rules of law as its primary if not exclusive object of concern. As a textual practice of reading and commentary it is a study of the meaning of the language of the legal text. It seeks to systematize rules, to elaborate legal concepts and articulate legal principles. 'Black letter' scholarship is still dominated by a desire to celebrate and preserve law as an archaic and esoteric language, to invest it with special significance, to police its meanings and to invest its practitioners with privileged access to the truth of law. Neither the impact of the society, economics, culture or politics upon law nor law's impact upon the world is thought of as a fit matter for legal scholarship.

Sexuality, legal scholarship and the impact of lesbian and gay scholarship

While matters of same sex genital relations might at best have been confined through much of the history of the dominant tradition of legal scholarship to discussions about the meaning of buggery or sodomy or at worst treated as matters beyond the concerns of legal scholarship, there is a long history of scholarship concerned with matters of same sex sexuality and law that is to be found elsewhere. The modern origins of this work are to be found in a wide range of scientific disciplines, particularly in sexology, psychology, psychiatry, that were put to work to explain law-breaking and to find a solution to the problem of criminality. Important texts within this corpus of writing include Krafft-Ebing's *Psychopathia Sexualis* (1947) and Havelock Ellis's *Studies in the Psychology of Sex, Vol. 1 Sexual Inversion* (1897). Cesare Lombroso's classic study, *The Female Offender* (1895), is an example of the use of these developments within the sciences to explain female criminality in the context of a new discipline: criminology. In much criminological writing same sex sexual relations were thought of as a cause of and a sign of deviance.[4] Other work relating to same sex sexual identity and law emerged in the context of debates about decriminalization (Lauritsen and Thornstad, 1974; Moran, 1996: Ch.1). Writings by Magnus Hirschfeld (1898), on German law and John Addington Symonds's (1928) on English law are good early examples of this type of scholarship.

Lesbian and gay studies provides a more recent body of work focusing on sexuality. Where the focus has been upon the social and cultural practices of exclusion, law has often appeared as one of the social practices taken as an object of study. However, this interest in law has a different point of departure and emerges in a very different context from the 'psy sciences' and emerging social sciences such as criminology. In the lesbian and gay context same sex sexuality is not so much a dangerous deviation from the norm as another possible legitimate identity and way of life. The shift from dangerous deviation to identity and style of life is reflected in the way lesbian and gay scholarship has produced a wealth of material about the significance of same sex sexuality not only within the confines of the criminal law but in other areas of law. It is impossible to document all instances, but the following is a short selection of work that has paid attention to matters of same sex sexual identity and the law.[5]

History scholars have produced a great deal of material. For example Goodich's work, *The Unmentionable Vice: Homosexuality in the Later Mediaeval Period* (1979) and Boswell's study, *Christianity, Social Tolerance and Homosexuality* (1980) provide much detail about the history of law, in particular the regulation of same sex relations through the canon law of the Catholic Church in Europe in the medieval period. Bray's *Homosexuality in Renaissance England* (1982) gives an insight into the historical shift from regulation of same sex relations through the law of the Church to regulation through the secular law of the state in early modern England. Mary McIntosh's groundbreaking study, *The Homosexual Role* (1968) and Norton's *Mother Clap's Molly House* (1992) document the operation of law in early eighteenth-century England. The study by Copley (1989) is an instance of work in the civilian legal tradition. Katz (1992) and Wotherspoon (1991) provide historical studies of the operation of the common law tradition across the globe by way of colonization, in the USA and Australia. Lillian Faderman's work is a still rare example of work that makes reference to lesbians and law (1981, 1983). In total this work has opened up an agenda in the historical study of law that had been completely neglected by legal scholars.

The social sciences and literary and cultural studies addressing questions of lesbian and gay sexuality also have significance for legal studies. For example Laud Humphreys's work *The Tearoom Trade* (1970) can be read as a sociological study of the impact of law on the behavioural practices of men who have sex with men. Work by Burke, *Coming out of the Blue* (1993), Leinen's *Gay Cops* (1993) and more recently Buhrke's *A Matter of Justice* (1997) are studies of gay and lesbian sexuality in the context of policing and more generally in the administration of law and order in Anglo-American contexts. Herek and Berill's work, *Hate Crimes: Confronting Violence against Lesbians and Gay Men* (1992) and Gary Comstock's 1991 *Violence against Lesbians and Gay Men* raise new questions about the operation of criminal law and the process of criminal justice; about the ability of law to recognize systematic violence, to protect individuals from that violence, and to punish those who perpetuate that violence. Work by Lobel (1986) and Taylor and Chandler (1995) has put aspects of lesbian and gay domestic relationships on the agenda. In the realm of literary and cultural studies Linda Hart's *Fatal Women* (1994) examines the relationship between lesbian sexuality and violence by women in popular culture and in criminological texts. Sally Munt's study of feminist interventions in the field of detective fiction, *Murder by the Book?* (1994) raises some important questions about lesbian sexuality, law enforcement and the legal order in popular culture.

Where law and legal practice have been a focus of study within lesbian and gay scholarship in the social sciences and the arts a wealth of information about same sex sexuality and law has been generated. Any attempt to understand the reception of this scholarship within legal studies has to take as its starting point the nature of the object of study of law, and must take account of the dominant methodological traditions of legal study.

Sexuality and contemporary legal scholarship

I now want to consider how legal scholars have responded to the rise of lesbian and gay activism and scholarship that has begun to document the wide-ranging impact of law on same sex sexual relations. To pursue this objective we will look at the dominant tradition and at other approaches to legal scholarship.

Within the dominant positivist approach, at best contemporary legal scholars have been concerned with cataloguing and describing those written and unwritten (judge-made) rules and juridical practices which overtly and covertly work to outlaw sexual relations between persons of the same sex and thereby render them illegitimate. This scholarship tends to pursue this objective through an examination of established topics of legal scholarship such as the criminal or civil code, through categories such as sexual offences, or family law, civil rights and human rights. Within this approach two responses are available to any conclusion that the law discriminates against lesbians and gay men. On the one hand the evidence of discrimination is presented as a need to change the law. As such it might be understood as being no longer a question of law but one of the politics or morality that informs the law. The lawyers' only role would be to use 'existing' legal concepts and legal language in the design of new legislation. On the other hand, having declared the law and its inadequacies for lesbians and gay men, the scholar steeped in the positivist tradition might embark upon a search for an 'existing' legal rule or 'underlying' principle which might meet the needs of the current inadequacies in the law. This might take the form of the application of old principles to forge new links or an exposition of new distinctions in existing laws. This mode of scholarship seeks to preserve the methodological requirement that law be seen as an autonomous practice which is defined by way of legal doctrine. In the final instance, while this approach may respond to the political, social and moral issues raised by lesbian and gay experience, activism and scholarship it denies that these concerns are the stuff of legal scholarship.

In the dominant tradition much pioneering work has been done to document the law and to produce guides to the law that address the legal needs of lesbians and gay men (Crane, 1982). Much recent work is to be found in the field of domestic and international human rights law (Heinze, 1995; Waaldijk, 1993; Wintermute, 1995). An expressed or assumed argument in this scholarship is that domestic and international human rights laws, while often silent about lesbian, gay or sexual orientation, already contain principles and rules which make the inferior legal status of same sex sexual relations contrary to human rights. To date, the rule and principle that has proved to be most successful in certain situations is that of privacy.[6] Anti-discrimination rules and principles have become a more recent focus of attention (Majury, 1994; Wintermute, 1995).

The virtues of this approach to scholarship are various. Here the existing law is both the problem and the solution for lesbians and gay men. Resort to concepts and principles that are said to be previously unarticulated or unspoken offers a solution that appears to be already present in the law. This solution avoids the trials and tribulations of reform through the political process. In particular it avoids the dangers of majoritarianism which are a feature of any democratic process and a problem to be overcome if the demand for reform is made by a minority. Resort to legal principle is also presented as a better option, as it is resort to the cool reason of law rather than the passion of politics. It is a resort to the certainty of tradition and continuity that is said to be the law rather than the uncertainty of novelty and change that is politics. As such it seeks to preserve the divide between law and sexuality and more generally law and politics and society.

A slightly different response to lesbian and gay studies is to be found within legal scholarship that is more closely aligned with legal philosophy, which in the Anglo-American world is called jurisprudence. Here, contemporary debates about lesbian and gay sexuality have their origins in Anglo-American scholarship that emerged out of proposals produced by a UK governmental committee, the Wolfenden Committee (1957), to decriminalize certain sexual relations between men over the age of 21 in private in England and Wales. These proposals for reform gave rise to a debate between H.L.A. Hart and Lord Devlin about the relationship between law and morality. The reform proposals were supported by Hart in *Law, Liberty and Morality* (1963) by way of a libertarian political philosophy. In *The Enforcement of Morals*, Devlin (1965) resorted to a utilitarian/communitarian position to argue against reform. This debate and commentaries around it originate in the context of concerns about 'homosexuality' as a deviation and demands for decriminalization rather than in the more recent political activism and scholarly interventions of 'lesbian and gay' which have focused upon sexual identity as a legitimate way of life.

In the wake of 'lesbian and gay', interest in the law and morality question has returned to the Hart/Devlin debate. More recently the terms of this debate have shifted to debates about natural law and natural rights. Those who adopt a natural law and natural rights position argue that there is a set of fundamental laws or rights that are basic to any good ordered society. As such, these rights reflect a fundamental morality. Their origin and authority are not in the institutions of the state or the practices of democracy; instead their origin is divine or they are inherent in the very idea of good order in society. They provide both a yardstick by which the worth of man-made laws might be challenged and a goal that law makers ought to aim for when reforming the law or making new laws.

This particular brand of legal philosophy has traditionally been a philosophical and jurisprudential stance hostile to lesbian and gay rights. A good example of this is to be found in the writings of John Finnis (1983, 1993). Finnis argues that the heterosexual couple and the family based upon the heterosexual couple are the basic building-blocks of any well-ordered society. For Finnis natural law and natural rights are the fundamental laws and rights that produce the social order as a heterosexual order. In this scheme of things lesbian and gay rights are antithetical to any well-ordered society and must be denied.

Gay philosophers and legal scholars have challenged this hostile stance and attempted to rewrite natural law/rights for a lesbian and gay politics. Good examples of this work are to be found Richard D. Mohr's book *Gays/Justice* (1988) and in Nicholas Bamforth's study, *Sexuality, Morals and Justice* (1997). Both argue *for* a humanist metaphysics of morals (natural rights) as a moral basis for the recognition of lesbian and gay rights and law reform. Mohr provides a critique of US constitutional law while Bamforth pursues his project by a critique of various schools of legal philosophy. Both demonstrate the viability of a natural law/natural rights position in support of recognition of lesbian and gay rights.

In general, by bringing morality into the frame of legal studies, this brand of legal scholarship departs from the dominant positivist position. Law is not just a set of rules but a moral order intimately concerned with justice. Legal scholarship might here focus more attention on critical analysis of the rules and the concepts deployed. Sources of authority might include references to philosophical texts and argument. At the same time the turn to morality often continues to focus upon the rules of law as the source of underlying moral principles. This points to the fact that an interest in questions of morality and justice is not inimical to many of the methodological requirements of positivist legal scholarship nor to the principles and concepts found in that approach to legal studies.

Beyond these two approaches there is, particularly within the common law world, much more diversity. In the twentieth century various schools of thought have emerged: the law in context movement, sociolegal studies, sociology of law, critical legal studies and legal studies informed by Marxism, theories of race and feminism. While it is impossible to go into any detail about these different schools, in different ways each brings the social and the political within the parameters of legal study. Each demands that legal scholarship engage with questions of power, the politics of social order (and disorder), the nature of social inclusion and social exclusion. In various ways they challenge the methodological assumptions and practices of positivist legal scholarship, and seek to incorporate work undertaken in the social sciences and the humanities into legal studies.

In a world where the study of law is dominated by the black letter tradition any attempt to incorporate work undertaken in the social sciences and the humanities into legal studies, whether in the context of the law of business organizations, the law of contract, or questions relating to gender or sexuality, has met with hostility. At best this work has been tolerated and marginalized, and at worst denied the status of legal scholarship and actively excluded from the institutions of legal learning. The focus and novelty of lesbian and gay issues has threatened to compound the will to exclude and the violence of exclusion.

Legal scholarship seeking to incorporate such work challenges both a positivist response to lesbian and gay issues and legal scholarship that gives importance to philosophies informed by utilitarianism, libertarianism or natural law/natural rights. One criticism of both positivist and law and morality legal scholarship is that both continue to reproduce the dominant terms of a very specific juridical agenda. As such they fail to respond to a considerable body of scholarship, particularly Marxist and post-Marxist, that offers important critiques of these approaches. In particular they fail to take account of the proximity of law and politics and law and society. More specifically, sexuality remains before or beyond the law, thereby reproducing the law/sexuality divide.

Legal scholarship that seeks to locate legal studies within the social sciences, to incorporate knowledge and the methods of the social sciences and, more recently, the arts, has begun to engage with lesbian and gay issues. This work is informed not only by lesbian and gay scholarship and more recently queer theory, but also by Marxist, post-Marxist/post-structuralist theory, and feminism (Halley, 1993, 1994; Herman, 1994; Herman and Stychin, 1995; Moran, 1996, 1997; Moran et al., 1998; Robson, 1992, 1998; Stychin, 1995). While this work is diverse, it has certain common characteristics. Taking law as the object of study, these scholars approach it by resort not only to legal theory but also to literary, political and social theory. The critiques that emerge challenge the divide between law and politics. They seek to examine and explore the place of law within the wider social order. Here law is both constituted by and constitutive of the wider social order. Sexuality is not so much outside the law, and something the law might respond to, but as always already in the law as a social and political practice, generated through legal categories and legal practices.

It is in this context that material generated by lesbian and gay studies, such as lesbian and gay historiography, cultural studies, sociology and so on, has become a part of legal studies alongside more traditional material such as legislation and judicial decisions. In the incorporation of lesbian and gay, and more recently queer material into legal studies there is the possibility of the generation of a new approach to legal studies which blurs boundaries, uses new methodologies and produces new objects of study. Other disciplines in the social sciences and arts offer a knowledge about law and legal practice from perspectives remote from the methodological obsessions that have over time generated law as a distinctive object of study within the scholarly practice of legal studies. It would be wrong to suggest that this challenge to the meaning and parameters of legal studies is a challenge unique to knowledge generated by lesbian and gay studies. These methodological challenges arise from the distinction between legal studies and the social sciences and legal studies and the arts. However, any challenge to the disciplinary boundaries within lesbian and gay studies in the social sciences and the arts might have an impact on the significance of those disciplines on legal studies.

The limits of lesbian and gay in legal studies

My analysis of the impact of lesbian and gay experience, activism and scholarship upon legal studies suggests that there are many responses available within legal scholarship. There is much to celebrate in the rise of such a rich and complex body of legal work.

However, there is a need for some caution here. It would be wrong to assume that legal scholarship that addresses lesbian and gay issues has found a home within institutions of legal education. In part this is a reflection of the continuing domination of positivist legal studies. Here lesbian and gay matters might continue to be thought of as matters of politics, or as raising issues that are appropriate in disciplines other than law. At best positivist legal scholarship on lesbian and gay issues has been confined to those still rare instances where it is possible to read a reference to same sex encounters on the face of the text: criminal law. Here, gay (and to a lesser extent, lesbian) scholarship struggles to find a home in the context of established divisions of law. It continues to be possible for institutions to ignore lesbian and gay issues altogether, or at best make brief passing reference to them. Nor does it necessarily follow that those institutions less hostile to other approaches to legal studies will take lesbian and gay issues more seriously. When they appear they may still be confined within the parameters of criminal law or family law. Legal studies remains predominantly heterocentric in its view of the world and there continues to be great hostility to issues relating to lesbians and gay men.

In scholarship that does address lesbian and gay matters much work has focused upon same sex sexuality in the context of men and the decriminalization of sexual relations between men. There has been a failure to take account of the growing evidence, much of it inspired by feminist work on law, that in general women's experience of law is different and in particular that lesbians' experience of law is very different from that of gay men (Majury, 1994: Mason, 1995; Mason and Tomsen, 1997; Robson, 1992, 1998). To read the law's response to genital relations between men as the same as its response to the regulation of genital relations between women would be a mistake. To date much of the history of legal practices has focused upon men. In part this reflects the general relative absence of references to the sexuality of women in law and the particular silence relating to sexual relations between women in law. As histories of the sexual relations between women in law emerge it becomes clear that same sex sexual relations between women, rather than being absent from the field of law, were policed in different ways using different legal categories in different spheres of law, for example by way of the regulations of the family and patriarchal relations found in private law rather than by way of public law, in particular the criminal law (Faderman, 1981, 1983; Robson, 1992; Crompton, 1980). In addition there has been a failure to take account of the different economic position, social status and priorities of women, and their different social experiences (Majury, 1994).

More recently, particularly where decriminalization has been achieved and where a strong feminist and lesbian and gay movement has emerged, legal scholarship is becoming more diverse. This reflects and produces a recognition of the close relationship between sexuality and gender and the idea of sexuality as an identity and a lifestyle. As a lifestyle, lesbian and gay engagement with the law and demands for law reform are no longer confined to criminal law or the prohibition of specific (homo)sexual practices but expand into aspects of private law: domestic relations, employment, property, housing and succession, taxation, parenthood and children. In the realm of public law the wider ambit of relations between the state and the individual is being addressed: lesbian and gay exclusion from the military, access to state education (especially sex education), freedom of expression, censorship and the media, prisons, access to welfare benefits, and the protection of sexual minorities in the state constitution. More recently international law, in particular the international law of human rights, has become a site of intervention and critique. Furthermore, the popularity and usefulness of legal concepts such as 'privacy' (Thomas, 1992), 'equality' (Majury, 1994) and the use of 'sexual orientation' as the basis for anti-discrimination initiatives (Majury, 1994 and Wintermute, 1995) have been challenged on the basis that all may have had limited success but in turn all have imposed new limits on the progress of change for the benefit of lesbians and gay men.

Lesbian and gay legal studies?

Signs of an emerging discipline of lesbian and gay legal studies are to be found in various contexts. There is a growing number of law monographs dealing with lesbian and gay matters. It is evidenced in the publication of special editions of existing scholarly journals (*Harvard Law Review*, the *Virginia Law Review* and *Social and Legal Studies*) and in the emergence of specialist legal journals dedicated to sexuality and the law such as the *Journal of Law and Sexuality* and the *Australasia Lesbian and Gay Law Journal*. However, it would be wrong to conclude that this activity has been sufficient to create a recognized discipline. In many instances the only reference to lesbian and gay issues within the extensive agenda of legal studies is to criminal law, and perhaps more recently to questions of the welfare of children and the role of the mother. Beyond a limited number in the USA few law schools offer courses in lesbian and gay legal studies.

There remains the question of whether there ought to be a separate category of lesbian and gay legal scholars, a distinct form of scholarship unique to lesbian and gay legal scholarship or a discipline of lesbian and gay legal studies. While the activities of all legal scholars and students engaging with lesbian and gay matters are informed by a politics of identity focusing upon lesbian and gay sexuality much pedagogic violence would have to be done to mould the rich diversity of topics, questions and approaches into a single topic or a range of discrete subjects. Much violence would have to be done to reduce the complexity of scholarship to the identity of those who undertake particular types of work. To do so might produce the ghettoization of matters lesbian and gay and of scholars who undertake such work. The issues of sexuality, identity, sex and gender raised within legal scholarship focusing on lesbian and gay issues have a wide significance, from questions relating to specific legal problems to questions that address the very nature of law and of legal scholarship. Nor can such legal scholarship be reduced to scholarship that is informed only by matters of sexual identity. In the many different approaches to legal scholarship on lesbian and gay matters attention is drawn to the fact that a multiplicity of factors informs scholarly practice. Finally, the establishment of a discrete discipline is neither necessary nor inevitable. While strategic considerations may support the move towards lesbian and gay legal studies, to counteract the pervasive heterocentric view of the world and the violence of exclusion that it is built upon, at best such developments should be thought of as stages in a process rather than an end in themselves.

The significance of legal studies for lesbian and gay scholarship

To pose the question, 'What is the significance of legal studies for lesbian and gay studies?' raises many problems. It seems to presuppose and reproduce existing divisions within disciplines (between law and the social sciences, between the social sciences and the arts) which in its most challenging manifestation lesbian and gay studies might problematize and refuse. Perhaps the question has significance in another way: it draws attention to the marginality of legal studies within the lesbian and gay studies that have to date arisen and been most successful in the context of the arts, cultural studies and the social sciences. The inclusion of legal studies in this volume is exceptional in the field of texts that purport to plot the field of 'lesbian and gay studies'. The failure to incorporate legal studies may point to assumptions within the established social sciences and the arts about the nature of legal studies which seek to confine it to dominant positivist conceptions of legal scholarship. Thereby lesbian and gay scholars have reproduced the dominant tradition of legal scholarship and distanced legal scholarship, perpetuating its marginalization within the social sciences and arts. While some types of legal scholarship might confirm some of these assumptions and divisions, in its diversity legal studies offers a dramatic challenge to them.

While there are many references to law and legal practice within lesbian and gay studies, legal scholarship in all its diversity may offer many challenges to the way matters of law have been raised and addressed in lesbian and gay studies. These challenges may be diverse. For example positivist legal scholars might challenge the limited understanding of the technical aspects of law evidenced in references to law within other disciplines. A legal scholarship that incorporates work undertaken in the social sciences and the humanities into legal studies might challenge assumptions in this work about law and legal studies. New insights into the nature of law and legal practice might be provided and new insights into the application of, for example, semiotics, historiography, post-structuralism or queer scholarship to law and legal practice, might be given. There is the potential to transform the way law is thought about in other disciplines.

Conclusion

As a legal scholar, for me the conjunction of matters lesbian, gay and legal generates important and exciting challenges. On the one hand it opens up a space for new adventures within and between legal studies. It makes available new opportunities for dialogue between disciplines. It offers to transform perceptions of the world, objects of enquiry, and methodologies of scholarly production. On the other hand it raises an important ethical question about scholarship within existing disciplinary boundaries. The institutions of legal scholarship that produce and perpetuate those disciplinary boundaries are places where much violence occurs in the name of truth. They are institutions that seek to silence and marginalize work that questions established practices and poses new questions. The ethical challenge for the institutions of legal scholarship is a demand for respect for new questions and new approaches to legal studies. At the same time there is an ethical challenge for those engaged in new scholarship: to respect different modes of scholarship. The future lies in struggles that produce the pleasures and pains of scholarship. These encounters will demand energy and commitment from those involved. They will provide great opportunities for reflection on the nature of scholarship.

Notes

1   There is much evidence that from early medieval times the regulation and prohibition of same sex genital acts has been referred to in written law. This knowledge might generate an expectation that the relevant legal rules would have been the object of study within the dominant tradition of legal scholarship. As rules of canon law (the laws generated and adminstered by the Catholic Church) and later in Criminal Law the regulation of same sex genital relations was outside the parameters of early modern legal scholarship that focused upon the dead corpus of Roman law. Furthermore neither were fit objects of academic study as they did not relate to the law of property or the law of obligations, which were the predominant concern of legal scholars. At best they were referred to, briefly, in the scholarly writings of those who practised law in the courtroom.

2   In that branch of the Western legal tradition that has developed out of English law a second source of law is recognized: unwritten law, or the law declared by judges.

3   As the legal method presupposed the existence of a code its deployment in the context of a living law that was not codified (for example in England) is particularly interesting. Far from changing the method of legal scholarship, in the absence of a code the project of legal scholarship became an attempt to organize the complex of written and unwritten law into a code-like text; to synthesize the existing complex body of ad hoc legislation and judicial decision into a single coherent logical synthesis of underlying principles and specific rules.

4   There are however exceptions to this, such as D.J. West's work, *Homosexuality* (1960), which is a plea for understanding and tolerance.

5   Wayne Dynes' *Homosexuality: a Research Guide* (1989) provides a rich bibliography of material.

6   For example in the European Court of Human Rights, Dudgeon (1981, 1982), Norris (1989) and Modinos (1993) and more recently under the International Convention on Civil and Political Rights, the case of Toonen (1994).

References

Bamforth, N. (1997) *Sexuality, Morals and Justice*. London: Cassell.

Berman, H. (1983) *Law and Revolution*. Cambridge, MA: Harvard University Press.

Boswell, J. (1980) *Christianity, Social Tolerance and Homosexuality*. Chicago: University of Chicago Press.

Bray, A. (1982) *Homosexuality in Renaissance England*. London: Gay Men's Press.

Buhrke, R.A. (1997) *A Matter of Justice*. London: Routledge.

Burke, M. (1993) *Coming Out of the Blue*. London: Cassell.

Coke, Sir E. (1628) *Institutes of the Laws of England*.

Comstock, G.D. (1991) *Violence against Lesbians and Gay Men*. New York: Columbia University Press.

Copley, A. (1989) *Sexual Morality in France 1780–1980*. London: Routledge.

Crane, P. (1982) *Gays and the Law*. London: Pluto.

Crompton, L. (1980) 'The myth of lesbian impunity', *Journal of Homosexuality*, 6 (1–2): 11.

Devlin, P. (1965) *The Enforcement of Morals*. Oxford: Oxford University Press.

Dynes, W.D. (1989) *Homosexuality: a Research Guide*. New York: Garland Press.

Ellis, H. (1897) *Studies in the Psychology of Sex, Volume 1, Sexual Inversion*. London: London University Press.

Faderman, L. (1981) *Surpassing the Love of Men*. New York: William Morrow.

Faderman, L. (1983) *Scotch Verdict*. New York: William Morrow.

Finnis, J. (1983) *Natural Law and Natural Rights*. Oxford: Clarendon Press.

Finnis, J. (1993) 'Law, morality and "sexual orientation"', *Notre Dame Law Review*, 69: 1049.

Goodich, M. (1979) *The Unmentionable Vice: Homosexuality in the Later Mediaeval Period*. Santa Barbara, CA: Ross-Erikson.

Goodrich, P. (1986) *Reading the Law*. Oxford: Blackwell.

Halley, J.E. (1993) 'The construction of heterosexuality', in M. Warner (ed.), *Fear of a Queer Planet: Queer Politics and Social Theory*. Minneapolis: University of Minnesota Press.

Halley, J.E. (1994) 'Bowers v. Hardwick in the Renaissance', in J. Goldberg (ed.), *Queering the Renaissance*. Durham, NC: Duke University Press.

Hart, H.L.A. (1963) *Law, Liberty and Morality*. Oxford: Oxford University Press.

Hart, L. (1994) *Fatal Women*. Princeton, NJ: Princeton University Press.

Heinze, E. (1995) *Sexual Orientation: A Human Right*. Dordrecht: Martiinus Nijhoff.

Herek, G. M. and Berill, K.T. (1992) *Hate Crimes: Confronting Violence against Lesbians and Gay Men*. London: Sage.

Herman, D. (1994) *Rights of Passage: Struggles for Lesbian and Gay Legal Equality*. Toronto: University of Toronto Press.

Herman, D. and Stychin, C. (eds) (1995) *Legal Inversions*. Philadelphia: Temple University Press.

Hirschfeld, M. (1898) *Paragraph 175 Reichsstrafgezetzbuchs: Die homosexuelle Frage im Urteile der Zeitgenossen*. Leipzig: Spohr.

Humphreys, L. (1970) *The Tearoom Trade*. London: Duckworth.

Katz, J.N. (1992) *Gay American History: Lesbians and Gay Men in the USA*. New York: Meridian.

Krafft-Ebing, R. (1947) *Psychopathia Sexualis* (originally published in 1876), trans. F.J. Rebman. New York: Pioneer Publications.

Lauritsen, J. and Thorstad, D. (1974) *The Early Homosexual Rights Movement (1864–1935)*. New York: Times Change Press.

Leinen, S. (1993) *Gay Cops*. New Brunswick, NJ: Rutgers University Press.

Lobel, K. (ed.) (1986) *Naming the Violence: Speaking out about Lesbian Battering*. Boston: Seal Press.

Lombroso, C. (1895) *The Female Offender*. London: Fisher Unwin.

McIntosh, M. (1968) 'The homosexual role', in K. Plummer (ed.) (1981) *The Making of the Modern Homosexual*. London: Hutchinson.

Majury, D. (1994) 'Refashioning the unfashionable: claiming lesbian identities in the legal context', *Canadian Journal of Women and the Law*, 7 (2): 286.

Mason, G. (1995) '(Out)laws: acts of proscription in the sexual order', in Margaret Thornton (ed.), *Public and Private: Feminist Legal Debates*. Oxford: Oxford University Press.

Mason, G. and Tomsen, S. (eds) (1997) *Homophobic Violence*. Sydney: Hawkins Press.

Mohr, R.D. (1988) *Gays/Justice: A Study of Ethics, Society and Law*. New York: Columbia University Press.

Moran, L.J. (1996) *The Homosexual(ity) of Law*. London: Routledge.

Moran, L.J. (1997) Special edition of *Social and Legal Studies 'Legal Perversions'*. London: Sage.

Moran, L.J., Monk, J. and Beresford, S. (1998) *Legal Queeries*. London: Cassell.

Munt, S. (1994) *Murder by the Book?* London: Routledge.

Norton, R. (1992) *Mother Clap's Molly House*. London: Gay Men's Press.

Robson, R. (1992) *Lesbian (Out)law*. Ithaca, NY: Firebrand.

Robson, R. (1998) *Sappho Goes to Law School*. New York: Columbia University Press.

Stychin, C. (1995) *Laws Desire*. London: Routledge.

Symonds, J.A. (1984) *Sexual Inversion*. Reprint of 1928 edn. New York: Bell Publishing.

Taylor, J. and Chandler, T. (1995) *Lesbians Talk Violent Relationships*. London: Scarlet Press.

Thomas, K. (1992) 'Beyond the privacy principle', *Columbia Law Review*, 92: 1431.

Waaldijk, K. (1993) *Homosexuality: A European Community Issue*. Dordrecht: Martinus Nijhoff.

West, D.J. (1960) *Homosexuality*. London: Penguin.

Wintermute, R. (1995) *Sexual Orientation and Human Rights: the United States Constitution, the European Convention, and the Canadian Charter*. Oxford: Clarendon Press.

Wolfenden, J. (1957) *Report of the Departmental Committee on Homosexual Offences and Prostitution*. Cmnd 247. London: HMSO.

Wotherspoon, G. (1991) *City of the Plain: History of a Gay Sub-Culture*. Sydney: Hale & Iremonger.

7 The Private and the Public: Gay and Lesbian Issues in Political Science

André Krouwel and Jan Willem Duyvendak

The public and the private sphere

Gay and lesbian movements' attitudes towards the state are ambivalent, to say the least: on the one hand, gays and lesbians politicize issues related to the private sphere, on the other hand, they demand that the state not make any claim on what they consider their 'private' affairs. Clearly, some gay and lesbian movements are looking for a more inclusive definition of the public, while others are after a more restricted definition of the public and, consequently, the political. But what is 'the political'? And what then is 'the private'?

We read in textbooks that political science examines those human activities and institutions that are related to the exercise of power and the regulation of conflict in the allocation of scarce resources.[1] Since power and conflict are part and parcel of all human (inter)action, the textbooks need to define political activities more precisely. So, it is argued, human behaviour is considered political only insofar as it is related to the public sphere, that is, to the state and society. Public power relations, the acquisition and exercise of power, political authority and the social counterforces that challenge power-holders are all claimed to be relevant phenomena for political scientists. The separation of the private from the public realm is what characterizes the process of modernization of politics and distinguishes liberal democracy from other political systems.

The public realm seems, for most textbooks, to be a self-evident given; precise analyses of shifts in the relationship between the private and public spheres are rare in mainstream political science. For instance, many political scientists will simply state that sexual behaviour or orientation is not to be considered 'public'. Yet, religious and political public institutions have attempted for centuries to regulate the most intimate expressions of human nature, such as sexuality, and condemned, prosecuted and murdered 'sodomites'. These institutions thereby ordained (homo)sexuality a public matter.

The Constituent Assembly of Revolutionary France in 1791 was the first political authority in modern European history to omit the 'crime of sodomy' from the penal code and the ensuing Code Napoléon upheld this secularized view of criminal law. Recriminalization of same sex behaviour occurred, however, in 1871 in the German states, unified under the Prussian regime and its legal system; other

European countries soon followed suit. As a response to this increasing oppression in Northern Europe since the late nineteenth century, several 'scientific' sexual reformist organizations emerged and strove to integrate homosexuals into hetero- sexual society by activating a public debate (Lauritsen and Thorstad, 1974; Weeks, 1977).

A second wave of political oppression was instigated by both Communists and anti-Communists. The destruction of Hirschfeld's Wissenschaftlich-Humanitäres Komitee (Scientific Humanitarian Committee) and the murder of Ernst Röhm and other SA leaders in 1934 by German Fascists are well-known examples. In the Soviet Union, Stalin outlawed homosexuality in 1934 after a period of relatively liberal legislation that was instituted in 1917. In the United States, McCarthy's inquest to root out 'dangerous communist elements' marked the most vigorous government persecution of homosexuals in modern America.

The repressive social climate evidenced by McCarthy's witchhunt eventually triggered the emergence in the late 1960s of 'new' gay and lesbian movements in the United States and elsewhere. These radical movements shifted the boundaries of the political even further; stimulated by the feminist movement, gays and lesbians intentionally blurred the lines between the political and private spheres by claiming that 'the personal is political'. Lesbians and gays put homosexuality on the political agenda.[2] Furthermore, starting in the 1970s gays and lesbians 'openly' gained a foothold in political parties and local councils, mostly in West European countries. Then, AIDS struck in the 1980s. As this epidemic became the mobilizing force and reoriented gay political activism towards public spending on health, relations between the state, civil society and 'private life' changed once again. This time the authorities were forced to give explicit information to the public on very 'intimate' sexual behaviour in order to prevent the spread of HIV.

Since the 1960s, social movements such as the gay and lesbian movement have been putting forward political demands in the moral and social sphere, seeking to politicize civil society and asking for equality before the law (Offe, 1985). At the same time, social movements have been challenging the state's authority and demanding maximum autonomy from official institutions and interventions (Samar, 1991). It is precisely this intriguing ongoing battle on the boundaries between the private and the public (Meijer and Duyvendak, 1988) that political scientists should analyse.

Departing from this deeply ambivalent relationship between (homo)sexuality and traditional political institutions, this chapter will focus on the attention given to homosexuality within the field of political science. Additionally, we shall deal with the question of the extent to which the 'political sphere' is incorporated in the field of gay and lesbian studies. Finally, we shall try to explain why homosexuality is such a difficult topic in political science and why politics is such a troubling factor in gay and lesbian studies.

No sex please, we're political scientists

Traditionally, political science is strongly oriented towards historical and judicial aspects of politics: the format and function of formal political institutions constitute the core of political science. Institutionalists focus on both the constitution and the political impact of the legislature, legal system, state and other administrative, political and economic institutions. In the institutional framework, formal laws and structures are examined to explain actual political behaviour.

This static approach to politics and the need for more comparative concepts provoked a counter-reaction in the 1950s and 1960s. The so-called 'behavioralist revolution' in political science shifted scholarly attention to values, attitudes and behaviour. Behaviouralism concentrated on what actually happened within the legal framework and political institutions, rather than on normative statements of what the best institutions are and what ought to happen. In order to analyse political behaviour, behaviouralists collected empirical data for statistical analysis. This 'scientific' approach sought to establish law-like generalizations about political phenomena (Easton, 1965; Wiarda, 1991).

The sharp distinction behaviouralists made between moral or ethical arguments and 'scientific' argumentation provoked a reaction from scholars, who argued that this empiricism was mere 'data-crunching' that had no explicit theoretical focus and neglected the moral underpinning of social interactions. In the early 1970s, this radical criticism of the dominant behaviouralist paradigms of political science emanated especially from neo-Marxist scholars who argued that scientific analysis should be combined with a critical stance towards society. Additional criticism, expressed by post-structuralists, was directed at the manner in which 'empirical facts' were presented as 'objective'; they showed that these facts were socially constructed and therefore 'subjective' by definition.

The revival of Marxism reintroduced the concept of the state into mainstream political science. Behaviouralist theories, stressing the characteristics, attitudes and behaviour of individuals, were unable to explain cross-national differences. Thus, social scientists were forced to reincorporate institutions into their explanations (Evans et al., 1985). These neo-institutionalists now define institutions more broadly as either the 'rules of the game' or as the 'patterns of behaviour', in order to include in their analyses both formal organizations and the informal rules and procedures that structure political behaviour. In the neo-institutional approach a wide range of state and societal institutions are considered to influence the way in which actors pursue both their interests and 'values'.

An opposite shift occurred in the 1980s, coinciding with a wave of 'new right' thinking: the new paradigm regards individual and collective behaviour as a result of a rational utility-maximizing choice between 'given' alternatives. This rational choice approach, which considers individuals as decontextualized 'atoms', has had a strong influence in political science to this very day.

The neglect of (homo)sexual issues in political science is partly due to the field's initial institutional focus on the function and form of constitutions, parliaments, courts and other political organizations. Under the implicit assumption that sexual orientation and activity have little or no bearing on the political process and structures, (homo)sexuality was practically absent from political science until the 1970s. Only when the behaviouralist approach became dominant were some studies concerning gay and lesbian issues undertaken. With respect to sexual orientation, the behaviouralists no longer analysed homosexuality from a social-psychological perspective or from a judicial angle; instead they related the phenomenon to the social structure and organization of society (Lautman, 1977). Additionally, neo-Marxists and (neo-)structuralists devoted some attention to sexuality issues, yet focused primarily on the dominant (heterosexual) discourses and practices in capitalist society as explanations for the repression of (homosexual) minorities.[3] Apart from these analyses at the periphery of political science, political science kept silent. Moreover, due to the recent dominance of the rational choice approach, mainstream political science almost disappeared once again from the field of sexuality.

We may therefore conclude that the conceptual tools of political science have not often been applied to analyse homosexuality and its social and political manifestations. As an American survey showed, the amount of research on gay and lesbian topics being undertaken by political scientists is very limited and many do not consider it 'serious political science'. Gay and lesbian politics and courses on lesbian and gay themes are largely marginalized in most political science departments in the United States (Ackelsberg and Rayside, 1995).

The gap between political science and gay and lesbian studies has not been bridged from the latter side, either. Most perspectives have failed to consider the 'official' political context and institutions. In the initial stage in the 1970s, gay and lesbian studies considered almost everything 'political' and consequently the concept had a different meaning in most gay and lesbian studies than it did in political science. The broader concept favoured by gays and lesbians, who considered the personal as being part of the political, did not result in a more inclusive definition within mainstream political science. On the contrary, after a brief interlude in the 1970s, political science opted for a more limited definition of its object in the 1980s. Furthermore, the methods used in the analyses in gay and lesbian studies deviated from the general trend in political science towards more quantitative analysis. Lesbian and gay studies is mainly qualitative: scholars trained in a constructivist tradition are reluctant to collect and use what they consider to be 'quasi-objective' quantitative data. This divergence in conceptualization as well as research method contributes to the estrangement of gay and lesbian studies from mainstream political science.

However, some recent developments seem to announce a somewhat brighter future. Some openings for gay and lesbian studies seem to be occurring, especially in social movement research, with its strong focus on 'identities', and in political theory. Additionally, recent research in gay and lesbian studies attempts to apply the dominant theories and methods of political science. In order to put this general picture in perspective, the remainder of this chapter gives an overview of some relevant debates and literature on lesbian and gay issues within the different subdisciplines of political science.

Analyses of the legislative process and public policy

As argued above, the study of the political institutions of the state, Parliament and government has traditionally marked the boundary of political science. Still, some studies addressing issues related to (homo)sexuality have been published. For example, an historical overview of the legal regulation of sexuality, including homosexuality, can be found in Posner (1992; see also Plummer, 1981). A recent and interesting comparative research project regarding the differences in legislation on homosexuality is Tielman and Hammelburg's 1993 study, 'World Survey on the Social and Legal Position of Gays and Lesbians'.[4] While these studies analyse existing laws and formal regulations on homosexuality, the institutional analyses lack investigations of how these laws come into existence (see also Chapter 6 on law in the present book). An interesting yet underdeveloped field of institutional analysis is the study of the voting behaviour of (individual) parliamentarians. These parliamentary studies could show which politicians and political parties facilitate or hamper gay and lesbian emancipation; yet longitudinal and cross-national research is not available. The most vigorous government persecution of homosexuality in the United States, McCarthy's prosecution of 'dangerous elements', has been studied only cursorily (see, for example, D'Emilio, 1983; Katz, 1976). In Europe, only one study of voting behaviour of members of the British House of Commons on homosexuality has been conducted, that of Read et al. (1994). Although other studies (Laver, 1995; Laver and Hunt, 1992) have analysed the position of political parties on moral issues, such as abortion and homosexuality, with the help of expert surveys, rigorous enquiries are lacking.[5]

Furthermore, the analysis of the impacts of different political systems, different electoral processes (majoritarian versus proportional representation), various voting procedures in parliaments, and other political institutions on the aggregation and mediation of the interests of gays and lesbians is still almost completely ignored by political scientists. The effects, for example, of different types of welfare statism on issues related to homosexuality – such as the Christian Democratic parties' dominance in Italy, Germany, Belgium and the Netherlands, which resulted in welfare statism where social rights are attached not to individuals (as is the case in Social Democrat-dominated Scandinavia) but to the family (Bussemaker and Kersbergen 1994) – have remained largely unexplored.

Additionally, there are few studies of the influence of political institutions on the positions of gays and lesbians in society at large, and vice versa. In electoral studies, for example, constituencies are primarily broken down into class and religious denomination; gender and sexual identity are seldom used as variables (for an exception see Norris, 1987). This is a surprising situation since electoral studies and analyses of coalition formation, which are at the core of contemporary political science, could shed some light on developments in permissiveness as well as repression of gays and lesbians. For example, the growing electoral success of extreme right-wing politicians and parties and the increasing strength of other anti-democratic and conservative forces can easily result in a more repressive climate. The presence of xenophobic or Fascist parties in the national parliaments of Belgium, France, Italy and Romania is an indicator that political repression of homosexuality still lurks around the corner. But gays and lesbians are not just 'passive victims' of electoral shifts. Political scientists could also pay attention to the gay and lesbian vote (the 'lavender vote'), which can be of decisive importance, especially in local elections in majoritarian electoral systems.

Political developments at the electoral and governmental level are particularly interesting in relation to public policy studies. When an official response from authorities was required in reaction to the rapid spread of HIV, the reactions differed significantly from one industrial country to the next. The disease actually generated a renewed sense of solidarity among gays. This led to the development of community AIDS organizations (Altman, 1994) and scholarly interest in the impact of AIDS on the gay and lesbian movement (see, for instance, Gamson, 1989). A large number of (comparative) studies of local (Joseph, 1992) and national policies on homosexuality and especially AIDS-prevention and related health policies emerged.[6]

Research concerning the legal protection of lesbians and gays shows that anti-discrimination laws differ substantially from country to country.[7] More often, rather than taking a positive stance, public authorities have attempted to repress explicit visibility of gay and lesbian lifestyles. The policy positions of authorities on issues such as 'gay marriage' or domestic partnership and parenthood and adoption by lesbians and gays have received some scholarly attention.[8]

In political science in general much attention is paid to the mass media's influence on policy-making, and mass-communication studies have developed into an important discipline in social science. However, only a few studies on gay and lesbian issues take the mass media into account (Berridge, 1991; Siegel, 1991). In contrast to the propensity of some popular media to 'accuse' persons of homosexuality, thereby 'destroying their careers', political authorities have often attempted to censor expressions of lesbian and gay identities. Many countries have official Boards of Censorship or other institutions to uphold dominant ideologies. This official censorship, especially in relation to pornography, is an interesting subject for investigation that lacks the attention it deserves (Dupagne, 1994; Kimmel, 1990). In particular, the conflict between this type of state regulation and the democratic principles of freedom of expression deserves more attention in relation to homosexuality.

The same topic, the freedom to be 'out', is pertinent in two other policy fields as well: the armed forces and local politics. National policies on homosexuality in the armed forces has only recently attracted much attention (Enloe, 1993). Following Bill Clinton's 1992 election promise to address the position of gays in the armed forces, some American studies of this subject were conducted (Cole and Eskridge, 1994) and these have led to some comparative reflection (Butler et al., 1993). In contrast to the armed forces, densely populated urban areas were always considered tolerant environments for lesbians and gays. The field of local policies, however, is largely unexplored in relation to homosexuality (Cooper, 1994; Tobin, 1990). This is all the more surprising as recent social and political developments may threaten the city's supposed tolerance. In this respect it would be interesting to study popular attitudes and official policy positions in the cities in Western Europe where xenophobic and racist parties have gained a substantial number of seats in local councils (Antwerp, Marseilles, Rotterdam and some cities in Northern Italy).

In conclusion, the manner in which different political regimes deal with (homo)sexuality is rarely a subject of empirical research and comparative enquiry in the dominant fields and approaches of political science. Still, where political science and sociology meet there have been some promising developments.

Political sociology

Political sociology researches the relation between the society and the state, focusing among others things on the social context of political decision-making, social movements, and the composition and behaviour of political elites. It emphasizes the way social structures are reflected in and reinforced by political institutions. Political sociology sometimes reverses this causality and investigates how political behaviour is related to social factors such as economic stratification and cultural, lingual, ethnic and religious groups. Some of these societal 'cleavages' are politicized, others are not. Conflicts and fundamental change seem to be 'normal' in the development of societies; consensus and stability are the exceptions (Bernard, 1983; Dahrendorf, 1958). Even if a large majority of the population fundamentally shares the dominant values and norms of a given society, the social order is challenged every once in a while by individuals or collectivities who feel deprived, discriminated against or dominated by others and see opportunities to change this. Thus, political sociological tools of analysis are well designed to study the social norms that regulate sexuality and the social and political institutions that structure and enforce these norms. Given its research topics, this subdiscipline of political science might provide insight into both public attitudes towards gays and lesbians and gay and lesbian political self-organization.

The discrepancy between conventional social norms governing sexuality and actual sexual behaviour in the United States first became apparent after the publication of Kinsey's reports (Kinsey et al. 1948, 1953) showing that homosexual activity was more widespread than assumed. This finding had an enormous emancipatory impact on American society. The liberalization of public attitudes towards homosexuality and lesbian and gay self-organization eventually resulted from broader societal developments rather than from Kinsey's publications. Significant economic growth and technological developments have radically changed the socio-economic structure of advanced capitalist societies since World War II, while the expansion of the welfare state increased living standards, eroding traditional class divisions and religious structures. Furthermore, the traditional fabric of society disintegrated as a result of increased social as well as geographical mobility, higher levels of education, and processes of urbanization and secularization. These developments have impinged on the long-term evolution of norms and values. For many younger citizens in the Western world who were raised in the affluent American society or the European welfare state, identity, personal development and lifestyle have become more important than material welfare. The general direction of value change, in which independence, self-fulfilment, individuality and emancipation are the key concepts, is usually referred to in political science as post-materialism (Inglehart, 1977, 1990). Research into the general population's attitudes towards homosexuality has shown that an increasing number, especially of the younger cohorts of the population, now regard sexual freedom as more important than traditional sexual morality. Within the older age cohorts a large proportion still rejects a homosexual lifestyle, but in comparison with other minorities, gays and lesbians are 'tolerated' better than previously by a large part of the general population (Thomassen, 1994).

In this more permissive context, gay men and lesbians are more visible than ever before, and their level of mobilization is quite impressive (Duyvendak, 1995a). In a nutshell, gay and lesbian movements attract people by new types of 'identity politics' that replace traditional interest mediation on the basis of, for example, an ideology related to class or religion. More precisely: identities are the interests around which the gay and lesbian movements mobilize. Like racial, ethnic, religious and (other) sexual minorities, gays' and lesbians' demands try to strike a balance between the right to be proudly different and the right simply to be treated as equals.

Diversity and heterogeneity are new ideals for many, often conflicting, groups. This plurality of interests makes representation and binding decision-making difficult. The question of policy-making in a multicultural, multisexual society seems to be the most urgent one facing political scientists, but amazingly enough, it has been left mainly to political theorists to struggle with these types of issue (see the section on political philosophy and political theory).

The topic of identity is, however, relevant not only from the perspective of multiculturalism. It is also important for political scientists to understand how a positive gay or lesbian self-identity is formed through subcultural activity and, conversely, how a common sexual preference may function as an incentive for individuals to mobilize and organize. The gay liberation movements of the 1960s gave sexual identities a political meaning by challenging the dominant cultural and religious beliefs with a 'coming out'-strategy (Altman, 1971). Since 'identity formation' has been the pivotal topic in theorizing about (new) social movements in recent years, these studies are highly useful for analyses of other social cleavages based upon identity rather than material interests, e.g., new religious movements, ethnic movements and movements of the elderly and handicapped. The development of the gay and lesbian movement offers a fascinating subject for political science from an empirical point of view, as well as from a more theoretical angle. There remains, however, a remarkable discrepancy: while political science research on social movements has expanded enormously since World War II, research on the gay and lesbian movements has lagged behind, and while theories on new social movements ('identity movements') abound and cross-national research in this field is booming, even here the study of gay and lesbian movements remains somewhat underdeveloped.[9] Studies of the history of these movements have largely been restricted to a particular geographical area, while comparative research has been carried out only since the mid-1980s.

Nevertheless, research on the gay and lesbian movement from a social movement theory perspective has generated some case studies and comparative research.[10] The comparative analyses reveal striking similarities in the development of subcultures and movements that cut across all political differences. At least in all Western capitalist countries, from the 1980s onwards there has been an enormous boom in cultural activities and the number and range of social movement organizations. These cross-country similarities do not mean, however, that the identities espoused by gays and lesbians in the various countries are identical as well. In some countries these identities have been strongly politicized whereas in other countries 'the personal' is not considered to be 'political' at all either by gays and lesbians or by society at large (Adam et al., 1999).

In some of the literature it is argued that lesbians and gays played the decisive role in 'gay liberation': the liberation of homosexuality is in this reasoning caused by the rise of the gay and lesbian movement itself (Cruikshank, 1992). The claim of 'self-liberation' seems to be exaggerated, however, since the start of the movement often followed rather than preceded the liberalization of opinions in society and politics (Duyvendak, 1994). Having said that, we must add that each movement did appear to influence the further transformation of dominant values in both politics and society as soon as it was established.

Unfortunately, data on the facilitation of the gay and lesbian movement by political parties are lacking, as are reliable data on the political representation of homosexuals in politics. There is one notable exception to this rule: an issue of the *Journal of Homosexuality* devoted exclusively to the connections between *Gay Men and the Sexual History of the Political Left* (Hekma et al., 1995). Gays and lesbians have been active, have even made political careers within several political parties in Western countries. Yet political activism within the traditional political structures has received little attention. Nor has the influence of lesbian and gay activism within political parties on the ideology or policy of the parties been analysed. The sole exception is a comparative analysis of party platforms in 27 countries (for a description see Budge et al., 1987) which gives data that can be used to identify party emphasis on (sexual) minorities and traditional moral values such as family, divorce and abortion.

So political sociology provides fertile theoretical and methodological ground for analysing lesbian and gay issues, as testified by the growing number of studies on homosexuality within this subdiscipline.

Political history

The field of political history pays somewhat more attention to homosexuality than other subdisciplines do. Some of the better-known general accounts of the history of (homo)sexuality give a contextualized overview, including political factors, of the 'transformation of intimacy' (D'Emilio and Freedman, 1988; Giddens, 1992; Seidman, 1991; Weeks, 1981, 1985, 1995). Many more authors and works could be mentioned, but this section focuses only on accounts that deal with political history in relation to (homo)sexuality (see Chapter 4 on history for a more complete overview).

In the United States, Katz (1976) studied the history of homosexuality from the sixteenth century to the mid-1970s. The history of the modern American movement in its formative stages, from the Mattachine Society's founding in Los Angeles in 1950 to the Stonewall riot in 1969, is analysed by D'Emilio (1983). The events at Stonewall have become, in the minds of most American authors, icons of the birth of lesbian and gay social organization, whereas in reality homophile movements had existed for decades. The Dutch COC (Cultural and Recreational Centre) was founded as early as 1946. Similar groups were created in Denmark (1948), West Germany (1949), Sweden (1951), Belgium (1954), France (1954) and Britain (1959). In the Netherlands, books by Tielman (1982) and Schuyf (1994) extensively describe the emerging gay and lesbian movement. The situations in the United States and the Netherlands (Krouwel, 1994) show that there is a strong correlation between the strength of the movement and the extent to which the movement and the issues it is fighting for are documented. In both countries significant attention has been given to the history of (homo)sexuality,[11] though the political context does not get the attention it deserves in the work of professional sociologists and historians.[12]

Studies in the field of political history in Germany have dealt with the negative attitude towards homosexuality related to the ideology and politics of the left-wing parties (KPD and SPD) in the Weimar Republic (Eissler, 1980) and the struggle for sexual reformation and gay rights in Wilhelminian Germany and the opposition to the movement by 'morality-movements' (Fout, 1992). Books concerning the (modern) gay and lesbian movement directly are rare, though there is increasing interest in the history of the movement.[13]

In France the situation is little better. No attention has been paid to the history of the gay and lesbian movement since its decline in the 1980s. Whereas the work of Girard (1981) covers the movement's rise in the 1960s and 1970s, only Duyvendak (1995b) and Martel (1996) deal with the movement's decline in the 1980s. Still, the rise of AIDS-related movements such as Act Up is better analysed and understood.[14] Books dealing with the history of (homo)sexuality in France mostly cover the rich gay and lesbian literary history; the political history is often neglected.[15]

In Great Britain the state of the art is somewhat more positive: not only are there books dealing with sexuality in general (Giddens, 1992) and the history of homosexuality in particular (Weeks, 1977, 1981, 1985); there are also some (other) movement-specialist published accounts as well.[16]

In the ongoing battle at the boundaries of the private and the public, (auto)-biographies of politicians in whose lives homosexuality played an important part are another underdeveloped field. The most well-known accounts are usually those of political scandals and *causes célèbres* in which politicians' homosexual activity was the cause of the scandal (Allen et al., 1990). These political scandals are at the thin line between the public and private realm when a public figure visibly violates the sexual mores of his or her society. From the events at the German court of William II in 1907, described in Steakley (1975), to the case of Jeremy Thorpe, the leader of the British Liberal Party who was forced to resign after being charged with conspiracy to murder his homosexual lover (Gaster, 1988), the political role of 'accusations of homosexuality' clearly emerges.

In summary, while the politico-historical analyses of gays and lesbians in the Western world are developing, the political history of lesbian women and gay men in other parts of the world, such as Eastern Europe, Asia, Africa, Central and South America and the Middle East, as yet remains largely unwritten.

Political philosophy and political theory

The last part of this chapter is not the least important. On the contrary, political theory and philosophy might perhaps even be considered the most flourishing part of the discipline.[17] Building on the abundance of literature on identity politics,[18] many authors dealing with multiculturalism – communitarians and liberals alike – discuss the meaning of communities, often including sexual ones. But whereas, for instance, Kymlicka, in distinguishing between types of culture in his trend-setting books *Multicultural Citizenship* (1995a) and *The Rights of Minority Cultures* (1995b), defines gay and lesbian cultures out of the field of multi-culturalism, other authors[19] put gays and lesbians at the heart of postmodern, multicultural politics.

Many of these authors are American. The absence of European authors, except for some British authors who have contributed to new theoretical developments such as queer theory and the sexual citizenship debate,[20] is quite striking. Even in the battle over Foucault's intellectual heritage, apart from his French biographer Didier Eribon (1989, 1994), Americans are preponderant.[21] This is in sharp contrast to the epistemological and political debate of the 1980s on (de)constructivism and essentialism, where continental Europeans were among the leading contributors. Their absence is the more remarkable since 'queer theorizing' might be considered the direct offspring of the deconstructivist position; the first elaborating on the anti-'naturalist' and historical perspective of the latter. At best, some of the con-structivist scholars in Europe show a sceptical attitude toward recent postmodern theorizing (see, for instance, Hekma, Chapter 5 in this book).

This shift from continental Europe towards the English-speaking world actually occurred during the past decade. Whereas in the 1960s and 1970s Europeans still dominated the Marxism debate in gay and lesbian circles, the first real shift became manifest with the constructivism/essentialism debate. Although important confer-ences dealing with these different approaches were held in Europe, Americans increasingly became the main contributors. In the 1990s, continental Europe lost its intellectual avant-gardist position. The paucity of articles by Europeans in, for instance, the *Gay and Lesbian Reader* is not due only to American chauvinism; it also shows that the main locus of theory development has shifted from one side of the Atlantic to the other.

Yet this is more than just a geographical shift. In fact, there seems to be a deepening cleavage in the kinds of theories developed in continental Europe and the United States (whereas Britain is, again, somewhere in between). As good political scientists, we claim that the differences in theorizing should be related to diverging political contexts. Whereas the Americans, mainly due to the catastrophe of AIDS, developed new political strategies and new 'queer' practices (Act Up, Queer Nation), in most European countries equal rights politics set the agenda. Some European countries have seen a different line of development. Here the authorities reacted just as slowly and homophobically as the US authorities to the AIDS crisis (for instance in France and Britain), resulting in the development of radical and new political 'queer' practices as well. In most European countries, however, gay and lesbian movements on the one hand and political authorities on the other proved capable of co-operating, leading to a 'normalization' tendency in both political practices and political theory (Duyvendak, 1996).

The rise of postmodernism in political theory (at least in the USA) has resulted in openings for gay and lesbian studies. In particular, 'queer theory' made gay and lesbian studies more prominently represented on the English-speaking political science stage (Phelan, 1994, 1997). The scholars who are developing queer theory are, however, not necessarily political scientists by training. It is most striking that scholars originating from cultural studies and the arts are in the forefront of this development of 'queering' and 'politicizing' theory (see Chapter 11, by Hoogland). In so doing, they are also causing turmoil in the field of political theory, which had excluded issues of gender and sexuality for such a long time.

Conclusion

Though gay and lesbian movements struggled for shifts in the boundaries between the private and the public, gay and lesbian voices and topics were for a long time neglected in political science. Moreover, scholars who carried out research on homosexuality seldom paid serious attention to the political context and usually did not apply the dominant theories, approaches and topics within political science.

Following the analyses of this chapter, the lack of attention paid to homosexuality in mainstream political science seems to be caused by a number of elements. First, we have the general homophobic attitude in academia, which was articulated in political science, with its ambition to be 'respectable'. Secondly, the difference in the definition of politics between political science on the one hand and gay and lesbian studies on the other explains why they seldom met. Although the boundaries of the concepts of 'private', 'public' and 'politics' have been shifting all the time, most political scientists favoured a rather narrow delimitation of politics, defining homosexuality out of their field. Thirdly, there is a paradigmatic gap between mainstream political science and gay and lesbian studies that shows up in divergences in methodology, epistemological presuppositions and the connections between theory and empirical research. This gap is not easy to bridge.

Some changes are occurring, however. A substantial amount of historical research is being carried out in which the political context is increasingly taken into account. Most important, however, is the contribution of gays and lesbians to the fields of political sociology and political theory, particularly compared with the rather weak position of gay and lesbian topics in public policy analysis. Most of the progress has been made in the fields of political science which border on either philosophy or sociology. The core of political science research on political institutions, election studies and mass communication studies and public policy analyses address homosexuality only marginally or ignore it completely. The political science community is still hesitant to acknowledge that the study of homosexuality can be of theoretical and empirical importance to the field. Scholars of lesbian and gay phenomena, on the other hand, still have to recognize that political science offers interesting tools and perspectives for their analyses of the rapidly growing lesbian and gay community throughout the world.

Notes

1 See Dahl (1963), Lasswell (1930), Schattschneider (1942).

2 See, for instance, Adam (1987), Duberman (1993).

3 See Adam (1978), Altman (1971), Gay Left Collective (1978), Hocquenghem (1978), Mieli (1980).

4 There are many case studies that describe the development of legislation on equal treatment of gays and lesbians (see Chapter 6, on law). A more general investigation into the legal principles of gay rights and anti-discrimination can be found in Riggle (1994) and Schacter (1994).

5 There are interesting unpublished studies on the position of parties with regard to homosexuality, for example, Vierhout (1976) on the Dutch case.

6 See, for instance, Altman (1986), Bayer (1991), Duyvendak (1995c), Duyvendak and Koopmans (1991), Favre (1992), Herdt and Lindenbaum (1992), Misztal and Moss (1990), Pollak (1988, 1994), Pollak et al. (1991), Vleeskruijer (1992).

7 For an overview see Waaldijk et al. (1991). For country studies see Hendriks et al. (1993) and Sylvestre (1994).

8 See, for instance, Bucher (1992), Rimmele (1993), Rubenfeld (1994), Stoddard and Fein (1990), Sullivan (1996).

9 For instance, the book edited by Laraña, Johnston and Gusfield, *New Social Movements. From Ideology to Identity* (1994), does not deal with the gay and lesbian movement at all, nor do Dalton and Kuechler (1990).

10 See Taylor and Whittier (1993) and Tarrow (1994) for interesting case studies; for a few comparative analyses see Plummer (1992, 1995), Adam (1987) and Duyvendak (1995a, 1995b).

11 See Cruikshank (1992), Duberman (1993), Duyvendak (1993), Duyvendak et al., (1992), D'Emilio (1992), Marcus (1992), Marotta (1981), Warmerdam and Koenders (1987) and further under the section political sociology in this chapter.

12 See D'Emilio and Freedman (1988), Hekma et al. (1989), Oosterhuis (1992), Seidman (1992).

13 See, for instance, Salmen and Eckert (1989), Steakley (1975) and Stümke (1989).

14 See Arnal (1993), Pollak et al. (1991).

15 With the exception of Copley (1989), Mossuz-Lavau (1991), Mendès-Leite (1994) and, of course, Foucault (1976), no books dealing with the political historical context of sexuality have been published.

16 See Hollibaugh (1980), Jeffrey-Poulter (1991), Kaufman and Lincoln (1991).

17 Since there is no separate chapter on philosophy, political philosophy is understood here in a rather broad way.

18 See, for instance, Bech (1992), Butler (1990, 1991), Cohen (1991), Duyvendak (1991), Epstein (1990), Fuss (1989), Weeks (1985).

19 Such as Aranowitz (1995), Fuss (1991), Phelan (1994, 1997), Nicholson and Seidman (1995), Kosofsky Sedgwick (1990, 1993), Seidman (1993, 1994, 1995, 1996, 1997), and Warner (1993).

20 See, for instance, Cooper (1994), Evans (1995), Herman (1995), Weeks (1995), Wilson (1995).

21 See, for instance, Bersani (1995), Blasius (1992, 1994), Halperin (1995), Miller (1993).

References

Ackelsberg, M. and Rayside, D. (eds) (1995) 'Report on the status of lesbians and gays in the political science profession', *American Political Science Association News*, September: pp. 564–72.

Adam, B.D. (1978) *The Survival of Domination*. New York: Elsevier/Greenwood.

Adam, B.D. (1987) *The Rise of a Gay and Lesbian Movement*. Reprinted in 1995. Boston: Twayne.

Adam, B.D., Duyvendak, J.W. and Krouwel, A. (1999), *Gay and Lesbian Movements Beyond Borders: National Imprints of a Worldwide Movement*. Philadelphia, PA: Temple University Press.

Allen, L. et al. (1990) *Political Scandals and Causes Célèbres since 1945, an international compendium*. London: Longman.

Altman, D. (1971) *Homosexual Oppression and Liberation*. New York: Outerbridge & Dienstfrey.

Altman, D. (1986) *AIDS and the New Puritanism*. London: Pluto Press.

Altman, D. (1994) *Power and Community: Organizational and Cultural Responses to AIDS*. London: Taylor & Francis.

Aranowitz, S. (1995) 'Against the liberal state: ACT-UP and the emergence of postmodern politics', in Nicholson and Seidman (1995), pp. 357–83.

Arnal, F. (1993) *Résister ou disparaître? Les homosexuels face au sida: la prévention de 1982 à 1992*. Paris: L'Harmattan.

Bayer, R. (1991) 'AIDS: the politics of prevention and neglect', *Health Affairs*, 10 (1): 87–91.

Bech, H. (1992) 'The disappearance of the modern homosexual, or: homo-genizing difference', in *Sexual Cultures in Europe*. Amsterdam: Forum on Sexuality/SISWO.

Bernard, J.B. (1983) *The Consensus–Conflict Debate. Form and Content in Social Theories*. New York: Columbia University Press.

Berridge, V. (1991) 'AIDS, the media and health policiy', *Health Education Journal*, 50 (4): 179–85.

Bersani, L. (1995) *Homos*. Cambridge and London: Harvard University Press.

Blasius, M. (1992) 'An ethos of lesbian and gay existence', *Political Theory*, 20 (4): 642–71.

Blasius, M. (1994) *Gay and Lesbian Politics: Sexuality and the Emergence of a New Ethic*. Philadelphia: Temple University Press.

Bucher, T. (1992) *Lebensformenpolitik für gleichgeschlechtliche Partnerschaften in der Schweiz*. Zurich: Zart & Heftig.

Budge, I., Robertson, D. and Hearl, D. (1987) *Ideology, Strategy and Party Change: Spatial Analysis of Post-war Election Programmes in 19 Democracies*. Cambridge: Cambridge University Press.

Bullough, V.L. (1979) *Homosexuality. A History*. New York: Wiley.

Bussemaker, J. and Kersbergen, K. van (1994) 'Gender and welfare states: some theoretical reflections', in D. Sainsbury (ed.), *Gendering Welfare States*. London: Sage. pp. 8–25.

Butler, J. (1990) *Gender Trouble: Feminism and the Subversion of Identity*. New York and London: Routledge.

Butler, J. (1991) 'Imitation and gender subordination', in D. Fuss (ed.), *Inside/out. Lesbian Theories, Gay Theories*. New York and London: Routledge. pp. 13–31.

Butler, J.S. et al. (1993) 'Homosexuality and military culture', *Society*, 31 (1): 13–47.

Cohen, E. (1991) 'Who are "we"? Gay "identity" as political (e)motion', in D. Fuss (ed.), *Inside/out. Lesbian Theories, Gay Theories*. New York and London: Routledge. pp. 71–92.

Cole, D. and Eskridge, W.N. (1994) 'From hand-holding to sodomy: First Amendment protection of homosexual (expressive) conduct', *Harvard Civil Rights Civil Liberties Law Review*, 29 (2): 319–51.

Cooper, D. (1994) *Sexing the City: Lesbian and Gay Politics within the Activist State*. London: Rivers Oram Press.

Copley, A. (1989) *Sexual Moralities in France 1780–1980. New Ideas on the Family, Divorce and Homosexuality*. London and New York: Routledge.

Costera Meijer, I., Duyvendak, J.W. and Van Kerkhof, M.P.N. (eds) (1991) *Over normaal gesproken*. Amsterdam: Schorer.

Cruikshank, M. (1992) *The Gay and Lesbian Liberation Movement*. New York and London: Routledge.

Dahl, R.A. (1963) *Modern Political Analysis*. Englewood Cliffs, NJ: Prentice-Hall.

Dahrendorf, R. (1958) *Class and Class Conflict in Industrial Society*. Stanford, CA: Stanford University Press.

Dalton, R.J. and Kuechler, M. (eds) (1990) *Challenging the Political Order: New Social and Political Movements in Western Democracies*. Cambridge: Polity Press.

D'Emilio, J. (1983) *Sexual Politics, Sexual Communities: the Making of a Homosexual Minority in the United States*. Chicago: Chicago University Press.

D'Emilio, J. (1992) *Making Trouble. Essays on Gay History, Politics and the University*. New York and London: Routledge.

D'Emilio, J. and Freedman, E. (1988) *Intimate Matters: History of Sexuality in America*. New York: Harper & Row.

Duberman, M. (1993) *Stonewall*. New York: Penguin Books.

Dupagne, M. (1994), 'Regulation of sexually explicit videotext services in France', *Journalism Quarterly* 71 (1): 121–34.

Duyvendak, J.W. (1991) 'De uitdaging van de homoseksuele subcultuur: de marges van de normaliteit en de normen van de marginaliteit', in Costera Meijer et al. (1991), pp. 124–34.

Duyvendak, J.W. (1993) 'Une Communauté homosexuelle en France et aux pays-Bas? De blocs, tribus et liens', *Sociétés*, 39: 75–82.

Duyvendak, J.W. (ed.) (1994) *De verzuiling van de homobeweging*. Amsterdam: SUA.

Duyvendak, J.W. (1995a) 'Gay subcultures between movements and markets', in H. Kriesi, R. Koopmans, J.W. Duyvendak and M. Giugni (eds), *New Social Movements in Western Europe. A Comparative Analysis*. London: UCL Press. pp. 165–80.

Duyvendak, J.W. (1995b) *The Power of Politics. France: New Social Movements in an Old Polity*. Boulder, CO: Westview Press.

Duyvendak, J.W. (1995c) 'De Hollandse aanpak van een epidimie: Of waarom Act Up! in Nederland niet kon doorbreken', *Acta Politica*, 15 (2): 189–214.

Duyvendak, J.W. (1996) 'The depoliticization of the Dutch gay identity, or why Dutch gays aren't queer', in Seidman, S. (ed.) *Queer Theory/Sociology*. Cambridge, MA: Blackwell Press. pp. 421–38.

Duyvendak, J.W. and Koopmans, R. (1991) 'Résister au sida: destin et influence du mouvement homosexuel', in Pollak et al., (1991), pp. 421–38.

Duyvendak, J.W., Heijden, H.A. van der, Koopmans, R. and Wijmans, L. (1992) (eds) *Tussen verbeelding en macht. 25 jaar nieuwe sociale bewegingen in Nederland*. Amsterdam: SUA.

Easton, D. (1965) *A Framework for Political Analysis*. New York: Prentice Hall.

Eissler, W.U. (1980) *Arbeiterparteien und Homosexuellenfrage. Zur Sexualpolitik von SPD und KPD in der Weimarer Republik*. Berlin: Verlag Rosa Winkel.

Enloe, C. (1993) *The Morning After: Sexual Politics at the End of the Cold War*. Berkeley: Univerisity of California Press.

Epstein, S. (1990) 'Gay politics, ethnic identity: the limits of social constructionism', in E. Stein (ed.), *Forms of Desire. Sexual Orientation and the Social Constructionist Controversy*. New York and London: Garland Publishing, pp. 239–93.

Eribon, D. (1989) *Michel Foucault*. Paris: Flammarion.

Eribon, D. (1994) *Michel Foucault et ses contemporains*. Paris: Fayard.

Evans, D.T. (1995) '(Homo)sexual citizenship: a queer kind of justice', in Wilson (1995), pp. 110–35.

Evans, P.B., Rueschemeyer, D. and Skocpol, T. (1985) *Bringing the State Back In*. Cambridge: Cambridge University Press.

Favre, P. (ed.) (1992) *SIDA et politique. Les premiers affrontements (1981–1987)*. Paris: L'Harmattan.

Foucault, M. (1976) *Histoire de la sexualité* Vol. 1: *La Volonté de savoir*. Paris: Gallimard.

Fout, J.C. (1992) 'Sexual politics in Wilhelmine Germany: the male gender crisis, moral purity, and homophobia', *Journal of the History of Sexuality*, 2 (3): 388–421.

Fuss, D. (1989) 'Lesbian and gay theory: the question of identity politics', in *Essentially Speaking. Feminism, Nature and Difference*. New York and London: Routledge, pp. 205–15.

Fuss, D. (ed.) (1991) *Inside/Out: Lesbian Theories, Gay Theories*. New York and London: Routledge.

Gamson, J. (1989) 'Silence, death and the invisible enemy: AIDS activism and social movement "newness"', *Social Problems*, 36 (4): 351–67.

Gaster, R. (1988) 'Sex, spies, and scandal: the Profumo affair and British politics', in A.S. Markovits and M. Silverstein (eds), *The Politics of Scandal: Power and Process in Liberal Democracies*. New York: Holmes & Meier. pp. 62–89.

Gay Left Collective (1978) *Homosexuality: Power & Politics*. London: Allison & Busby.

Giddens, A. (1992) *The Transformation of Intimacy. Sexuality, Love and Eroticism in Modern Societies*. Cambridge: Polity Press.

Girard, J. (1981) *Le Mouvement homosexuel en France 1945–1980*. Paris: Editions Syros.

Halperin, D.M. (1995) *Saint Foucault. Towards a Gay Hagiography*. New York and Oxford: Oxford University Press.

Hekma, G., Kraakman, D., Lieshout, M. van and Radersma, J. (1989) *Goed verkeerd. Een geschiedenis van homoseksuele mannen en vrouwen in Nederland*. Amsterdam: Meulenhoff.

Hekma, G., Oosterhuis, H. and Steakley, J. (eds) (1995) *Gay Men and the Sexual History of the Political Left*. New York and London: The Haworth Press.

Hendriks, A., Tielman, R. and Veen, E. van der (1993) *The Third Pink Book. A Global View of Lesbian and Gay Liberation and Oppression*. Buffalo, NY: Prometheus Books.

Herdt, G. and Lindenbaum, S. (1992) *The Time of Aids. Social Analysis, Theory and Method*. London: Sage.

Herman, D. (1995) 'A jurisprudence of one's own? Ruthann Robson's lesbian legal theory', in Wilson (1995), pp. 146–75.

Hocquenghem, G. (1978) *Homosexual Desire*. London: Allison & Busby.

Hollibaugh, A. (1980) 'Right to rebel', in Gay Left Collective.

Inglehart, R. (1977) *The Silent Revolution: Changing Values and Political Styles among Western Publics*. Princeton, NJ: Princeton University Press.

Inglehart, R. (1990) 'Values, ideology, and cognitive mobilization in new social movements', in Dalton and Kuechler (1990), pp. 43–66.

Jeffrey-Poulter, S. (1991) *Peers, Queers and Commons. The Struggle for Gay Law Reform from 1950 to the Present*. London: Routledge.

Joseph, S.C. (1992) *Dragon within the Gates: the Once and Future Aids Epidemic*. New York: Carroll & Graf.

Katz, J. (1976) *Gay American History: Lesbians and Gay Men in the USA. A Documentary*. New York: Crowell.

Kaufman, T. and Lincoln, P. (eds) (1991) *High Risk Lives. Lesbian and Gay Politics after the Clause*. Bridport, Dorset: Prism Press.

Kimmel, M.S. (ed.) (1990) *Men Confront Pornography*. New York: Crown Publications.

Kinsey, A.C., Pomeroy, W.P. and Martin, C.E. (1948) *Sexual Behavior in the Human Male*. Philadelphia, PA: W.B. Saunders.

Kinsey, A.C., Pomeroy, W.P., Martin, C.E. and Gebhard, P.H. (1953) *Sexual Behavior in the Human Female*. Philadelphia, PA: W.B. Saunders.

Kosofsky Sedgwick, E. (1990) *Epistemology of the Closet*. Berkeley: University of California Press.

Kosofsky Sedgwick, E. (1993) 'How to bring your kids up gay', in Warner (1993), pp. 69–81.

Krouwel, A. (1994) 'Beweging en subcultuur in vijf Westeuropese landen', in Duyvendak (1994), pp. 40–61.

Kymlicka, W. (1995a) *Multicultural Citizenship. A Liberal Theory of Minority Rights*. Oxford: Clarendon Press.

Kymlicka, W. (ed.) (1995b) *The Rights of Minority Cultures*. Oxford: Oxford University Press.

Laraña, E., Johnston, H. and Gusfield, J.R. (eds) (1994) *New Social Movements. From Ideology to Identity*. Philadelphia: Temple University Press.

Lasswell, H. (1930) *Politics: Who Gets What, When and How?* New York: World Publishing.

Lauritsen, J. and Thorstad, D. (1974) *The Early Homosexual Rights Movement (1864–1935)*. New York: Times Change.

Lautman, R. (1977) *Seminar: Gesellschaft und Homosexualität*. Frankfurt am Main.

Laver, M. (1995) 'Party policy and cabinet portfolios in the Netherlands 1994' *Acta Politica*, 30 (1): 3–28.

Laver, M. and Hunt, M. (1992) *Policy and Party Competition*. New York: Routledge.

Marcus, E. (1992) *Making History. The Struggle for Gay and Lesbian Equal Rights 1945–1990*. New York: HarperCollins.

Marotta, T. (1981) *The Politics of Homosexuality. How Lesbians and Gay Men Have Made Themselves a Political and Social Force in Modern America*. Boston: Houghton Mifflin.

Martel, F. (1996) *Le rose et le noir: Les homosexuels en France depuis 1968*. Paris: Seuil.

Meijer, I.C. and Duyvendak, J.W. (1988) 'A la frontière: le lesbian et l'homosexuel considérés en tant que conflits frontaliers autour du sexe et de la sexualité, du politique et du personnel', *Sociétés*, 17.

Mendès-Leite, R. (ed.) (1994) *Sodomites, invertis, homosexuels. Perspectives historiques*. Lille: Cahiers Université 5.

Mieli, M. (1980) *Homosexuality and Liberation. Elements of a Gay Critique*. London: Gay Men's Press.

Miller, J. (1993) *The Passion of Michel Foucault*. New York and London: Anchor Books/Doubleday.

Misztal, B.A. and Moss, D. (eds) (1990) *Action on AIDS: National Policies in Comparative Perspective*. New York: Greenwood Press.

Mossuz-Lavau, J. (1991) *Les Lois de l'amour: les politiques de la sexualité en France (1950–1990)*. Paris: Payot.

Nicholson, L. and Seidman, S. (eds) (1995) *Social Postmodernism. Beyond Identity Politics*. Cambridge: Cambridge University Press.

Norris, P. (1987) *Politics and Sexual Equality: The Comparative Position of Women in Western Democracies*. Boulder, CO: Reinner Publishers.

Offe, C. (1985) 'New social movements: challenging the boundaries of institutional politics', in *Social Research*, Winter: 817–68.

Oosterhuis, H. (1992) *Homoseksualiteit in katholiek Nederland. Een sociale geschiedenis 1900–1970*. Amsterdam: SUA.

Phelan, S. (1994) *Getting Specific. Post-modern Lesbian Politics*. Minneapolis: University of Minnesota Press.

Phelan, S. (ed.) (1997) *Playing with Fire: Queer Politics, Queer Theories*. New York and London: Routledge.

Plummer, K. (ed.) (1981) *The Making of the Modern Homosexual*. London: Routledge.

Plummer, K. (ed.) (1992) *Modern Homosexualities: Fragments of Lesbian and Gay Experience*. London: Routledge.

Plummer, K. (1995) *Telling Sexual Stories: Power, Change and Social Worlds*. London: Routledge.

Pollak, M. (1988) *Les Homosexuels et le sida. Sociologie d'une épidémie*. Paris: A.M. Métailié.

Pollak, M. (1994) *The Second Plague of Europe. AIDS Prevention and Sexual Transmission among Men in Western Europe*. New York: Harrington Park Press.

Pollak, M., Mendès-Leite, R. and Borghe, J. van den (1991) *Homosexualité et sida*. Lille: Cahiers Université 4.

Posner, R.A. (1992) *Sex and Reason*. Cambridge, MA: Harvard University Press.

Read, M., Marsh, D. and Richards, D. (1994) 'Why did they do it?: voting on homosexuality and capital punishment in the House of Commons', *Parliamentary Affairs*, 47 (3): 374–86.

Riggle, E.D. (1994) 'Political tolerance of homosexuals: the role of group attitudes and legal principles', *Journal of Homosexuality*, 26 (4): 135–47.

Rimmele, H. (1993) *Schwule Biedermänner? Die Karriere der 'schwulen Ehe' als Forderung der Schwulenbewegung: Eine politikwissenschaftliche Untersuchung.* Hamburg: Männerschwarm.

Rubenfeld, A.R. (1994) 'Sexual orientation and custody: constitutional protections are often denied same sex parents', *Human Rights*, 21 (1): 14–17.

Salmen, A. and Eckert, A. (1989) *20 Jahre bundesdeutsche Schwulen-bewegung, 1969–1989.* Cologne: Bundensverband Homosexualität.

Samar, V.J. (1991) *The Right to Privacy: Gay, Lesbians, and the Constitution.* Philadelphia: Temple University Press.

Schacter, J.S. (1994) 'The gay civil rights debate in the States: decoding the discourse of equivalents', *Harvard Civil Rights Civil Liberties Law Review*, 29 (2): 283–317.

Schattschneider, E.E. (1942) *Party Government.* New York: Rinehart & Co.

Schuyf, J. (1994) *Een stilzwijgende samenzwering. Lesbische vrouwen in Nederland 1920–1970.* Amsterdam: IISG.

Seidman, S. (1991) *Romantic Longings. Love in America 1900–1980.* New York and London: Routledge.

Seidman, S. (1992) *Embattled Eros. Sexual Politics and Ethics in Contemporary America.* New York and London: Routledge.

Seidman, S. (1993) 'Identity and politics in a "postmodern" gay culture: some historical and conceptual notes', in Warner (1993), pp. 105–42.

Seidman, S. (1994) 'Symposium: queer theory/sociology: a dialogue', *Sociological Theory*, 12: 166–77.

Seidman, S. (1995) 'Deconstructing queer theory or the under-theorization of the social and the ethical' in Nicholson and Seidman (1995), pp. 116–41.

Seidman, S. (ed.) (1996) *Queer Theory/Sociology.* Cambridge, MA: Blackwell Press.

Seidman, S. (1997) *Difference Troubles.* Cambridge: Cambridge University Press.

Siegel, P. (1991) 'Lesbian and gay rights as a free speech issue', in M.A. Wolf and A.P. Kielwasser (eds), *Gay People, Sex and the Media.* New York: Harrington Park Press. pp. 203–59.

Steakley, J. (1975) *The Homosexual Emancipation Movement in Germany.* New York: Arno.

Stoddard, T. and Fein, B. (1990) 'Gay marriage: should homosexual marriages be recognized legally?' *ABA Journal*, 76 (1): 42–3.

Stümke, H.G. (1989) *Homosexuelle in Deutschland. Eine politische Geschichte.* Munich: C.H. Beck.

Sullivan, A. (1996) *Virtually Normal. An Argument about Homosexuality.* New York: Alfred A. Knopf.

Sylvestre, R. (ed.) (1994) *De l'illégalité à l'égalité: rapport de la consultation publique sur la violence et la discrimination envers les gais et lesbiennes.* Quebec: Commision des droits de la personne de Québec.

Tarrow, S. (1994) *Power in Movement. Social Movements, Collective Action and Politics.* Cambridge: Cambridge University Press.

Taylor, V. and Whittier, N.E. (1993) 'Collective identities in social movement communities: lesbian feminist mobilization', in A.D. Morris and C. McClurg Mueller (eds), *Frontiers in Social Movement Theory*, New Haven, CT: Yale University Press. pp. 105–42.

Thomassen, J. (1994) 'Support for democratic values', in H.D. Klingemann and D. Fuchs (eds), *Citizens and the State.* Oxford: Oxford University Press. pp. 383–416.

Tielman, R. (1982) *Homosexualiteit in Nederland. Studie van een emancipatiebeweging.* Boom: Meppel.

Tielman, R. and Hammelburg, B. (1993) 'World survey on the social and legal position of gays and lesbians', in Hendriks et al. (1993) *The Third Pink Book, A Global View of Lesbian and Gay Liberation and Oppression*. Buffalo, NY: Prometheus Books.

Tobin, A. (1990) 'Lesbianism and the Labour Party: the GLC experience', *Feminist Review*, (34): 56–66.

Vierhout, M. (1976) *De houding van de politiek partijen in Nederland t.o.v. homosexualiteit en het COC van 1945–1976*. Utrecht: Utrecht University.

Vleeskruijer, C. (1992) 'Aids-voorliching: een internationaal vergelijkend onderzoek'. University of Amsterdam.

Waaldijk, K. et al. (1991) *Tip of an Iceberg. Anti-lesbian and Anti-gay Discrimination in Europe 1989–1990: A Survey of Discrimination and Anti-discrimination in Law and Society*. Utrecht: International Lesbian and Gay Association.

Warmerdam, J.N. and Koenders, P. (1987) *Cultuur en ontspanning. Het COC 1946–1966*. Utrecht: University of Utrecht, Publicatiereeks Homostudies, 10.

Warner, M. (1993) *Fear of a Queer Planet? Queer Politics and Social Theory*. Minneapolis: University of Minnesota Press.

Weeks, J. (1977) *Coming Out. Homosexual Politics in Britain, from the Nineteenth Century to the Present*. London: Quartet.

Weeks, J. (1981) *Sex, Politics and Society. The Regulation of Sexuality since 1800*. London: Longman.

Weeks, J. (1985) *Sexuality and its Discontents. Meanings, Myths & Modern Sexualities*. London: Routledge & Kegan Paul.

Weeks, J. (1995) *Invented Moralities: Sexual Values in an Age of Uncertainty*. Cambridge: Polity Press.

Wiarda, M.J. (eds) (1991) *New Directions in Comparative Politics*. Boulder, CO: Westview Press.

Wilson, A.R. (ed.) (1995) *A Simple Matter of Justice?* London: Cassell.

8 Geographies of Sexuality – A Review of Progress

Jon Binnie and Gill Valentine

This chapter evaluates the growth of work on lesbian, gay and bisexual sexualities within geography. It is a rapidly expanding area of publication. As more and more writers on sexuality from outside the discipline of geography, such as Kath Weston (1995) and Elspeth Probyn (1995, 1996) are now writing about space and place, we wish to examine what is distinctive about geography's contribution to the study of lesbian, gay and bisexual sexualities. We do not claim to be authoritative arbiters of the field, but feel that a review of the literature may be helpful to those approaching the subject for the first time. In doing so we wish to articulate the omissions, exclusions and failures of this emerging body of literature. In addition we wish to assess the contribution of work produced in geography towards our understanding of how sexuality informs our understanding of social, cultural economic and political transformations.

We have chosen to focus our review on three key areas where the greatest volume of work has been conducted: urban geography; geographies of the rural/urban opposition; geographies of sexual citizenship. The prevalence of material in these areas reflects the fact that they have been among those most receptive to feminist and postmodern critiques, and so have been among the most open towards work on sexuality.

Urban geography

The earliest work on sexuality and space sought to map the most visible lesbian and gay spaces within the North American city. While Loyd and Rowntree (1978) and Weightman (1981) were the first to publish geographies of the 'gay landscape', it is Manuel Castells (an urban sociologist) whose work is most widely cited. In *The City and the Grassroots*, Castells (1983) presented material from his study of lesbian and gay spaces in San Francisco. This work was most easily and unproblematically 'spatial'. The boundaries of specific gay male neighbourhoods and commercial districts were marked and defined by dots on maps: the dots being lesbian and gay facilities such as bars and other businesses gleaned from gay guides and business directories. Castells argued that the geography of gay men and the geography of lesbians reflected their respective gender roles and gendered behaviour. Gay men acted primarily as men and were therefore more territorial, had more disposable income, and desired the visible spatially defined commercial scene. Accordingly, lesbians acted primarily as women, were not territorial, were reliant on informal networks rather than commercial facilities, were more politicized than gay men and created lesbian space within feminist networks. The corollary of Castells' assumptions about what lesbians and gay men 'looked like' was that they led lives distinct from each other and from straight society. These simplistic assumptions would be considered highly problematic and less tenable today.

Castells' work on San Francisco did at least draw urban sociologists' and geographers' attention to the fact that there was a spatial basis to gay identity; and that gay men in particular were playing an important role in the gentrification of the city and more generally in the so-called 'urban renaissance' in North American cities. Since Castells' work on San Francisco, surprisingly few writers within urban sociology and urban geography have examined the role of gay men in urban regeneration. Larry Knopp has been the most diligent in researching this area, conducting studies in New Orleans and Minneapolis, and has published a string of papers on the involvement of gay men in the urban political economy (Knopp, 1987, 1990a, 1990b). More recently Benjamin Forest (1995) has focused on the complex relationship between gay identity, space and place in West Hollywood.

Until very recently, lesbian urban communities had been very much neglected in these studies of gay male space. However, Sy Adler and Joanna Brenner's study on an unspecified lesbian community in a city in the north-west of the United States challenged Castells' simplistic assumptions about lesbian identity and behaviour (Adler and Brenner, 1992). In their paper they argued that lesbians did concentrate in specific neighbourhoods of the city in question but that these 'communities' were 'quasi underground' and ephemeral. The same characteristics were observed in studies of lesbian residential areas in other North American, British and French cities (see for example Davis and Kennedy, 1986; Ettore, 1978; Peake, 1993; Valentine, 1995; Winchester and White, 1988). Indeed, both Ettore (1978) and Peake (1993) have demonstrated the political importance to lesbians of establishing local territorial bases. Peake (1993: 427), writing in relation to Grand Rapids, a lesbian neighbourhood in the US, states that 'the formation of a lesbian residential area represents a political act aimed at securing access to residential areas of the city which are not mediated through relations with men'.

Work by Tamar Rothenberg on the Park Slope lesbian community in Brooklyn, New York represents the most sophisticated treatment of an actually existing lesbian community to date (Rothenberg, 1995). Central to her study was the whole intensely problematic notion of what constitutes a lesbian community. Rothenberg argues that while economic factors, in particular the availability of inexpensive rented housing, have shaped and influenced the development of a lesbian-identified neighbourhood, lesbian imaginings of community and the 'symbolic' importance that has been attached to Park Slope have also facilitated the growth and development of this neighbourhood into an area with 'perhaps the heaviest concentration of lesbians in the US' (1995: 169). Rothenberg's work is a reflection of the fact that work on the urban has become more sophisticated in its treatment of lesbians and gay men. It is now also examining wider relationships between political economy of space and the politics of sexuality. Knopp has attempted to explore the links between sexuality and capitalism in a broader context (Knopp, 1992, 1995). In addition, a number of writers have explored the links between sexualized cultures of consumption and the production of sexualized space (see Binnie, 1995a, 1995b; Mort, 1995; Munt, 1995).

Equally significant has been the blossoming of work examining sexualized urban space outside of the major North American gay centres. In response to the dramatic growth and development of urban gay villages in the heart of British cities in the 1990s there has been an upsurge of work on London's Soho (Binnie, 1995a), and a string of studies on Manchester's 'Gay Village' (Corton, 1993; Hindle, 1994; Quilley, 1995; Whittle, 1994). Beyond the UK and North America, there have been several studies on Amsterdam (Binnie, 1995a, 1997a; Duyves, 1992a). For another Northern European perspective there is the work of Henning Bech (1992, 1997, 1999). Matthias Duyves (1992a, 1992b, 1995) and Jon Binnie (1995a) have both examined the phenomenon of lesbian and gay tourism, the economic potential of which has been recognized in many quarters recently (Duyves, 1992a).

Later work has extended the scope of lesbian and gay geographies beyond the more material manifestations on the urban landscape towards examining lesbian informal networks and institutions (Valentine, 1993a, 1993c), and the management of multiple identities in everyday life (Valentine, 1993b). In contrast to the early work which identified visible gay neighbourhoods and consumption spaces within cities, these studies have been significant for stressing the importance of studying the less visible aspects of lesbian and gay communities. Likewise, the work of Canadian geographer Celeste Wincapaw (forthcoming) is also broadening geographical understandings of lesbian and gay 'communities'. Rather than focusing on 'real time' face-to-face lesbian communities her research is beginning to explore the negotiation of lesbian and bisexual identities in the virtual space of 'lesbian-focused' electronic mailing lists on the Internet. Such work, which draws heavily on the burgeoning cultural studies literature on identity and performativity but which also attempts to theorize the notion of 'lesbian' space in complex ways, offers new possibilities for geographical work to both inform, and be informed by, the work of other social science disciplines. As geographers we have indeed progressed a long way from marking 'dots on maps' in our understanding of the multiple and fluid ways that sexual 'communities' are imagined, negotiated and contested as demonstrated by the essays in Duncan (1996) and Ingram et al. (1997).

Geographies of the rural/urban opposition

In the mid-1990s, there was an upsurge of interest in the rural as a specific focus for work on sexual geographies. The pioneering work of Jerry Lee Kramer on lesbian and gay communities in North Dakota (Kramer, 1995), and work by David Bell and Gill Valentine on rural Britain (Bell and Valentine, 1995a) both mark a significant development in the geography of sexuality, and clearly reinforce the need for lesbian and gay studies to consider issues of space and place. Bell and Valentine (1995a) argue that studies of the rural have thus far failed to examine the experiences of lesbian and gay men. These few studies of rural sexual geographies demonstrate how much we take for granted that lesbian and gay lives are lived in the urban environment. The urbanism of lesbian and gay existence only really becomes visible when contrasted with the rural. In 'Queer country' Bell and Valentine (1995a) trace a cartography of lesbian and gay rural existence and experience. They stress the ambivalence of the rural in the sexual imaginary as simultaneously utopian and dystopian – a place of escape or becoming, as well as a place to escape from. They draw a distinction between those lesbians and gay men who have been brought up in a rural environment who migrate to the city to escape the oppressive moral landscape of the rural; and those lesbian and gay city dwellers who migrate to the countryside actively seeking a rural lifestyle in preference to the city. For those raised in rural communities, the city is most likely to be seen as a place to escape to, where one can define oneself as lesbian or gay. For those who actively choose rural life the attractions are manifold, the reasons for migration less clear.

In the 1970s lesbian separatist communities were established in rural parts of the United States (Valentine, 1997). These communities adhere to a folkish rural utopianism. For many women membership of these communities may embody a rejection of the man-made city, and perceived masculinity of the urban built environment. Here, place-bound identity is all-important. For as Bell and Valentine (1995a) argue, those engaged in same sex activity in rural areas may not define themselves as lesbian or gay due to the lack of a developed social and political gay and lesbian community infrastructure. Informal networks, telephone dating and cottaging and cruising may constitute the rural spaces of these communities. Rural dwellers enjoying same sex activity may not share the identity of the urban lesbian or gay man. This point is reinforced by the few case studies on the rural lives of lesbians and gay men.

A fascinating case study of one rural sexual geography is provided by Jerry Lee Kramer's study of a rural lesbian and gay rural community in North Dakota. Kramer reinforces the need for lesbian and gay studies to examine sexualities of the rural: 'in gay and lesbian studies, empirical research into the strategies, behaviours and motivations of non-metropolitan gays and lesbians can provide further insights into the wide diversity of the homosexual experience' (1995: 200). It is significant and fascinating that Kramer conducted his interviews with 'exiled' North Dakotans in the conurbation of Minneapolis–St Paul. Though his study is mostly concerned with gay men, he does acknowledge that North Dakotan lesbians are generally likely to be more isolated than gay men who at least have public spaces such as restrooms where they can meet other men for sex. Kramer (1995) argues that for lesbians the only escape was to visit Minneapolis and other big cities.

In 'Get thee to a big city' Kath Weston (1995) argues that the urban/rural dichotomy is crucial to how many make sense of their lesbian and gay identity. She stresses that: 'This symbolic contrast was central to the organization of many coming out stories' (1995: 255). Weston adds that it is possible and useful to make sense of the rural through the study of the urban. Neither can be studied in isolation. Weston's work brings into focus the tension between the rural and urban in the production of a 'gay imaginary'. Unlike other studies, however, Weston's research depicts a more pessimistic view of rural life for lesbians and gay men.

As both Kramer's (1995) and Weston's (1995) work suggests, the significance of migration in lesbian and gay lives and identities needs to receive greater attention. As Bob Cant says in the introduction to *Invented Identities*, 'lesbians and gay men differ from other groups of migrants in that there is no homeland that can validate our group identity' (Cant, 1997: 1). While lesbians and gay migrants share the experience of migrating to escape prejudice and forge an identity, Cant, through his editing of the life stories of eighteen lesbians and gay men, is keen to demonstrate the diversity of this experience, and specifically the significance of economic constraints on migration. A fascinating survey on London gay men's mobility *How Far Will You Go?* (Kelley et al., 1996) published by the London-based Gay Men Fighting AIDS (GMFA), points to a complex pattern of gay men's movement to and within London, the city that dominates the British gay culture. The results of the GMFA survey demonstrate that only 23 per cent of the gay men they interviewed were originally from London, and that gay residents tend to cluster in the inner London boroughs such as Islington, Hackney and Wandsworth. Of course, it is not only rural–urban differences or regional differences that encourage lesbians, gay men and bisexuals to migrate. In the next section we consider the relationship between international migration and sexual citizenship.

Geographies of sexual citizenship

Geographers have begun to theorize the relationship between sexuality and the state – how these are mutually constituted at different spatial scales. The focus on spatial scales, and how sexual citizenship is constructed at different scales, is a major strength of Michael Brown's study of AIDS activism in Vancouver (Brown, 1994, 1995a, 1995b, 1997). David Bell has examined the ways in which an intimate citizenship is constructed and contested through the politics of public sex and the Operation Spanner trial in the UK (Bell, 1995a, 1995b). These studies constitute a challenge to an urban, political geography hitherto ignorant of sexuality. They also reflect a growth of interest in sexuality and the state more generally in social and legal theory (Cooper, 1994, 1995; Stychin, 1995; Wilson, 1995). While many of these studies ignore the spatial, for others issues of public and private space and the deployment of spatial concepts is central to their arguments. For example in her study of symbolic centrality of race and sexuality in New Right discourse in contemporary Britain, Anna Marie Smith (1994) deploys Derridean perspectives on space, identity and difference. She argues that the post-war production of British national identity was predicated on the exclusion of otherness, specifically the figure of the black immigrant in Powellism, and the queer in Thatcherism. Shane Phelan (1995) also discusses space in her deconstructive reading of queer politics, while Leslie Moran (1996) places his discussion of the contested and performative uses of space in his elegant study of the place of sexuality within English law, *The Homosexual(ity) of Law*. Moran is concerned with how English law creates a distinction between public and private space, one which is reinforced by the policing of public sex between men. Focusing on the space of the public convenience as a discursive and real space (also discussed in Woodhead, 1995), Moran (1996: 141–2) argues that:

> the public, non-sexualized, convenience is always already imagined as a sexualized space of private encounters; its very existence speaks not only of a taboo around urination/defecation and the fact that it now has to be undertaken in private but that the removal of these functions into a private space generates other private dangers. The private and the sexualized nature of that space is written in the division between male and female space; in the use of frosted glass that might provide natural light but prevent a public display; in the design of the stalls; in the erection of barriers between the stalls to secure individuality during the private act of urination; in the separation of space into individual private cubicles; in the provision of lockable doors to secure that individual space etc.

While lawyers such as Moran have explored the links between sexuality, public order and space, an evolving literature on architecture and sexuality (Colomina, 1992; Sanders, 1996; Urbach, 1996) has examined how buildings embody concerns about the proper social order. Other writers have examined the policing of public sex (Califia, 1994; Dangerous Bedfellows, 1996).

From the discussion of the literature on lesbian and gay geographies thus far it is clear that movement and migration loom large in the lives of lesbians and gay men. However, there have been few studies of sexual citizenship and the politics of international migration (though see Chauvel, 1994; Jessurun D'Oliveira, 1993). For lesbians and gay men, migration across national boundaries can be immensely problematic, especially when it comes to obtaining full rights of citizenship based on same sex relationships. There has been little discussion of the transnational dimension in sexual cultures. Binnie's work on international migration and tourism hints at a connection between consumption and sexual citizenship (Binnie, 1995a, 1997a). While it may be hard for some to resist the temptation to stereotype gay men as uniformly affluent and mobile, the persistence of laws that fail to recognize same sex partners for the purpose of rights of residence and affording of citizenship status represents a barrier to movement of lesbians and gay men across national boundaries (Valentine, 1996).

Work on international lesbian and gay tourism needs to challenge the homophobia often implicit within disembodied accounts of Western tourists engaged in sex tourism. Lynda Johnston (1996) has criticized the study of tourism within disciplines such as geography, arguing that it produces hegemonic, disembodied and masculinist knowledge. Her work on the HERO parade, New Zealand's largest gay pride parade, and the Sydney Mardi Gras in Australia, offers a new perspective on tourism and the complex power relations it involves. By taking an embodied approach to the study of these festivals, Johnston's research not only subverts the masculinism of tourism discourse but also, like the work of Binnie and Bell, represents a significant attempt to liberate sexuality from the ghetto of community studies within the discipline, marking another step on the path towards making it a fundamental issue to be considered in all aspects of human geography enquiry.

One major feature of the work discussed so far is the predominance of writers from the English-speaking world, especially North America and the United Kingdom – with perhaps some of the most innovative work on feminist geography and sexuality and space now coming from geographers at the University of Waikato in Hamilton, New Zealand (Longhurst, 1995; Peace, forthcoming). Criticizing the ethnocentricity of lesbian and gay geographers and their preoccupation with the developed world Glen Elder asks: 'How are sexualities constructed and negotiated in peripheral economies, and how do these spatial processes feed into the emergence of amongst other things, "gay and lesbian culture" in "First World" settings?' (Elder, 1995: 57). Unfortunately, there are still few answers to these questions (though see Bravmann, 1994; Drucker, 1996; Murray, 1995; Robson, 1991; Skelton, 1995).

Each of these subsections has considered progress in specific fields of geographical study where the interplay of sexualities, acts and identities with space and place has been paramount. The discussion of race and nationhood – as the studies of community have also shown – shows that the whole notion of a uniform universal lesbian and gay identity and community has become untenable in both politics and theory. We will now go on to discuss work done by geographers which has sought to critically evaluate the politics of lesbian and gay identity, in the light of the challenges posed by queer politics and theory.

Queer geographies: the trouble with identity politics

Geographers have recently explored a range of perspectives based on queer theory and sexual practice. This is a reaction against earlier work on lesbian and gay geographies outlined above, which perhaps had an uncritical all-embracing concept of lesbian and gay identity. Queer geographies have attempted to scrutinize the desirability of identity politics. Work by writers such as Julia Cream (1992, 1995), Alison Murray (1995), Bell et al. (1994) has challenged established notions of fixed identities. David Bell's mapping of a bisexual geography is significant here in subverting the hegemony of lesbian and gay geography, which had hitherto ignored bisexuality (Bell, 1994). For Bell, bisexuality is very much 'a place on the margins'. In challenging the placelessness and homelessness of bisexuality in queer politics, and lesbian and gay geographies, Bell offers a powerful critique of biphobic notions that bi's are tourists in lesbian and gay spaces (Bell, 1994). However, while remaining ever sympathetic towards queer's transgressive project to subvert identity, he also remains highly cynical of queer's utopianism, and in particular the way queer politics has almost become a parody of itself, reinforcing the marginalization of discussions of 'race' and bisexuality, among other thorny issues (Bell, 1994).

There have been few studies explicitly concerned with sexuality and the geographies of 'race' and racism (though see Davis, 1995; Peake, 1993; Skelton, 1995). Moreover, geographers studying this have been culpable of neglecting sexuality in their discussions, despite the growth of material on the intersections of race and sexuality elsewhere (for instance see Gilman, 1985; Mercer, 1993;

Smith, 1994; Smyth, 1995). Disability is another neglected area of geographical research on sexuality and space (though see Butler, 1999). Work outside of geography has addressed the links between homophobia and ableism. In *Untold Desires: the Sexual Politics of Disability* Tom Shakespeare, Kath Gillespie-Sells and Dominic Davies (1996) provide a starting point for an examination of both the homophobia within the disability movement and ableism within the lesbian and gay scene. They argue that while there are studies of sexuality and disability they fail to acknowledge the experiences of disabled people themselves (1996: 3):

> There is quite an industry producing work around the issue of sexuality and disability, but it is an industry controlled by professionals from medical and psychological and sexological backgrounds, the voice and experience of disabled people is absent in almost every case. As in other areas, disabled people are displaced as subjects, and fetishized as objects.

While such critiques of the concept of a lesbian and gay identity represent one example of queer geographies, a second strand of work has sought to understand how the theoretical insights of queer theory's critique of identity politics may be applied to discussions of space. In 'All hyped up and no place to go' Bell et al. (1994), inspired by the work of Judith Butler (1990), attempted to explore the importance of the spatial specificity of the performance of gender identities. Employing Butler's notion that gender is not simply an aspect of what one is, but is something one does repetitively in interactions with others, Bell et al. try to assess whether similar arguments can be made for the production of spaces. While Butler (1990) suggests that gender as performance is no longer limited by sex, so Bell et al. (1994) suggest that public heterosexual space may not be restricted to heterosexuality. Using the examples of the lipstick lesbian and the gay skinhead, they asked questions about whether the performance of these identities can ever disrupt the heterosexuality of straight space, questioning whether, in Butler's words, 'it is the site of parodic contest and display that robs compulsory heterosexuality of its claims to naturalness and originality'. Concluding their paper Bell et al. remain ambivalent about the politics of proclaiming the queer transgression and subversion of identity, pointing out that the performances of these identities are read differently by different people in different places. The paper and the respective replies to it demonstrate the limits of thinking through the tensions between discursive bodies and material spaces.

Conclusion

Despite the critical tone of the latter stage of this chapter we hope we have demonstrated that geographies of sexualities have come a long way in the last decade. Progress in the study of the lives of dissident sexualities has been striking, notably in three key areas: urban geography; rural lesbian and gay geographies; and the geography of sexual citizenship. In each of these areas there have been significant developments in geographical understandings of lesbian, gay and bisexual lives and signs that sexual dissidents are beginning to have an impact on the heteronormative nature of geographical knowledge (Binnie, 1997b).

Work on geographies of sexualities has to date been characterized by an emphasis on both the material and the everyday – how sexualities are lived out in particular places and spaces. This is the major contribution that geographers can offer other disciplines concerned with sexuality. Geographical work provides a corrective to the tendency within some post-structuralist writing on queer to divorce considerations of sexual politics from wider political economic debates. It is a strength of the more contextualized geographies of sexuality that they do not treat sexual politics in isolation and that wider political economic forces and considerations are at play in the production of sexualized spaces (Binnie, 1993, 1995a; Quilley, 1995). As Michael Warner (1993: x) argues in his introduction to *Fear of a Queer Planet*, 'the energies of queer studies have come more from rethinking the subjective meaning of sexuality than from rethinking the social'. Geographers could occupy a central place in the rearticulation of queer theory to include a much needed social or material dimension (Warner, 1993). There is an urgent need, expressed by Richard Cornwell (1997) among others, to create a queer social theory and queer political economy which acknowledges both the importance of capital to the formation of sexual cultures and communities, and the exclusion and marginalization from economic activity engendered by homophobia, as well as recognizing the homophobia implicit within the commonplace assumption that gay men are uniformly white and affluent.

While there is now almost an abundance of published material on local lesbian and gay communities, less has been written linking lesbian and gay geographies to processes of globalization. Geographers could gain much from material produced elsewhere on the transnational basis of sexual identity (Manalansan IV, 1995), nationalism (Mosse, 1985; Parker et al., 1992) and imperialism and globalization (Hyam, 1990; Lane, 1995). Unfortunately we have yet to witness much work on the geography of sexuality in these areas, and the ethnocentricity of the literature on sexuality and space remains largely unchallenged.

Indeed, there are many areas within the discipline of geography where discussion of sexuality has been notable for its absence, for example transport geography and population geography. The different philosophical approaches that dominate different subdisciplinary areas may explain the uneven impact of work on dissident sexualities within geography. Geography remains a highly contested enterprise. While social and cultural geography have been very receptive to contemporary developments in social theory (e.g. the postmodern emphasis on 'difference') and therefore towards dissident sexualities, many other fields of geographical enquiry remain wedded to their positivist tradition. However, this does not explain why the hegemonic sexual identity, heterosexuality, has thus far received so little attention from geographers (notable exceptions being Linda McDowell's 1995 work on heterosexual masculinities in city workplaces and Phil Crang's 1995 work on the performance of masculinities and femininities in restaurants). Perhaps then what we need is not so much a queer reading of space as a queer reading of the discipline of geography itself.

Acknowledgements

Thanks to Susan Smith and David Bell for their comments on earlier versions of this chapter.

References

Adler, S. and Brenner, J. (1992) 'Gender and space: lesbians and gay men in the city', *International Journal of Urban and Regional Research*, 16: 24–34.

Bech, H. (1992) 'The disappearance of the modern homosexual, or homo-genizing difference'. Paper presented at the Sexual Cultures in Europe conference, Amsterdam, June.

Bech, H. (1997) *When Men Meet*. Cambridge: Polity.

Bech, H. (1999) 'Citysex: representing lust in public', in M. Featherstone (ed.) *Love and Eroticism*. London: Sage. pp. 215–41.

Bell, D. (1994) 'Bi-sexuality – a place on the margins', in S. Whittle (ed.), *The Margins of the City. Gay Men's Urban Lives*. Aldershot: Ashgate. pp. 129–41.

Bell, D. (1995a) 'Pleasure and danger: the paradoxical spaces of sexual citizenship', *Political Geography*, 14: 139–53.

Bell, D. (1995b) 'Perverse dynamics, sexual citizenship and the transformation of intimacy', in D. Bell and G. Valentine (eds), *Mapping Desire. Geographies of Sexualities*. London: Routledge. pp. 304–17.

Bell, D. and Valentine, G. (1995a) 'Queer country: rural lesbian and gay lives', *Journal of Rural Studies*, 11: 113–22.

Bell, D. and Valentine, G. (eds) (1995b) *Mapping Desire. Geographies of Sexualities*. London: Routledge.

Bell, D., Binnie, J., Cream, J. and Valentine, G. (1994) 'All hyped up and no place to go', *Gender, Place and Culture*, 1: 31–47.

Binnie, J. (1993) 'Invisible cities/hidden geographies: sexuality and the city'. Paper presented at Social Policy and the City conference, University of Liverpool, July.

Binnie, J. (1995a) 'Trading places: consumption, sexuality and the production of queer space', in D. Bell and G. Valentine (eds), *Mapping Desire. Geographies of Sexualities*. London: Routledge. pp. 182–99.

Binnie, J. (1995b) 'The trouble with camp', *Transgressions: A Journal of Urban Exploration*, 1: 51–8.

Binnie, J. (1997a) 'Invisible Europeans: sexual citizenship in the new Europe', *Environment and Planning A*, 29: 237–48.

Binnie, J. (1997b) 'Coming out of geography: towards a queer epistemology', *Environment & Planning D: Society and Space*, 15: 223–37.

Bravmann, S. (1994) 'The lesbian and gay past: it's Greek to whom?', *Gender, Place and Culture*, 1: 149–67.

Brown, M. (1994) 'The work of city politics: citizenship through employment in the local responses to AIDS', *Environment and Planning A*, 26: 873–94.

Brown, M. (1995a) 'Sex, scale and the "new urban politics": HIV-prevention strategies from Yaletown, Vancouver', in D. Bell and G. Valentine (eds), *Mapping Desire: Geographies of Sexualities*. London: Routledge. pp. 245–63.

Brown, M. (1995b) 'Ironies of distance: an ongoing critique of the geographies of AIDS', *Environment and Planning D: Society and Space*, 13: 159–83.

Brown, M. (1997) *Replacing Citizenship: AIDS Activism and Radical Democracy*. New York: Guilford Press.

Butler, J. (1990) *Gender Trouble: Feminism and the Subversion of Identity*. London: Routledge.

Butler, R. (1999) 'Double the trouble or twice the fun? Disabled bodies in the gay community', in R. Butler and H. Parr (eds), *Mind and Body Spaces: Geographies of Illness, Impairment and Disability*. London: Routledge.

Califia, P. (1994) *Public Sex: The Culture of Radical Sex*. Pittsburgh, PA: Cleis Press.

Cant, B. (ed.) (1997) *Invented Identities: Lesbians and Gays Talk about Migration*. London: Cassell.

Castells, M. (1983) *The City and the Grassroots*. Berkeley: University of California Press.

Chauvel, C. (1994) 'New Zealand's unlawful immigration policy', *Australasian Gay and Lesbian Law Journal*, 4: 73–84.

Colomina, B. (ed.) (1992) *Sexuality and Space*. Princeton, NJ: Princeton Architectural Press.

Cooper, D. (1994) *Sexing the City: Lesbian and Gay Politics within the Activist State*. London: Rivers Oram.

Cooper, D. (1995) *Power in Struggle: Feminism, Sexuality and the State*. Buckingham: Open University Press.

Cornwell, R. (1997) 'Queer political economy: the social articulation of desire', in A. Gluckman and B. Reed (eds), *Homoeconomics. Capitalism, Community, and Lesbian and Gay Life*. London: Routledge. pp. 89–122.

Corton, S. (1993) 'Anal street: Manchester's gay village – dissection of a "community"'. Undergraduate dissertation in Geography, University of Manchester. Copy available from the author, Department of Geography, University of Manchester, Oxford Road, Manchester, UK.

Crang, P. (1995) 'It's showtime: on the workplace geographies of display in a restaurant in southeast England', *Environment and Planning D: Society and Space*, 12: 675–704.

Cream, J. (1992) 'Sexing shapes. Sexuality and space network lesbian and gay'. Geographies Conference Proceedings. Copy available from D. Bell, Department of Cultural Studies, University of Staffordshire, College Road, Stoke on Trent, UK.

Cream, J. (1995) 'Re-solving riddles: the sexed body', in D. Bell and G. Valentine (eds), *Mapping Desire. Geographies of Sexualities*. London: Routledge. pp. 31–40.

Dangerous Bedfellows (eds) (1996) *Policing Public Sex*. Boston, MA: South End Press.

Davis, M. and Kennedy, E. (1986) 'Oral history and the study of sexuality in the lesbian community: Buffalo, New York, 1940–60', *Feminist Studies*, 12: 7–26.

Davis, T. (1995) 'The diversity of queer politics and the redefinition of sexual identity and community in urban spaces', in D. Bell and G. Valentine (eds), *Mapping Desire: Geographies of Sexualities*. London: Routledge. pp. 284–303.

Drucker, P. (1996) '"In the tropics there is no sin": sexuality and gay-lesbian movements in the Third World', *New Left Review* 218: 75–101.

Duncan, N. (ed.) (1996) *Bodyspace: Destabilising Geographies of Gender and Sexuality*. London: Routledge.

Duyves, M. (1992a) 'The inner-city of Amsterdam: gay show-place of Europe?' Paper presented at the Forum on Sexuality conference, Sexual Cultures in Europe, Amsterdam, June.

Duyves, M. (1992b) 'In de ban van de bak: openbaar ruimtegebruik naar homoseksuele voorkeur in Amsterdam', in J. Burgers (ed.), *De uitstaad: Over stedelijk vermaak*. Utrecht: Uitgeverij Jan van Arkel. pp. 73–98.

Duyves, M. (1995) 'Framing preferences, framing differences: inventing Amsterdam as gay capital', in J. Gagnon and R. Parker (eds), *Conceiving Sexuality. Approaches to Sex Research in a Postmodern World*. London: Routledge. pp. 51–66.

Elder, G. (1995) 'Of moffies, kaffirs and perverts: male homosexuality and the discourse of moral order in the apartheid state', in D. Bell and G. Valentine (eds), *Mapping Desire. Geographies of Sexualities*. London: Routledge. pp. 56–65.

Ettore, E. (1978) 'Women, urban social movements and the lesbian ghetto', *International Journal of Urban and Regional Research*, 2: 499–519.

Forest, B. (1995) 'West Hollywood as symbol: the significance of place in the construction of a gay identity', *Environment and Planning D: Society and Space*, 13: 133–57.

Gilman, S. (1985) *Difference and Pathology. Stereotypes of Sexuality, Race and Madness.* Ithaca, NY: Cornell University Press.

Hindle, P. (1994) 'Gay communities and gay space in the city', in S. Whittle (ed.), *The Margins of the City. Gay Men's Urban Lives.* Aldershot: Ashgate Publishing. pp. 7–25.

Hyam, R. (1990) *Empire and Sexuality. The British Experience.* Manchester: Manchester University Press.

Ingram, B.G., Bouthilette, A.M. and Retter, Y. (eds) (1997) *Queers in Space: Communities, Public Places, Sites of Resistance.* Seattle: Bay Press.

Jessurun d'Oliveira, H.U. (1993) 'Lesbians and gays and the freedom of movement of persons', in K. Waaldijk and A. Clapham (eds), *Homosexuality: a European Community Issue. Essays on Lesbian and Gay Rights in European Law and Policy.* Dordrecht: Martinus Nijhoff. pp. 289–316.

Johnston, L. (1996) 'Embodying tourism. Proceedings of Tourism Down Under' II Conference, 3–6 December, University of Otago, Dunedin, New Zealand. Copy available from author, Department of Geography, University of Edinburgh, Drummond Street, Edinburgh EH8 9XP, UK.

Kelley, P., Pebody, R. and Scott, P. (1996) *How Far Will You Go? A Survey of London Gay Men's Migration and Mobility.* London: GMFA.

Knopp, L. (1987) 'Social theory, social movements and public policy: recent accomplishments of the gay and lesbian movements in Minneapolis, Minnesota', *International Journal of Urban and Regional Research*, 11: 243–61.

Knopp, L. (1990a) 'Some theoretical implications of gay involvement in an urban land market', *Political Geography Quarterly*, 9: 337–52.

Knopp, L. (1990b) 'Exploiting the rent-gap: the theoretical significance of using illegal appraisal schemes to encourage gentrification in New Orleans', *Urban Geography*, 11: 48–64.

Knopp, L. (1992) 'Sexuality and the spatial dynamics of capitalism', *Environment and Planning D: Society and Space*, 10: 651–69.

Knopp, L. (1995) 'Sexuality and urban space: a framework for analysis', in D. Bell and G. Valentine (eds), *Mapping Desire. Geographies of Sexualities.* London: Routledge. pp. 149–61.

Kramer, J.L. (1995) 'Bachelor farmers and spinsters: gay and lesbian identities and communities in rural North Dakota', in D. Bell and G. Valentine (eds), *Mapping Desire. Geographies of Sexualities.* London: Routledge. pp. 200–13.

Lane, C. (1995) *The Ruling Passion. British Colonial Allegory and the Paradox of Homosexual Desire.* Durham, NC: Duke University Press.

Longhurst, R. (1995) 'Geography and the body', *Gender, Place and Culture*, 2: 97–105.

Loyd, B. and Rowntree, L. (1978) 'Radical feminists and gay men in San Francisco: social pace in dispersed communities', in D. Lanegran and R. Palm (eds), *Invitation to Geography.* New York: McGraw Hill. pp. 78–88.

McDowell, L. (1995) 'Bodywork', in D. Bell and G. Valentine (eds), *Mapping Desire. Geographies of Sexualities.* London: Routledge. pp. 75–95.

Manalansan IV, M. (1995) 'In the shadow of Stonewall: examining gay transnational politics', *GLQ: A Journal of Lesbian and Gay Studies*, 2: 425–38.

Mercer, K. (1993) 'Reading racial fetishism: the photographs of Robert Mapplethorpe'. in E. Apter and W. Pietz (eds), *Fetishism as Cultural Discourse.* Ithaca, NY: Cornell University Press.

Moran, L. J. (1996) *The Homosexual(ity) of Law.* London: Routledge.

Mort, F. (1995) 'Archaeologies of city life: commercial culture, masculinity, and spatial relations in 1980s London', *Environment and Planning D: Society and Space*, 13: 573–90.

Mosse, G.L. (1985) *Nationalism and Sexuality: Middle Class Morality and Sexual Norms in Modern Europe.* Madison: University of Wisconsin Press.

Munt, S. (1995) 'The lesbian flâneur', in D. Bell and G. Valentine (eds), *Mapping Desire: Geographies of Sexualities.* London: Routledge. pp., 114–25.

Murray, A. (1995) 'Femme on the streets, butch in the sheets (a play on whores)', in D. Bell and G. Valentine (eds), *Mapping Desire. Geographies of Sexualities*, London: Routledge. pp. 66–74.

Parker, A., Russo, M., Sommer, D. and Yaeger, P. (eds) (1992) *Nationalisms and Sexualities*. London: Routledge.

Peace, R. (forthcoming) 'Abject sexualities: lesbian identity, geography and policy', in D. Bell, J. Binnie, R. Longhurst, R. Peace, D. Wakeford and D. Woodhead (eds), *Pleasure Zones. Bodies, Cities and Spaces*. Syracuse, NY: Syracuse University Press.

Peake, L. (1993) '"Race" and sexuality: challenging the patriarchal structuring of urban social space', *Environment and Planning D: Society and Space*, 11: 415–32.

Phelan, S. (1995) 'The space of justice: lesbians and democratic politics' in A. Wilson (ed.), *Simple Matters of Justice: Theorising Lesbian and Gay Politics*. London: Cassell. pp. 193–220.

Probyn, E. (1995) 'Lesbians in space: gender, sex and the structure of missing', *Gender, Place and Culture*, 2: 77–84.

Probyn, E. (1996) *Outside Belongings*. London: Routledge.

Quilley, S. (1995) 'Manchester's "village in the city": the gay vernacular in a post-industrial landscape of power', *Transgressions: A Journal of Urban Exploration*, 1: 36–50.

Robson, E. (1991) 'Space, place and sexuality in Hausaland, Northern Nigeria'. Paper presented at ERASMUS Geography and Gender Course, University of Durham.

Rothenberg, T. (1995) '"And she told two friends": lesbians creating urban social space', in D. Bell and G. Valentine (eds), *Mapping Desire. Geographies of Sexualities*. London: Routledge. pp. 165–81.

Sanders, J. (ed.) (1996) *Stud: Architectures of Masculinity*, Princeton, NJ: Princeton Architectural Press.

Shakespeare, T., Gillespie-Sells, K. and Davies, D. (1996) *Untold Desires: The Sexual Politics of Disability*. London: Cassell.

Skelton, T. (1995) '"Boom, bye, bye": Jamaican ragga and gay resistance', in D. Bell and G. Valentine (eds), *Mapping Desire. Geographies of Sexualities*. London: Routledge. pp. 264–83.

Smith, A.M. (1994) *New Right Discourse on Race and Sexuality: Britain, 1968–1990*. Cambridge: Cambridge University Press.

Smyth, C. (1995) 'Crossing the tracks', *Perversions*, 5: 43–53.

Stychin, C. (1995) *Law's Desire: Sexuality and the Limits of Justice*. London: Routledge.

Urbach, H. (1996) 'Closets, clothes, disclosure', in D. McQuorquodale, K. Ruedi and S. Wigglesworth (eds), *Desiring Practices: Architecture, Gender and the Interdisciplinary* London: Black Dog Publishing. pp. 246–63.

Valentine, G. (1993a) '(Hetero)sexing space: lesbian perceptions and experiences of everyday spaces', *Environment and Planning D: Society and Space*, 11: 394–413.

Valentine, G. (1993b) 'Negotiating and managing multiple identities: lesbian time-space strategies', *Transactions of the Institute of British Geographers*, NS, 18: 237–48.

Valentine, G. (1993c) 'Desperately seeking Susan: a geography of lesbian friendships', *Area*, 25: 109–16.

Valentine, G. (1995) 'Out and about: geographies of lesbian landscapes', *International Journal of Urban and Regional Research*, 19: 96–112.

Valentine, G. (1996) 'An equal place to work? Discrimination and sexual citizenship in the European Union', in M.D. Garcia-Ramon and J. Monk (eds), *Women of the European Union: the Politics of Work and Daily Life*. London: Routledge. pp. 111–25.

Valentine, G. (1997) 'Making space: lesbian separatist communities in the United States', in P. Cloke and J. Little (eds), *Contested Countryside Cultures*. London: Routledge.

Warner, M. (ed.) (1993) *Fear of a Queer Planet. Queer Politics and Social Theory*. Minneapolis: University of Minnesota Press.

Weightman, B. (1981) 'Commentary: towards a geography of the gay community', *Journal of Cultural Geography*, 1: 106–12.

Weston, K. (1995) 'Get thee to a big city: sexual imaginary and the great gay migration', *GLQ: A Journal of Lesbian and Gay Studies*, 2: 253–77.

Whittle, S. (1994) 'Consuming differences: the collaboration of the gay body with the cultural state', in S. Whittle (ed.), *The Margins of the City. Gay Men's Urban Lives.* Aldershot: Ashgate Publishing. pp. 27–41.

Wilson, A. (ed.) (1995) *A Simple Matter of Justice: Theorising Lesbian and Gay Politics.* London: Cassell.

Wincapaw, C. (forthcoming) 'Lesbian, bisexual women's electronic mailing lists as sexualised spaces', *Journal of Lesbian Studies.*

Winchester, H. and White, P. (1988) 'The location of marginalized groups in the inner city', *Environment and Planning D: Society and Space*, 6: 37–54.

Woodhead, D. (1995) '"Surveillant gays": HIV, space and the constitution of identities', in D. Bell and G. Valentine (eds), *Mapping Desire. Geographies of Sexualities.* London: Routledge. pp. 231–44.

9 Gay Male Literary Studies

Marco Pustianaz

Literary studies are still often seen as a highly specialized field, relevant only within the restricted area of academia. On the contrary, gay literary studies developed as a set of counter-reading strategies connected with the 'rise' of homosexual subjects and with the organization of gay liberation movements. Their political content is therefore embedded in their foundation as a counterdiscourse.

Despite the prevalent myth that posits Stonewall as the originating moment of homosexual visibility and pride, the existence of a cultural agenda emphasizing a 'homosexual identity' actually predates the Stonewall era. Issues of literariness, literary creativity and biography were present in the interests of early-century sexual reformers. M. Hirschfeld's *Jahrbuch für sexuelle Zwischenstufen* repeatedly published in its nine issues (Leipzig, 1899–1908) long case studies centred on the psychological biography of historical and literary figures.

This early focus on specific key-figures and texts is of crucial importance. The possibility of a 'homosexual tradition' relies on the singling out of founding fathers, propelled by the desiring gaze cast on certain writers and texts turned into recognized icons of identification. Gay literary studies have often relied on evidence pointing to the homosexuality of literary figures, thus implying that the outing of homosexual worthies may stand for the liberation of all homosexual practices and feelings. The singling out of authors and texts was already happening in the nineteenth century, especially in the quest for Greece and its classical tradition of 'manly affection' and 'Platonic love'. Thus, even before the modern male homosexual was able to name himself there was already an interpretive community selecting a canon, which the early 'Uranian' poets and sexual reformers endorsed and empowered.[1]

Two world wars, the increasingly repressive psychiatrization of homosexuals and the strictly disciplinary organization of post-war literary studies intent on rebuilding a core of Western humanist ideology, all helped to disperse the loose but nonetheless congruent strands of early twentieth-century homosexual 'knowledge'. The dominant agenda of post-war heterosexual humanism required either the silencing of all homosexual traces or their ethico-medical correction.

What changed dramatically in the 1970s was both the activist refusal to collaborate with institutional homophobia and the positive assertion of a counter-culture. Out of this radical break with the past emerged the first conscious attempts to write homosexual desire back into the history of Western culture, and therefore the first outspoken affirmations of the need to bring back to light a homosexual tradition in literature. If homoerotic writing had, it seemed, existed for a long time, what was still lacking was a literary and political criticism that was committed to witness and 'out' that tradition. What set apart early gay literary studies from previous occasional glimpses of recognition (e.g. Leslie Fiedler's *Love and Death in the American Novel*, 1960) was the sense of a collective purpose binding the affirmation of an oppositional counterculture to its political subject. Gay literary studies were inseparable from gay political practices and broke decisively with what (little) homosexual discourse could survive within the institutions. No wonder that gay literary studies around the Stonewall era grew mainly outside academic spaces. As Rictor Norton, one of the earliest founders of gay criticism in the United States, bluntly wrote in a 1974 article for the magazine *Gay Sunshine*, 'More accurate information and perceptive commentary on homosexual literature and authors can be gleaned from such periodicals as *Arcadie, Gay Sunshine, Gay News, Him* and *Fag Rag* [and the now defunct *International Journal of Greek Love*] than from all the scholarly journals indexed in the Modern Language Association's annual 80,000-item bibliography'.[2]

The first generation of gay literary and cultural critics had a very clear notion of the urgent tasks at hand. Gay literary criticism identified two urgent needs: the rediscovery of hidden and suppressed 'sexually heretic' texts, and the restoration of the homosexual subtext and context of major classics tampered by heterotextual cleansing (e.g. Whitman's 'ameliorated' editions). The oppositional project of emerging gay literary criticism also questioned a number of broader political and theoretical assumptions typical of male bourgeois culture. On the one hand gay critics set out to dismantle the assumption that the artistic expressions of gay male sexuality could never represent universal values and feelings, and for that reason were outside the bounds of 'common morality' and 'common culture'. On the other hand, a long-standing battle was waged against the cruder versions of (Freudian) psychoanalysis which targeted homosexuality as both an individual and a social perversion.

Along with the liberation of gay literature from the claws of censoring homo-phobia came a number of very important editorial projects: the gathering of gay bibliographies and anthologies of past homosexual literature. Given the crucial relationship of gay literary criticism with a community struggling for a sense of identity, the collection of loose homosexual strands into a single homotextual continuum should not be underestimated. The appeal of gay anthologies testifies to the remarkable figure of the male homosexual as 'reader', becoming a subject thanks to the gathering of the multiple texts in which he finds his 'voice'. In the 1970s such anthologies as B. Reade's *Sexual Heretics* and I. Young's *The Male Muse: A Gay Anthology* came to complement earlier collections couched in more ambiguous terms (e.g. Anderson and Sutherland's *Eros: An Anthology of Male Friendship*, 1963).[3]

The gay liberation movement did not start to make headway in the academic institutions until the late 1970s, and then only through the effort of single-minded pioneers. There was a handful of gay scholars but not yet a discipline of 'gay studies' recognized as academically relevant or scientifically 'sound'. Much of the knowledge stimulated by the gay liberation movement found its natural place in the small gay independent presses; similarly, the first gay academic essays were published either by gay publishers or by local presses not affiliated with the universities. Thus, even though in 1974 Louis Crew and Rictor Norton devoted a seminal issue of *College English* magazine to the 'Homosexual imagination – in literature – in the classroom – in criticism', their first book-length gay studies came out respectively for New York's Revisionist Press and for ETC Publications in Palm Springs.

The key concept for the development of gay literary studies during this phase of 'identity politics' was the idea of 'homosexual tradition'. The post-Stonewall gay male critic was interested in liberating the homosexual author and his text from the cultural vacuum to which heterosexual criticism had consigned them, consequently liberating the homosexual reader as well from his existential vacuum by handing back to him a literature he could relate to. The literary and political task was thus to re-establish severed connections, and by doing so allow them to spread out into the future. The strong sense of a tradition was particularly felt and emphasized in American gay literary studies.[4] Even books published more than a decade later, while acknowledging a much more complex interplay in the genealogy of a 'gay tradition', effectively pay homage to and build upon a canonical consensus made possible by the earlier tradition-builders in gay literary studies.[5]

Constructing the canon meant re-establishing the organic relationship between the 'historical milieu and biography' that 'can deepen our understanding of an author's work'[6], and tracing how the 'author's awareness of himself as a homosexual has affected how and what he wrote'.[7] Even though some critics felt that gay literary studies had as their own specific field 'homotextuality',[8] rather than the fleshing out of a homosexual 'Hall of Fame', the homosexual canon could hardly dispense with an implicit reliance on some kind of lived and felt experience of the 'founding fathers'. The bond between reader and writer fashioned by the gay critics (as builders of a symbolic community sharing a common treasure of texts) was somehow patterned after the bond of mutual recognition and father–son relationship. In a way the homosexual literary tradition refigures younger readers (and writers too) as 'children', thus providing a powerful alternative model of cultural parenthood, all the more necessary for a gay subject who has lacked peer socialization and has been brought up as an alien in heterocentred families.

Stabilizing concepts such as 'homosexual identity', 'tradition' and 'continuity' have helped to build a pattern of visibility for gay writing, reading and self-consciousness. It would be inaccurate, however, to portray the early phase of gay literary criticism as blind to the contradictions inherent in a rigid dichotomous view of the homo/hetero binary. The essay on 'Ganymede raped' by Rictor Norton, for instance, did not limit itself to a purely liberationist politics of textual restoration.[9] After pointing out the difficulty of defining 'homosexual literature' Norton actually rejected the idea of a separate homosexual monolith and surprisingly went on to suggest that 'before one knows what's happening, *the entire Western literary tradition will be subsumed by the homosexual literary tradition*' (Norton's italics). The metaphor of rape was provocatively turned upside down. As polymorphous forms of 'positive or negative, dominant or subordinate, overt or latent' homosexuality were gradually seen to permeate all texts, there was eventually no heterosexual left to speak of! In Norton's essay heterosexuality is always already undermined by diffuse homosexualization. The reappropriation of fantasies of gay counter-dominance can be indulged in because the Western literary canon embodies the contradictory nature of a male heterosexuality both dominant and subverted.

Clearly, the notions of self-affirmative gay criticism, tradition-building and historical reconstruction still left a great number of unanswered questions. These, as shown by Norton's stunning reversal, basically have to do with the conceptual definition of an autonomous, self-evident and empirically discrete 'thing' named homosexual experience, translating itself into texts and recognized by the homosexual reader as something pertaining to his own being. Could such autonomy, self-evidence and empirical nature be taken as a matter of fact? The task of canon construction which was (and is) so important for all gay literary criticism based on identity politics also left a legacy of open questions. What criteria of selection and exclusion will shape our gay canon?[10] How does one discriminate between *degrees* of homotextuality? Need a homosexual tradition comprise only positive images of the homosexual, and if so how to reconcile and evaluate the coded indirectness of much (though not all) pre-Stonewall 'gay literature', which furthered not only positive forms of subcultural recognition but also dominant homophobic stereotypes? How can one subscribe to the notion of a separate, or separable, homosexual tradition without accounting for the fact that what renders a text 'homosexual' may either be the biographical homosexuality of the author, its hidden homosexual coding, its latent homosexual meaning, its textual reception, all of these or a variable combination of these? The complex negotiations of meaning that make a text 'homotextual', and the interpretive strategies, no less political than literary, that are brought to bear on the texts in order to 'deliver' a homosexual tradition were already glimpsed in the early phase of gay literary criticism, but the theoretical and methodological tools used by many of those gay radicals did not help to illuminate those aspects of 'homotextual construction'.

In other words, there was the occasional acknowledgement of the problematic nature of the opposition between a homosexual and a heterosexual tradition, but the interpretive paradigm and the ethical-political imperative of gay liberation turned those unsolved problems into a kind of 'necessary blindspot'. Things changed greatly with the decisive influence of Michel Foucault's *History of Sexuality* on gay literary studies, especially from the mid-1980s onwards.[11] The historicity of the notion of sexuality and the investigation of its multiple construction in modern Western culture has had a number of radical consequences and has pointed to a widely different approach to 'gay criticism'. If sexuality is no longer thought of as a basically natural drive unchangeable throughout human history, then the notion of a 'homosexual tradition' running from classical Greece to twentieth-century modernity will itself be an ideological construct, tied to a specific moment in the construction of modern 'sexual identity'. Hence the so-called 'constructionist' approach to homosexuality, which is critical of all illusions of naturalness in the identities that we employ. It is worth stressing that the move towards theories of socio-ideological construction of sexuality antedated Foucault's book (cf. anthropologist Mary McIntosh[12] and sociologist Jeffrey

Weeks)[13] and were more generally in keeping with post-structuralist critiques of the autonomy of the subject and of its scope for agency. It was Foucault's impact, nevertheless, that gave new impetus to a revision of traditional (radical, liberal or Marxist) models of gay oppositional subjectivity.

The empirical basis for the 'detection' of homosexuality through the ages was also undermined. Since for Foucault knowledge is always implicated with power, the medical discourse that originated many of the categories of sexual identity now taken for granted (including 'homosexuality' itself) is more an active producer than a simple discoverer of them. Therefore whenever gay literary critics choose to uncover a 'homosexual' tradition spanning the ages they are themselves making a power move, whose consequences are to be critically viewed. Gay literary critics will select their field of enquiry and their methodological approaches to the texts in a very different manner according to the strategy each wishes to pursue: whether he wants to produce 'identification' by way of 'finding the same', or to promote 'disidentification' by way of 'finding the different and the divergent', both within the field of homosexuality and across the homo/hetero binary. The two divergent approaches of recent gay discourse have often been termed 'essentialist' and 'constructionist' (a terminology largely borrowed from analogous controversies in feminism).

Gay literary critics, influenced by Foucault, have furthered at least three complementary strategies, often divisively contrasting with priorities held by gay 'essentialists': the move (a) towards cultural studies; (b) towards history; (c) towards 'queer'.

(a) The privileged focus on homosexual 'authors' should be challenged by an emphasis on 'discourse'. The meaning of homosexuality is defined less by the intentional meaning invested in the author as by the general conditions that allow 'sexuality' to be articulated, communicated, interpreted, or indeed spoken about at all, according to specific sociocultural constraints. Hence the move from purely literary to cultural studies.

(b) Foucault argued that sexuality is a relatively modern specialized discourse, a form of aetiological and taxonomical knowledge. If so, students of early modern literature should learn to discard assumptions about what now qualifies as homosexuality and employ other interpretive and descriptive tools. Hence the move to historical investigations of how sexuality was conceptualized and represented in early modern[14] and modern texts, with an emphasis on discontinuities.

(c) If there is no 'homosexual monolith' but a mutually implicated homo/hetero binary that, in analogy with gender binaries, unstably binds one to the other (each depends on the other in order to be intelligible at all), the gay literary critic should cease to view gay literature as a self-enclosed subject, and broaden its scope to take into account the historical and relational nature of his/her definitional categories. Hence the need to investigate the nexus that binds together male homo- and heterosexuality in our gender system rather than posit their transhistorical opposition.[15]

Gay literary studies inflected by Foucauldian genealogies of sexuality and by queer/ feminist readings emphasizing the mutual implication of sexuality and gender have produced a second discontinuity after the Stonewall revolution. Gay criticism is increasingly interested in how 'gay discourse' engages in a dialectical relationship with dominant forms of culture. Part of gay and lesbian criticism has abandoned its early 'minoritizing' strategy (cf. E.K. Sedgwick, *Epistemology of the Closet*, 1990)[16] centred on identity politics and entered the 'queer moment' – that is, an oppositional discourse not bound to identity politics.[17]

The by no means easy 'passage' from a gay to a queer paradigm can be compared to queer literary criticism increasingly questioning the matter-of-fact homosexuality of authors and texts and taking on board all the interpretive elements of sexual dislocation and instability, particularly when sexual identities are intersected by race, class and gender identities that complicate them. The queer critic will tend to emphasize gay effects at least as much as gay identities, never seeing those identities as inseparable from discursive practices, including those of dissident reading.[18] In this light what 'homosexual' means is never just one thing but a 'cluster' of meanings developing across different 'locations'. Especially relevant to queer literary studies will be all those strategies that involve crossings and transitivity, such as camp style and performativity in general (for example in theatrical cross-dressing practices).[19]

Leaving behind the homosexual in order to embrace queer cross-identifications may indeed seem a gross misconduct and even a betrayal of our responsibilities towards the gay community and its hard-won traditions of cultural (and physical) survival. Many gay critics feel uncomfortable in relinquishing safe knowledges that have been proved empowering. The case can be argued that even now there is a certain backlash against queer theory, which is seen as a weakening of homosexual subjectivities. The appeal of a 'gay canon' is still evident in titles such as *The Gay Canon*, by Robert Drake, or *Unlimited Embrace. A Canon of Gay Fiction, 1945–1995*, by Reed Woodhouse, showing a definite impatience with queer deconstruction or feminist contaminations. Even new gay literary histories (Mark Lilly, Gregory Woods) speak to a resilient desire for a kind of historical permanence and separate visibility that will counteract the ravages of AIDS.[20]

On the other hand it may be that forms of betrayal are necessary not so much for the survival of the homosexual but for the continued possibility of perverse resistance to dominant discourses – a possibility that the homosexual has, at specific historical junctures, found him/herself to embody. By trying to leave open those outward-opening connections, a queering practice may foreground the visibility of other differences, some of them uneasily enclosed by the blanket term 'homosexuality', others exceeding it (transsexuals, bisexuals . . .).

Notes

1 On the canon of homosexually identified readings at the turn of the century see James Gifford, *Dayneford's Library. American Homosexual Writing 1900–1913* (Amherst:

Massachusetts University Press, 1995). Walt Whitman's early transatlantic fortune is well documented in Robert K. Martin, *The Homosexual Tradition in American Poetry* (Austin: Texas University Press, 1979; new expanded version Iowa City: Iowa University Press, 1998).

On Victorian sexual politics and culture see at least Richard Dellamora, *Masculine Desire: the Sexual Politics of Victorian Aestheticism* (Chapel Hill: North Carolina University Press, 1990); Linda C. Dowling, *Hellenism and Homosexuality in Victorian Oxford* (Ithaca, NY: Cornell University Press, 1994); Joseph Bristow, *Effeminate England: Homoerotic Writing after 1885* (New York: Columbia University Press, 1995). On the centrality of Oscar Wilde's trial see Ed Cohen, *Talk on the Wilde Side* (London: Routledge, 1993).

For further bibliography of literary-historical essays cf. the massive *Lesbian and Gay Studies Reader*, ed. Henry Abelove, Michele A. Barale and David M. Halperin. (New York: Routledge, 1993).

2 Rictor Norton, 'Ganymede Raped. Gay Literature. The critic as censor', *Gay Sunshine Journal 23* (Nov–Dec 1974), reprinted in Winston Leyland (ed.), *Gay Roots. Twenty Years of Gay Sunshine. An Anthology of Gay History, Sex, Politics and Culture* (San Francisco: Gay Sunshine Press, 1991), pp. 328–36.

3 Ian Young, *The Male Muse: A Gay Anthology* (Trumansburg: Crossing Press, 1973); Brian Reade *Sexual Heretics: Male Homosexuality in English Literature from 1850 to 1900* (London: Routledge, 1970); Alistair Sutherland and Patrick Anderson (eds), *Eros: An Anthology of Male Friendship* (New York: Citadel Press, 1963).

4 Rictor Norton, *The Homosexual Literary Tradition* (New York: Revisionist Press, 1974); Roger Austen, *Playing the Game: The Homosexual Novel in America* (Indianapolis: Bobbs-Merrill, 1977); Robert K. Martin, *The Homosexual Tradition in American Poetry* (Austin: Texas University Press, 1990). A recent restatement in Claude J. Summers, *Gay Fiction: Wilde to Stonewall. Studies in a Male Literary Tradition* (New York: Continuum, 1990).

5 Cf. David Bergman's *Gaiety Transfigured. Gay Self-Representation in American Literature* (Madison: Wisconsin University Press, 1991).

6 Rictor Norton, 'Ganymede Raped', p. 331.

7 Robert K. Martin, *Homosexual Tradition in American Poetry*.

8 A term proposed by Jerome Stockinger in the groundbreaking collection edited by Louie Crew, *The Gay Academic* (Palm Springs: ETC Publications, 1978).

9 Norton, 'Ganymede Raped', pp. 328–36.

10 The eclectic nature of canon selection gets even wilder in Gregory Woods's *History of Gay Literature. The Male Tradition* (New Haven and London: Yale University Press, 1998), which manages to sweep from Homer to David Leavitt; his transcultural historical narrative can be achieved only by allowing in equal measure works by openly gay men, works in which homosexual activity occurs, and works that manifest a gay 'sensibility'.

11 Michel Foucault, *The History of Sexuality. Vol.1 An Introduction* (New York: Pantheon Books, 1978).

12 Mary McIntosh, 'The Homosexual Role', *Social Problems* 16, 2 (1968), pp. 182–92.

13 Jeffrey Weeks, *Coming Out: Homosexual Politics in Britain from the 19th Century to the Present* (London: Quartet Books, 1977).

14 The seminal study for Renaissance gay historical studies inflected by Foucauldian analysis is Alan Bray, *Homosexuality in Renaissance England* (London: Gay Men's Press, 1982). On 'sodomy' as a historically specific category not easily translatable in terms of 'homosexual identity' see Jonathan Goldberg, *Sodometries. Renaissance Texts, Modern Sexualities* (Stanford, CA: Stanford University Press, 1992) and Jonathan Goldberg (ed.), *Queering the Renaissance* (Durham, NC: Duke University Press, 1994).

15 A 'feminist model' for such a nexus was provided since 1985 by Eve K. Sedgwick, *Between Men. English Literature and Male Homosocial Desire* (New York: Columbia University Press). The strategy employed in *Between Men* is to foreground 'homosociality' rather than homosexuality, i.e. 'the whole range of male bonds that shape the social constitution'.

16 Eve Kosofsky Sedgwick, *Epistemology of the Closet* (Hemel Hempstead: Harvester Wheatsheaf, 1991).

17 Cf. David Halperin's book on Foucault as precursor of queer theory and activism: *Saint Foucault. Towards a Gay Hagiography* (New York and Oxford: Oxford University Press, 1995). According to Halperin, 'queer is by definition whatever is at odds with the normal, the legitimate, the dominant'. Queer is a possible reaction to the objectification of sexual identities produced by twentieth-century sexual discourse. By embracing resistance to the binary assimilation of sexual identities and by multiplying the chances for cross-identification, queer discourse and practice is clearly responding, according to Halperin, to a Foucauldian imperative of dislocation and invention, rather than harking back to the earlier myth of a stable homosexual subject endowed with full rights of citizenship in Western liberal society.

On the 'queer' turn in literature cf. Robert McRuer, *The Queer Renaissance: Contemporary American Literature and the Reinvention of Lesbian and Gay Identities* (New York: New York University Press, 1997).

18 In England dissident readings are emphasized from a cultural materialist standpoint by Alan Sinfield, *Cultural Poetics–Queer Reading* (Philadelphia: Pennsylvania University Press, 1994) as well as by Jonathan Dollimore, *Sexual Dissidence: Augustine to Wilde, Freud to Foucault* (Oxford: Clarendon Press, 1991).

19 David Bergman (ed.), *Camp Grounds: Style and Homosexuality* (Amherst: Massachusetts University Press, 1993); Moe Meyer (ed.), *The Politics and Poetics of Camp* (London: Routledge, 1994) with further bibliography.

20 Robert Drake, *The Gay Canon* (New York: Doubleday Anchor Books, 1998); Reed Woodhouse, *Unlimited Embrace. A Canon of Gay Fiction, 1945–1995* (Amherst: Massachusetts University Press, 1998); Gregory Woods, *A History of Gay Literature: The Male Tradition* (New Haven: Yale University Press); Mark Lilly, *Gay Men's Literature in the Twentieth Century* (New York: New York University Press, 1993).

10 Lesbian Literary Studies

Liana Borghi

Like gay studies, lesbian literary studies can be said to have developed as a counter-reading strategy. We can envisage a development from individual acts of solitary or shared pleasure in reading, loving, and tracking down forgotten texts, to wider cultural projects involving political self-awareness and community-building.

In North America, Jeannette Foster's 'Foreword' to *Sex Variant Women in Literature* (1956) foregrounded the connection between real-life experience and scholarly research – in her case, a forty-year-long path, from a homophobic episode to the study of scientific texts, and eventually to literary history and criticism. 'Lesbian literary studies' thus revealed from its official inception the main ingredients of a possible development: the double-cross of sexuality and cultural identity with issues of affiliation and readership.

When Foster's path-breaking study of French, German and English literature was published, Barbara Grier was just 23 years old. She had been on a lesbian track for seven years, and from her meeting with Foster stemmed the literary criticism of the pioneering lesbian magazine *The Ladder* (1956–70), aimed at mapping lesbian writing past and present – mostly minor characters in high literature, or pulp fiction. The essays collected in the 1975 edition of *The Lesbian in Literature* reviewed over 2,000 books.[1]

It almost seemed as if establishing a literary tradition was merely a question of retrieving 'the pearls of our lost culture', but studies in lesbian and gay cultures were then, and have been since, a construction hectically under way.[2] 'We believe that lesbian studies is essentially a grassroot movement,' stated Margaret Cruikshank in her introduction to *Lesbian Studies*, outlining at the same time the difficulties encountered by lesbians, personally and professionally, in the academic world.[3]

By that time lesbian feminism was firmly established in a troubled but strong alliance with the women's movement. A marker of this alliance, and of the non-sexualized political lesbianism of the 1970s, was Adrienne Rich's theorization of a lesbian continuum that posits for all women a cross-cultural and transhistorical latency of lesbianism, parallel to the grounding of every lesbian identity in (female) constructions of sex and gender.[4] If again it seemed a question of retrieving the pearls of a common identity, differences as well as difference among, between and within women were also under theoretical construction.

Audre Lorde, who had been one of the first to insist on 'how important differences are in our lives', said in an interview: 'The poem happens when I, Audre

Lorde, poet, deal with the particular instead of the "UNIVERSAL".'[5] But her friend Adrienne was not far behind in refiguring identity, earlier as a 'coat of many colors', and later, in 'The politics of location', as a form of hybrid consciousness, unmasking doctrines of objectivity and sustaining the possibility of cross-racial political solidarity based on location, embodiment and experience.

Narrative, observes Judith Roof, cannot exist or operate separately from 'identity, ideology, subjectivity, and sexuality – by which we organize existence and experience'.[6] It is not surprising, therefore, that the main topics under discussion in the 1970s became the much-revised core of subsequent lesbian literary studies:[7] the definition and theorization of the lesbian subject and lesbian literature in all its complex inner specificity and diversity; the 'ghosting', the spiriting away of lesbian characters and authors; the creation of a lesbian reader and text; the transmission of lesbian literature (media, publishing, the arts, the new technologies, teaching); and the relationship between heterosexual narrative structure and lesbian plots.

Over the past ten years – as the gay and lesbian canon expanded in breadth and depth, lesbian bodies became overtly sexualized, and lesbian identity fragmented and contradicted – these questions have been asked in a more complex language rooted both in feminist and gay theory, and in a variety of critical trends, from deconstruction to cultural studies. Lately, with the focus shifting from feminism to the gender-effacing challenge of queer theory, lesbian representation has reached yet another of its recurrent crisis points.

Although Sally Munt writes hopefully that 'our literary tradition is a history of the linguistic traces of a common identity',[8] according to Sue-Ellen Case 'the very term "lesbian" is slipping semiotically on the banana peel of mainstream and academic fashion'. In certain circles it has been evacuated and overwritten by the queer-derived *dyke*.[9] Indeed, nowadays the lesbian is not only apparitional and liminal but also metaphorical: a sexual subject position indicating not only a situation in space but the possibility of a heterotopia.[10] And if 'lesbian' is a contested word subjected to continuous renegotiation – a term that both constitutes and is constituted by subjectivities defined around sets of sexual desires – lesbian literature can only be an equally contested space where the process of defining subjects, contexts and meanings is constantly represented. Thus the transition (individual or collective) from gender rebellions to nameless but dangerous intimacies, to concepts of identity, and now to queer politics, involves issues of identification and representation that closely concern literary criticism. Establishing a canon and mapping fluid cultural parameters is a crucial commitment for writers, readers and critics alike.

After over three decades of militancy, as homosexuality becomes more visible and mainstream, the question of what exactly a gay or lesbian book is becomes harder to answer, and it is not by chance that so many critical texts of the past decade begin by interrogating that same question. Although we may surmise that Jeanette Winterson was nominated for the Lambda Award because she is an out lesbian, the fact that in 1993 she received the award for *Written on the Body*, a novel the gender of whose protagonist is never revealed, shows how much has changed from lesbian feminist days, when such golden tags were reserved for novels written by lesbians for lesbians featuring lesbian characters and reflecting lesbian political concerns.

If the utopian stage is over, the deconstructing stage is on. A wealth of new criticism is opening up new fields of enquiry where feminism may meet queer theory, sexuality interrogate narrative, passing and queering reflect upon each other, lesbian performance address the end of print culture, and Freud himself become a friendly fetish. The postmodern, post-structuralist shift established in the late 1980s now coexists happily with declaredly lesbian feminist publications.[11] If for a time these seemed a little too concerned with authorial identities, too thematic and descriptive, prone to what Eve Sedgwick has called 'weak theoretical acts'[12] as compared to the strong (and sometimes abstruse) critical performance of queer theory, the gap has now almost closed. The latest full-length studies, especially those by Julie Abraham, Carolyn Allen, Marilyn Farwell, Sally Munt and Judith Roof,[13] have given us narratological tools that link reading strategies to the reconstruction of the lesbian canon pursued by so many of us in different fields and countries. Although Gabriele Griffin, among others, fears that the construction of lesbian 'classics' may constitute an exclusionary practice, there can be little doubt about the value of Emma Donoghue's and Lisa Moore's reconstruction of a British 'sapphic' literary canon of the seventeenth and eighteenth centuries, which has shown yet again the importance of understanding changes in concepts of sexual identity in distant as well as recent history. Judith Schuyf's discussion, in this book, of the concept of 'knowledge' as central in the development of lesbian identity is a good case in point.[14]

But reconstructing the canon may certainly be viewed as a power move, and not just because we tend to read the past according to our wants and needs – to paraphrase Sedgwick, was there ever a lesbian Sappho? Most answers to that primary question, 'What is lesbian literature?' or 'What counts for lesbian literature?' (as Sally Munt asks, echoing Diana Fuss) involve issues of power and resistance to the varied and complex heteropatriarchal practice of eradicating lesbian desire. How not/to elide lesbianism by avoiding self/censorship is a topic also covered by Terry Castle's argument on the dematerialization of the lesbian – the well-known 'ghosting' effect in cinema, art and culture which materially re/inscribes lesbian in/visibility. Possibly because of lesbian investment in women's politics, the feminist effacement of lesbianism (Cheshire Calhoun's 'gender closet') has also been scrutinized time and again; recently by renée hoogland who explores various patterns of disclosure and concealment prescribing 'participative thinking' as an antidote. The term, borrowed from Bakhtin, indicates, more than a reading practice, 'a mode of *un-indifferent* thinking which entails engagement, commitment, involvement, concern, and indeed, *interest*'. On a similar wavelength, Kathleen Martindale laments the self-inflicted damage done by lesbians who do not read enough. By resisting reading they make lesbian theory and literature invisible, and fail to take advantage of their transforming power. This resistance appears especially regrettable in view of the traditional scarcity of lesbian texts.[15]

Indeed, literary visibility depends on access to publishing. Rightly, Catharine Stimpson reminds us of the power of reviewers, and many of us who are in print could add stories about the importance of adequate circulation, and the tyranny of sales figures. Many authors and critics discuss in books and magazines the concomitant weight of sexual, social and racial factors on the access to publishing. It may hearten some that Isabel Miller's novel *Patience and Sarah* (1973) was self-published, but umpteen other texts, especially those of lesbians who are less privileged and/or live in countries of stronger homophobia and/or fewer resources, may never see print. Homophobic censorship has caused lesbian references to be encoded (Gertrude Stein's 'Cow', Daphne Du Maurier's 'Cairo') and hidden behind masks and symbolic markers. Astute reading strategies, like Judith Butler's 'queering', are needed to enable the reader to detect a 'passing' text. Other impediments, as Kathleen Martindale and Sue Ellen Case have also pointed out, may be caused by the discriminatory distinction between high and low cultures, and others still by the dearth of translations from non-hegemonic cultures. Whereas the use of French lesbian/feminist theories is quite common in lesbian criticism from English-speaking countries, theories from other countries are seldom 'imported'. A rare application of the theories developed by the Milan Women's Bookstore Collective is to be found in an essay on lesbians in literature by Gabriele Griffin. The figuration of the symbolic mother and the concept of empowerment are used by Griffin to read the negotiation of power differentials by the mother–daughter–lover triangle in Radclyffe Hall's *The Unlit Lamp*.[16]

Obviously, a passion for theory permeates recent criticism. Dualisms and dichotomies have become literary sins of our postmodern times, and open-ended texts are virtuous in more senses than one. Sally Munt frowns on the reactionary constraint of dualisms used in literary criticism, as in the case of the moralistic attitude evidenced in Gillian Spragg's critique of Jane Rule's *Desert of the Heart*. Unfashionable forms of utopian separatism (as critiqued by Sonia Andermahr) also fall under her stern scrutiny. But she looks with approval at forms of textual and political freedom, like Jeanette Winterson's crossing over from marginal to dominant culture and vice versa in her fiction, or Lisa Henderson's avoidance of dichotomies like pornography/censorship in her critical work.[17]

There are many other examples of a similar position-taking. Teresa De Lauretis also writes some of her texts with the intent of defusing polarities. Her reading of Sheila MacLaughlin's 1987 film *She Must Be Seeing Things* disarms both the butch/femme and the s/m themes by casting the argument in terms of the relationship between fantasy and the real. Her essay 'The essence of the triangle' depolarizes the controversy between essentialism and constructionism, which has affected literary criticism as much as any other field.[18]

We find evidence of the 'intimate' intertextuality typical of lesbian criticism – an intricate pattern of careful cross-references often based on friendships, alliances, shared experience, esteem – in Tamsin Wilton, who uses similar strategies to defuse polarizations concerning identity, and to construct positive links with queer theory. In *Lesbian Studies*, in a short section on 'the metaphorical dyke', she dubs identity essentialist and redundant, and opts instead for identification, which is an interactive concept. But the likely attack on the politics of identity does not materialize. Rather, Wilton makes a detour into feminist theory and ends up justifying the contingent use of the term 'lesbian' on the basis of Julia Kristeva's politically expedient use of the term 'woman'.[19]

Paulina Palmer also tackles the representation of identity in fiction. In *Contemporary Lesbian Writing* she discusses the shift in recent lesbian narrative toward postmodernist strategies that highlight the fictionality of a text, moving away from identity politics towards unstable sexual and textual identities. The tortuousness of sexual identification and our lack of control on choice are exemplified by showing the 'queer' interaction of sex and fantasy in the work of Jeanette Winterson, Sarah Schulman and Jane DeLynn. In her book on the erotics of loss, Carolyn Allen also reads Winterson alongside Djuna Barnes and Rebecca Brown so as to reconstruct a narrative genealogy. Her neo-Freudian approach blends in fascinating ways with post-structuralism to uncover the dynamics of obsessive love, fusion and desperate lack performed in their narratives and to open up dark places, sexual as well as epistemological, between women lovers.

Those of us, from Sandra De Perini to Teresa De Lauretis, who would agree that it takes two women, not one, to make a lesbian, should read Julie Abraham's book on lesbian writing and modernist historical fiction, *Are Girls Necessary?*. Her opinion is that, for the timespan she deals with, all it takes to make a lesbian 'is one woman and a novel' (xvii). But the novel, unfortunately, is a formula fiction based on the very heterosexual plot which lesbian writers have attempted to circumvent in so many ways. This is why Willa Cather, Gertrude Stein, Djuna Barnes, Virginia Woolf, Mary Renault, Marguerite Yourcenar, Sylvia Townsend Warner and Bryher turned to history to reach beyond the limits imposed by the formulaic nature of the lesbian novel. Abraham, of course, is not the only one to address the lesbian subversion of heterosexual plots and plot structure. Elizabeth Meese, Terry Castle, Teresa De Lauretis and Janet Montefiore have also worked on this topic.[20] In her latest book, *Come As You Are*, Judith Roof focuses specifically on the rhetoric of visibility in coming-out narratives, which however tends to relocate homosexual characters within the larger heteronarratives from which they had been excluded.

The suspicion arises that critics may be driven to look for forms of lesbian narrative subversion by that romantic hope to validate lesbian identity described by Sally Munt in *Heroic Desire* (1998). And this validation is not only directed toward authors and characters, but also extended to readers. Most of the critical strategies I have outlined so far both address and create an ideal lesbian reader who can be somehow repositioned, 'changed' (and perfected?) by intervening in our understanding of storytelling and the functioning of narrative. Because, as Marilyn Farwell hopefully explains, the metaphoric lesbian subject exceeds discursive and narrative boundaries whether in experimental or traditional narratives, and by so doing may secure narrative agency for women readers. And this is perhaps the sustaining metanarrative of our lesbian literary studies.[21]

Notes

1 See Jeannette Foster's foreword to her own *Sex Variant Women in Literature* (Baltimore, MD: Diana Press, 1975), and Barbara Grier's afterword to that same text, p. 356, for a description of the various editions of *The Lesbian in Literature*. Noteworthy

is also Barbara Grier et al., *The Lesbian in Literature: A Bibliography* (Tallahassee, FL: Naiad Press, 1981).

2 The quotation is from Suzanne Raitt (1995) in her edited collection, *Volcanoes and Pearl Divers. Essays in Lesbian Feminist Studies* (London: Harrington Park Press, 1995).

3 Margaret Cruikshank *Lesbian Studies. Present and Future* (Old Westbury, NY: The Feminist Press, 1982), p. xiv.

4 Marilyn Farwell argues that 'the lesbian subject of this century is dependent on the expansion of the narrated categories of woman' in *Heterosexual Plots & Lesbian Narratives* (New York: New York University Press, 1996), p. 18. See also her discussion on feminism and the black lesbian community, especially, p. 157. I am including Monique Wittig in the 'non-sexualized' category, although her constructionist position ('one is not born a lesbian') does not fit cultural lesbianism.

5 Interview in Claudia Tate (ed.), *Black Women Writers at Work* (New York: Continuum, 1984), pp. 114, 109.

6 Judith Roof, *Come As You Are. Sexuality & Narrative* (New York: Columbia University Press, 1996) p. xvi. Adrienne Rich, 'Notes toward a politics of location', in Adrienne Rich *Blood, Bread, and Poetry: Selected Prose 1979–1985* (New York: Norton, 1986).

7 I am thinking in particular of Jane Rule, *Lesbian Images* (Garden City, NY: Doubleday, 1975); Lillian Faderman, *Surpassing the Love of Men. Romantic Friendship and Love between Women from the Renaissance to the Present* (New York: Morrow, 1981); Judy Grahn, *The Highest Apple. Sappho and the Lesbian Poetic Tradition* (San Francisco: Spinsters Inc., 1985); Bonnie Zimmerman, *The Safe Sea of Women. Lesbian Fiction 1969–1989* (Boston: Beacon, 1990); Paulina Palmer, *Contemporary Lesbian Writing. Dreams, Desire, Difference* (Buckingham: Open University Press, 1992); Elizabeth Meese, *(Sem)Erotics* (New York: New York University Press, 1992); Patricia Duncker, *Sisters & Strangers. An Introduction to Contemporary Feminist Fiction* (Oxford: Blackwell, 1992); Terry Castle, *The Apparitional Lesbian. Female Homosexuality and Modern Culture* (New York: Columbia University Press, 1993); Gabriele Griffin, *Heavenly Love? Lesbian Images in Twentieth-Century Women's Writing* (Manchester: Manchester University Press, 1993); Annamarie Jagose, *Lesbian Utopics* (London: Routledge, 1994). I am not listing Adrienne Rich or Audre Lorde, whose literary essays deserve a special discussion.

8 Sally Munt (ed.) *New Lesbian Criticism. Literary and Cultural Readings* (London and New York: Harvester, 1992), p. xi.

9 Sue-Ellen Case, *The Domain-Matrix. Performing Lesbian at the End of Print Culture* (Bloomington: Indiana University Press, 1996), p. 1.

10 For a discussion of these figurations see Marilyn Farwell, Elizabeth Meese and Bonnie Zimmerman in *Professions of Desire. Lesbian and Gay Studies in Literature*, ed. Bonnie Zimmerman and George E. Haggerty (New York: NLA, 1995); and Liana Borghi 'Liminaliens and others – but mostly vamps, dragons and women's SF', in G. Covi (ed.), *Critical Studies on the Feminist Subject* (Trento: Università di Trento, 1997) pp. 101–25. See also the discussion on the 'lesbian' as a utopian space in Jagose *Lesbian Utopics*. De Lauretis has dealt with the concept of heterotopia, and so does Sally Munt at the end of *Heroic Desire: Lesbian Identity and Cultural Space* (London: Cassell; New York: New York University Press, 1998). According to Foucault, a heterotopia is an absent commonality between a large number of possible orders. A simple definition of the term would point to a conceptual space where a new and different perspective is possible. In her discussion, Munt describes it as an 'enabling idea which permits the imagination to reconfigure space' (pp. 168–9).

11 See three publications on postmodern culture of the 1980s: respectively British, American and Canadian: *The Good, the Bad and the Gorgeous: Popular Culture's Romance with Lesbianism*, ed. Diane Hamer and Belinda Budge (London: Pandora, 1994), *The Lesbian Postmodern*, ed. Laura Doan (New York: Columbia University Press, 1994), and Kathleen Martindale, *Un/Popular Culture. Lesbian Writing after the Sex Wars* (Albany, NY: SUNY Press, 1997) and Sonya Andermahr's overview, ' "There's nowt so queer as

folk": lesbian cultural studies', in *Straight Studies Modified. Lesbian Interventions in the Academy*, ed. Gabriele Griffin and Sonya Andermahr (London: Cassell, 1997).

12 Eve K. Sedgwick, 'Paranoid reading and reparative reading', in *Novel Gazing. Queer Readings in Fiction* (Durham, NC: Duke University Press, 1997), p. 23.

13 Julie Abraham, *Are Girls Necessary? Lesbian Writing and Modern Histories* (New York: Routledge, 1996); Carolyn Allen, *Following Djuna. Women Lovers and the Erotics of Loss* (Bloomington: Indiana University Press, 1998); and Sally Munt, *Heroic Desire*.

14 Emma Donoghue, *Passions between Women. British Lesbian Culture 1668–1801* (London: Scarlet Press, 1993); Lisa Moore, *Dangerous Intimacies. Toward a Sapphic History of the British Novel* (Durham, NC: Duke University Press, 1997).

15 Cheshire Calhoun, 'The gender closet. Lesbian disappearance under the sign "women"', *Feminist Studies*, 21 (1) (Spring 1995); repr. in *Lesbian Studies. A Feminist Studies Reader*, ed. Martha Vicinus (Bloomington: Indiana University Press, 1996), pp. 209–32. renée hoogland, *Lesbian Configurations* (New York: Columbia University Press, 1997), p. 135; Martindale, *Un/Popular Culture*, pp. 35–36, 40.

16 See Catharine Stimpson, 'Afterword: lesbian studies in the 1990s', in *Lesbian Texts and Contexts*, ed. Karla Jay and Joanne Glasgow (New York: New York University Press, 1990), pp. 377–81; Judith Butler, *Bodies That Matter: On the Discursive Limits of 'Sex'* (New York: Routledge, 1994); Gabriele Griffin, '"We are family": lesbians in literature', in Griffin and Andermahr, *Straight Studies Modified*.

17 See Munt's introduction to *New Lesbian Criticism*, pp. xx–xxi.

18 See 'Sexual indifference and lesbian representation', *Theater Journal*, 40 (2) (1988): 155–77; 'The essence of the triangle', *Differences*, I (Summer 1989): 3–37 and also her most recent book, *The Practice of Love* (Bloomington: Indiana University Press, 1996).

19 Tamsin Wilton, *Lesbian Studies. Setting an Agenda* (London: Routledge, 1995), pp. 42–3.

20 Janet Montefiore in 'Listening to Minna: realism, feminism, and the politics of reading', in Raitt *Volcanoes*, pp. 123–46. See also Jean E. Kennard, 'Ourselves behind ourself: a theory for lesbian readers' (1984), in *Gender and Reading*, ed. Elizabeth A. Flynn and Patrocinio P. Schweickert (Baltimore: Johns Hopkins University Press, 1986) and Maaike Meijer, 'Poetry and seduction. On reading as a lesbian', in *Beyond Limits. Boundaries in Feminist Semiotics and Literary Theory*, ed. Liesbeth Braiwer (Groningen: Rijksuniversiteit, 1990), pp. 97–110.

21 See Munt *Heroic Desire*, p. 10 and Farwell, *Heterosexual Plots*, pp. 17–19.

11 Fashionably Queer: Lesbian and Gay Cultural Studies

renée c. hoogland

Presenting an overview of lesbian and gay cultural studies is no easy task. The phrase 'cultural studies' means different things to different people, depending on their institutional, sociocultural and geographical vantage points. Even in the English-speaking world, the term may refer to highly different fields of scholarly practice and critical enquiry. Indeed, if we allow for the diverse definitions that serve to demarcate 'cultural studies' as a specific domain within distinct sections of the Western academy, the label itself can be seen to branch off into more narrowly defined traditions of critical practice, emerging under various subheadings in the catalogues of academic book publishers, such as 'cultural theory', 'history of culture', 'literary and cultural studies', 'cultural criticism' and numerous other categorizing terms. Still, the central meanings of the term 'cultural studies' in the context of the Anglo-American academy, while clearly not unrelated or even incompatible, point to what are now commonly acknowledged as two divergent tendencies within its overall project. The British sociologist Stuart Hall, who is widely regarded as the founder of cultural studies as such, described these divergent tendencies as, in effect, two different paradigms (1980).

In the United Kingdom, often considered the discipline's 'homeland', the label 'cultural studies' is largely reserved for its sociological wing. Having its roots in the traditions of the Frankfurt School and the Centre for Cultural Studies at the University of Birmingham, British cultural studies is fundamentally political in nature, grounded in essentially Marxist assumptions, and takes the concept of ideology as its central point of orientation. The work of culture critics such as Richard Hoggart, Raymond Williams, E.P. Thompson and Stuart Hall himself can be seen to lie at the heart of a distinct although not strictly defined field of sociocultural analysis that has, since its founding in the late 1950s, evolved through the theoretical moments of culturalism, structuralism, Gramscian Marxism and, subsequently, post-structuralism and postmodernism (Storey, 1996).[1] The lasting influence of these 'founding fathers' is reflected in British gay and lesbian studies, recognizable in, for instance, an emphasis on the sociological analysis of the reception and audiences, and in the ways groups and classes reproduce and use cultural texts.

Current usage of the term 'cultural studies' in the US, while by no means apolitical in overall thrust, designates a realm of scholarly practice whose main focus is, in contrast, on the problem of textuality. Variously influenced by semiotics, psychoanalysis and theories of the subject (among other strands of so-called (post-)structuralist and deconstructive theory), this tradition of cultural studies in the first place explores how texts become effects for and in their readers. Rather than relying on various forms of sociological analysis, US cultural studies largely draws its inspiration from the more abstract forms of thought commonly referred to as 'continental philosophy' or 'French theory'. Important names here include those of such dissimilar figures as Roland Barthes, Louis Althusser, Jacques Lacan, Michel Foucault, Jean-François Lyotard and Jacques Derrida.

The practice of cultural studies both within and across disciplinary boundaries is as diverse as its theoretical foundations. While its earliest encounters were with literary criticism and social history, cultural studies today is variously produced at the intersections of more traditional fields like history, cultural anthropology, ethnography, the sociology of culture, philosophy and literary criticism, as well as more recent interdisciplinary fields, such as film theory and criticism, media and communication studies, and, most importantly, feminist, gender and multicultural or post-colonial studies. The term, then, designates a particularly elusive site on the current map of critical investigation, especially since its usage is not restricted to the Anglo-American academy. Still, even though culture critics on different parts of the European continent continue to produce their own distinct configurations of the field, the two central paradigms, or the textual and sociological wings characterizing Anglo-American cultural studies, can be seen to overlap to various degrees and intertwine within them.[2] Rather than tracing such distinctions in detail, I shall steer a middle course among the many different varieties of current cultural critique and foreground their significance for lesbian and gay studies.[3] In addition to discussing specifically lesbian, gay and queer cultural practices, I shall focus on the critical and theoretical concerns these interrelated fields of scholarly enquiry have in common.

A first point of overlap is, indeed, the complexity of demarcating the respective domains. In their shared (inter)disciplinary breadth and cross-disciplinary significance, lesbian, gay and cultural studies underscore a point made by cultural anthropologist Clifford Geertz, who described the boundaries of cultural studies as 'essentially contestable' (1973: 29). The ability to engage a variety of critical and cultural practices, ranging from both popular and 'high' forms of art and literature to philosophy, history, ethnography, as well as certain social scientific discourses, attests to the relevance of cultural analysis for Western scholarship generally, and for lesbian and gay studies in particular. But the reverse holds equally true: cultural studies has been important for the development of lesbian and gay cultural critique, but the latter forms of intellectual practice have also been influential in reshaping the project of cultural studies.

The establishment of lesbian and gay studies in the Western academy reflects the profound inter-implication of the two fields. Lesbian and gay collaboration in the academy is of relatively recent date. While uniting them in the quest for equal civil rights, the launching of the 'gay revolution' in 1969 also marked the beginning of a gradual parting of the ways between lesbians and gay men, a drifting apart that became most visible in their different forms of social organization and cultural practice. While large numbers of gay men in the early 1970s began to celebrate their sexual liberation by participating actively in a rapidly expanding gay bar culture (and its unprecedented opportunities for casual sex), many lesbians became involved in the simultaneously burgeoning women's liberation movement. As a result, lesbian feminist scholars tended to ally themselves with their straight 'sisters' rather than their gay brothers to further the cause of women's lib generally and of feminist criticism in particular. As Teresa De Lauretis points out, throughout the 1970s and early 1980s, white gay male scholarship evolved quite separately from white lesbian feminist critical theory and practice, especially in the USA (1991: v). Only from the second half of the 1980s onwards did these distinct critical traditions begin to coalesce to constitute the diversified field now known as lesbian and gay studies. The AIDS crisis, which led to new sociopolitical alliances among all kinds of sexual 'outcasts', and a growing sense of frustration among lesbians with the (largely unquestioned) heterocentrism prevailing in much feminist discourse, played different yet equally determining roles in this process of increased collaboration.

The tradition of white gay male critical discourse resembles the project of cultural studies in the British sense of the term, in that it developed more or less in line with the central disciplines in which it finds its starting points, i.e. (literary) historiography and sociology. Lesbian cultural critique, in contrast, closely parallels the 'textual wing' of cultural studies, finding its main inspiration in Anglo-American feminist thought and various post-structuralist theoretical models that came to prominence in the course of the 1980s via French feminism. So, by trying to integrate these divergent traditions, the establishment of lesbian and gay studies in the Western academy marks a successful coming together of the two tendencies, or paradigms, subtending (and dividing) the domain of cultural studies as a whole.

This merger across both disciplinary and gender lines should not, however, be seen only in the light of recent sociopolitical developments. Despite their distinct institutional origins and disciplinary backgrounds, lesbian and gay scholars have always had several basic ideas and assumptions in common. There is, first, the presupposition that practices of culture are by definition *social* practices, that is to say, intrinsically bound up with structures of power and ideology. Secondly, lesbian and gay scholars share a joint focus on the position of the subject, as opposed to the object, of cultural practice; in other words, they each in their own ways pay particular attention to the role of the individual in the production, distribution and reception of cultural texts. The significance of these concerns will soon become clear.

Not unlike other 'minority' discourses (feminist, black, and a variety of post-colonial and interethnic studies), lesbian and gay cultural critics of the late 1960s–early 1970s initially set out to bring to light the largely neglected (or suppressed) but in fact extensive historical traditions of gay and lesbian life and artistic production. They also began openly to re-read what had generally been received as unambiguously heterosexual texts. Their aim was, first, to demonstrate that gay and lesbian culture was not so much 'non-existent' as insistently 'hidden' from history within mainstream scholarly practice,[4] and therewith to provide viable role models for lesbian and gay readers, writers and critics alike. Secondly, they sought to show up the largely unnoticed (or repressed) homosexual subtexts of dominant cultural production and to expose Western society's deep-rooted tradition of homophobia.[5] Employing our own 'perverse' perspectives to produce such different, alternative readings of mainstream history and cultural texts had, of course, been part and parcel of gay and lesbian experience long before the 1970s, if only because of the virtual non-existence of (even potentially) gay/lesbian cultural representations during the pre-Stonewall era. As 'sexual deviants,' lesbians and gays had been forced to read between the lines of ostensibly straight texts well before such strategies of reading 'against the grain' became the established theoretical paradigm in the age of deconstruction. Sally Munt hence rightly observes:

> We are particularly adept at extracting our own meanings, at highlighting a text's latent content, at reading 'dialectically', at filling the gaps, at interpreting the narrative according to our introjected fictional fantasies, and at foregrounding the intertextuality of our identities. (1992: xxi)

There was, however, a particularly radical edge to the 'different' re-readings lesbian and gay scholars began to incorporate into their writings. By doing so, they not only openly questioned 'common-sense knowledge' about the presumed natural-ness of sexual identities, but also challenged, from within the 'official' theoretical arena, the so-called authenticity of identity categories *per se*. Alternative cultural readings generated by various previously 'excluded' groups, but by gay and lesbian critics in particular, would have an impact on the project of cultural studies as a whole, moving far beyond the as yet limited realms of 'minority' studies proper.

Gay and lesbian scholarship newly corroborated the idea that any form of cultural production is inherently ambivalent. Textual meanings can never be fixed once and for all, and all cultural production is subject to a continuing process of re-vision and re-appropriation. Perhaps more importantly, however, these critiques also made clear that the production of meaning(s) does not depend only on the signifying operations of a given text, but is also critically informed by the desires, fantasies and assumptions each reading/spectating subject brings to it. The exposure of the profoundly subjective nature of all cultural practice, especially though not only where (unconscious) sexual preferences are concerned, helped to enforce upon the larger critical community the realization that, just as members of 'minority' groups bring 'special interests' to cultural texts in order to construct their own 'specific' truths, so are mainstream critics (that is, white, heterosexual, middle-class males) equally engaged in the production of partial, rather than 'universal', meanings. While all subsequent modes of lesbian, gay and, lately, queer practices of cultural critique continue to emphasize the subject's constitutive role in the production of cultural meanings, it is possible to trace various shifts in focus, both within the respective traditions of lesbian feminist and gay male scholarship and in what is now also called the 'new studies of sexuality'.[6]

Where lesbian and gay cultural critics were initially concerned primarily with exposing the heterosexist operations of mainstream cultural processes (Becker et al., [1981] 1995; Wood, [1978] 1995), they soon also directed attention to the growing stream of new, openly lesbian and gay cultural production entering the (popular) cultural market from the early 1970s onwards. Not content merely to criticize the negative stereotypes and pathologizing discourses on 'deviant' sexualities that prevailed in dominant cultural – and, indeed, critical – practice, scholars and social scientists also strove to highlight the positive images and articulations of lesbian and gay desires in newly burgeoning countercultural activities (Jackson and Persky, 1982). Additional efforts were made to recover such forms of cultural practice as had flourished in the gay and lesbian underground in previous decades despite severe social pressure (Bronski, 1984; Garber, 1992; Hadleigh, 1991; Russo, 1981 [1987]). Both the search for positive images and the recovery of an autonomous tradition of lesbian and gay culture fitted well within the larger picture of liberatory politics that characterized the post-revolutionary era in most Western societies (Miller, 1995). In the course of the 1980s, however, the growing visibility of gays and lesbians in the sociocultural realm increasingly became overshadowed by the ongoing AIDS crisis and a swell in homophobic and misogynous sentiment concomitant with the rise of the New Right, anti-feminism, and a 'politically correct' backlash.

These contradictory developments – growing visibility of a variety of 'abnormal' people within an (at least in the US and a large part of Western Europe) increasingly conservative political climate – provided the impetus for the emergence of new modes of cultural and critical practice that came to the fore in the second half of the 1980s under the term *queer*. Queer, originally a pejorative term used to underscore the pathological nature of sexual 'deviants', was adopted by some gays and lesbians as a positive term of reinforcement and self-empowerment (De Lauretis, 1991; Signorile, 1993). At once serving to cast off the chains of heterosexist oppression in society at large and to escape from the subcultural rules of political correctness (frequently perceived as equally confining), 'queer' has since 'become an attractive and oppositional self-label that acknowledges a new cultural context for politics, criticism, reception-consumption, and production' (Creekmur and Doty, 1995: 6).[7]

Instead of focusing strictly on gay- and lesbianness, queer criticism insists on expanding its purview to include other forms of sociocultural exclusion, for instance, along the lines of gender, race/ethnicity, class, age and nationality. Not to be understood as additional differences to be enumerated alongside – or indeed, subordinated to – sexual differences, multiple forms of differentiation are regarded as fully interdependent forms of personal identity and sociocultural stratification. Hence, Creekmur and Doty argue, queer critics

> not only resist mainstream definitions of sexuality and identity but put themselves in positions to question gay and lesbian orthodoxies that, for example, continue to marginalize black gay men or Chicana lesbians, or that isolate gay men from lesbians, or that have strict and narrow political positions on controversial issues like drag, pornography, sadomasochism, fetishism, and bisexuality. (1995: 6)

Queer theorists, in line with activist groups like ACT UP and the Lesbian Avengers, tend to adopt an 'in-your-face' approach both to their objects of analysis and to their envisaged audiences. As a response to the cultural mainstreaming of gay and lesbian 'lifestyles' and as a rejection of (increasingly successful) attempts of certain gays and lesbians, especially in the more affluent parts of Western Europe and the USA, actively to blend into the mainstream, the slogan 'We're here, we're queer, get used to it!' adequately reflects this confrontational attitude. In critical writings, the term 'queer' therefore functions next to but distinct from 'lesbian and gay' to mark, in the words of Teresa de Lauretis, a 'certain critical distance from the latter, by now an established and often convenient formula' (1991: iv). The editors of a recent collection of essays in fact go so far as to claim that 'Queer Theory is no more "about" lesbians and gay men than Women's Studies is "about" women' (Burston and Richardson, 1995: 1).

While not all self-identified queers would be willing to let go of a direct connection between sexual 'deviancy' and queer practice, there appears to be general agreement that queer criticism does not so much seek to enhance gay and lesbian visibility as to challenge cultural readings that fail to take sufficiently into account the operations of all forms of (sexual) differentiation. What Jeffrey Hilbert has remarked with respect to the radical drag community, then, could be said to hold true for queer culture and criticism as a whole: both are centrally motivated by a 'desire to get audiences thinking about their own sexuality' in whatever terms they define themselves (1995: 469). An effective strategy for accomplishing this is to show up queerness at the very heart of dominant culture. With suggestive titles like *Queering the Pitch* (Brett et al., 1994), *Making Things Perfectly Queer* (Doty, 1993), and *Fear of a Queer Planet* (Warner, 1993), recent volumes of gay and lesbian criticism hold up for scrutiny the undeniably queer aspects of those often revered, canonized products of a cultural mainstream that insists on seeing itself as sexually 'normal' – hence normative. Such work furthermore brings out into the open that queer viewing, reading and listening practices are not the sole prerogative of self-identified queers. Since 'abnormal' sexual meanings are an intrinsic, though repressed, part of both established and popular culture, 'taking queer pleasure' in cultural production, whether secretly or openly indulged in, is a form of practice available to even the 'straightest' of audiences (Gevers et al., 1993; Sinfield, 1994).

Its amenability to co-optation and re-signification by both mainstream and 'minority' audiences has made the realm of mass culture (film, television, popular music, photography, advertising, fashion) a particularly productive site for radical lesbian, gay and queer investigation.[8] It is worth while to look at some of this work in slightly more detail.

Popular culture has of old constituted a 'privileged' domain in gay and lesbian lives and experiences. One reason for this is that, like other 'disenfranchised' groups, queers of all stripes and colours have historically been denied equal access, or perhaps more precisely, access on their own terms to the prevailingly heterocentric realm of more elite forms of cultural expression. While some literary figures, such as Oscar Wilde, Henry James, E.M. Forster, Virginia Woolf, André Gide and Marcel Proust, succeeded in gaining 'official' recognition despite their unspeakable (and often unspoken) inclinations, most gay and – especially – lesbian authors could traditionally establish themselves only by hiding behind 'straight' masks or by encoding 'queer' meanings in such a way as to make them practically unrecognizable to mainstream audiences. Before gay liberation began to take effect in the Western world, the majority of homosexual writers and artists had been largely confined to the subcultural realm of underground literature, special screenings, and private clubs for stage performances. If they made it into the mainstream, they were usually forced to keep their 'perverse' preferences hidden, either by leaving them unarticulated altogether or by using such complex modes of imagery and codification that they would go unnoticed by general audiences and, more importantly, by (both official and unofficial) censors. Still, while censorship laws and fear of social approbation put severe limitations on lesbian and gay cultural practice in the days before Stonewall, the paradigms of life 'in the closet' – a common metaphor for a private or subcultural space where one can experience one's 'forbidden' identity without fear of exposure – also produced what some regard as gay culture's most 'crucial contribution to modernism', that is, the discourse of *camp* (Creekmur and Doty, 1995: 2).[9]

Brought into the mainstream in the early 1960s, primarily through Susan Sontag's controversial 'Notes on camp' ([1964]1982), camp initially emerged as a kind of attitude, a sensibility, in the gay subcultures of earlier decades. Increasingly recognized as a gay phenomenon, flamboyant camp performances employed sophisticated forms of parody, presenting 'different' readings of the social text in order to 'deflate the pretensions of mainstream culture while elevating what that same culture devalued or repressed' (Creekmur and Doty, 1995: 2). At once 'casual and severe, affectionate and ironic', camp was both a means to rewrite and disturb dominant meanings and values and a mode of 'insider's' knowledge to express and circulate whatever was in vogue in the subcultural domain (ibid.).

Camp, in Philip Core's phrase, is 'the lie that tells the truth' (1984), and as such, a form of sub- or countercultural resistance. Gay liberation, especially its insistence on visibility and 'outness', caused many gays in the early 1970s nonetheless to turn away from it. The new, politicized visibility of lesbian and gay culture did not mean that camp was altogether lost, however. While 'old camp', in its closeted guise, continued to flourish in certain subcultural niches, new modes of camp have since been variously reintroduced, emerging in specific styles, attitudes and performances with a notably gay, lesbian or, indeed, queer quality. 'New camp' primarily seeks to inscribe 'queerness' on the margins of mainstream culture, to articulate the special relationship between sexual deviance and the popular, by, for example, exploiting humorously the queer significance of such lesbian and gay icons as Bette Davis, Judy Garland and Marlene Dietrich, or, in a slightly different vein, Diana Ross, Barbra Streisand and, more recently, Madonna (Doty, 1993; Frank and Smith, 1993; Schwartz, 1993). New camp, apart from offering high-class entertainment, emphatically questions the 'notion of a mainstream culture or preferred (read straight, white, middle-class male) cultural readings' (Creekmur and Doty, 1995: 4).

Although lesbians in the 1950s and 1960s occasionally used campy styles to articulate their relationship to popular culture, such engagement more often took shape through 'reading strategies involving identification (sometimes cross-gendered) and erotics' (Creekmur and Doty, 1995: 5). If only because lesbians, even more than gay men, have historically had (and continue to have) great difficulty in gaining positions of power and control in popular culture industries, little lesbian cultural production predates the 1970s. While recent efforts in lesbian criticism have brought to light an extensive canon of lesbian films, movie stars (Weiss, 1993), and opera divas (Castle, 1993), as well as a long-standing tradition of lesbian (popular) literature and pulp fiction (Radstone, 1988; Zimmerman, 1990), a more 'out' form of lesbian culture flourishing throughout the 1970s, especially in West Germany and the US, was what was obliquely labelled 'women's (womyn's) music' (Stein, 1994). The most important contribution of lesbians to mainstream, feminist, gay and queer critical practices, however, was the development of advanced theoretical tools to analyse both mainstream and subcultural production.

In the late 1970s, lesbian feminist film critics in the US, writing in the then recently founded journal *Jump Cut*, were already producing complex ideological analyses of media representations of women, as well as incisive accounts of the politics involved in the production, distribution and reception of (mainstream) film, television and video (Becker et al., [1981] 1995). Such theoretical sophistication extends well into current modes of lesbian studies and continues to inform many other contemporary forms of radical cultural critique (Butler, 1991, 1994; De Lauretis, 1994; Hart, 1994; hoogland, 1997; Mayne, 1990; Munt, 1992; Roof, 1991).

The influence of queer practice on the overall critical community clearly testifies to the relative openness of the popular realm, which has enabled some lesbian and gay writers and artists to achieve both prominence and power within it. However, as the gradual assimilation of the discourse of camp also reflects (Ferris, 1993; Garber, 1992; Straayer, 1992), the inevitable side-effect of such mainstreaming is that radical gay/lesbian cultural production loses some of its critical edge once it is embraced by general audiences. Moreover, the process of co-optation necessarily works both ways, allowing for mutual appropriation by dominant and non-dominant sociocultural groups alike. A poignant illustration of this is provided by a form of popular culture that has played a central role in (re)defining gay/lesbian identities throughout the century, that is, popular and showbiz music.[10]

If there is a single musical style that has become closely associated with gay culture, it is disco (Hughes, 1993). Rather than merely a form of music, disco represents, in Richard Dyer's view, a 'certain sensibility' encompassing historically and culturally specific 'kinds of dancing, club, fashion, film' (1990: 407). In the liberated atmosphere of the pre-AIDS era, disco formed, as it were, the soundtrack to the white gay males' celebration of their new freedom in the openness of the public dance floor. While rapidly spreading into the mainstream, going on to affect the overall sound of pop, the roots of 1970s disco music, however, do not lie in white gay dance clubs, but go back, as Anthony Thomas points out, to the 'small underground gay black clubs of New York City' ([1989] 1995: 438). Like so many other popular models influenced by African and African-American cultural traditions, disco acquired commercial viability only after having been 'white-washed' through its appropriation by the predominantly white, gay male population of North American dance clubs.

The history of disco illustrates that any popular cultural form is by definition appropriable, whether by other 'minority' groups or by the avant-gardes of the cultural majority. While the adoption of gay black musical styles into white gay male dance culture is an example of the former, the incorporation of queer fashion styles into the commercial world of advertising and the capitalist clothing industry forms a striking example of the latter (Fuss, 1992). The inherent reciprocity of the process of cultural reappropriation, and hence of potential re-signification, is directly linked to the nature and purposes of consumer culture as such.

Unlike traditional forms of art and literature, pop cultural products are commodities to be consumed. Produced to make a profit rather than to elevate its recipients to the lofty realms of high aesthetic pleasure, pop needs a mass audience both to ensure and to legitimize its existence.[11] Consumer products tend to appeal to the widest range of possible audiences, to speak to many different (groups of) people at once. Mass culture is thus by definition more 'generic' in form and content than any of the so-called high art forms that deliberately address more partial, specialized audiences. This is not to say that the latter are necessarily less 'commercial' or less 'capitalist' than popular culture, for Western consumerism does not stop at the imaginary boundaries set up to protect high culture against vulgarizing influences from below. It means that pop culture 'ideally' – that is, when it succeeds in making large profits – does not target any clearly defined group to the exclusion of all others, by, for instance, appealing to a certain kind of snob appeal or 'in-crowd' feeling. On the contrary, mass culture tries to embrace as many segments of the (globalized) consumer market as it possibly can. Any popular cultural form may therefore be as unapologetically sexist, homo/lesbophobic, racist, ageist, looksist and classist, as it may occasionally attempt to be 'politically correct'. Still, because of the power and money involved in the production of consumer culture, the former is much more likely than the latter.

Partly as a result of the growing visibility of queer 'lifestyles' in Western societies, the fundamental ambiguity of the popular realm has become a key issue in lesbian and gay critical practice. While such visibility is hailed by some as a sign of greater social tolerance and acceptability, Essex Hemphill aptly reminds us that dominant cultural production, however many 'kinky lifestyles' it may wish to assimilate or cash in on, is not made for those of us who have no choice but to live the sociopolitical consequences of our 'marginality': '[Popular culture] is not intended for *our* consumption but for the consumption by mass audiences who have no understanding of us, no desire to understand us' ([1990] 1995: 393). Consumer culture, then, whether produced by (formerly) disenfranchised groups or by the multinational corporations of capitalist industry is inherently ambivalent, in that any popular text is as amenable to reactionary as it is to subversive (re)appropriation. The difference is in the specific sociocultural location of its receiving audience.

An illuminating example of this is provided by the sexual thriller *Basic Instinct* (directed by Paul Verhoeven, 1992), a controversial product of the commercial cultural industry *par excellence*, Hollywood cinema. From its opening night – slightly overshadowed by loud protests of US gay and lesbian activists objecting to its negative portrayal of 'lesbianism' – Verhoeven's multimillion-dollar fantasy proved almost as appealing to lesbians as to its targeted general (read, straight) audience. The apparent appeal of what is, essentially, no more than a postmodern version of the classic lesbian vampire story is explained partly by the sheer scarcity of lesbian images in the Western cultural domain as a whole. However, *Basic Instinct* was also one of the first films to present sexy, alluring and powerful 'lesbians' on the big slick screen of commercial cinema, instead of the traditional ugly old spinster, frumpy schoolmarm, or desperate adolescent trapped in the solitude of her 'doomed' existence, and eventually committing suicide to escape from her unspeakable sexuality.[12] The appearance of sexy and powerful 'lesbians' on the big movie screen was thus an unprecedented cultural event in which many lesbians took considerable pleasure. Yet, while the alluring images of Sharon Stone and some of the other 'designer dykes' displayed in the popular media may gratify the tastes of a specific group of spectators starved of any form of cultural representation, mainstream audiences indisputably see a different film while consuming the 'kinky thrills' of films like *Basic Instinct*.[13] What they see is probably what they think to have 'known' about lesbians all along, for Verhoeven is neither the first nor will he be the last filmmaker to capitalize on the long-standing connection between lesbianism and excessive (sexual) violence in the Western collective imagination (Hart, 1994).

In its blatant portrayal of lesbian serial killers, *Basic Instinct* can easily be exposed as the anxious product of straight white male fantasy. Other recent films with a lesbian theme, such as *Heavenly Creatures* (1995), *Sister My Sister* (1995), and *Butterfly Kiss* (1996), though ostensibly more 'artistic' and politically responsible, likewise reinscribe stereotypical associations of lesbianism with aggressive (female) sexuality and violence. But because these films throw a more complexly 'serious' veil over the lesbian's presumed regressive tendencies and uncontainable passions, they are much more difficult to criticize. In such instances, it is important not only to take into account a cultural product's wider sociopolitical context, but also the structural power involved in its production, distribution and reception. As with so-called crossover culture, with its appeal to minority and majority consumers alike, the question of audience location thus acquires crucial significance.[14] Much work in lesbian and gay cultural studies in the past few years has, in fact, shifted direction to focus on the specificity of reception and uses, rather than content and form, of (mainstream) popular cultural production.[15]

The rapid expansion of the consumer market has unquestionably enabled lesbians and gay men, among other non-dominant groups, to enter the realm of popular culture. Yet, as we have seen, such cultural incorporation does not always turn out to be an unmixed blessing. As the popularity of murderous lesbians or the endless appearance of gay drag in dominant media demonstrate, mainstream co-optation of subcultural forms may easily lead to a reinforcement of precisely those negative images and insidious stereotypes that non-dominant, countercultural forms call into question and try to subvert. These complicated, contradictory effects are the direct results of the fundamental ambivalence at the heart of the popular market, and will continue to set the agenda for radical lesbian, gay and queer cultural critiques, both now and in the future.

The point of cultural studies is not so much to determine what popular culture is, or even to trace its variously developing patterns and models. In what distinguishes it from other forms of queer scholarship, the project of lesbian and gay cultural studies is therefore not all that different from its objects of analysis.

As Creekmur suggests, popular culture's 'real value' is located 'in its cultural context and use rather than artistic form' (1995: 405). Gay and lesbian cultural critics have the important task of helping to create the conditions that will allow all queer consumers to put these perishable goods to politically empowering use.

Notes

1 Key texts are Hoggart ([1957] 1990); Williams ([1958] 1963, [1961] 1965); Thompson ([1963] 1996); Hall & Whannel (1964); Hall et al. (1980); Hall (1987).

2 Such elusiveness is adequately reflected in each of the more than 20 essays that make up a recent, appropriately named reader *What Is Cultural Studies?* (Storey, 1996).

3 For a discussion of the distinctions between cultural criticism and critique see Con Davis and Schleifer (1991).

4 See, for example, several contributions to Duberman et al. (1991); and Miller (1995).

5 An interesting case in this context is Alfred Hitchcock, whose films have served to do both, being extensively subjected to critique by lesbian, feminist and gay film critics alike. See the section 'Dossier on Hitchcock,' in Creekmur and Doty (1995).

6 The phrase 'new studies of sexuality' is Domna C. Stanton's (1992).

7 For interventions into lesbian and gay critical discourses on race/ethnicity see Goldsby (1990); Hemphill (1991); Julien and Mercer (1988). On lesbian pornography and S/M see Gibson and Gibson (1993); on gay porn see Watney ([1985] 1995). On drag see Tyler (1991) and on fetishism see De Lauretis (1994), Grosz (1991). On bisexuality see Garber (1995).

8 For extended bibliographies on these various fields see Abelove et al. (1993) and Creekmur and Doty (1995).

9 On the sociocultural function and effects of 'the closet' see Russo ([1981] 1987), Sedgwick (1990) and Hadleigh (1991). A selection from the extensive literature on camp would include Core (1984), Meyer (1994), Newton ([1972] 1979).

10 On music generally see Hadleigh (1991); on rock see Robinson (1989); on house, Currid (1995).

11 On the implication of gay/lesbian culture in capitalist consumerism see D'Emilio (1983) and Rand (1994).

12 The quotation marks around the word lesbian here serve to suggest that there is not a lesbian character in *Basic Instinct* (hoogland, 1997); also see Hart (1994).

13 On the contemporary phenomenon of the 'designer dyke,' a.k.a. the 'lipstick' or 'lifestyle' lesbian, see Clark (1991); O'Sullivan (1994). Critical work on the function of the sexualized look and/or 'the gaze' in film is too extensive to list here. For specifically lesbian contributions to the debate see Straayer (1990).

14 Think, for instance, of highly popular crossover stars like k.d. lang, Elton John, Melissa Etheridge, Janis Ian, Jimmy Somerville and Marc Almond.

15 For representative examples of such work, consult Case et al. (1995); Doan (1994); Roof and Wiegman (1995).

References

Abelove, H., Barale, M.A. and Halperin, D.M. (eds) (1993) *The Gay and Lesbian Studies Reader*. New York: Routledge.

Becker, E., Citron, M., Lesage, J. and Rich, B.R. [1981] (1995) 'Lesbians and film', in Creekmur and Doty (1995), pp. 25–43.

Brett, P., Wood, E. and Thomas, G. (eds) (1994) *Queering the Pitch: The New Gay and Lesbian Musicology*. New York: Routledge.

Bronski, M. (1984) *Culture Clash: The Making of Gay Sensibility*. Boston: South End.

Burston, P. and Richardson, C. (eds) (1995) *A Queer Romance: Lesbians, Gay Men and Popular Culture*. London and New York: Routledge.

Butler, J. (1991) 'Imitation and gender subordination', in D. Fuss (ed.), *Inside/Out: Lesbian Theories, Gay Theories*. New York: Routledge. pp. 13–31

Butler, J. (1994) *Bodies That Matter: On the Discursive Limits of 'Sex'*. New York: Routledge.

Case, S.-E., Brett, P. and Foster, S.L. (eds) (1995) *Cruising the Performative: Interventions into the Representation of Ethnicity, Nationality, and Sexuality*. Bloomington and Indianapolis: Indiana University Press.

Castle, T. (1993) *The Apparitional Lesbian: Female Homosexuality and Modern Culture*. New York: Columbia University Press.

Clark, D. (1991) 'Commodity lesbianism', *Camera Obscura*, 25–6: 181–201.

Con Davis, R. and Schleifer, R. (1991) *Criticism & Culture: The Role of Critique in Modern Literary Theory*. London: Longman.

Core, P. (1984) *Camp: The Lie That Tells the Truth*. New York: Delilah.

Creekmur, C.K. (1995) 'Dossier on popular music: introduction', in Creekmur and Doty (1995), pp. 403–6.

Creekmur, C.K. and Doty, A. (eds) (1995) *Out in Culture: Gay, Lesbian, and Queer Essays on Popular Culture*. Durham and London: Duke University Press.

Currid, B. (1995) '"We are family": house music and queer performativity', in Case et al. (1995), pp. 165–96.

De Lauretis, T. (1991) 'Queer theory: lesbian and gay sexualities: an introduction', *Differences*, 3: iii–xviii.

De Lauretis, T. (1994) *The Practice of Love: Perverse Desire and Lesbian Sexuality*. Bloomington and Indianapolis: Indiana University Press.

D'Emilio, J. (1983) 'Capitalism and gay identity', in A. Snitnow, C. Stansell and S. Thompson (eds), *Desire: The Politics of Identity*. London: Virago. pp. 140–54.

Doan, Laura (ed.) (1994) *The Lesbian Postmodern*. New York: Columbia University Press.

Doty, A. (1993) *Making Things Perfectly Queer: Interpreting Mass Culture*. Minneapolis: University of Minnesota Press.

Duberman, M.B., Vicinus, M. and Chauncey Jr, G. (eds) (1991) *Hidden from History: Reclaiming the Gay and Lesbian Past*. London: Penguin.

Dyer, R. (1990) 'In defense of disco', in S. Shepard and M. Wallis (eds), *On Record: Rock, Pop, and the Written Word*. New York: Pantheon.

Ferris, L. (ed.) (1993) *Crossing the Stage: Controversies on Cross-Dressing*. New York: Routledge.

Frank, L. and Smith, P. (eds) (1993) *Madonnarama: Essays on Sex and Popular Culture*. Pittsburgh: Cleis.

Fuss, D. (1992) 'Fashion and the homospectatorial look', *Critical Inquiry*, 18: 713–37.

Garber, M. (1992) *Vested Interests: Cross-Dressing and Cultural Anxiety*. New York: Routledge.

Garber, M. (1995) *Vice Versa: Bisexuality and the Eroticism of Everyday Life*. New York: Simon and Schuster.

Geertz, C. (1973) *The Interpretation of Cultures*. New York: Basic Books.

Gevers, M., Parmar, P. and Greyson, J. (eds) (1993) *Queer Looks: Perspectives on Lesbian and Gay Film and Video*. New York: Routledge.

Gibson, P.C. and Gibson, R. (eds) (1993) *Dirty Looks: Women, Pornography, Power*. London: BFI.

Goldsby, J. (1990) 'What it means to be colored me', *Out/Look*, 9: 8–17.

Grosz, E. (1991) 'Lesbian fetishism?', *Differences*, 3: 37–54.

Hadleigh, B. (1991) *The Vinyl Closet: Gays in the Music World*. San Diego: Los Hombres.

Hall, S. (1980) 'Cultural studies: two paradigms', *Media, Culture and Society*, 2: 57–72.

Hall, S. (1987) *The Real Me: Postmodernism and the Question of Identity*. London: ICA.

Hall, S. and Whannel, P. (1964) *The Popular Arts*. London: Pantheon Books.

Hall, S., Lowe, A. and Willis, P. (eds) (1980) *Culture, Media, Language*. London: Hutchinson.

Hart, L. (1994) *Fatal Women: Lesbian Sexuality and the Mark of Aggression*. Princeton, NJ: Princeton University Press.

Hemphill, E. (ed.) (1991) *Brother to Brother: New Writings by Black Gay Men*. Boston: Alyson.

Hemphill, E. [1990] (1995) 'In living color: toms, coons, mammies, faggots, and bucks', in Creekmur and Doty (1995), pp. 389–401.

Hilbert, J. (1995) 'The politics of drag', in Creekmur and Doty (1995), pp. 463–9.

Hoggart, R. [1957] (1990) *The Uses of Literacy*. Harmondsworth: Penguin.

hoogland, r.c. (1997) *Lesbian Configurations*. Cambridge: Polity Press; New York: Columbia University Press.

Hughes, W. (1993) 'Feeling mighty real: disco as discourse and discipline', *Village Voice Rock and Roll Quarterly*, 7, 10–11, 21.

Jackson, E. and Persky, S. (eds) (1982) *Flaunting It! A Decade of Gay Journalism from the Body Politic*. Vancouver and Toronto: New Star/Pink Triangle.

Julien, I. and Mercer, K. (1988) 'True confessions: a discourse on images of black masculinity', in R. Chapman and J. Rutherford (eds), *Male Order: Unwrapping Masculinity*. London: Lawrence & Wishart.

Mayne, J. (1990) *The Woman at the Keyhole: Feminism and Women's Cinema*. Bloomington and Indianapolis: Indiana University Press.

Meyer, M. (ed.) (1994) *The Politics and Poetics of Camp*. New York: Routledge.

Miller, N. (1995) *Out of the Past: Gay and Lesbian History from 1869 to the Present*. New York: Random House/Vintage Books.

Munt, S. (ed.) (1992) *New Lesbian Criticism: Literary and Cultural Readings*. Hemel Hempstead: Harvester Wheatsheaf.

Newton, E. [1972] (1979) *Mother Camp: Female Impersonators in America*. Chicago: University of Chicago Press.

O'Sullivan, S. (1994) 'Girls who kiss girls and who cares?', in D. Hamer and B. Budge (eds), *The Good, the Bad and the Gorgeous: Popular Culture's Romance with Lesbianism*. London: Pandora. pp. 78–95.

Radstone, S. (ed.) (1988) *Sweet Dreams: Sexuality, Gender, and Popular Fiction*. London: Lawrence & Wishart.

Rand, E. (1994) 'We girls can do anything, right Barbie? Lesbian consumption in postmodern circulation', in Doan (1994).

Robinson, T. (1989) 'A conversation about rock, politics, and gays', in S. Shepherd and M. Wallis (eds), *Coming on Strong: Gay Politics and Culture*. London: Unwin Hyman.

Roof, J. (1991) *A Lure of Knowledge: Lesbian Sexuality and Theory*. New York: Columbia University Press.

Roof, J. and Wiegman, R. (eds) (1995) *Who Can Speak? Authority and Critical Identity*. Urbana and Chicago: University of Illinois Press.

Russo, V. [1981] (1987) *The Celluloid Closet: Homosexuality in the Movies*. New York: Harper & Row.

Schwartz, D. (1993) 'Madonna and Sandra: like we care', in A. Sexton (ed.), *Desperately Seeking Madonna*. New York: Delta.

Sedgwick, E.K. (1990) *Epistemology of the Closet*. Berkeley: University of California Press.

Signorile, M. (1993) *Queer in America: Sex, the Media, and the Closets of Power*. New York: Random House.

Sinfield, A. (1994) *Cultural Politics–Queer Reading*. New York and London: Routledge.

Sontag, S. [1964] (1982) 'Notes on camp', in *A Susan Sontag Reader*. Harmondsworth, Middlesex: Penguin. pp. 105–19.

Stanton, D.C. (ed.) (1992) *Discourses of Sexuality: From Aristotle to AIDS*. Ann Arbor: University of Michigan Press.

Stein, A. (1994) 'Crossover dreams: lesbianism and popular music since the 1970s', in

D. Hamer and B. Budge (eds), *The Good, the Bad, and the Gorgeous: Popular Culture's Romance with Lesbianism*. London: Pandora. pp. 15–27.

Storey, J. (1996) *What Is Cultural Studies? A Reader*. London: Arnold.

Straayer, C. (1990) 'The hypothetical lesbian heroine: *Voyage en Douce* (Michele Deville, 1980), *Entre Nous* (Diane Kurys, 1983)', *Jump Cut*, 35: 50–7.

Straayer, C. (1992) 'Redressing the "natural": the temporary transvestite film', *Wide Angle*, 14: 36–55.

Thomas, A. [1989] (1995) 'The house the kids built: the gay black imprint on American dance music', in Creekmur and Doty. pp. 437–46.

Thompson, E.P. [1963] (1966) *The Making of the English Working Class*. New York: Vintage.

Tyler, C.-A. (1991) 'Boys will be girls: the politics of drag', in D. Fuss (ed.), *Inside/Out: Lesbian Theories, Gay Theories*. New York: Routledge. pp. 32–70.

Warner, M. (ed.) (1993) *Fear of a Queer Planet: Queer Politics and Social Theory*. Minneapolis: University of Minnesota Press.

Watney, S. [1985] (1995) 'Men's pornography: gay versus straight', in Creekmur and Doty (1995), pp. 307–27.

Weiss, A. (1993) *Violets and Vampires: Lesbians in Film*. New York: Penguin Books.

Williams, R. [1958] (1963) *Culture and Society 1780–1950*. Harmondsworth: Penguin.

Williams, R. [1961] (1965) *The Long Revolution*. London: Penguin.

Wood, R. [1978] (1995) 'Responsibilities of a gay film critic', in Creekmur and Doty (1995), pp. 12–24.

Zimmerman, B. (1990) *The Safe Sea of Women: Lesbian Fiction 1969–1989*. Boston: Beacon Press.

12 Crossing Borders – A Debate on the Perspectives of Women's Studies and Gay and Lesbian Studies

Theo Sandfort and Hansje Galesloot

In collaboration with

Irene Costera Meijer, Stefan Dudink, Geertje Mak and Ine Vanwesenbeeck

At first glance, these women's studies and gay/lesbian studies may appear to be closely related. Both women's studies and gay/lesbian studies analyse the way in which the concepts of masculinity and femininity make themselves felt in popular culture and in individual lives. Gender, sex and sexuality are important aspects on the agenda of both. Despite the fact that these disciplines have become more academic, the majority of practitioners in both fields still have a social objective: to create insight into the social imbalances based on gender and sexual preference, the mechanisms that continuously reproduce these imbalances and the results thereof. One would think that this would have created a bond. However, the relationship between women's studies and gay/lesbian studies has always been a difficult one. This chapter focuses on the reasons for this strained relationship and the future prospects of a more fruitful co-operation.

This contribution differs from the other chapters here, in that it is based on a debate between four experienced scholars in the field of women's studies and gay/lesbian studies. This format was chosen to allow each individual perspective on women's studies, and lesbian and gay studies its rightful place. Due to the fact that it is nearly impossible to place these interdisciplinary fields of study under one theoretical banner, not to mention attempting to summarize the research carried out, this discussion will focus on the development of theories. In fact, the theoretical aspects of the relationship between these two disciplines are particularly intriguing.

Stefan Dudink, Geertje Mak, Irene Costera Meijer and Ine Vanwesenbeeck took part in the debate. Despite their academic differences, their personal careers reflect a viable border crossing between women's studies and gay/lesbian studies.

Irene Costera Meijer works in the Department of Communication Studies at the University of Amsterdam. She started her university career in women's studies, specializing in lesbian studies, but is now integrating the two points of view into more generic research and education. 'Although I am still doing the same work,

I now call it something else.' She completed her doctorate on the history of feminist awareness in the Netherlands, 'a subject with clear lesbian aspects'. She is currently occupied with the relationship between media and citizenship, particularly advertising, infotainment and more popular forms of journalism.

Stefan Dudink is a political scientist, whose doctorate is on social liberalism in the Netherlands at the end of the nineteenth century. He has also written a number of articles in the field of gender and gay studies. He is currently a lecturer in gay studies at the Catholic University in Nijmegen, where lesbian/gay studies is part of the Centre for Women's Studies. 'I like this combination: I am comfortable in the field of tension between gender and gay studies.' This is clear from his current research topic: the significance of masculinity in Dutch political culture around 1800. His contribution to the debate is expressed particularly when it focuses on gay studies.

Geertje Mak studied history, and first worked on gay and lesbian studies in Amsterdam and later on women's studies in Utrecht. She wrote a dissertation on nineteenth-century masculine women. 'I was continuously suspended between the two disciplines. My dissertation is also like that: while dealing with women's history, it is also clearly a dissertation on lesbianism. And it specifically seeks out areas of tension between the two.'

Ine Vanwesenbeeck is a social psychologist, who has been working at the Department of Women's Studies in Tilburg since 1984. She also works at the Netherlands Institute of Social-Sexological Research. She did policy research into the well-being of prostitutes, and wrote her dissertation on the same topic. As an extension of this, she became increasingly involved in the field of sexology, with current research topics covering media and body attitudes, the monitoring of the effects of changes in legislation on prostitution, sexual risks and gender-specific sex education.

All participants in the debate are Dutch and their statements frequently refer to the Dutch situation and to past events in the Netherlands. However, this is done in an exemplary fashion. It is, however, relevant to know that gay/lesbian studies in the Netherlands has not only been a discipline in which individual scholars have been active, but has also become institutionalized. In other words, unlike in nearly every other country, working groups or departments in the Netherlands occupied themselves with this subject. Only the Catholic University of Nijmegen still has such a department. In Amsterdam and Utrecht, where research was done from a social-constructionist, and a more emancipating and policy-directed perspective respectively, it seemed that neither group was able to maintain its position within the academic system.

The broadening of women's studies

Women's studies has become a wide field of scientific study, covering a number of disciplines. It is difficult to characterize in a general fashion, also because the nature of women's studies has changed fundamentally over the past thirty years. What would you describe as the essence of women's studies?

Mak: 'What makes women's studies so complicated and exciting is the fact that on the one hand it investigates women and femininity, while on the other hand, it continuously questions these concepts and their meaning.[1] In other words, you make women and femininity visible, you give it a place, but at the same time, you bring it down. I think that nearly all research in women's studies takes place in this area of tension.'

Meijer: 'I want to emphasize the opposite. Today, nearly everyone emphasizes the deconstructive effect of women's studies: fortunately, we have moved away from the fixed roles and identities. In theory, I agree with that, but it allows too little room for the positive connotation that the concept of femininity can have. It does not only mean being compartmentalized, it also has creative potential. However, too often the issue is that if you formulate it positively, you risk being marginalized, something along the lines of: women are different. It is precisely this 'differentness' of women that can be positively applied. Somehow everyone is always very hesitant to do this. Femininity is never allowed to have merit, it is always something that stigmatizes. Therefore, it cannot be interpreted as behaviour which simply serves specific purposes and which you can evaluate on its effectiveness.'

Mak: 'I agree with you that one should also allow for a positive interpretation of femininity, but even then I think that the research in women's studies can never avoid this tension, because a concept such as femininity is determined socially and culturally and should always be critically questioned.'

Vanwesenbeeck: 'In this, women's studies has undergone development. Initially, the aim was to make women and femininity visible in research and theory, because the lives of women and women's activities were completely invisible, and because all sorts of assumptions on humanity were made based on research among men. Therefore, it was about making women visible, contextualizing femininity, and in that sense, constructing femininity. From a historical perspective, the deconstruction and questioning of femininity was secondary to this. There is, however, a second area of tension that I find characteristic of women's studies. In the initial phase, the primary desire was to develop a feminist scientific method. This ideal has faded into the background, because it is so difficult to achieve, but the question still remains: does a specific feminist research method exist?'

Mak: 'And there you see extreme specialization, because it has now turned into a philosophical, epistemological debate, with complete books being devoted to the subject: is there feminine knowledge? what is the relationship between experience and knowledge? These types of questions have developed extensively in the meantime.'

Has women's studies become less political as a result of this?

Vanwesenbeeck: 'Well, I think it has become more diverse, broader. Everyone involved in women's studies still intends to contribute to the well-being of humanity, particularly women, but the distance between the goal and the means has only become much greater.'

Mak: 'Subdisciplines have developed, some of which are so specialized that the uninitiated cannot follow it. For example, many people find a psychoanalytical feminist exposition completely incomprehensible. Entire bookcases have been filled with research in the area of women's studies. Whereas previously you could only find one little shelf with feminist books, now entire libraries are filled with them. Women's studies has developed several separate branches of its own.'

Vanwesenbeeck: 'In addition, you find a separation between feminist-empiricists, who continue to view the individual as a unit of analysis, to which I belong, and the constructivists such as Rosi Braidotti who say that this type of empirical perspective is not important at all.[2] According to them, there are a variety of images and linguistic expressions, and it is sufficient to study these critically. The study of cognition, emotions and behaviour of individuals will not add anything substantial to this. However, for me, as a psychologist, the way people experience things offers an interesting perspective with which to address people directly. It is difficult to merge these two approaches in a fruitful manner. The division recurs in the structure of research groups and collaborations.'

Mak: 'Although this gap does exist, I would like to emphasize another phenomenon: if *anything* is well developed in women's studies, it is precisely this interdisciplinary element. There are very few fields of study in which the thought processes are so interdisciplinary. This is a major strength of women's studies, but it also requires a lot of effort, as you have to immerse yourself in a different terminology, a different methodology. However, this effort has been made and it makes women's studies special. Diversity as a source of creativity. Except, of course, across the gap mentioned by Ine.'

Meijer: 'I don't see it like that. In recent years, an empirical section has also developed within cultural studies. Here one specifically examines people's perceptions and one is not satisfied with the analysis of the content of texts. Methods to analyse texts and images have been developed within cultural studies and, depending on your research topic, you can decide to apply these methods or not. Constructivists will never claim that empirical research is worthless. They will only argue that empirical data are also text, and I agree with this point of view. As soon as you transcribe an interview, it becomes text and you handle it as text, and not as something that is an experience.'

Vanwesenbeeck: 'The way people reflect on their lives is also text, of course. So, in that sense, all psychology becomes text at some point, but this is text that refers to a lived reality. Respondents' statements are also viewed from this perspective.'

Mak: 'Ultimately, the difference is that you empiricists actually do acknowledge it – agreed, the interview or questionnaire has been solidified into text – but then you do not take any of it to heart. You apply everything you have learnt to it, to determine whether something is a significant difference, whether something clinches it. In short, you apply a variety of statistical methods to get to the bottom of your research material, while people who are strongly in favour of the decon-structivist approach, will always argue that realities are being created here, *how* are they created, *why* they are created. They are almost critical by definition. The disadvantage of this is that you never produce facts, since you always criticize their existence and the way in which they came into being, in which ideological context: which practices or which cash flows form the basis of the facts that come to light through such a survey. In theory, these are beautiful analyses, very informative, but they don't enable them to say, to the policy-makers for instance, that this problem has to be dealt with because it is serious. It serves a different purpose, it is meant more as cultural criticism, a continuous warning: what we are involved in here is not reality. On the other hand, you need all the provisional truths from empirical research to be able to think ahead, plan and build. This is a completely different perspective, and both perspectives are necessary within women's studies.'

So methodologically, women's studies has developed dramatically, whereby new scientifically critical insights and new specialities have developed. If you look at it with regard to content, has there been a shift in topics over the past thirty years?

Mak: 'Initially, the most important aim was to make women visible, considering in which areas women were disadvantaged. This resulted in a movement of protest against the implied standards, that women were to become equal to men, just as visible and present in various situations. That movement took a radical turn to the other side by researching femininity as the greater good. The fact that both lesbian and ethnic studies insisted that the differences between women should also be explored, caused the contrast between these two approaches to disappear. This finally resulted in the concept of gender studies, which not only focuses on women as the research topic, but on the relationship between the sexes in general. In addition, a distinction was made between sex and gender: sex as a biological concept, while gender was seen as a historical and social construction of male and female behaviour. The concept of gender made it possible to submit stereotypes and certain assumptions about male and female behaviour to a critical analysis. The way in which culture, the structure of a society and the interactions between people, continuously steers towards stereotypical behaviour for both sexes was analysed in a variety of studies. Now the final step is that the concept of sex has also been entered in the debate. The transgender movement and queer studies argue that sex is not a clear-cut concept that is determined 'naturally' at all. In terms of content, it is therefore possible to demonstrate a tendency towards a continuous expansion of the focal area and the increasingly critical examination of concepts such as masculinity and femininity.'

Meijer: 'In terms of the expansion, an interesting development is that the terminology of women's studies has become sexually neutral in many cases. The spotlight is, for example, no longer on 'housekeeping', but on 'everyday life', not on 'violence against women', but on sexual violence. The disadvantage of this, is that the genderedness of the experience – at least in the Dutch language – disappears. The good thing is that the focal area is much broader. A year ago, the editorial team of the magazine *Tijdschrift voor Vrouwenstudies*,[3] of which I am the editor, decided to change the name to *Tijdschrift voor Genderstudies* – a development that is actually seen worldwide. We opted for the term 'gender studies' to indicate that we want to continue to focus on the relationships between the sexes. The down side to this approach is that women's studies might not receive the credit it deserves, but on the positive side, you reach and convince people who previously weren't interested in women's studies. However, you risk getting lost in the mainstream.'

Mak: 'Of course it was always true of women's studies that it is a very vague type of discipline. Lecturers and ideas are to be found all over, and not necessarily under the explicit heading of women's studies. The same is true of lesbian/gay studies – and it is indeed true that this is increasingly so. I also presented a course on women's history, for which few students registered, so, of course, that simply makes you change the title. It is the same with lesbian/gay studies. If students aren't interested in learning something of the history of homosexuality, just call it the history of sexuality.'

Is that just a politically strategic decision to attract more students and generate more research funding, or does the content also ask for a wider approach?

Mak: 'Then you arrive at the issue of whether women's studies has succeeded in placing its key issues on the agenda of other disciplines. Otherwise you risk the disappearance of your own research questions. I honestly think that this has failed horribly.'

Vanwesenbeeck: 'Well, come on, I don't think that is true all over.'

Mak: 'I am just testing your response.'

Meijer: 'Political philosophy, for instance, has clearly been influenced. It led to the ethics of care in its entirety, the consideration of the value of care and thoughtfulness. Psychology is another example: a lot of attention is paid to the female psyche, which was done before, but now it is done critically.'

Mak: 'In my subject, history, nobody in the mainstream is interested in it. And if they are, it is on the most banal level: oh dear, we also have to have a woman. Women's topics are considered to be trivial by institutions that fund research. I am very pessimistic about how we can move away from this marginalization.'

Dudink: 'In England and America you find that historians are influenced by postmodernism and examine concepts such as gender and sexuality in a critical manner. However, in the Netherlands and countries like Germany, Belgium and France, this occurs far less frequently.'

Vanwesenbeeck: 'A number of topics and approaches adopted from women's studies have become important in social sciences. Certain scientific themes, such as the workings of stereotyping, have been strongly influenced and stimulated by women's studies. Coping with sexual trauma, and also aggression, these are some of the topics that would never have developed in this manner without the stimulus of women's studies. The feminist movement in science has also changed something in what is accepted as a researchable and important topic. The topic of prostitution comes to mind. When I started working on it, I was also looked at askance. People were not sure how to deal with it: as a scholar you were stigmatized to the same degree as the prostitutes about whom you were writing. Over the past fifteen years, this has changed to such an extent that I can now even study burnout amongst prostitutes, so to speak. This is a truly enormous change.'

Meijer: 'At which point can you state that something originated in women's studies? The feminists have boosted all the issues of inequality, for example in the field of law where it has now become fairly common to keep the influence of gender in mind. But can you still claim that? Innovations such as these are usually not claimed by or attributed to women's studies. I think that is also typical of women's studies: as soon as it has taken hold, it disappears. Then the credit is no longer yours.'

Vanwesenbeeck: 'But haven't you reached your goal when you've managed to put the topics on the agenda? Even if it is not under the banner of women's studies?'

Meijer: 'What do you mean by achieved your goal? Why should you be so selfless and self-sacrificing? I would also like to be able to claim that we achieved that. For some reason, this is impossible within women's studies: as soon as you claim it under the title of women's studies, you disqualify yourself. The subject has absolutely no status whatsoever.'

Vanwesenbeeck: 'That is true. And even if you claim it under the banner of gender studies . . .'

Meijer: 'No, it doesn't matter. It is slightly more neutral, at least they dare to use the word.'

The rise and fall of lesbian studies

What research has been done within women's studies with regard to homosexuality?

Meijer: 'You are speaking about lesbian studies, since male homosexuality was only glanced at in a highly theoretical sense, and not actually researched. In the early 1980s a lesbian approach grew strongly within women's studies. Everybody swooned about Adrienne Rich's book on compulsory heterosexuality,[4] and wondered which possibilities the term "female friendships" offered as a binding concept. All over, groups occupied with lesbian studies could be detected within women's studies. Many early practitioners of women's studies were lesbians and thought that that could be connected to their scientific practice.'

Mak: 'Feminism in its totality had a lesbian wave, which was reflected in feminist science,[5] although the beginning was very dogmatic. Rich introduced the terms "lesbian existence" and "lesbian continuum", detaching the definition of lesbianism from sexual preference and expanding it to all emotional ties between women. In retrospect, the way in which feminism took over lesbianism was widely criticized. This excluded a variety of lesbian subcultures.'

Meijer: 'Yes, the butch–femme cultures were not allowed, as the profiling of male and female roles within lesbianism was not regarded as feminism. The sadomasochistic culture was also wrong, as differences in power were cultivated in the area of sexuality.'

Mak: 'The feminist interpretation of lesbianism was very judgmental. It concerned the meaning of female friendships and the way in which mutual solidarity could be used to weaken the heterosexual norm. Apart from the fact that certain subcultures were excluded in this way, the specific problems of lesbians were also neglected – at least in lesbian/gay studies in Amsterdam. In Utrecht, on the other hand, this emancipation perspective was the central issue. There they were mainly occupied with policy-focused research into concrete problems in the living situation of homosexual men and lesbian women. This was called essentialism, because the concept of homosexuality was not problematized, but taken as a given. In Amsterdam however, the deconstructivist school came into being, with lesbian studies as an important initiator. From this point of view, issues such as "what is lesbian, how is it defined, what is 'woman' actually", were being raised. So lesbian studies actually led to questioning and problematizing those women with whom feminism was concerned.'

Meijer: 'I have another story, perhaps one that precedes this. The term "female friendships" is now being belittled, but the interesting thing was that it specifically did not focus on the compartments lesbian or heterosexual. What was crucial was the introduction of the term "female friendship", which symbolized a crucial moment in the history of the feminist movement: women started to value relationships, friendships between women in political terms. This was contrary to the idea that your most important relationships were always with men.[6] This was an extraordinarily radical perspective, particularly – but certainly not exclusively – for heterosexual women. The value of womanhood had to be reassessed, the value to oneself and to others.'

Mak: 'As such, it was a very good movement, virtually placing the fundamental solidarity between women on a pedestal, but by labelling this as lesbian sight was lost of a different experience. The traditional way of being lesbian was marginalized precisely because of the sexuality, which suddenly was no longer allowed to determine the border.'

Meijer: 'That is true, but often only that is mentioned and the initial idea, the creativeness of shaping a collective identity for women, is lost. That is such a loss. The importance of this phase to the development of feminist consciousness should not be underestimated. However, you are correct that lesbianism as a separate lifestyle had vanished in this way.'

Mak: 'Lesbianism as an explicit subject for research within women's studies has also disappeared.[7] This is true for the Netherlands, but also for most other countries. It is only in the United States that lesbian studies has been continued in queer studies; it has never disappeared there. However, here many people who were busy with lesbian studies moved on to other things in the late 1980s. Perhaps they did some more work on the subject under the banner of women's studies, as a sideline, but not as a central theme. It just disappeared off the agenda, while looking at women's studies, a strikingly high percentage of those involved were still lesbians.'

What caused the disappearance of the specifically lesbian?

Mak: 'I think it was seen as too small a topic, too limited. It continuously focused on the precise definition of lesbian. People grew tired of it.'

Vanwesenbeeck: 'Many topics that were deemed important within women's studies also had a strong heterosexual connotation.'

Mak: 'Yes, that is another point. I think that feminism, but also women's studies that was based upon this feminism, started from the problems of women which are strongly related to heterosexuality, to the position of women in relation to men. As a consequence, the concept of woman was implicitly heterosexually charged. However, by focusing on these issues, you confirm the interpretation of womanhood. It was actually only in later years that fierce theoretical criticism developed in response to this, for example by Judith Butler.'[8]

Meijer: 'I disagree. The concept of a woman, as it was then focused on, was not interpreted as heterosexual or lesbian. It involved problems that lesbian women also encountered, like being made the object of the male stare. Most lesbian women are also not that different from heterosexual women. Concepts always display trends, a concept becomes popular and then it is unmasked, as white, middle class or hetero, etc. – this happens in waves. I think that these are fruitful discussions, but I find it too easy to say that lesbian women were excluded. Many heterosexual women could also not identify with the feminist concept of the woman. Moreover, if you call the concept heterosexual, then you exclude lesbian women who might identify with a more motherly, or feminine conceptualization of "women". In my opinion, concepts are continuously changing to include and exclude. That is incredibly interesting to study, specifically because of the distinctions that do not make it possible to think in terms of unambiguous contrasts. Lesbian women with children, for example, have always felt excluded, because the norm was that "we lesbians" didn't have children, that was for heterosexuals. There is no systematic exclusion of particular groups, it shifts from time to time and from group to group.'

Mak: 'That might be true, but nevertheless, I detect a dominance of the heterosexual perspective in women's studies. If I use my own field of study as an example, it is clear that women concerned with lesbian history are continuously occupied by the question of how lesbian women relate to feminism.[9] However, if women are concerned with the women's movement from the point of view of women's history, they never ask the question of how the women's movement has related to the lesbian movement, and what effect this has on the definition of woman, women's movements and feminism. Lesbian women are always overlooked.'

Vanwesenbeeck: 'That is because they were not very noticeable in history.'

Mak: 'If they are mentioned, it is as a separate little section that has no influence on the fundamental concepts that are applied, the concepts of woman and femininity, or even more importantly, the concept of sexuality. Since the end of the previous century, sexuality has been defined in such a way that it is difficult to give lesbianism a proper place, as lesbian sexuality does not involve polarized tension. Within the current definition, there is little room for sexuality based on a form of equality. In that respect, I can see what Irene says, that there are continuous movements of inclusion and exclusion, and that there are continuous negotiations, and that lesbianism itself also creates exclusions. However, in the meantime it is true that in its current form women's studies does not consider what would happen if, more fundamentally, lesbianism or being black is included in the theorizing. This type of criticism can however be seen at a meta-level. People such as Butler and De Lauretis try to intervene in the feminist discourse from a lesbian point of view.[10] In practice, however, this has scarcely had any effect.'

Vanwesenbeeck: 'I think that indeed, during the past years, a whole lot of themes in women's studies centred around heterosexuality, and that most research concerned the interaction between men and women. This doesn't automatically exclude lesbian women, because they also encounter problems such as these. However, as their position is often not explicitly mentioned, or is only included as a type of side note, I think that lesbian women have not felt themselves represented strongly enough.'

Mak: 'I am not only concerned with representation, let me just correct that. I am also concerned with the problematization of heterosexuality, of particular types of femininity as being self-evidently feminine.'

Vanwesenbeeck: 'But that happened all over the place. Adrienne Rich's argument on compulsory heterosexuality is widely read within women's studies. That had a major impact as this way of thinking was so closely related to definitions of masculinity and femininity.'

What is the situation now? Who now expresses the lesbian perspective or a critical position towards heterosexuality?

Vanwesenbeeck: 'On the one hand, the realization is clearly present that sexual identity is under pressure from a number of standards, specifically the heterosexual standard, and that research is one way in which one has to try to break it open. On the other hand, I don't know of any research projects that are explicitly aimed at homosexual groups or homosexuality as a theme. Research into sexual risks, which I am working on now, mainly concerns heterosexuality, and if it does concern homosexuality, it concerns men.'

Mak: 'Even in the humanities nobody is involved in researching the themes related to lesbianism any more. I find that that was something of a disappearing act. Lesbian subjects have almost silently disappeared from all programmes: women who used to be involved in them started to do other things. And that is detrimental, as nothing has taken their place. Look, I think it is perfectly fine when the lesbian approach is included in broader research, that is the way it should be. But often this perspective has simply disappeared. Possibly homosexuality has become too self-evident, at least in the Netherlands: with the result that it is no longer regarded as an interesting enough subject to justify any attention being paid to it. I really think that that is a pity, an enormous waste. At a certain point in time, you will have to start all over again. Say it is taken up again in ten years' time, then a great deal of the memory will have been lost as the ongoing discipline is lacking. Building on traditions makes one immeasurably stronger than when everything has been broken down and ten years later you have to pick up all the pieces. I am convinced that it is a criminal waste. You no longer function as a contact for students who want to do this type of research. They have to rediscover everything for themselves.'

The love–hate relationship between women's studies and gay studies

What kind of relationship exists between women's studies and gay studies?

Meijer: 'There has been a lot of tension since the beginning. The following story will explain it clearly. The first international gay and lesbian studies conference was organized in Amsterdam in 1983 by gay studies in co-operation with women's studies.[11] I participated in the organization as a representative of women's studies. That conference was bulging with conflicts between "the male homosexual", the Queen (with a capital Q) and "the feminist lesbian". The conference was devoted to homosocial arrangements: group formation among women and among men. The gay men wanted it to be called "Among men, among women", while the women wanted it reversed. After all, women's history had a tradition of studies of female friendships and other networks between women, while men's studies were just starting off. In addition, "among women" had always been much more problematic, much less obvious. Historically speaking, female institutions such as schools or convents were less powerful and visible than male institutions such as sport or the army. So, for both reasons, we thought the women should be mentioned first. It may seem a simple debate, but does illustrate something fundamental. Finally, the man who was responsible for the announcement simply called it "Among men, among women" without the matter being finalized.'

Mak: 'Ten years later, during the next conference, an attempt was made in Amsterdam to bring together gay studies, women's studies and sexology. Once again everything went wrong. The men refused to see the problematic side of sexuality, which naturally was put forward by the women. That was put down as female whining. One used such different terms to talk about sexuality and what it meant to people.'

Meijer: 'It also has something to do with flirting with power, something the gay scholars tended to do. In 1983, they wanted to initiate studies of clubs of football supporters, or the Rotary – all of those male networks that combine power and manhood. Meanwhile, what were the women doing? Studies of convents, female education. All of those non-powerful, non-spectacular phenomena. This difference in power suddenly became clear after the introduction of the term "homosocial arrangements". The term suggested symmetry rather than asymmetry. Male arrangements are, however, a lot more powerful and visible than the female ones. And the gay men would not see this at all. On the contrary. They were perfectly happy now that they were finally being brought into the mainstream academic world by studies such as these. Which excluded women's issues, just as usual, nothing new, but now gay men were avoiding questions of power and gender, and that hurt. At the 1991 conference on sexuality, the lines were indeed drawn in precisely the same manner: the men wanted to put the public celebration of sexuality on the stand. Women's sexuality, by virtue of its more private character was once again threatening to fall out of the boat. So it started going wrong even at the moment the issue was defined.'

Mak: 'In retrospect, one thinks that it is important to examine what happened back then, but at the time you're too involved to see things objectively. I sensed a certain amount of gender-blindness in those kinds of discussions. Contrasts between the sexes strongly influenced the debate, without being problematized.'

Meijer: '"Among men, among women" involves an imbalance. In principle, the "among women" is powerless, and the "among men" is powerful. This asymmetry works between gay men and lesbians as well. What we at women's studies found a particular problem was that these men, who were in principle just as marginal as we were, were reluctant to problematize the issue. Their attitude was "this is our salvation, this is our lunge for power". Suddenly they were in line with mainstream science, something which encountered its limits later, by the way. This only applied to the men at gay studies in Amsterdam. The men from Utrecht were critical of that flirting with power right away, not because they had more affinity with the arguments of the Amsterdam feminists, but because of their affiliation with emancipation studies. Male networks, such as among football supporters, are based on exclusion – not only of women, but of gay men as well. So there were certainly interesting theoretical correlations between women's studies and gay studies, but it stands or falls by whether or not the issue of power is taken into account in the definition of the problem. In women's studies this tension field between the homosocial and the homosexual was precisely what we wanted to debate as the central issue, but at that time the men were not interested in facing the problem. They just wanted to focus on all-male bonding. To some extent, conflicts such as these recur in queer studies.'

Dudink: 'By the way, you should keep in mind that later a different, critical concept of homosociality did become successful, not only within gay studies, but also within feminist literary studies. This is a concept in which gender relations, exclusion mechanisms and hierarchies are explicitly taken into account. An analysis is made of the way in which homosociality creates gender inequality on the one hand, and on the other hand develops as a result of the exclusion of homosexuality. There are two axes: the way in which homosexuality is excluded to allow the homosociality of men to function, and the way in which gender inequality is created in this way. Something not realized at the time finally did emerge at a later stage.'[12]

Do the twin concepts construction and deconstruction, that are so characteristic of women's studies, also apply to gay and lesbian studies?

Mak: 'Yes, I think so. By doing research and collecting data, homosexuality is made visible, but at the same time you are continually criticizing the categories with which you are working. And it is precisely this area of tension that makes it interesting, just as it does in women's studies. Naturally, it concerns other knowledge, other terms are the focal point. But the disciplines overlap, most clearly when you talk about sexuality and gender, the terms apply to both. If you do not define gender, you cannot talk about homosexuality: that does not exist without gender. Because sexuality plays an incredibly large role in gender relationships, you cannot study that subject outside the context. Therefore, theoretically, a large overlap exists between women's studies and gay studies, although in practice they are still mostly segregated. The themes are different.'

Dudink: 'I think that homosexuality as a positive category, the active constructing of it, is less developed on the gay studies side. You mainly see it in lesbian studies, in lesbian ethics for instance, but not in gay studies. There you see that although transgressing borders and sexual radicalism are celebrated, it is hardly programmatic.'

Meijer: 'Well, we've had that phase. Cherishing boyhood friendships, the pedagogic Eros, initiation rites in New Guinea, all those things.'

Dudink: 'Yes, but never as a political programme. And now that too has gone. I think that it is related to the fact that being gay, just like masculinity, is no longer a sufficiently subjective starting point for an oppositional political programme.'

Mak: 'That lesbianism had to fight harder to gain such a subject position: wanting to become visible.'

Meijer: 'But say that a great tradition of men's studies develops, would it be possible then? Could homosexuality then become a sobriquet?'

Dudink: 'No, because men's studies is focused on the opposite. Although men's studies turns masculinity into a specific subject, it is not based on the idea that masculinity must then become the point of departure for a philosophy or a political theory or an ethical programme.'

Meijer: 'Then it almost becomes a fascist . . .'

Dudink: 'Yes, you will indeed create a monster then. If you first highlight it and then say, now let's do something good with this.'

Meijer: 'However, that danger certainly exists. Advertising and marketing research, for example, uses popular masculine cultural icons such as *Iron John*[13] next to versions of the new man – Sissy Boy and James Dean clones not excluded – to advertise for Coca-Cola Light and Levi's jeans.'

Dudink: 'But do you see this in gay studies? I think that the Foucault-like approach to the beautiful life, the male friendships, was always purposely defined in vague terms, as a possibility, not as a programme.'

Meijer: 'Well, take for instance subjects such as the art of male friendships or the art of public sex, the latter framed in the politics of the sexual use of public toilets. I would say that there are several manifestations of gay politics which celebrate gay forms of "mainstream" culture. (Friendship or public toilet visiting is not limited to gay people.) But it is quite different from the cultivation of lesbianism. What is beautiful among men is never quite as beautiful as for example lesbian ethics, because of its normative, ideal, almost angelic quality. It exudes equality, in a way that almost turns your stomach. With men cultural politics often also involves the beauty of what is ugly or dangerous as well. Pleasure and danger can go together with men, for women they look mutually exclusive. Sexual violence among gay men could make a good story: you have all these movies like Fassbinder's *Querelle* [1983] in which rape is the order of the day: homosexuality as a beautiful danger. Apart from lesbian pornography, such as Pat Califia's, sexual violence has seldom been used as an attractive topic in lesbian studies. It lacks the erotic attraction it has among men.'

Mak: 'Now that we are talking so programmatically anyway: I think there has been a lack of such analyses of similarities and differences, such comparisons between gay and lesbian studies. And actually it is still an interesting issue. You should have research programmes that explicitly examine the cultural differences between gay men and lesbians, because it is fascinating.'

So actually lesbian and gay studies are very far removed from each other?

Mak: 'We were forced to attend conferences and working groups together. No, seriously: could you formulate it in this way? It is quite weird actually.'

Meijer: 'In Utrecht gay men and lesbians worked together in gay studies, on the basis of equal oppression, you could say. Because there emancipation studies was the central issue, it created a joint basis for research into shared problems of discrimination.'

Mak: 'We keep talking about the relationship between gay studies and lesbian studies. But if we could just go back to the relationship between women's studies and gay studies I would like to make a case for taking a much better look at the way in which they define and implicate each other. How gender and sexuality affect each other. This does not happen nearly often enough, on either side. Women's studies should be more aware of how the definitions of sexuality – heterosexuality and homosexuality – are related to concepts of masculinity and femininity, of gender in effect. And vice versa, gay studies should also keep that relation in mind. Lesbian studies is still on the cutting edge the most, I think.'

Vanwesenbeeck: 'This type of research is already happening within women's studies.'

Meijer: The development of women's studies into gender studies is geared to this.'

Mak: 'Many people do say that this is what should happen, but I find that in practice it is quite disappointing what people do with it. You could get more out of it.'

Meijer: 'Actually it is quite strange. For more than fifteen years we have been aware of the powerful interaction of sexuality, gender and sex. Still, the issue keeps sliding away. If you now again elevate it to the status of a programme, you will first have to find out why it is so difficult. Have we not come full circle?'

Mak: 'No, because even a conversation such as this would not have been possible twenty years ago. Exactly the same is happening with blacks and whites. Women of colour have also raised issues of which we white women thought, what on earth are they talking about? Or which infuriated us, or whatever. Those conversations were an absolute failure, although people were trying to understand each other, they did hurt each other. Some people are still upset about that. But that period has more or less been closed and now you see that people observe: Good heavens, women's studies is going to look into the differences between women. Well, twenty years ago we were also looking into these differences, so that is not new, but suddenly there is leeway to make it fruitful, it is not so threatening any more. This could now also apply to the relationship between women's studies and gay studies. Effectively, the debate hardly developed during the past ten years, hardly anyone was working on it. So the issue still remains – and it is an amazing issue.'

Meijer: 'The differences in other countries seem even more marked than they are in the Netherlands. In the USA, Germany and England lesbian and gay studies are still worlds apart. Historically this can be explained because the Netherlands is one of the few countries with a decades-old mixed gay and lesbian movement and a mixed start of the feminist movement. Although some part of the women's movement remained open to the participation of men, after 1972 most of Dutch feminism turned itself into an all-female activity.[14] Having mixed (male, female, gay and lesbian) political organizations appears to be a tradition here. And that generates exciting debates.'

The wide perspectives of queer theory

Queer theory is on the rise, certainly in the United States: a movement, emerging from gay/lesbian studies, which wants to break away radically from fixed identities on the basis of gender and sexual preference. Border crossings between the sexes and between homosexuality and heterosexuality are the new programme. Transgenders, transvestites, transsexuals and gender benders are the most radical exponents of these blurring borders. Instead of allowing themselves to be marginalized, these groups are turning their deviancy into a weapon: their very existence proves that normality is fictitious. Does queer theory really offer the grandiose perspectives it boasts about?

Vanwesenbeeck: 'On the one hand, I find queer theory fascinating and intellectually challenging. But I can hardly use it in the research into women's studies in which I am involved. The gap between the empirical and this type of theory development is huge. If you want to apply the questions to concrete psychological mechanisms, concrete groups of people . . .'

Meijer: 'So what about prostitution? Just take the American movie *Paris is Burning* [1991]. It is about young boys who are competing in professional dressing-up parties to give themselves a new identity. They take months to become for example a genuine boarding-school girl, some even have operations. On the one hand they earn their money through prostitution, while on the other hand continuously playing a game with gender, a professional game. To some extent, this is their downfall and to some extent this is how they get their kicks. If you then see how prostitution is organized in Amsterdam, it is also more and more related to a gender game. Brazilian and Argentinian whores are very sophisticated when it comes to that.'

Vanwesenbeeck: 'Yes, that is a new segment in prostitution. But what fascinates me even more about prostitutes is that they represent a form of turn-around in the relationship between gender and power. They seem to be the most exploited category of women, but in the meantime, they have power over men. In my study I spoke to many prostitutes who claim to be in power over male desires, to be subjects instead of being their object of desire.'

Meijer: 'But it is precisely this turn-around in the balance of power which is what queer theory is all about! And what is so interesting is that the prostitutes themselves raised the issue of power. They publicly opposed the feminist idea that they are completely powerless. And then you see that practice ensures that the terms are turned around, or the wall turned the ship, as we say in Dutch.'

Vanwesenbeeck: 'You could indeed place prostitutes in the whole line-up of gender bending and all other transgressions of sexual definitions. But even so: I may consider that to be a great phenomenon and I may find it exciting to wonder where it is heading, but in my opinion it does not contribute to formulating research questions.'

Dudink: 'But does that not apply to any theoretical or meta-programme? It could offer a context from which you may arrive at these questions.'

Mak: 'Differences between the Netherlands and the US also play a role, which is what makes it rather abstract to Dutch scholars. Queer is rooted in the radical subcultures of the United States, which are extremely insulated. A great deal happens within the protection of these subcultures, at least in certain districts. In the Netherlands, the situation is quite different: here homosexuality has become quite ordinary, you can be a gay or lesbian wherever you like. The point is now, transgressive behaviour demands a great deal if you do not live in a community where it is accepted – and even then it takes a lot. It exists in the United States by grace of the fact that there are subcultures in which you can still survive to some extent. But it would be absurd to try that on your own here in the Netherlands. You will never survive. This sort of queer optimism really makes me angry, that it is only fun to cross all borders. It may be revolutionary and exciting and fantastic, but it simply destroys people. And it is an absolutely isolated phenomenon within those subcultures. Because outside those subcultures, America is, of course, a terrible place for homosexual men and women.'[15]

Dudink: 'But there is another side to queer theory which is extremely interesting. It not only involves the practice of transgressions, but also the systematic consideration of the instability and contradictions of the "normal". So queer could inspire analyses of mechanisms that operate in the construction or deconstruction of what is normal. Queer theory is a project to understand how normality functions. That it is much less stable, self-evident and coherent than it pretends to be.'[16]

Mak: 'Yes, but the instability of the normal is always demonstrated with examples of transgressions. For instance, biological gender is not stable at all, push a cloth down your pants and you're a man. Stories like that, as if it were that simple. What is more, is it really true that systems can so easily be thrown off balance when borders are crossed? Systems have so many different kinds of answers to that, with the result that deviations are easily neutralized. You can demonstrate that the systems in themselves are not true, but compared to their stability that is peanuts.'

Vanwesenbeeck: 'That is indeed an interesting question. Under which conditions, where and by whom can normality be perverted, and for the sake of whose happiness, how does that turn out.'

Mak: 'Queer remains stuck in giving examples that demonstrate that nothing natural or self-evident exists, which I am quite willing to accept. But if you look at the historical studies in which whole cans of weird types are opened, then I simply think, what happened to them, what did these transgressive types actually achieve? Well, nothing.'

Vanwesenbeeck: 'They were all marginalized, just as prostitutes are continuously being marginalized.'

Mak: 'And that happens in various ways. This is precisely what I want to study: which mechanisms are used to put people back in their places or to keep the systems intact. Then you see how incredibly vulnerable individuals are to exclusions and contempt, so that things are not all that joyful after all.'

Dudink: 'I agree with you there. The self-evident celebration of transgression is the most debatable point of queer theory.'[17]

Mak: 'The transgressions only demonstrate that gender is not natural, that it is constructed. Theoretically it is easy to see this in all the intersexes. But in practice the border crossings can be warded off quite easily.'

Meijer: 'But you do see that absolute borders change into relative borders. For instance, homosexuality is no longer the third gender, but a variation of the normal. Everyone has some element of homosexuality in them. If you make this border itself the subject of a study, you can see how the status of the border changes. The

Netherlands certainly has an interesting history when it comes to debating gender and sexuality borders. Look at the students today: there you come across those temporary lesbians, cross-border traffic has become much easier. Or just look how many men have taken to kissing these days. And advertising: how gay eroticism is emerging. The twilight zone is expanding all the time.'

Vanwesenbeeck: 'And yet the stability of the normal is huge, it is an incredible stronghold.'

Meijer: 'I find it not very informative or useful to cover all that under the term "stability". Absolute or relative borders, it makes quite a difference.'

Could queer theory lead to closer co-operation between women's studies and gay studies?

Mak: 'I think that now with queer theory certain alliances are developing between women's studies and gay studies, but one of the problems with that is that queer studies has again isolated itself as a completely separate ghetto. In some strange way it has cut itself off from traditions that already existed. And so the revolutionary – if queer can be called so – remains suspended without one being able to link it properly to other academic practices. It never serves any purpose to just crash about wildly, it should have a relation to something and if the connection is lost, it becomes rather meaningless. I would prefer that queer studies developed in relation to women's studies, for example.'

Meijer: 'It is simply an attempt to attain uniqueness, exclusivity – and it works. You can see that it projects a new *élan*. After all, part of queer theory is certainly involved in a debate with women's studies, gay studies and lesbian studies. The innovative aspect in queer is that people are exploring the space to remain outside general categories: how can you think of being different as not being different, but almost as power.'

Dudink: 'That is precisely why I find the relationship of queer theory to women's studies, gay studies and lesbian studies to be problematical. The continual appeal to being in the revolutionary vanguard, the continual pressure to flee to the front, to assume a position – *the* position – from which normality can be deconstructed. I find that complicated, because I do not believe that it works that simply, and because too little of the historical nature of the outcast position is acknowledged in queer theory. Without analysing it properly and placing it in a social and historical context, the outcast position is used as a weapon to beat up on normality. As far as that is concerned, I find that what is happening in women's studies, gender studies and some areas of lesbian and gay studies is much stronger: they make the dual move of deconstruction on the one hand while on the other hand they simply study the given categories.'

Mak: 'Yes, that is precisely why I find it so damaging that queer theory is isolating itself so. You see that women who do not feel comfortable with the concept of women as used in women's studies – because they find it to be too heterosexual or too feminine or whatever – move to queer studies. And that becomes a garbage can of everyone who no longer feels that they fit in with women's studies, either theoretically or in terms of their own identity. As a result, the critical tension disappears between women's studies and everything that does not fit in seamlessly with that. And it is precisely that tension that makes women's studies so interesting. There should always be a relationship between simply having fun and the normality, the normal woman. Once that tension disappears, both have lost their point of departure. Then neither is interesting any longer.'

Dudink: 'Queer theory prides itself on the fact that everything can be included in it, while at the same time you see that a lot of analytical dimensions are swept under the table. I particularly think of the complicated relationship between gender and sexuality.[18] We are always saying that they are mutually constitutive, but it remains difficult to imagine a research practice in which you study both and in which you actually justify that basic premise. So, sometimes it looks as if we have not made any progress at all in recent years. But to me, the biggest gain of all the debates on gender and sexuality – that actually started with the debate on class and gender – is that this continual reflection on the various categories has been a tremendous driving force behind the conceptualization of the contingent nature of these categories: it enabled us to think of them as unstable and as historical. So in that respect, these debates have made a valuable contribution to the deconstructive project. And that in itself is a reason to keep the debate going.'

Notes

1 Teresa De Lauretis, *Technologies of Gender. Essays on Theory, Film and Fiction* (Bloomington: Indiana University Press, 1987).

2 Rosi Braidotti is Professor in Comparative Women's Studies geared to language and image. See Rosi Braidotti (ed.) *Poste Restante. Feministic Messages to Postmodernism* (Kampen: Kok Agora, 1994).

3 The *Tijdschrift voor Vrouwenstudies* is a Dutch scientific magazine, founded in 1980.

4 Adrienne Rich, 'Compulsory heterosexuality and lesbian existence', in *Blood, Bread and Poetry, Selected Prose 1978–1985*. (London: Virago Press, 1986).

5 Leslie Feinberg, *Stone Butch Blues* (Ithaca, NY: Fireband Books, 1993); Esther Newton, 'The mythic mannish lesbian: Radclyffe Hall and the new woman', in E. Friedman et al. (eds), *The Lesbian Issue: Essays from Signs* (Chicago: University of Chicago Press, 1985), pp. 7–25; Joan Nestle, *A Restricted Country* (Ithaca, NY: Firebrand Books, 1987).

6 Irene Costera Meijer, *Het persoonlijke wordt politiek. De geschiedenis van feministische bewustwording 1965–1980* (Amsterdam: Het Spinhuis, 1996).

7 renée c. hoogland, *Lesbian Configurations* (Cambridge: Polity Press, 1997).

8 Judith Butler, *Gender Trouble. Feminism and the Subversion of Identity* (New York: Routledge, 1990).

9 Geertje Mak, 'Wo sprechen zum Schweigen wird. Die historische Beziehung zwischen "Frau" und "Lesbe"', in Kati Röttger and Heike Paul (eds), *Differenzen in der Geschlechterdifferenz. Geschlechterdifferenz und Literatur. Publikationen des Münchener Graduiertenkollegs*, Vol. 8. (Munich: Erich Schmidt Verlag, 1998); Dorelies Kraakman, 'Vijfmaal nul is nul. Ofwel de betekenis van een Frans vrouwengeschiedenis project voor lesbische geschiedenis', in Josine Blok et al. (eds), *Deugd en ondeugd. Jaarboek voor vrouwengeschiedenis 13* (Amsterdam: Stichting beheer IISG, 1993), pp. 137–47.

10 Butler, *Gender Trouble*; Teresa de Lauretis, *The Practice of Love: Lesbian Sexuality and Perverse Desire* (Bloomington and Indianapolis: Indiana University Press, 1994).

11 Mathias Duyves, Myriam Everard, Saskia Grotenhuis, Gert Helina, Paula Koelmÿ and Jan Willem Tellegen (eds) (1983) *Among Men, Among Women. Sociological and Historical Recognition of Homosocial Arrangements.* Amsterdam: Sociologisch Instituut, Universiteit van Amsterdam.

12 Eve Kosofsky Sedgwick, *Between Men: English Literature and Male Homosocial Desire* (New York: Columbia University Press, 1985).

13 Robert Bly, *Iron John. A Book about Men* (New York: Addison-Wesley, 1990).

14 Costera Meijer *Het persoonlijke wordt politiek.*

15 Butler, *Gender Trouble*; Marjorie Garber, *Vested Interests: Cross-dressing and Cultural Anxiety* (New York and London: Routledge, 1992); Julia Epstein and Kristina Straub, *Body Guards. The Cultural Politics of Gender Ambiguity* (New York and London: Routledge, 1991); Teresa de Lauretis (ed.) 'Queer theory. Lesbian and gay sexualities', *Differences. A Journal of Feminist Cultural Studies*, 3 (2); Julia Epstein, *Altered Conditions. Disease, Medicine, and Storytelling* (New York and London: Routledge, 1995). Less optimistic, based more on the experiences of 'queers' themselves (not 'queer theory'): Leslie Feinberg, *Transgender Warriors. Making History from Joan of Arc to RuPaul* (Boston: Beacon, 1996); Kate Bornstein, *Gender Outlaw. On Men, Women and the Rest of Us* (New York: Vintage Books, 1994).

16 Eve Kosofsky Sedgwick, *Epistemology of the Closet* (Berkeley and Los Angeles: University of California Press, 1990); Michael Warner (ed.) *Fear of a Queer Planet? Queer Politics and Social Theory* (Minneapolis: University of Minnesota Press, 1993).

17 Biddy Martin, 'Extraordinary homosexuals and the fear of being ordinary', in Biddy Martin (ed.), *Femininity Played Straight: The Significance of Being Lesbian* (London: Routledge, 1996), pp. 45–70.

18 Judith Butler, 'Against proper objects', in Elizabeth Weed and Naomi Schor (eds), *Feminism Meets Queer Theory* (Bloomington: Indiana University Press, 1997), pp. 1–30; Biddy Martin, 'Sexualities without genders and other queer utopias', in Biddy Martin (ed.), *Femininity Played Straight: the Significance of Being Lesbian* (London: Routledge, 1996), pp. 45–70.

13 Fighting the Epidemic: Social AIDS Studies

Rommel Mendès-Leite and Onno de Zwart

AIDS has been a central element in the lives of most gay men over the last fifteen years. It has become an integral part of the gay and lesbian community and culture. AIDS has also generated a lot of research: research about public sex environments where men have sex with men and the frequency of sexual acts by gay men all around the globe, male sex workers and their clients, gay communities and their responses to AIDS, and how gay identity is constructed in prevention. This research can be described as social AIDS studies.

In this chapter we shall analyse how social AIDS studies have contributed to the knowledge and understanding of homosexuality, thereby paying special attention to most important discussions within social AIDS studies. Furthermore we shall describe what the relationship between social AIDS studies and gay and lesbian studies has been and might be in the future.

Social AIDS studies

Most of the chapters in this book deal with the relationship between gay and lesbian studies and a specific scientific discipline. Many of these disciplines are well established within the scientific community. Social AIDS studies is a new field of study rather than a single discipline. It would therefore be quite possible to produce a book like this one about the contribution of various scientific disciplines to our understanding of AIDS and its consequences.

Social AIDS studies is not one single field, although there is a common theme. It can be considered a construction that is aimed at collecting studies on AIDS that do not come within the framework of medicine or basic science. It encompasses studies done within different disciplines such as epidemiology, sociology, anthropology, health psychology and sexology. Within social AIDS studies distinct methodologies such as large-scale cohort studies, questionnaires and interviews about sexual behaviour, anthropological observation and discourse analysis are being used. This diversity in disciplinary background, methodology and approach makes discussion within the field sometimes quite difficult. In this chapter we shall limit ourselves to social AIDS studies related to homosexuality.

Whether social AIDS studies is a single offshoot of different disciplines or not remains an open question. In this chapter we consider it as a developing field. After all, social AIDS studies has existed for only fifteen years and although considerable research has been done over this short period, these studies are still under construction.

Compared with other health problems, AIDS has generated a lot of social research. This cannot be explained only by the fact that AIDS is a communicable disease, so that social studies can help to identify factors influencing behaviours which make transmission possible. Nor is it due only to the fact that AIDS is a deadly disease. When in the 1980s, however, it became clear that medicine could not produce a magic bullet to stop or cure AIDS, social AIDS studies made it clear that the knowledge it produced was necessary to the understanding and promotion of behavioural change (Patton, 1990), and behavioural change was the only option to stop the epidemic from spreading.

The fact that AIDS is a deadly epidemic and that behaviour change was the only way to slow the epidemic's spread has influenced social AIDS studies in many respects. It has affected discussions about what kind of knowledge is needed and thereby influenced the research agenda. At the start of the epidemic it seemed that social AIDS studies should provide guidance to prevent more gay men from becoming infected with HIV. Studies were urgently needed to give insight into sexual behaviour, factors influencing behaviour and behaviour change, and the effectiveness of prevention. Related to this sense of urgency was a debate about whether the target of prevention should be safe sex (meaning 100 per cent safety) or safer sex (as much safety as possible), and thus whether research should con-tribute to developing such 100 per cent safety prevention campaigns. Analysis of this discussion shows that many factors played a role in it, e.g., the different disciplinary backgrounds of the researchers involved (epidemiology and health psychology versus sociology and anthropology), the geographical location and often thereby also the level of the epidemic (US-based studies versus studies done in Europe and Australia), etc. Social AIDS studies has to a large extent been very utilitarian. The sense of urgency present in many makes them different from many other studies related to homosexuality. Over the years this perspective has modified (Mendès-Leite and de Busscher, 1993). This is due to the fact that AIDS has become a permanent factor in the lives of gay men and despite all research cannot be totally stopped. Social AIDS studies has outlined the complexity of behaviour change, which has resulted in a change in the research agenda.

Six perspectives

Within social AIDS studies it is possible to distinguish six main themes and perspectives. We have outlined them briefly below:

The first perspective consists mostly of research focusing on sexual behaviour, risk management and behaviour change. This is an ever-expanding field of research and is receiving most of the attention and funding. It includes studies using quantitative methods, such as large-scale cohort studies, and studies using a more qualitative or anthropological approach.

Studies that deal with AIDS and its relationship to policies, communities and movements are a second theme. These include studies that look into groups like Act Up! as a new social movement, studies that analyse the so-called AIDS industry, and studies evaluating the impact of AIDS on the gay and lesbian community.

The third approach focuses on discourse and social representation analysis. Research here ranges from in-depth analyses of the media coverage to the development of prevention discourse. Social representations that identify the disease with 'otherness' and so-called deviant behaviours have also been analysed within this field (Clatts and Mutchler, 1989; Gilman, 1988; Leap, 1995; Llamas, 1995; Mott, 1985). The role of social representations of homosexuality is central to the development of discourses on AIDS (Fausto Neto, 1991; Plexoussaki and Yannacopoulos, 1996; Watney, 1993) – among which some discourses are clearly homophobic (Llamas, 1997; Treichler, 1988).

Fourthly, we have research concentrating on persons living with HIV/AIDS (PLWHA). This approach focuses on the needs of PLWHAs (Adam, 1992), the quality of their lives (Laurindo da Silva, 1993, 1999b), the construction of an identity as a person living with HIV or AIDS (Ariss, 1997; Delor, 1997; Kowalewski, 1988; Packwood, 1992–93; Whittaker, 1992), their sexuality (Delor, 1997; Green, 1995; Keogh and Beardsell, 1997), their social integration or lack thereof, the level of social tolerance towards them, the effects of different forms of psychosocial interventions to promote the quality of their lives, the impact of being HIV positive on the relationships with family and friends (whether these individuals are HIV positive or negative), and issues related to new treatments.

A fifth category of research relates to art analysis. These studies list and research literary and cinematographic works as well as other expressions of art relating to the epidemic. The influence of AIDS on current art culture has been impressive (Aliaga, 1997b; Aliaga and Cortes, 1993; Gott, 1994; Klusacek and Morrison, 1992; Miller, 1992; Nelkin et al., 1991; Roman, 1997). The greater number of these studies are found in the field of literary analysis, ranging from research on specific authors (Boulé, 1995; Heathcote, 1995; Smith, 1997) and selected narrative forms (Duncan, 1995; Edelman, 1994; Pratt, 1995; Robinson, 1995) to more comprehensive analyses (Harvey, 1992; Murphy and Poirier, 1993; Watney, 1994).

Let us finally also mention studies on the construction of AIDS knowledge, those relating to the influence of HIV/AIDS medical research on the production of scientific knowledge, both in epidemiological (de Busscher, 1997; Levine, 1992; Seidman, 1997) and methodological terms (Boulton, 1993; Kotarba, 1990) but also those adopting a sociological and philosophical angle (Altman, 1989; Cardin, 1990; Duttmann, 1995; Weeks, 1991, 1995). These studies range from analysing the major shift in sex-related studies – and especially those about male homosexuality – towards an AIDS 'focus' (Gagnon, 1992; Giami, 1992, 1996), to the possible impact of AIDS on applying methodologies that are commonly used in social sciences, such as participant observation (Mendès-Leite and de Busscher, 1993; Wight and Barnard, 1993), moral and ethical problems raised during first-hand observation of sexual behaviour patterns in bathhouses or outdoor cruising places (Bolton, 1995; Broqua, 1997) or researchers' closeness to infected people and the influence of this on their personal involvement in their research. Community activism, especially in the USA, rooted as it is in the gay community, has also influenced science (Epstein, 1996; Nguyet-Erni, 1994; Wachter, 1991). In his groundbreaking study, Epstein made it clear how community activism has altered the way clinical science and trials have been constructed and carried out, and how activism has made drugs more readily available.

In this chapter we shall concentrate on the first two perspectives and their connections to gay studies. These perspectives are the most extensive and have also played a major role in prevention directed at gay men. In some countries, especially in the English-speaking world, the lesbian community has been involved with AIDS since the beginning of the epidemic (Schneider, 1992; Stoller, 1997; Winnow, 1989). However, research into sexual behaviour of lesbian women in the light of AIDS, like research into the consequences of AIDS on the lesbian community (Schneider, 1997), has been scarce. The situation of lesbians requires specific attention, more than can be given in this chapter. The scant research on these issues that does exist was conducted mostly in the United States (cf. for instance Chu et al., 1992; Dicker, 1989; Hollibaugh, 1994; Young et al., 1992) and Italy (Raiteri et al., 1994). However scarce it is, it does indicate that, even though the actual risks of transmission of HIV in sex between women is very low, being lesbian does not exclude all risks. Lesbian women run risks in other ways, i.e. when they have sex with men (bisexuality), when they use drugs or are destitute (Bevier et al., 1995; Lemp et al., 1995). It is therefore essential to discriminate between these two factors and the possibility of the sexual transmission of AIDS among lesbians when one partner has been infected by HIV (Lhomond, 1996). Confusing these issues may lead to approaching the subject only from the viewpoint of sexually related infection, thereby possibly minimizing, even negating, social exposure, however real it is (Lhomond, 1992). This points to the difficulties related to different forms of categorization in research and AIDS prevention (Kitzinger, 1994; Richardson, 1988, 1994). Epidemiological categorization can differ from self-representations, which can differ from how HIV/AIDS is represented. It is therefore important to take the social and political context into account both in research and in developing prevention not only for lesbians, but for any population.

Sexual behaviour, risk management and behaviour change

This approach is the most common (Riedmann and Kraus, 1994). It dominates the research agenda because the results of these studies can help to explain the spread of the epidemic as well as being used for the development and evaluation of preventive interventions. Within this approach, an individualistic, cognitive paradigm, using models such as the Theory of Planned Behaviour, Health Belief Model and AIDS Risk Reduction Model, is prominent in the English-speaking world, especially in the US (Flowers et al., in press). This prominence is related to the fact that AIDS came at a time when theories about rational decision-making were (and still are) the ruling paradigm within (health) psychology in the US. Since most US research was rooted in health psychology and most of the research has been conducted in the US, it is not surprising that these theoretical models have dominated the field ever since.

Social AIDS studies first of all contributed to more knowledge of gay men's sexual behaviour. Before AIDS only three major studies had dealt with sexual behaviour of gay men: those of Bell and Weinberg (1978), Bon and D'Arc (1974), and Dannecker and Reiche (1974). Since then, a lot of research has been carried out, and the resulting cohort studies have given the first detailed descriptions of sexual behaviour over a longer period of time (Coxon, 1996; Davies et al., 1993; De Wit, 1994; Ekstrand and Coates, 1990).

These studies, along with cross-cultural comparisons, show that a great many gay men have more partners than heterosexual men do (Sandfort, 1998). The most popular sexual activities for gay men are masturbation – which, since AIDS, is practised even more – and oral sex (Bochow et al., 1994). Two-thirds of gay men practise anal sex, although more often with regular than with casual partners. Some of these studies have also yielded information about self-identification, membership of gay organizations and acceptance of homosexuality by family, friends and colleagues. These studies have contributed greatly to increasing knowledge about gay men. We know now more about the sex – and probably also social – lives of gay men than at any time before.

These studies and cross-sectional studies, some of which were repeated at various intervals (Adam and Schiltz, 1996; Bochow, 1994; Pollak, 1988; De Vroome et al., 1998), indicate that many changes have taken place in gay sexual behaviour since the early 1980s. These changes include a decrease in the number of sexual partners, including anonymous partners; a decrease in unprotected anal sex, and an increase in protected anal sex (Schiltz and Adam, 1995). The changes have been accompanied by a decrease in the rate of seroconversion to HIV and a decrease in sexually transmitted diseases (STDs) among gay men (Donovan et al., 1994). Most studies in the 1980s identified a change in the sexual behaviour by which gay men reduced their risk exposure. However, in the early 1990s some studies reported that some gay men were engaging again in risky sexual practices (De Wit et al., 1993; Prieur, 1990). Researchers used the term 'relapse' to describe this return to former practices. The use and implications of this term led to a fierce debate within social AIDS studies. Some researchers, mostly from the US, considered it the right term to use; others, especially in Europe and Australia, opposed its use, condemning the implicit connection with addiction. More importantly, they argued that equating unprotected with unsafe sex did not take account of sexual behaviour's context (Adam and Schiltz, 1996; Bochow, 1991; Davies and The Project Sigma, 1992; Hart et al., 1992).

Many social AIDS studies have tried to include different sorts of men who have sex with men. It soon became clear that the term 'gay' was not sufficient to describe all the relevant experiences and identities. The need to acknowledge the diversity of gay men was also noticed in prevention, as some prevention materials did not appeal to all the intended readers. The term 'men having sex with men' was therefore used. Although this enabled social AIDS studies to use a purely descriptive term, it is interesting to notice the parallel with gay and lesbian studies. In the 1990s gay and lesbian studies in United States incorporated the use of the term 'queer'. Both terms aim to acknowledge the range of situations accounted for, with 'men having sex with men' rooted in the description of sexual behaviour and 'queer' rooted in the awareness of the limits of the notion of the gay identity.

The will to include a diversity of men who have sex with men has not only led to a different terminology. Recent research carried out in the UK has shown large numbers of men – tens of thousands – do not identify themselves as gay or bisexual, but have sexual contacts with other men who often do not identify themselves as gay or bisexual either (Weatherburn et al., 1996). Research on men with bisexual practices and/or identities (Parker and Carballo, 1990; Tielman et al., 1991; Weinberg et al., 1994) has shown that some of them consider themselves heterosexual. The category that is socially labelled 'bisexual' becomes much more of a problem than some researchers would care to admit, especially those who rely on the epidemiological approach.

These studies have also demonstrated that a sizeable percentage of men with bisexual behaviour base their safer sex management on their partner's gender, i.e. that they tend to take more precautions during homosexual sex, but noticeably less when their partners are female. This is all the more true because to some men, women represent a 'normal' world (i.e. a heterosexual world, without homosexuality, where prostitution and using intravenously injectable drugs is proscribed), a world that they often imagine to be almost completely safe from AIDS-related risks (Mendès-Leite et al., 1996). Research and prevention policies based on sexual identities should therefore also be considered from the angle of sexual practices (Messiah and Mouret-Forme, 1993), without neglecting the importance of ambivalent identities in categories that were considered non-problematic for so long – including by scientists – that they are now taken for granted (Mendès-Leite and Deschamps, 1997).

Since HIV in the gay male community is transmitted mostly through sexual contact, many social AIDS studies have focused on factors that influence sexual behaviour. Although most studies limit themselves to identifying 'risk factors', such factors can be placed in a broader context. Most studies have looked into individual factors influencing decisions about sexual behaviour. This individual focus is related to the influential social-cognitive paradigm. Others have pointed out the importance of interpersonal aspects and the context of sexual contact (Davies et al., 1993; Dowsett, 1995, 1996; Flowers et al., in press). One of the main factors influencing decisions about safety is whether sexual contact occurs within a stable partnership or with a casual partner. Other factors that have been observed, and debated by some, include age, geographical location, the use of alcohol and drugs, education, attitudes, social influence, social standards, the ability to use condoms, and risk perception (Hospers and Kok, 1995).

The notion that sexual behaviour with steady partners differs from that with casual partners, in that more unprotected anal sex takes place with steady partners, has sparked the most recent debate within social AIDS studies. Realizing that many gay men in partnerships decide not to use condoms with each other, Australian researchers have coined the term 'negotiated safety'. This term is used to describe unprotected anal sex by HIV-negative partners in a relationship that is contingent on the partners' having made safety agreements about sex with others. Based on this notion, prevention strategies have been developed in Australia, the UK, Belgium and the Netherlands. Others, however, have fiercely criticized this strategy and called it 'negotiated danger'. Whereas most studies see this behaviour, researchers doubt whether men will stick to their agreements and thus if such a strategy is really safe. This debate is related to the earlier discussion about whether 100 per cent safety should be the goal or not. From a '100 per cent safety' perspective negotiated safety seems nonsense; from a more contextual view it is a logical and justifiable option.

HIV-related risk factors have been identified mostly in large-scale quantitative studies. More in-depth qualitative analyses have led to more knowledge about certain aspects of sexual behaviour and factors influencing risk-taking. The meaning that anal sex has for gay men, how anal sex is organized and how this is related to the use of condoms have received more attention, ableit relatively late in the epidemic (Davies et al., 1993; Prieur, 1990; Van Kerkhof et al., 1995). Studies have also addressed the issues of gay identity, one's relations to the gay community and (un)protected sexual behaviour (Sandfort, 1995). Through the use of sexual diaries, social AIDS studies has been able to map in detail a select group's sexual behaviour over time (Coxon, 1996). The diary method has yielded the most detailed diachronic description of sexual behaviour, thereby showing that other methods are less reliable in recording exact sexual behaviour.

Research conducted in France (Mendès-Leite, 1998) has revealed a phenomenon labelled 'imaginary and symbolic protections'. These studies reveal that most individuals acknowledge the need to use various preventive techniques to avoid HIV infection. Yet people sometimes apply the official prevention guidelines with a different meaning. This process of reassigning meaning involves a kind of symbolic 'manipulation' of preventive techniques that allows these practices to be drawn closer to the person's own cognitive framework. On the other hand, when it comes to their representations of what is safe and what is not, these men sometimes admitted to taking risks, which they considered as actual, i.e. potentially dangerous, even though from an epidemiological standpoint they were not. These declarations are related to social imagery associating some styles of sexuality or sexual practices with perversion, filth, sexual deviance and, consequently, infection and the spread of these imaginary dangers.

Some studies have concentrated on specific scenes or services, such as the gay dance scene and sex cinemas. Consequently they have yielded information not only about sexual behaviour, but also about the nature and function of these scenes or services for gay men (Henriksson, 1995; Lewis and Ross, 1995). Other studies, although not directly based on the same subject and applying different methodologies, have their own way of playing down traits that were stigmatized by the homosexual subculture, including impersonal/casual sex, multi-partner sex and the availability of places where this type of sex can take place. Throughout the study of the eroticization of space, a number of researchers (Bolton, 1992a; Henriksson, 1995; Henriksson and Mänsson, 1995; Mendès-Leite and Proth, 1998; Mendès-Leite and de Busscher, 1997) have discovered a new field of meanings, visible only to a trained eye. In most of these eroticized areas, verbal communication is replaced by body language. Social and sexual potential is directly related to the specific geographical characteristics of the locus. These characteristics lead to a particular use of space and to symbolic boundaries defining different areas and activities.

This type of finding points to the different ways in which these loci are taken over, which in turn could lead to differentiated prevention policies. A study conducted in Belgium (Bolton et al., 1994) has also shown that the availability of preventive material and tools (flyers, posters, condoms, etc.) makes it easier to learn prevention messages, provided that the symbolical appropriation of this material is integrated into the social actors' rationales. This research amounts to saying that multi-partnership may also facilitate the adoption of preventive behaviour, especially if negotiation processes are repeated.

Collective responses to the epidemic

The fact that AIDS was first identified in gay men and struck the gay community first had a profound impact on different communities' responses to the pandemic. Community-based organizations sprang up all around the globe, often because of the lack of official reaction. Some authors described how many of these organizations were rooted in the gay and lesbian community and were influenced by earlier experiences of gay activism (Altman, 1994; Broqua et al., 1997; Duyvendak and Koopmans, 1991; Epstein, 1999; Fillieule and Duyvendak, 1999). An interesting example of the link between gay activism and community reactions to AIDS is the use of the phrase 'coming out'. Originally, 'coming out of the closet' meant starting an openly gay lifestyle. This expression, which originated in the US, was soon used in gay communities throughout the English-speaking world. Within the AIDS movement it took on the meaning of being open about one's positive HIV status. Since then it has become widely used for being public about other diseases as well.

Creating safer sex as a practice and bringing it into widespread use within gay communities deeply influenced AIDS prevention and turned it into a crucial notion in societies worldwide. However, safer sex approaches and techniques are not always identical. They depend on complex processes of dialectical influences and mediation among distinct social agencies such as gay activism, the fight against AIDS, public health institutions, etc. (de Busscher, 1996; De Zwart et al., 1998). Social factors (broadly defined to include religious, political and cultural influences as well) must also be considered. The successfulness of gay prevention as measured by the new case index varies from one country to another (Pollak, 1993a). Similarly, negotiations between authorities, both governmental and medical, and AIDS organizations (especially non-profit and activist organizations) on developing prevention policies – where safer sex occasionally assumes the status of hardcore ideology (de Busscher, 1995) – have at times been very conflictual (MacRae, 1987a, 1987b; Mott, 1989). This is certainly one reason why highly politicized, militant organizations were created and developed in several countries, the best example being Act Up! (Carter, 1992; Crimp, 1987; Crimp and Rolston, 1990; Elbaz, 1995; Gamson, 1989).

AIDS has had a paradoxical effect on the gay subculture. On the one hand, especially in the US, it led to changes in the commercialized and sex-oriented subculture. In some countries, such as the US and UK, bathhouses were closed down at the beginning of the epidemic. This was due not only to political pressure, but was also linked to the diminishing number of clients and the criticism voiced by some segments of the gay community. At the same time AIDS has probably contributed largely to the development of new activities within the gay subculture, sport clubs being the best example. As sex became overshadowed by the virus, gay men and lesbians sought more non-sexual ways to meet and enjoy themselves. The rise of new activities, culminating in the success of the Gay Games, has continued. The downturn, however, of the traditional subculture seems to have been a temporal phenomenon. Acknowledgement of diversity within the gay community has given rise to a growing subculture and sex-oriented institutions have reopened and regained popularity. The last trend is not uncontroversial, again especially in the US, where it has become part of the so-called 'sex wars'.

Researchers have identified the strengths and weaknesses of community-based organizations (Altman, 1994). They have also made it clear that the success of AIDS activism is related to national political structures and the specificities of the gay community (Arnal, 1993; Berridge, 1996; de Busscher and Pinell, 1996; Duyvendak, 1995a; Kayal, 1993; Kirp and Bayer, 1992; Llamas and Vila, 1997; Padgug and Oppenheimer, 1992). In this respect, the Netherlands is an interesting example (De Zwart et al., 1998). AIDS prevention in Holland was started by the gay community in close co-operation with some medical and political authorities. As in the Scandinavian countries and Australia, community-based organizations worked closely with the government. In the Netherlands, however, this also resulted in a more inflexible prevention message about anal sex ('Don't fuck and if you can't stop, use a condom') and an absence of activist organizations like Act Up! compared with France and the US (Duyvendak, 1995b). Co-operation and inclusion made radical protest less feasible and it has been suggested that part of the price was a more conservative message. The influence of AIDS activism was unprecedented and has influenced other organizations of people living with diseases.

It has become difficult to imagine the gay community without AIDS, although that exact image is used in some prevention materials (for example by the Gay City project in Seattle, in which the image of a gay community is applied, not characterized by red ribbons). AIDS has profoundly influenced gay communities over the last fifteen years (Dowsett, 1996; Rofes, 1996; Van Kerkhof et al., 1991). Dowsett pointed out the importance of taking into account the specific local situation. In analysing the gay communities in Melbourne and Sydney he has distinguished the rise of a 'post-AIDS' culture originating from two different situations. Whereas 'post-AIDS' in Sydney stands for a younger generation who have incorporated AIDS into their lives and consider it a part of everyday gay life, 'post-AIDS' in Melbourne stands for a community that has been only slightly affected. This makes it clear that despite AIDS's omnipresence in gay culture, specific situations do differ and the seroprevalence rate within a specific community (ranging from more than 50 per cent of gay men in some US cities to less than 5 per cent in some large cities in Western Europe) influences communities' responses (King, 1993).

Other authors have tried to describe the impact AIDS has had on gay communities (Aliaga, 1997a; Levine et al., 1997; Rofes, 1996; Van Kerkhof et al.,

1991; Wright 1996). In recent years specific attention has been paid to the issue of an 'AIDS survivor syndrome' within the gay community. Such a syndrome encompasses the reactions of the men and women who have lost many partners, friends, roommates and colleagues. Some authors (Odets, 1995; Wright, 1996) described individual men having such experiences; others, such as Rofes (1996), focused on the gay community and how it handles death and survival. Several studies delved into community response to mourning and the social construction of cultivating the memory of people who have died from AIDS (Sherr, 1995), sometimes insisting on the relationships between mourning and militancy (Broqua, 1998; Crimp, 1989) or between collective memory and citizenship (Brown, 1997).

In connection with the issue of a survivor syndrome, attention has been drawn to the situation of HIV-negative men in the US. In his influential study, Odets (1995) showed that in some US cities, becoming HIV positive is a rite of passage that seems to be an inevitable part of a gay life course for some people. He argued that, apart from specific attention to the social and psychological needs of gay men with HIV or AIDS, men also need special attention.

An important element in all research on gay communities is its specificity. Although AIDS is an element in all gay communities, the contexts everywhere are different. The differences extend to the levels of seroprevalence, the number of people aware of their serological status, social support systems, and the legal situation. Taking the specific gay community's local and historical context into account is a prerequisite in analysing communities and – although it is too often forgotten – in using studies to develop preventive and other actions (cf. Adam et al., 1999).

Conclusion: counting sexual acts or analysing sexuality?

The first case of what later came to be known as AIDS was diagnosed in the US in 1981. This was also the year that *The Making of the Modern Homosexual*, edited by Ken Plummer, was published. This book can be considered a landmark in gay and lesbian studies as it focused the discussion for years to come on the topic of essentialism versus constructionism. With hindsight, it also made it clear that gay and lesbian studies at that time concentrated mostly on sociological and historical issues such as the construction of the homosexual identity and the social organization of homosexuals. Concrete sexual behaviour seemed of less interest.

According to Plummer (1992), in the 1970s gay and lesbian studies in the English-speaking world were especially influenced by sociology, psychology and history; in the 1980s by cultural studies, literary theory and postmodern feminism; and in the 1990s by the rise of queer theory. Other disciplines have influenced social AIDS studies, so that these studies emphasize different themes and use a different methodology.

Social AIDS studies have resulted in detailed knowledge about the sexual behaviour of gay men and some of the factors influencing it. These studies sometimes offered an opportunity to gather knowledge about other aspects of gay life as well. In some cases, they have given a better understanding of some of the complex issues related to gay men's sexuality, such as the meanings attached to different sexual acts and how this meaning relates to identity (Pollak, 1993b). The debates within the social AIDS studies approach have often been related to the underlying suppositions reflecting the split between researchers who define AIDS foremost as a health problem that needs to be cured and researchers who contextualize AIDS with the sexual and social behaviour of gay men. The latter approach resembles the development of gay and lesbian studies where more and more emphasis has been placed on context, lived reality and the construction of sexuality, gender and identity. It is not surprising that those researchers emphasizing context were themselves rooted in either gay and lesbian studies or related disciplines.

The need for, and significance of, research in humanities/social sciences and public health indisputably contributed greatly to more generous funding for prevention, and consequently to a boom in sex research. Research on male homosexuality certainly took on unprecedented proportions. Investigators studied matters that had already been researched, albeit on a smaller scale, such as male and transvestite prostitution (Estep et al., 1992; Laurindo da Silva, 1999a; Mendès-Lopes, 1995; Parker, 1991), young people starting a homosexual life (Lhomond, 1997), homophobia (Mott, 1996; Treichler, 1988; Welzer-Lang et al., 1994), male same sex couples (Hickson et al., 1992). But the situation also facilitated studies on issues that had been researched very little or completely ignored, such as male homosexual multi-partnership (Bedfellows, 1996; Bolton, 1992b; Crimp, 1988; Mendès-Leite, 1995) and the sexualization of space (Betsky, 1997; Mendès Leite and de Busscher, 1997; Mendès Leite and Proth, 1998; Woodhead, 1995), and research in countries or communities and cultural/ethnic groups where male homosexuality had been studied little or not at all (Carballo-Dieguez, 1989; Diaz, 1997; Huashan, 1996; Isaacs and McKendrick, 1992; Jeay, 1991; Murray, 1995; Pegge, 1994; Peterson, 1997; Sabogal et al., 1993). Last but not least, as yet untackled subject matters, such as homosexual mourning and related rites, were analysed. Other research fields, including those relating to lesbianism and infection risk management among females, are, as mentioned, still embryonic. It is clear, however, that research on sexualities in the light of the AIDS epidemic is approached differently from studies of sexualities *per se*, and homosexuality even more so. One consequence of the 'AIDSification' of social science research means that a certain (re-)medicalization of sexualities is happening. This phenomenon may conceal another one, i.e. a certain impoverishment of research where more emphasis is being placed on counting (quantitative approach) or describing (qualitative approach) sexual acts or behaviours with or without condoms than analysing social phenomena where sex is part of a complex issue on a larger scale. This happens, for example, when research is developed in a utilitarian framework, as is often the case with urgent situations, of which the AIDS epidemic is a perfect example, especially when sponsors push in that direction. By the same token, the power inherently wielded by decision-making sponsors allows them to ignore certain issues that are considered irrelevant from an epidemiological viewpoint, such as infection risks in lesbian sex, or because they are 'embarrassing' (sado-masochism, impersonal sex, etc.). Thus social AIDS studies has not only contributed to our understanding of homosexuality. It has also expanded the field of gay and lesbian studies, and social sciences in particular. A pertinent example is the revival, or at least the questioning, of traditional methodological know-how and the limits thereof, like participant observation being turned into 'observing participation' by certain researchers due to the requirements of fieldwork (Mendès-Leite and de Busscher, 1993). As pointed out previously, another contribution is the development of studies on new or as yet hardly researched topics, even a stronger multidisciplinarity in using a dual approach (both qualitative and quantitative) or reconsidering certain issues – such as the deconstruction of certain traditional concepts and notions – which, due to the issue of the epidemic, may now be questioned differently.

If one asks whether social AIDS studies would have been different if gay and lesbian studies had not existed, the answer has to be 'yes!' Although gay and lesbian studies still does not have the status which social AIDS studies rapidly received, it did establish the study of homosexuality as a legitimate scientific practice. With its roots within the gay and lesbian community, it also influenced gay men's involvement in research. Since the start of the AIDS epidemic more gay men than ever before have participated as 'research subjects'. Gay and lesbian studies has certainly meant that gay men have been taken seriously as research subjects. The attention paid to contextualizing behaviour, as well as contextualizing homosexuality, has been influenced by gay and lesbian studies. Although this approach is far from universal within social AIDS studies, far more attention has been paid to the context of behaviour with regard to AIDS than is the case for other diseases, which are often considered health problems only.

In this chapter we have tried to give some insights into social AIDS studies and its connections with gay and lesbian studies. What is missing is a thorough analysis of social AIDS studies on a par with Epstein's analysis of the biomedical sciences and AIDS activism. So many questions remain unanswered. For example, why has gay and AIDS activism hardly bothered with social AIDS studies? How have funding policies affected social AIDS studies over the years? How has the trend of scientificization influenced social AIDS studies? Social AIDS studies would benefit greatly if gay and lesbian studies took up this challenge.

Note

The authors wish to thank Pierre-Olivier de Busscher, Lucille Cairns, Brigitte Lhomond, Ricardo Llamas and Constantinos Phellas for their help on bibliographical research, and Christophe Broqua, Bruno Proth, Stuart Michaels and Theo Sandfort for their insightful review, comments and suggestions.

References

Adam, B. (1992) 'Sociology and people living with AIDS', in J. Huber and B. Schneider (eds), *The Social Context of AIDS*. London: Sage. pp. 3–18.
Adam, P. and Schiltz, M.-A. (1996) 'Relapse et cantonnement du risque aux marges de la communauté: deux idées reçues à l'épreuve de l'enquête presse gaie', in ANRS, *Les*

Homosexuels face au sida. Rationalités et gestions des risques. Paris: Agence Nationale de Recherches sur le Sida. pp. 11–24.

Adam, B., Duyvendak, J.-W. and Krouwel, A. (eds) (1999) *The Global Emergence of Gay and Lesbian Politics. National Imprints of a Worldwide Movement*. Philadelphia: Temple University Press.

Aliaga, J.V. (1997a) 'La comunidad gay, el SIDA y la sociedad española', in J.V. Aliaga and J.M. Cortés (eds), *Identidad y diferencia. Sobre la cultura gay en España*. Barcelona and Madrid: Egales-Editorial Gay y Lesbiana. pp. 89–107.

Aliaga, J.V. (1997b) *Bajo vientre. Representaciones de la sexualidad en la cultura y el arte contemporaneos*. Valencia: Generalitat Valenciana.

Aliaga, J.V. and Cortés, J.M. (1993) *De amor y de rabia. Acerca del arte y el sida*. Valencia: Universidad Politecnica de Valencia.

Altman, D. (1989) 'AIDS and the reconceptualization of homosexuality', in D. Altman, C. Vance, M. Vicinus, J. Weeks et. al (eds), *Homosexuality, Which Homosexuality?* Amsterdam and London: Uigeverij An Dekker-Schorer/Gay Men's Press. pp. 35–48.

Altman, D. (1994) *Power and Community: Organisational and Cultural Responses to AIDS*. London and Bristol: Taylor & Francis.

Ariss, R. (1997) *Against Death: the Practice of Living with AIDS*. Amsterdam: Gordon & Breach.

Arnal, F. (1993) *Résister ou disparaître? Les homosexuels face au sida. La prévention de 1982 à 1992*. Paris: L'Harmattan.

Bedfellows, D. (ed.) (1996) *Policing Public Sex. Queer Politics and the Future of AIDS Activism*. Boston: South End Press.

Bell, A.P. and Weinberg, M.S. (1978) *Homosexualities: A Study of Diversity among Men and Women*. London: Mitchell Beazley.

Berridge, V. (1996) *AIDS in the UK: the Making of Policy, 1981–1994*. Oxford: Oxford University Press.

Betsky, A. (1997) *Queer Space. Architecture and Same-Sex Desire*. New York: William Morrow.

Bevier, P.J., Chiasson, M.A., Hefferman, R.T. and Castro, K.G. (1995) 'Women at a sexually transmitted disease clinic who reported same sex contact: their HIV seroprevalence and risk behaviors', *American Journal of Public Health*, 85 (10): 1366–71.

Bochow, M. (1991) 'Le Safer Sex: une discussion sans fin', in M. Pollak, R. Mendès-Leite and J. Vandemborghe (eds), *Homosexualités et sida*. Lille: GKC.

Bochow, M. (1994) *Schwuler Sex und die Bedrohung durch AIDS Reaktionen homosexueller Männer in Ost- und West-Deutschland*. Berlin: Deutsche AIDS Hilfe.

Bochow, M. et al. (1994) 'Sexual behaviour of gay and bisexual men in eight European countries', *AIDS Care*, 6 (5): 533–49.

Bolton, R. (1992a) 'Mapping terra incognita: sex research for AIDS prevention. An urgent agenda for the 1990s', in G. Herdt and S. Lindenbaum (eds), *The Time of AIDS. Social Analysis, Theory, and Method*. London: Sage. pp. 124–58.

Bolton, R. (1992b) 'AIDS and promiscuity: muddles in the models of HIV prevention', in R. Bolton and M. Singer (eds), *Rethinking AIDS Prevention. Cultural Approaches*. Montreux: Gordon & Breach. pp. 7–85.

Bolton, R. (1995) 'Tricks, friends and lovers: erotic encounters in the field', in D. Kulick and M. Willson (eds), *Taboo: Sex, Identity and Erotic Subjectivity in Anthropological Fieldwork*. London: Routledge. pp. 140–67.

Bolton, R., Vincke, J. and Mak, R. (1994) 'Gay baths revisited. An empirical analysis', *GLQ, A Journal of Lesbian and Gay Studies*, 1 (3): 255–73.

Bon, M. and D'Arc, A. (1974) *Rapport sur l'homosexualité de l'homme*. Paris: Éditions universitaires.

Boulé, J.P. (1995) *Hervé Guibert. A l'ami qui ne m'a pas sauvé la vie and Other Writings*. Glasgow: University of Glasgow French and German Publications.

Boulton, M. (1993) 'Methodological issues in HIV/AIDS social research: recent debates, recent developments', *AIDS*, 7 (1): S249–55.

Broqua, C. (1997) 'Enjeux méthodologiques des recherches ethnographiques sur les sexualités entre hommes', *Transcriptase*, 52: 18–23.

Broqua, C. (1998) 'De Quelques Expressions collectives de la mémoire face au sida', *Ethnologie Française*, 28 (1): 103–11.

Broqua, C., Busscher, P.O. de and Pinell, P. (1997) 'Du Mouvement à la communauté homosexuelle', *Politique: la revue*, 5: 57–60.

Brown, M.P. (1997) *Replacing Citizenship: AIDS Activism and Radical Democracy*. New York: Guilford Press.

Busscher, P.O. de (1995) 'The development of safer sex as an ideology in France, 1989–1994', in D. Friedrich and W. Heckmann (eds), *AIDS in Europe: The Behavioural Aspect*, Vol. 3: *Frameworks of Behaviour Modification*. Berlin: Sigma. pp. 185–92.

Busscher, P.O. de (1996) 'L'Évaluation des outils de prévention en milieu homosexuel: pour une approche structurale', in Ex æquo, *Homosexualité(s), Sida et Prévention(s)*. Brussels: Ex æquo. pp. 117–22.

Busscher, P.O. de (1997) 'Les Enjeux entre champ scientifique et mouvement homosexuel en France au temps du sida', *Sociologie et Sociétés*, 29 (1): 47–60.

Busscher, P.O. de and Pinell, P. (1996) 'La Création des associations de lutte contre le sida', in S. Héfez (ed.), *Sida et vie psychique: approche clinique et prise en charge*. Paris: La Découverte.

Carballo-Dieguez, A. (1989) 'Hispanic culture, gay male culture, and AIDS: counseling implications', *Journal of Counseling and Development*, 68: 26–30.

Cardin, A. (1990) 'Una cierta sensación de fin', in A. Cardin, *Lo projimo y lo ajeno*. Barcelona: Icaria.

Carter, G.M. (1992) *Act Up. The AIDS War and Activism*. Westfield, NJ: Open Media.

Chu, S.Y., Hammett, T.A. and Buehler, J.W. (1992) 'Update: epidemiology of reported cases of AIDS in women who report sex only with other women, United States, 1980–1991', *AIDS*, 6 (5): 518–19.

Clatts, M. and Mutchler, K. (1989) 'AIDS and the dangerous other: metaphors of sex and deviance in the representation of disease', *Medical Anthropology*, 11 (2–3): 105–14.

Coxon, A. (1996) *Between the Sheets. Sexual Diaries and Gay Men's Sex in the Era of AIDS*. London: Cassell.

Crimp, D. (1987) 'AIDS: cultural analysis cultural activism', *October*, 43: 15.

Crimp, D. (1988) 'How to have promiscuity in an epidemic', in D. Crimp (ed.), *AIDS. Cultural Analysis Cultural Activism*. Cambridge, MA: MIT Press. pp. 237–71.

Crimp, D. (1989) 'Mourning and militancy', *October*, 51: 3–18.

Crimp, D. and Rolston, A. (1990) *AIDS Demographics*. Seattle: Bay Press.

Dannecker, M. and Reiche, R. (1974) *Der gewöhnliche Homosexuelle. Eine soziologische Untersuchung über männliche Homosexuelle in der Bundesrepublik*. Frankfurt am Main: Fischer.

Davies, P. and The Project Sigma (1992) 'On relapse: recidivism or rational response?', in P. Aggleton, G. Hart and P. Davies (eds), *AIDS: Rights, Risks and Reason*. London: The Falmer Press. pp. 133–41.

Davies, P.M., Hickson, F.C.I., Weatherburn, P. and Hunt, A.J. (1993) *Sex, Gay Men and AIDS*. London: The Falmer Press.

Delor, F. (1997) *Séropositifs. Trajectoires identitaires et rencontres du risque*. Paris: L'Harmattan.

De Vroome, E.M.M., Kok, G.J., Jager, J.C., Tielman, R.A.P. and Sandfort, T.G.M. (1998) 'The adoption and maintenance of safe sex in a national cohort of gay men in the Netherlands', in T.G.M. Sandfort (ed.), *The Dutch Response to HIV: Pragmatism and Consensus*. London: UCL Press. pp. 246–61.

De Wit, J. (1994) *Prevention of HIV Infection among Homosexual Men. Behavior Change and Behavioral Determinants*. Amsterdam: Thesis Publishers.

De Wit, J.B.F., Van Griensven, G.J.P., Kok, G.J. and Sandfort, T.G.M. (1993) 'Why do homosexual men relapse into unsafe sex? Predictors of resumption of unprotected anogenital intercourse with casual partners', *AIDS*, 7: 1113–18.

De Zwart, O., Sandfort, T.G.M. and Van Kerkhof, M.P.N. (1998) 'No anal sex please: we are Dutch. A dilemma in HIV prevention directed at gay men', in T.G.M. Sandfort (ed.), *The Dutch Response to HIV: Pragmatism and Consensus*. London: UCL Press. pp. 135–52.

Diaz, R.M. (1997) 'Latino gay men and psycho-cultural barriers to AIDS prevention', in M.P. Levine, P.M. Nardi and J.H. Gagnon (eds), *In Changing Times. Gay Men and Lesbians Encounter HIV/AIDS*. Chicago: University of Chicago Press. pp. 221–44.

Dicker, B.G. (1989) 'Risk of AIDS among lesbians', *American Journal of Public Health*, 79 (11): 1569.

Donovan, C., Mearns, C., McEwan, R. and Sugden, N. (1994) 'A review of the HIV related sexual behaviour of gay men and men who have sex with men', *AIDS Care*, 6 (5): 605–17.

Dowsett, G. (1995) 'Sexual contexts, HIV prevention and gay men', *Venereology*, 8 (4): 243–50.

Dowsett, G. (1996) *Practicing Desire: Homosexual Sex in the Era of AIDS*. Chicago: University of Chicago Press.

Duncan, D. (1995) 'Gestes autobiographiques: le sida et les formes d'expressions artistiques du moi', *Nottingham French Studies*, 34 (1): 100–11.

Duttmann, A.G. (1995) *La discordia del sida. Como se piensa y se habla acerca de un virus*. Madrid: Anaya & Mario Muchnik.

Duyvendak, J.W. (1995a) 'De la révolution à l'involution: la disparition du mouvement gai', in R. Mendès-Leite (ed.), *Un Sujet inclassable? Approches sociologiques, littéraires et juridiques des homosexualités*. Lille: GKC. pp. 87–98.

Duyvendak, J.W. (1995b) 'De Hollandse aanpak van een epidemie: of waarom Act Up! in Nederland niet kon doorbreken', *Acta Politica*, 15 (2): 189–214.

Duyvendak, J.W. and Koopmans, R. (1991) 'Résister au Sida: destin et influence du mouvement homosexuel', in M. Pollak, R. Mendès-Leite and J. Van Dem Borghe (eds), *Homosexualités et Sida*. Lille: GKC. pp. 195–224.

Edelman, L. (1994) *Homographesis: Essays in Gay Literary and Cultural Theory*. New York: Routledge.

Ekstrand, M.L. and Coates, T.J. (1990) 'Maintenance of sexual behaviours and predictors of risky sex: the San Francisco Men's Health Study', *American Journal of Public Health*, 80: 973–7.

Elbaz, G. (1995) 'Beyond anger: the activist construction of the AIDS crisis', *Social Justice*, 22 (4): 43–69.

Epstein, S. (1996) *Impure Science. AIDS, Activism and the Politics of Knowledge*. Berkeley: University of California Press.

Epstein, S. (1999) 'Gay and lesbian movements in the United States. Dilemmas of identity, diversity, and political strategy', in B. Adam and J-W. Duyvendak (eds), *The Global Emergence of Gay and Lesbian Politics. National Imprints of a Worldwide Movement*. Philadelphia: Temple University Press. pp. 30–90.

Estep, R., Waldorf, D. and Marotta, T. (1992) 'Sexual behavior of male prostitutes', in J. Huber and B. Schneider (eds), *The Social Context of AIDS*. London: Sage. pp. 95–112.

Fausto Neto, A. (1991) *Mortes em derrapagem. Os casos Corona e Cazuza no discurso da comunicaçao de massa*. Rio de Janeiro: Rio Fundo Editôra.

Fillieule, O. and Duyvendak, J.-W. (1999) 'Gay and lesbian activism in France. Between integration and community-oriented movements', in B. Adam and J-W. Duyvendak (eds), *The Global Emergence of Gay and Lesbian Politics. National Imprints of a Worldwide Movement*. Philadelphia: Temple University Press. pp. 184–213.

Flowers, P., Sheeran, P., Beal, N. and Smith, J.A. (in press) 'The role of psychological factors in HIV risk reduction among gay and bisexual men: a quantitative review', *Psychology and Health*, 12 (2): 197–230.

Gagnon, J. (1992) 'Epidemics and researchers: AIDS and the practice of social studies', in G. Herdt and S. Lindenbaum (eds), *The Time of AIDS. Social Analysis, Theory, and Method*. London: Sage. pp. 27–40.

Gamson, J. (1989) 'Silence, death and the invisible enemy: AIDS activism and social movement "newness"', *Social Problems*, 36 (4): 351–67.

Giami, A. (1992) 'Les Nouveaux Paradigmes de l'épidémie', *Le Journal du Sida*, 43–4: 38–40.

Giami, A. (1996) 'Représentations du sida: une théorie sexuelle', in S. Héfez (ed.), *Sida et vie psychique. Approche clinique et prise en charge*. Paris: La Découverte. pp. 275–90.

Gilman, S. (1988) *Disease and Representation: Images of Illness from Madness to AIDS*. Ithaca, NY: Cornell University Press.

Gott, T. (ed.) (1994) *Don't Leave Me This Way. Art in the Age of AIDS*. Canberra: National Gallery of Australia.

Green, G. (1995) 'Sex, love and seropositivity', in P. Aggleton, P. Davies and G. Hart (eds), *AIDS. Safety, Sexuality and Risk*. London: Taylor & Francis. pp. 144–8.

Hart, G., Boulton, M., Fitzpatrick, R., McLean, G. and Dawson, G. (1992) 'Relapse to unsafe sexual behaviour among gay men. A critique of recent behavioural HIV/AIDS research', *Sociology of Health and Illness*, 14 (2): 216–32.

Harvey, R. (1992) 'Sidéens/Sidaïques: French discourses on AIDS', *Contemporary French Civilization*, 16 (2): 308–35.

Heathcote, O. (1995) 'From cold war to AIDS war: narratives of identity from Gide's, *Retour de la Russie* to Guilbert's *Cytomégalovirus'*, *Modern and Contemporary France*, 3 (4): 427–37.

Henriksson, B. (1995) *Risk Factor Love. Homosexuality, Sexual Interaction and VIH Prevention*. Göteborg: Göteborgs Universitet.

Henriksson, B. and Mänsson, S.A. (1995) 'Sexual negotiations. An ethnographic study of men who have sex with men', in H-P. Brummelhuis and G. Herdt (eds), *Culture and Sexual Risk: Anthropological Perspectives of AIDS*. New York: Gordon & Breach. pp. 157–82.

Hickson, F. et al. (1992) 'Maintenance of open gay relationships: some strategies for protection against HIV', *AIDS Care*, 4 (4): 409–19.

Hollibaugh, A. (1994) 'Lesbian leadership and denial in the age of the AIDS epidemic: bravery and fear in the construction of a geography of risk', in B. Schneider and N. Stoller (eds), *Women Resisting AIDS: Feminist Strategies of Empowerment*. Philadelphia, PA: Temple University Press.

Hospers, H.J. and Kok, G. (1995) 'Determinants of safe and risktaking sexual behavior among gay men: a review', *AIDS Education and Prevention*, 7 (1): 74–96.

Huashan, Z. (1996) 'Les Camarades à l'ombre du sida', in Z. Huashan (ed.), *Histoires de 'camarades'. Les homosexuels en Chine*. Paris: Méditerranée. pp. 191–209.

Isaacs, G. and McKendrick, B. (1992) 'AIDS: the new homosexual crisis', in G. Isaacs and B. McKendrick (eds), *Male Homosexuality in South Africa. Identity Formation, Culture, and Crisis*. Cape Town: Oxford University Press. pp. 112–37.

Jeay, A. (1991) 'Homosexualité et sida au Mali: variations sur l'étrange et l'étranger', in M. Pollak, R. Mendès-Leite and J. Van Dem Borghe (eds), *Homosexualités et sida*. Lille: GKC. pp. 60–8.

Kayal, P.M. (1993) *Bearing Witness. Gay Men's Health Crisis and the Politics of AIDS*. Boulder, San Francisco and Oxford: Westview Press.

Keogh, P. and Beardsell, S. (1997) 'Sexual negotiations of HIV-positive gay men: the qualitative approach', in P. Aggleton, P. Davies and G. Hart (eds), *AIDS, Activism and Alliances*. London: Taylor & Francis. pp. 226–37.

King, E. (1993) *Safety in Numbers. Safer Sex and Gay Men*. London and New York: Cassell.

Kirp, D.L. and Bayer, R. (eds) (1992) *AIDS in the Industrialised Democracies: Passions, Politics and Policies*. New Brunswick: Rutgers University Press.

Kitzinger, J. (1994) 'Visible and invisible women in AIDS discourses', in D. Lesley, J. Naidoo and W. Tansmin (eds), *AIDS: Setting a Feminist Agenda*. London: Taylor & Francis. pp. 95–109.

Klusacek, A. and Morrison, K. (eds) (1992) *A Leap in the Dark: AIDS, Art and Contemporary Cultures*. Montreal: Véhicule.

Kotarba, J. (1990) 'Ethnography and AIDS. Returning to the streets', *Journal of Contemporary Ethnography*, 19 (3): 259–70.

Kowalewski, M.R. (1988) 'Double stigma and boundary maintenance: how gay men deal with AIDS', *Journal of Contemporary Ethnography*, 17 (2): 211–28.

Laurindo da Silva, L. (1993) 'The evolution of the AIDS illness and the polarisation of values', in R. Mendès-Leite and P.O. De Busscher (eds), *Gay Studies from the French Cultures*. New York: The Haworth Press. pp. 293–305.

Laurindo da Silva, L. (1999a) 'Travestis and gigolos. Male prostitution and HIV prevention in France', in P. Aggleton (ed.), *Men Who Sell Sex. International Perspectives on Male Sex Work and HIV/AIDS*. London: UCL Press. pp. 41–60.

Laurindo da Silva, L. (1999b) *Vivre avec le sida en phase avancée: une étude de sociologie de la maladie*. Paris: L'Harmattan.

Leap, W. (1995) 'Talking about AIDS: linguistic perspectives on non-neutral discourse', in H-P. Brummelhuis and G. Herdt (eds), *Culture and Sexual Risk: Anthropological Perspectives of AIDS*. New York: Gordon & Breach. pp. 227–38.

Lemp, G. et al. (1995) 'HIV seroprevalence and risk behaviors among lesbians and bisexual women in San Francisco and Berkeley, California', *American Journal of Public Health*, 85 (11): 1549–52.

Levine, M.P. (1992) 'The implication of constructionist theory for social research on the AIDS epidemic among gay men', in G. Herdt and S. Lindenbaum (eds), *The Time of AIDS. Social Analysis, Theory, and Method*. London: Sage. pp. 185–98.

Levine, M.P., Nardi, P.M. and Gagnon, J. (eds) (1997) *In Changing Times. Gay Men and Lesbians Encounter HIV/AIDS*. Chicago: University of Chicago Press.

Lewis, L.A. and Ross, M.W. (1995) *A Select Body. The Gay Dance Party Subculture and the HIV/AIDS Pandemic*. London: Cassell.

Lhomond, B. (1992) 'Lesbiennes: un risque moins sexuel que social', *Le Journal du Sida*, 43–4: 43–4.

Lhomond, B. (1996) 'Les Risques de transmission du VIH chez les femmes ayant des rapports sexuels avec des femmes', *Transcriptase*, 46: 8–10.

Lhomond, B (1997) 'Attirance et pratiques homosexuelles', in H. Lagrange and B. Lhomond (eds), *L'Entrée dans la sexualité. Le comportement des jeunes dans le contexte du sida*. Paris: La Découverte. pp. 183–226.

Llamas, R. (ed.) (1995) *Construyendo Sidentidades. Estudios desde el corazon de una pandemia*. Madrid: Siglo XXI.

Llamas, R. (1997) *Miss Media. Una lectura perversa de la comunicación de masas*. Barcelona: Ediciones de la Tempestad.

Llamas, R. and Vila, F. (1997) 'Spain: passion for life. Una historia del movimiento de lesbianas y gays en el Estado Español', in Xosé M. Buxan (ed.), *ConCiencia de un singular deseo. Estudios lesbianos y gays en el Estado Español*. Barcelona: Laertes. (English translation: Llamas, R. and Vila, F. (1999) 'Passion for life: a history of the lesbian and gay movement in Spain', in B. Adam, J-W. Duyvendak and A. Krouwel (eds), *The Global Emergence of Gay and Lesbian Politics. National Imprints of a Worldwide Movement*. Philadelphia: Temple University Press. pp. 103–22).

MacRae, E. (1987a) 'AIDS. Prevençao ou novo tipo de segregacionismo?', *Temas do IMESC*, 4 (1): 73–81.

MacRae, E. (1987b) 'Os homossexuais, a AIDS e a medicina', *Radis Tema*, 5: 41–7.

Mendès-Leite, R. (1995) '"Comment ou combien?" Le multipartenariat sexuel et gestion des risques de transmission du sida', *Quel Corps?* Special triple issue: 'Constructions sexuelles', 47, 48, 49: 70–91.

Mendès-Leite, R. (1998) 'Imaginary protections against AIDS', in M. Wright, S. Rosser and O. de Zwart (eds), *New International Directions in HIV Prevention for Gay and Bisexual Men*. New York: The Haworth Press. pp. 103–22.

Mendès-Leite, R. and de Busscher, P.O. (1993) 'Les Sciences humaines et sociales face à l'épidémie du sida: un bouleversement scientifique?', *Sociétés*, 42 Approches méthodologiques. pp. 351–6.

Mendès-Leite, R. and de Busscher, P.O. (1997) *Back-rooms. Microgéographie 'sexographique' de deux back-rooms parisiennes*. Lille: GKC.

Mendès-Leite, R. and Deschamps, C. (1997) 'Des Mots, des pratiques et des risques. La gestion différenciée de la parole et de la prévention du vih chez des hommes à comportements bisexuels en France', *Sociologie et Sociétés*. Special issue: 'Homosexualités: enjeux scientifiques et militants', 29 (1): 99–111.

Mendès-Leite, R. with Deschamps, C. and Proth, B. (1996) *Bisexualité: le dernier tabou*. Paris: Calmann-Lévy.

Mendès-Leite, R. and Proth, B. (1998) 'L'Itinéraire des désirs: déambulations masculines sur les lieux de drague à Paris', *French Cultural Studies. Special issue: AIDS in France*. Nottingham: University of Nottingham Press. pp. 367–83.

Mendès-Lopes, N. (1995) 'The transvestite, the woman and the client: a socio-anthropological approach of transvestite prostitution', in W. Heckmann and D. Friedrich (eds), *AIDS in Europe – The Behavioural Aspect*. Berlin: Sigma. pp. 247–53.

Messiah, A. and Mouret-Forme, E. (1993) 'Homosexualité, bisexualité. Éléments de socio-biographie sexuelle', *Population*. Special issue: 'Sexualité et sciences sociales' (ed. M. Bozon and H. Léridon), 48 (5), 1353–80.

Miller, J. (ed.) (1992) *Fluid Exchanges: Artists and Critics in the AIDS Crisis*. Toronto: University of Toronto Press.

Mott, L. (1985) 'AIDS: reflexoes sobre a sodomia', *Comunicações do ISER*, 4 (17): 32–41.

Mott, L. (1989) 'Os médicos e a AIDS no Brasil', *Ciência e cultura*, 5–12.

Mott, L. (1996) *Epidemic of Hate. Violation of Human Rights of Gay Men, Lesbians and Transvestites in Brazil*. San Francicso: IGLHRC.

Murphy, T. and Poirier, S. (1993) *Writing AIDS: Gay Liberation, Language and Analysis*. New York: Columbia University Press.

Murray, S.O. (1995) 'Homosexuality and AIDS in Latinos in the United States: an annotated bibliography', in S.O. Murray (ed.), *Latin American Male Homosexualities*. Albuquerque: University of New Mexico Press. pp. 170–9.

Nelkin, D., Willis, D. and Parris, S. (eds) (1991) *A Disease of Society: Cultural and Institutional Response to AIDS*. Cambridge: Cambridge University Press.

Nguyet-Erni, J. (1994) *Unstable Frontiers. Technomedicine and the Cultural Politics of 'Curing' AIDS*. Minneapolis: University of Minnesota Press.

Odets, W. (1995) *In the Shadow of the Epidemic. Being HIV Negative in the Age of AIDS*. Durham, NC: Duke University Press.

Packwood, A.N. (1992–93) 'Dialectical narratives in myths of healing: two stories told about gay and bisexual men living with HIV and AIDS', *Santé Culture Health*, 9 (2): 323–66.

Padgug, R.A. and Oppenheimer, G.M. (1992) 'Riding the tiger: AIDS and the gay community', in E. Fee and D.M. Fox (eds), *AIDS. The Making of a Chronic Disease*. Berkeley: University of California Press. pp. 245–78.

Parker, R. (1991) 'Male prostitution, bisexual behavior, and HIV transmission in urban Brazil', in T. Dyson (ed.), *Sexual Behavior and Networking: Socio-cultural Studies on the Transmission of HIV*. Liège: Ondina Editions.

Parker, R.G. and Carballo, M. (1990) 'Qualitative research on homosexual and bisexual behavior relevant to HIV/AIDS', *Journal of Sex Research*, 27 (4): 497–525.

Patton, C. (1990) *Inventing AIDS*. New York: Routledge.

Pegge, J. (1994) 'Living with loss in the best way we know how: AIDS and gay men in Cape Town', in M. Gevisser and E. Cameron (eds), *Deviant Desire. Gay and Lesbian Lives in South Africa*. Johannesburg: Ravan Press. pp. 301–10.

Peterson, J. L. (1997) 'AIDS-related risks and same sex behaviors among African American men', in M.P. Levine, P.M. Nardi and J.H. Gagnon (eds), *In Changing Times. Gay Men and Lesbians Encounter HIV/AIDS*. Chicago: University of Chicago Press. pp. 283–301.

Plexoussaki, E. and Yannacopoulos, K. (1996) 'Le Mal purifié. Manipulation du sida en Grèce', *L'Homme*, 139: 125–35.

Plummer, K (ed.) (1981) *The Making of the Modern Homosexual*. London: Hutchinson.

Plummer, K. (ed.) (1992) *Modern Homosexualities. Fragments of Gay and Lesbian Experience*. London: Routledge.

Pollak, M. (1988) *Les Homosexuels et le sida. Sociologie d'une épidémie*. Paris: Métailié.

Pollak, M. (1993a) *The Second Plague of Europe. AIDS Prevention and Sexual Transmission among Men in Western Europe*. New York: The Haworth Press.

Pollak, M. (1993b) 'Homosexuals' rituals and safer sex', in R. Mendès-Leite and P.O. de Busscher (eds), *Gay Studies from the French Cultures. Voices from France, Belgium, Brazil, Canada and The Netherlands*. New York: Harrington Park Press. pp. 307–17.

Pratt, M. (1995) 'De la désidentification à l'incognito, à la recherche d'une autobiographie homosexuelle', *Nottingham French Studies*, 34 (1): 70–81.

Prieur, A. (1990) 'Norwegian gay men: reasons for continued practice of unsafe sex', *AIDS Education and Prevention*, 2: 109–15.

Raiteri, R., Fora, R. and Gioannini, P. (1994) 'Seroprevalence, risk factors and attitude to HIV-1 in a representative sample of lesbians in Turin', *Genitourinary Medicine*, 70 (3): 200–5.

Richardson, D. (1988) 'Lesbians and AIDS', in D. Richardson (ed.), *Women and AIDS*. New York: Routledge. pp. 87–101.

Richardson, D. (1994) 'Inclusions and exclusions: lesbians, HIV and AIDS', in D. Lesley, J. Naidoo and W. Tansmin (eds), *AIDS, Setting a Feminist Agenda*. London: Taylor & Francis. pp. 159–70.

Riedmann, K. and Kraus, M. (eds) (1994) *Inventory of Psychosocial Behavioural AIDS/Drug Research throughout Europe*. Berlin: AIDSZentrum im Bundesgesundheitsamt.

Robinson, C. (1995) 'AIDS writing in France and the gay self-image', in *Scandal in the Ink: Male and Female Homosexuality in Twentieth-century French Literature*. London and New York: Cassell. pp. 117–43.

Rofes, E. (1996) *Reviving the Tribe. Regenerating Gay Men's Sexuality and Culture in the Ongoing Epidemic*. New York: Harrington Park Press.

Roman, D. (1997) *Acts of Intervention. Performance, Gay Culture, and AIDS*. Indianapolis: Indiana University Press.

Sabogal, F., Faigeles, B. and Catania, J. (1993) 'Multiple sexual partners among Hispanics in high-risk cities', *Family Planning Perspectives*, 25 (6): 257–62.

Sandfort T.G.M. (1995) 'HIV/AIDS prevention and the impact of attitudes towards homosexuality and bisexuality', in G.M. Herek and B. Greene (eds), *AIDS, Psychology, and the Lesbian and Gay Community*. Thousand Oaks, CA: Sage. pp. 32–54.

Sandfort, T.G.M. (1998) 'Homosexual and bisexual behaviour in European countries', in M.C. Hubert, N. Bajos and T.G.M. Sandfort (eds), *Sexual Behaviour and HIV/AIDS in Europe*. London: UCL Press. pp. 68–105.

Schiltz, M.A. and Adam, P. (1995) 'Reputedly effective risk reduction strategies and gay men', in P. Aggleton, P. Davies and G. Hart (eds), *AIDS: Safety, Sexuality and Risk*. London: Taylor & Francis. pp. 1–19.

Schneider, B.E. (1992) 'Lesbian politics and AIDS work', in K. Plummer (ed.), *Modern Homosexualities*. New York: Routledge. pp. 160–74.

Schneider, B.E. (1997) 'Owning an epidemic. The impact of AIDS on small-city lesbian and gay communities', in M.P. Levine, P.M. Nardi and J.H. Gagnon (eds), *In Changing Times. Gay Men and Lesbians Encounter HIV/AIDS*. Chicago: University of Chicago Press. pp. 145–69.

Seidman, S. (1997) *Difference Troubles. Queering Social Theory and Sexual Politics*. Cambridge: Cambridge University Press.

Sherr, L. (ed.) (1995) *Grief and AIDS*. Chichester: John Wiley.

Smith, P.J. (1997) 'La representación del sida en el Estado Español: Alberto Cardin y Eduardo Haro Ibars', in Xosé M. Buxan (ed.), *ConCiencia de un singular deseo. Estudios lesbianos y gays en el Estado Español*. Barcelona: Laertes.

Stoller, N.E. (1997) 'From feminism to polymorphous activism: lesbians in AIDS organizations', in M.P. Levine, P.M. Nardi and J.H. Gagnon (eds), *In Changing Times*.

Gay Men and Lesbians Encounter HIV/AIDS. Chicago: University of Chicago Press. pp. 171–89.

Tielman R., Hendriks, A. and Carballo, M. (eds) (1991) *Bisexuality and HIV/AIDS. A Global Perspective*. Buffalo, NY: Prometheus Books.

Treichler, P.A. (1988) 'AIDS, homophobia, and biomedical discourse: An epidemic of signification', in D. Crimp (ed.), *AIDS. Cultural Analysis, Cultural Activism*. Cambridge, MA: MIT Press. pp. 31–70.

Van Kerkhof, M., Sandfort, T. and Geensen, R. (1991) *Als je het nour van hard werken kreeg! Tien jaar AIDS en homocultuur*. Amsterdam: Veen.

Van Kerkhof, M.P.N., de Zwart, O. and Sandfort, T. (1995) *Van achteren bezien: anale seks in het aidstijdperk*. Amsterdam: Schorer.

Wachter, R.M. (1991) *The Fragile Coalition: Scientists, Activists and AIDS*. New York: St Martin's Press.

Watney, S. (1993) *Policing Desire: Pornography, AIDS and the Media*. Minneapolis: University of Minnesota Press.

Watney, S. (1994) *Practices of Freedom: Selected Writings on HIV/AIDS*. London: Rivers Oram Press.

Weatherburn, P. et al. (1996) *Behaviourally Bisexual Men in the UK. Identifying Needs for HIV Prevention*. London: Sigma Research.

Weeks, J. (1991) *Against Nature. Essays on History, Sexuality and Identity*. London: Rivers Oram Press.

Weeks, J. (1995) *Invented Moralities. Sexual Values in an Age of Uncertainty*. New York: Columbia University Press.

Weinberg, M., Williams, C. and Pryor, D. (1994) *Dual Attraction. Understanding Bisexuality*. Oxford: Oxford University Press.

Welzer-Lang, D., Dutey, P. and Dorais, M. (1994) *La Peur de l'autre en soi. Du sexisme à l'homophobie*. Montreal: VLB éditeur.

Whittaker, A.M. (1992) 'Living with HIV: resistance by positive people', *Medical Anthropology Quarterly*, 6 (2): 385–90.

Wight, D. and Barnard, M. (1993) 'The limits to participant observation in HIV/AIDS research', *Practicing Anthropology*, 15 (4): 66–9.

Winnow, J. (1989) 'Lesbians working on AIDS: Assessing the impact on health care for women', *Out/Look*, 5.

Woodhead, D. (1995) 'Surveillant gays. HIV, space and the constitution of identities', in D. Bell and G. Valentine (eds), *Mapping Desire. Geographies of Sexualities*. London and New York: Routledge. pp. 231–44.

Wright, M.T. (1996) *Und wir überleben. Gibt es ein AIDS Survivor Syndrom unter schwulen Männern in Deutschland?* Berlin: Deutsche AIDSHilfe e.V.

Young, R.M., Weissman, G. and Cohen, J.B. (1992) 'Assessing risk in the absence of information: HIV risk among women injection drug users who have sex with women', *AIDS and Public Policy*, 7 (3): 175–83.

14 Conclusion: Gay and Lesbian Studies at the Crossroads

Judith Schuyf and Theo Sandfort

The chapters in this book offer a variety of perspectives on what is usually known as lesbian and gay studies. Although the chapters are diverse, these two terms: *gay/lesbian* and *studies*, are precisely what they have in common. In this final chapter we will evaluate some of the common issues and debates addressed in the preceding chapters, and give some possible directions for the future, centring on the terms *gay/lesbian* and *studies*.[1] We will start, though, with a discussion of the term *homosexuality*, as one cannot understand gay and lesbian studies without its primary object of study, homosexuality.

What about homosexuality?

Nowadays you cannot use the term homosexuality without accounting for it. How should homosexuality be defined in the context of gay and lesbian studies? Is there a specific kind of homosexuality on which gay and lesbian studies focuses? It might seem evident that by adopting the label 'gay and lesbian studies', the understanding of homosexuality as being expressed in separate identities is implied. This understanding of homosexuality is certainly adequate for a substantial group of men and women in our current Western society, although the content of these identities, the way it is filled in and experienced, differs between persons as well as within persons over time. From a cultural and historical perspective, a general definition of homosexuality in terms of identity is of course not warranted at all.

The conceptualization of sex in the form of an identity is a product of a long, historic development. The idea that a person can (and should) have something like a sexual identity is a fairly recent one, perhaps dating from the eighteenth century, even apart from the realization that gender is a distinguishing or constitutive factor for such an identity (Trumbach, 1989).

We do not, however, have to go back in history – or to contemporary, non-Western cultures – to demonstrate that a definition of homosexuality in terms of identities is not all encompassing. Even in Western cultures, people can behave homosexually for parts of their lives (i.e. have either sexual or erotic involvement with somebody of the same sex) without ever identifying themselves as such. On the other hand, among modern homosexuals many refuse to identify as 'gay' or 'lesbian', for a number of different reasons. Some simply do not see any part of their personal identity as central, others refuse to label themselves, to resist categorization that they experience as limiting, just to be 'postmodern'. So, if homosexuality is not necessarily always an identity, what is it?

One way out would be to define homosexuality in terms of desires, but this, as well as the related concept of same sex desire, is also not without problems. We, at least most of us, do of course experience ourselves as having specific sexual desires, directed at specific classes or categories of people. This understanding of ourselves only became possible when sexual desires became classified according to the objects at which they are directed. There are other ways of classifying sexual desires, for instance on the basis of the kind of gratification one is looking for. It is obvious that without the presence of a distinct, generally acknowledged heterosexuality/homosexuality dichotomy, sexual desires must have been experienced quite differently. Besides, it is known that homosexual behaviour is not necessarily always inspired by homosexual desires (for instance between men in prisons). In the old days, one could accuse such people of either having a false consciousness or simply being 'not that far yet', but obviously the matter is more complex.

To us, homosexuality is part and all of the above. Homosexuality is the generic term for divergent ways in which sexuality, desires and emotions between people of the same sex are organized. It is more than 'gay and lesbian' as it does not focus on a collective of individuals but on homosexuality as a social phenomenon. This broad definition should be recognized in the work we are doing. This seems in contradiction to adopting the label of gay and lesbian studies. At the same time we have to realize that, by the very language we adopt, gay and lesbian studies, as a partner in a sexological discourse affecting the lives of individuals, has an impact on the way homosexuality is organized and expressed. It is about time to reflect on the role gay and lesbian studies plays in the reproduction and the maintenance of the current organization of (homo)sexuality.

The identity of gay and lesbian studies

Having first considered some aspects of the homosexual aspect of gay and lesbian studies, we will now turn to the studies part. Does gay and lesbian studies have a specific identity, which makes it recognizable in the world of academia?

Unlike traditional academic disciplines such as sociology or psychology, gay and lesbian studies cannot be defined as having a specific perspective on human behaviour. Instead it is constituted by the specific subject it focuses on, namely homosexuality, which is approached from almost all traditional perspectives. This makes it difficult to give it a place among the traditional disciplines in academia. As a consequence, this continuously weakens the position of gay and lesbian studies, and obstructs the achievement of academic respectability, hindering the allocation of research grants, which are usually discipline bound.

We agree with Jeffrey Weeks, when he stated in Chapter 1 that gay and lesbian studies is more 'a dialogue, across disciplines, experiences and differences' than one specific academic discipline. This description by Weeks opens up the possibility for transgression (by contesting fixed knowledge) and yet closely connects to existing ways of identity politics. As such, this book nicely fits this definition. In mapping out the contents we deliberately organized it around traditional academic disciplines – in order to explore the relationship of gay and lesbian studies with these disciplines and to show, where possible, the major contributions of gay and lesbian studies within specific disciplines. Partly as a consequence of this, the chapters by no means have a uniform perspective. To understand the way in which the individual chapters are related, we should look at the various paradigms underlying the perspectives. These are the major three paradigms current in academic research: positivism/post-positivism, constructionism, and critical theory.

Paradigms in gay and lesbian studies

Before discussing the various perspectives in lesbian and gay studies, we will map out the main characteristics of these three paradigms, following Egon Guba and Yvonna Lincoln's overview (1994). They define paradigms as dealing with first principles of research: these principles define the worldview of the researcher, and their ultimate truthfulness can never be established. Paradigms should be distinguished from interpretative perspectives, such as the gay and lesbian perspective, since the latter are not as solidified or well unified as paradigms and reflect even more a way of viewing the world from a particular standpoint.

Paradigms distinguish themselves by the assumptions they have concerning:

- the form and nature of reality and what can be known about reality; an *ontological* issue;
- the relationships between the knower and what can be known; an *epistemological* issue;
- how the enquirer can go about finding out whatever he/she believes can be known; a *methodological* issue.

Various positions are possible regarding these three issues, as will subsequently become clear.

Gay and lesbian studies have inherited a clearly *positivist or post-positivist* approach from the sexological tradition. Most psychological research is still performed along these lines. In this approach, knowledge of the 'way things are' is conventionally summarized in the form of time- and context-free generalizations. Some of these generalizations, formulated as supported hypotheses, take the form of cause–effect laws. Criteria for disciplined enquiry are internal and external validity, reliability and objectivity. Examples of studies based on this paradigm are found in journals such as *Archives of Sexual Behavior* and the *Journal of Sex Research*. Our 'own' *Journal of Homosexuality* also regularly includes papers of this type.

From the mid-1970s onwards, the generalizing positivist position was increasingly criticized for excluding interpretations based on individual studies, which within this position were not considered to be valid. Early research in the social sciences and humanities already reflected the point of view that what we now see as reality is always shaped by and part of historical and social processes. This also informed Foucault's groundbreaking work on the social and historical construction of sexuality. Foucault's work is a clear example of *constructionism*. Most postmodern research (in the social sciences, but mainly in the field of the humanities) is based on the assumption that there is not one objective and quantifiable reality, but a series of mental constructs shared by individuals and groups. The investigator and the object of investigation are assumed to be interactively linked so that the 'findings' are literally created as the investigation proceeds.

Constructionism dominated research agendas in the 1980s and led the way to queer studies in the 1990s, together with the *critical theory* approach. Critical theory originally arose out of the Frankfurt School before World War II, but is now generally understood to entail various forms of research that critique existing forms of power and enquiry. Critical theory assumes that all thought is mediated by power relations, that facts can never be isolated from the domain of values, and that language is central to the formation of subjectivity (Kincheloe and McLaren, 1994). Constructionist and critical theory approaches are united in their opposition to positivism and their commitment to the study of the world from the point of view of the interacting individual, producing knowledge that is both historical and structural. Inherently, critical theory seeks to produce transformations of the social order (Guba and Lincoln, 1994).

So how do the chapters in this book relate to existing hegemonic paradigms and interpretative perspectives in academic research? The individual authors have written from their own perspectives of academic enquiry, which are sometimes in agreement with the mainstream paradigm – as seems to be the case for the chapter on psychology – and at other moments less so – as with the chapters on law and geography, with the emphasis on critical theory. The paradigm adopted by the authors of course affects which studies and publications they refer to in their chapters.

Although the approaches in the chapters cannot be considered separately from their disciplinary origins, the book reflects its origins in space (with an emphasis on Western versus world perspectives and on European versus American perspectives, so that it misses out on ethnic perspectives as well as on the psychoanalytic turn in cultural and literary studies made popular by California-based scholars such as Teresa de Lauretis) and time (the almost universal absence of Marxist interpretative perspectives is quite remarkable, considering the fact that such perspectives were widely used in gay and lesbian studies in the 1980s).

On the whole, the book reflects a strong preference for interpretative, qualitative forms of enquiry. This seems logical, as experience is crucial to gay and lesbian lives. As a consequence, gay and lesbian studies mainly deals with the world of lived experience. This may well be a hallmark and, incidentally, may contribute to the fact that gay and lesbian studies are not considered academically respectable by the more positivist-dominated academia.

Standpoint homosexuality

Weeks sees lesbian and gay studies as taking a standpoint perspective on learning to live with differences, contesting existing knowledge and redefining who has the right to speak about homosexuality. As such, it is rooted in identity politics. This standpoint perspective is what unites gay and lesbian studies more than its apparent lack of a clearly defined common paradigm. Like feminist theory, standpoint homosexuality develops new ethical and epistemological criteria for evaluating research. It makes lived experience central to qualitative enquiry and develops criteria of evaluation based on the ethics of liberation, empowerment, personal responsibility and open dialogue.

We think that gay and lesbian studies should deal with research questions that might contribute to countering discrimination against homosexuality, to fostering its expression and to promoting sexual diversity. The ultimate aims of gay and lesbian studies are the critique and transformation of the social, political, cultural, economic, ethnic and gender situations around homosexuality. This implies that the definition of what gay and lesbian studies is is a political one, and that the existence and the identity of these studies is bound to the current social climate. It also implies that gay and lesbian studies has a relationship with the political and social group of which we are all part and parcel: the gay and lesbian movement. So we see that the standpoint perspective affects three separate areas of practice: ethics (how is homosexuality valued in the research design?), evaluation of research questions in terms of their relevance, and its relationship with the movement.

Ethics

The binding factor for gay and lesbian studies is that it deals with homosexuality in one way or another – however troublesome it might be to define what homosexuality is. Does this imply that all research addressing homosexuality should be seen as part of gay and lesbian studies? We don't think so. After all, why wasn't the name 'homosexual studies' adopted instead of 'gay and lesbian studies'? The reason for this is that we, as gay and lesbian researchers, share a specific attitude towards homosexuality. This attitude may – defensively – be characterized as follows: there is no reason to be defensive about homosexuality. Or, more affirmatively: there is a positive valuation of homosexuality as a self-evident part of sexual diversity.

The fact that it is necessary to adopt and to foster such an attitude indicates that homosexuality, in general, is not regarded as a legitimate form of sexual expression. Homosexuality is grounds for the marginalization, discrimination and exclusion of individuals, in whatever blatant or subtle form this is brought about. This societal climate offers the rationale for the existence of gay and lesbian studies, although not the only one. The current social context forms the matrix for our research questions and sets the aims of this research. It offers a frame of reference to define the relevance of research questions and to set research priorities. As a consequence, a prerequisite for gay and lesbian studies is a continuous reflection on and analysis of what is going on in society with respect to homosexuality.

Evaluation criteria

One of the consequences of adopting a standpoint perspective is that some of the issues that are studied in relation to homosexuality should be considered less relevant. To prevent any misunderstandings, we are not saying that these questions are not intriguing, or that nobody should be allowed to study them. We think that gay and lesbian studies should not study these questions, at least not prioritize them. From the perspective of gay and lesbian studies, one of the less relevant questions deals with the origins and biological co-varieties of homosexuality. Some of the research in this field has created quite a stir, such as Dörner's (1988) enquiry into hormones, LeVay's (1993) study of brains and Hamer's (Hamer et al., 1993) work on genes. We don't expect that answers to these questions will change anything about the position of homosexuality in society. This research is not central to gay and lesbian studies and neither is other research into the cause of homosexuality, be it animal studies or studies of homosexual twins. From the perspective of gay and lesbian studies it would be extremely relevant, though, to investigate why people think this makes interesting research, as this is clearly related to the way homosexuality is represented and evaluated within certain fields of academia as well as among the public at large.

We said that the criterion for a study to be relevant or worthwhile from a gay and lesbian perspective, is whether it will contribute, directly or indirectly, to improvements in the position of homosexuality or counteract discrimination against homosexuality. By stating this we do not imply that the outcomes of the study should be known beforehand. On the contrary, one of the most basic characteristics of scientific research is that outcomes are not known beforehand; indeed the research should be set up in such a way that all outcomes are equally possible. The issue of relevance relates to which issues are selected and how issues and research questions are conceived. An example might illustrate this. With respect to gay and lesbian parenthood several research questions can be formulated. One can focus on the consequences for the child of living in a family arrangement such as that; the implicit aim here is to find out whether lesbians and gays can be good parents and should be allowed to have access to legal parenthood. As a researcher one could also focus on the problems lesbian and gay parents encounter and on the responses they get from their surroundings, in order to bolster their position and that of future gay and lesbian parents. It is obvious to us that the latter focus should have priority, as this is empowering rather than defensive research.

We do not want to suggest that gay and lesbian studies should produce a pleasant, non-disturbing picture of homosexuality in order to promote its acceptance. We should not avoid difficult research topics, which might run the risk of reinforcing prejudices against gays and lesbians. 'Difficult' research topics can – and should indeed more than they are now – be addressed. Examples of 'difficult' research questions are enquiries into the relationship between homosexuality and psychological disorders, substance abuse, inter-partner violence and promiscuity. What is important is the direction of enquiry and analysis – regardless of the fact that, sometimes, the outcome of such an enquiry could be less than desired. Instead of running away from the truth – or specific versions of the truth – it may be beneficial and purifying for the gay and lesbian community to be confronted with these issues and to find ways of solving them.

Relationship to the gay and lesbian movement

Many of the people engaged in gay and lesbian studies have roots in the gay and lesbian (or feminist) movement. This is not surprising because the movement provides a discussion platform for political and social action. It is an empowering environment in which to start reflecting on the position of homosexuality in society. This does not mean, however, that gay and lesbian studies is an automatic extension of this movement. In fact, there often turns out to be an uneasy relationship between gay and lesbian scholars and the gay and lesbian movement, as Ken Plummer remarks in his chapter on sociology.

The uneasy relationship originates in the discrepancy between what Plummer calls 'folk essentialism', the idea that homosexuals are 'born that way' and the constructionist vision of most scholars. Research in the Netherlands has shown that this essentialist idea is much more common among gay men than among lesbians. This view that homosexuals are 'born that way' also has political consequences. This can be demonstrated in the differences between the US, where the emancipation movement is built on an ethnic (i.e. essentialist) model and Europe, where a human rights (i.e. constructionist) model is much more prevalent.

The gap between gay and lesbian studies and the movement in fact seems to be on the increase, because many people have difficulty in following the dense, queer way of theorizing, which does seem to lead further and further away from direct political action. This is contrary to how we think the relationships with the movement should be: gay and lesbian studies should be a critical follower of the movement and provide the movement with ideas, while not losing touch with actual social and academic questions on homosexuality.[2]

Future directions for lesbian and gay studies: organizational

Academization and de-academization

The past few years have seen a remarkable shift in the relative positions of gay and lesbian studies in the US and Europe. While the main centres of gay and lesbian studies used to be found in Europe, the balance has now shifted to the United States. In the US many universities now have sections where some form of gay and lesbian studies can be undertaken, and the number of academic journals is on the increase. Some of these journals are 'queer' in general, but many more address gay and lesbian issues within a specific field, such as therapy. In Western Europe the academic positions that were acquired with much difficulty are continuously under pressure. The United Kingdom seems to be an exception to this at the moment. No doubt, elsewhere practitioners of gay and lesbian studies within universities have been relegated to a relative outsider position, by the use of arguments against standpoint positions (versus 'value-free science'), as well as by the discrediting of its methodology and research questions.

Networking

Since its inception, gay and lesbian studies has thrived on international co-operation. In the 1980s large international conferences such as Among Men, Among Women (1984) and Homosexuality, Which Homosexuality? (1987) formed the beginning of long-term international co-operation in research and teaching. This must continue, for several reasons. In view of the small number of people involved in gay and lesbian studies and the little power it has in hegemonistic terms, exchange of ideas on a wider scale is of vital importance. It supports groups and individuals that have to carry out their research programmes in relative isolation and, last but not least, it serves as necessary reflection on what one is doing.[3]

Networks need some form of institutionalization in order to survive the vagaries of bureaucracy. E-mail is a necessary, but not a sufficient means of keeping in contact. Lobbying is also important, particularly to get funding for activities within large government or intercommunal programmes where the bulk of the money is usually directed at technological research and development. We in Europe can take as an example the successful lobby that the joint European women's studies (WISE) has directed at the European Commission.

Globalization and US-centrism

The Internet has made an enormous change in the way contacts are made and maintained in the academic world. As they say, we now live in a global village, but it is one in which English has become the universal language and American ways of thinking have become hegemonic. We may be global, but those of us who are native English speakers seem to be more global than others. Increasingly, discussions are dominated by Anglo-American issues, norms and values. Speakers of other languages have been relegated to the back benches, as can be seen if one consults the editorial boards of many international journals. This specifically applies to academic journals, but also to journals on gay and lesbian studies. Almost everybody on the editorial lists appears to be a native English speaker. As the larger European publishers tend to cater to the American market, it becomes more difficult to publish local studies for a wider audience.[4] This is a pity, because we clearly need to make our enquiries more global.

Future directions of lesbian and gay studies: content

Interdisciplinarity (or rather: multidisciplinarity)?

Since its inception, gay and lesbian studies has proposed a multidisciplinary agenda. This was clearly used in outlining the chapters for this book. Some topics were so multidisciplinary that we had to assign them to one of the possible authors. Some authors as a matter of fact suggested that particular research questions within their field could be much better dealt with from an interdisciplinary perspective.

The need for an interdisciplinary approach applies to a number of research questions within the field of history, e.g. questions about the formation of (sub)cultures (sociology, anthropology), identity development and maintenance (psychology, sociology). In the field of law it applies to the introduction of laws and their effect on daily life, to analysing and combating hate crimes (psychology, law, sociology). In Chapter 6, on law, Moran cites an impressive array of legal studies that have been 'informed by Marxist, post Marxist/post-structuralist theory and feminism' and uses not only legal, but also literary, political and social theory. Finally, existential questions about the nature of subjectivity can be dealt with in psychoanalysis and literature.

Such interdisciplinary actions are not simple and also not without their own dangers. What can be a legitimate practice within one discipline can be a deadly sin within another. Terminology among disciplines varies strongly, even though people may use the same term for something.

So what about the natural sciences?

The natural sciences are absent from this book, even though over the last few years research into homosexuality has been performed in biology. We have cited some examples from this type of research before. We have also stated that, from our perspective, these studies should not fall under the banner of gay and lesbian studies, because the research questions involved do not have much relevance for the position of homosexuality within society. However, this does not mean that the natural sciences are disqualified from the field of gay and lesbian studies. There are enough interesting research questions, for instance in the fields of medicine and biology, and especially related to issues of sickness and health. What we do need is to enter into a constructive dialogue with the natural sciences in order to develop joint research questions.

And what about queer?

On balance, this book is about gay and lesbian studies and not about queer studies. On re-reading the chapters it becomes apparent why this is the case: queer fits with difficulty into the standpoint and methodological perspectives taken by many of the authors.

The authors do not oppose the transgressive, destabilizing impact of queer – that has been done before (as Steven Epstein recently remarked about Jeffrey Weeks when he highlighted the long-term impact of Weeks's sexual identity politics on evacuating our sexual taxonomies of any stable meaning: Epstein, 1998). It is among other things the extreme relativist point of view taken by some authors on queer that does not go down well.

An interesting question would be whether a queer perspective produces knowledge that is useful from a standpoint perspective. In certain cases it certainly does, such as in AIDS studies. Here, focusing on identity would in fact obstruct an enquiry which should be more interested in actions. Queer might also be able to analyse the often confusing allegiances in which many people are placed by postmodern and multicultural societies.

We are not the first to critique queer theory. Former Marxists such as Elisabeth Wilson and Mary McIntosh criticized queer because of its non-political standpoint (McIntosh, 1993; Wilson, 1993). The queer idea that all life is text and not experience also seems to ignore daily reality, as pointed out by Plummer (Stein and Plummer, 1994). Due to its tendency to ignore the role of gender, of political, economic and social institutions, a queer perspective does not seem very useful in the analysis of current social issues. Plummer opposes queer because of its apparent lack of affinity with empiricism. This criticism of queer applies not only to sociology (which was what Plummer aimed at) but also to history. Queer challenges fixed identities, but only by putting shifting identities or multiple identities in their place. Queer theory is an interesting approach when studying the expression of (homo)sexuality and the formation of sexual lifestyles; it works well in those disciplines where critical enquiry is a viable method (such as in literature) but it works less well in disciplines where research methods are still more or less based on empiricism.

At its extreme, the queer theory approach requires us to give up the concept of gay and lesbian identities, which at this moment would probably turn out to be devastating. This does not imply that gay and lesbian scholars should be constrained within the narrow boundaries of lesbian and gay – a more inclusive perspective could be gender, because this can be used as a method of analysis that does not lose its political connotations, precisely because it takes social and political differences as its point of origin.

A research agenda for the next decade

It is not the purpose of this book to offer a clear-cut research agenda for gay and lesbian studies. Issues that should be addressed should emerge from an analysis of a specific social context and cannot be specified.

Nevertheless, the combined chapters in this book suggest the following set of ideas for research issues for the coming decade, which seem to have some common general priority.

- the effects of globalization (within sociology, anthropology and geography). One could think of the globalization of culture, the effects of the impact of the Western/American model of homosexuality on non-Western cultures, and the effects of transnational migration;
- the urban/rural division. This issue is relevant to psychology (with further elaboration of the thesis that urban cultures produce gay and lesbian identities and that the urban is not only a place where rural gays and lesbians flock to as a refuge) and geography (spatial basis to identities); and again, effects of migration (both urban/rural and transnational);
- diversity – this perspective is applicable to all disciplines and leads us away from a unified conception of homosexuality. Within sociology this leads to research into multiculturalism, increasing tolerance and its impacts on lifestyles;

- the historicization of gender and the body, and the development of the self and the soul. History and psychology would benefit from this approach, which gives us more insight into the development of gendered identities and sexualities;
- sexual lifestyles and behaviours, desire, and sexual socialization. Except for AIDS studies, it is striking that the sexual behaviour of gay men, and especially that of lesbians, is one of the least-explored issues in gay and lesbian studies;
- within sociology there is a plea for work that links to heterosexism, post-modernism, intimate citizenship and social worlds; for re-reading the classic theories and studies wearing gay/lesbian spectacles and for using strategic concepts such as modernity as a means of analysis.

Lesbians and gay men

In this chapter we have talked about gay and lesbian studies in the singular. The agendas of lesbian research and gay research do not however necessarily coincide, even though the basic principles we set forth are the same.

The differences between lesbian and gay research agendas start out from the fact that many lesbian researchers have a different world perspective, based on existing power differences between men and women in society. Therefore, much lesbian research starts from the point of difference, instead of from a unifying viewpoint which sees lesbians as basically the same as gay men, the latter viewpoint not infrequently adopted by gay researchers (if they notice women at all).

Many lesbian researchers adhere closely to feminist perspectives of research, in which the articulation of difference and diversity, not only in socio-economic positions but in lifestyles, was theorized and practised at a much earlier date than was the case in gay male studies. Different methodologies are also involved – the question of the (im)possibility of female subjectivity has dominated much lesbian research in the last decade, because the denial of female subjectivity was seen by many as the result of patriarchy. There was no need for gay men to address this problem.

As has been suggested, integrating gender into gay and lesbian research might be a way to cut this Gordian knot. If one sees gender as a complex, interacting model of analysis, touching on identity, sex, roles and representation, it is possible to theorize on both the relative positions of women and men and their relationships and individual strengths. If one sees gender as a model of constructionist social roles it can also be used to analyse one of the more pervasive stereotypes of homosexualities: that gay men are effeminate and lesbians are masculine. When analysing gender bending, gender can be deployed as a transgressive method of enquiry.

As said by Weeks in the introduction to this book, gender is one of the major sources of difference within gay and lesbian studies, next to age, generation, class, race and ethnicity, and nationality. These differences create various tensions, which are necessary if we are to make any progress. This progress is made by questioning the heterosexual orthodoxy and in a search for sexual justice, regardless of the way this is articulated. In this respect, at least, a continued dialogue between lesbians and gay men will also contribute to the further development of gay and lesbian studies.

Notes

1 Increasingly, the term 'queer studies' is being used, especially in the United States. Since its introduction, the term 'queer' has become to mean a variety of things. The meaning partly depends on one's particular location on earth: in Europe queer stands exclusively for postmodern, transgressive research in the humanities, while in the United States queer has become just another word for gay and lesbian. Although we prefer to continue using gay and lesbian studies, for at least some readers this concluding chapter is about queer studies as well.

2 In this sense, even historical research has actuality, as it can demonstrate that sex and gender are recent constructs, and not things that have always 'naturally' been there.

3 A good example of international co-operation was the Intensive Study Programme on Lesbian and Gay Studies, funded by the Erasmus Exchange Programme of the European Union, which under the directorship of the Universities of Utrecht and Essex flourished during the late 1980s and early 1990s. Students and professors of six countries participated in this programme.

4 There is one interesting consequence though, which is the advance of people from Australia (and New Zealand) who often show new and exciting ideas (e.g. Grosz and Probyn, 1995; Jagose, 1994).

References

Dörner, G. (1988) 'Neuroendocrine response to estrogen and brain differentiation in heterosexuals, homosexuals and transsexuals', *Archives of Sexual Behavior*, 17: 57–75.

Epstein, S. (1998) 'Review of Steven Seidman, *Difference Troubles*', *Sexualities*, 2 (2): 270–2.

Grosz, E. and Probyn, E. (eds) (1995) *Sexy Bodies: the Strange Carnalities of Feminism*. London: Routledge.

Guba, E.G. and Lincoln, Y.S. (1994) 'Competing paradigms in qualitative research', in N.K. Denzin and Y.S. Lincoln (eds), *Handbook of Qualitative Research*. Thousand Oaks, CA: Sage. pp. 105–17.

Hamer, D.H., Hu, S., Magnuson, V.L., Hu, N. and Pattatucci, A.M.L. (1993) 'A linkage between DNA markers on the X chromosome and male sexual orientation', *Science*, 261 (5119): 321–7.

Jagose, A. (1994) *Lesbian Utopics*. London: Routledge.

Kincheloe, J.L. and McLaren, P.L. (1994) 'Rethinking critical theory and qualitative research', in N.K. Denzin and Y.S. Lincoln (eds), *Handbook of Qualitative Research*. Thousand Oaks, CA: Sage. pp. 138–57.

LeVay, S. (1993) *The Sexual Brain*. Cambridge, MA: MIT Press.

McIntosh, M. (1993) 'Queer theory and the war of the sexes', in J. Bristow and A. Wilson (eds), *Activating Theory. Lesbian, Gay, Bisexual Politics*. London: Lawrence & Wishart. pp. 30–52.

Stein, A. and Plummer, K. (1994) 'I can't even think straight: queer theory and the missing sexual revolution in sociology', *Sociological Theory*, 12 (2): 178–87.

Trumbach, R. (1989) 'Gender and the homosexual role in modern Western culture: the eighteenth and nineteenth centuries compared', in D. Altman, C. Vance, M. Vinicus and J. Weeks (eds), *Homosexuality, Which Homosexuality?* Amsterdam and London: Schorer/Dekker, GMP. pp. 149–70.

Wilson, E. (1993) 'Is transgression transgressive?', in J. Bristow and A. Wilson (eds), *Activating Theory. Lesbian, Gay, Bisexual Politics*. London: Lawrence & Wishart. pp. 107–17.

Index